The MVVM Pattern in .NET MAUI

The definitive guide to essential patterns, best practices, and techniques for cross-platform app development

Pieter Nijs

BIRMINGHAM—MUMBAI

The MVVM Pattern in .NET MAUI

Group Product Manager: Kunal Sawant

Publishing Product Manager: Akash Sharma

Book Project Manager: Prajakta Naik

Senior Editor: Esha Banerjee

Technical Editor: Maran Fernandes

Copy Editor: Safis Editing

Proofreader: Safis Editing

Indexer: Pratik Shirodkar

Production Designer: Nilesh Mohite

Marketing Coordinator: Sonia Chauhan

First published: November 2023

Production reference: 1101123

Published by Packt Publishing Ltd.

Grosvenor House

11 St Paul's Square

Birmingham

B3 1RB, UK

ISBN 978-1-80512-500-6

www.packtpub.com

To my son, Gust, whom I had to disappoint too often while I was working on this book. Now I have time to play, let's go!

– Pieter Nijs

Foreword

Early in my career as a self-taught software developer, I realized I had a poor grasp of the terms being used by developers around me to describe application architecture. The role and responsibility of a View were obvious to me, but what about a model, presenter, mediator, service, factory, controller, or any number of other things? And what a ViewModel was really threw me! I often felt paralyzed about how to apply a pattern, which greatly slowed me down. I eventually discovered that while there are some rules you must not break, many things are also permissible once you understand the purposes behind a pattern.

Oh, how I wish I had had access to Pieter's book back then! He would have saved me a ton of time and spared me so much confusion.

I have interacted with Pieter for many years through the .NET community, and I know the size and scope of projects that he has been involved with. For that reason, I'm confident he's well suited to not only explain the MVVM pattern but to do so in a way that conveys the real-world application of it. This book will help you understand why the pattern exists, and whether to use it or not.

Of course, I'm thrilled that Pieter is teaching MVVM while also introducing you to the awesome power of .NET MAUI for building mobile and desktop applications. MVVM is by far the most common pattern we see used with .NET MAUI and is what we use in most of our product samples at Microsoft.

I can't wait to see what you build with .NET MAUI! Happy coding.

David Ortinau

Principal Product Manager @ Microsoft for .NET MAUI

Contributors

About the author

Pieter Nijs is a .NET consultant at Xebia in Belgium, with a keen interest in mobile and cloud development. He's been instrumental in diverse projects, from vast healthcare and telecom systems to compact LOB apps. Now, Pieter's exploring AI's potential to enhance customer projects innovatively. Passionate about technology, he actively experiments and shares knowledge as a conference speaker, trainer, and blogger at blog.pieeatingninjas.be. Pieter has been awarded the Microsoft MVP Award since 2017, reflecting his unwavering passion and expertise in serving the community.

Thank you, Stefanie, my constant, not just in the process of writing this book but in every step of life. Your unwavering love, encouragement, and belief in me have been the driving force behind everything I do and achieve, not just this book. I cannot measure your impact in mere words. Thanks also to my parents, who gave my brothers and me endless opportunities and a strong foundation.

About the reviewer

Gerald Versluis is a Senior Software Engineer at Microsoft working on .NET MAUI. Since 2009 Gerald has been working on a variety of projects, ranging from frontend to backend and anything in between that involve C#, .NET, Azure, ASP.NET and all kinds of other .NET technologies. At some point, he fell in love with cross-platform and mobile development with Xamarin, now .NET MAUI. Since that time, he has become an active community member, producing content online and presenting about all things tech at conferences all around the world.

Gerald can be found on X (formerly Twitter) @jfversluis, blogging at `https://blog.verslu.is`, or on his YouTube channel: `https://youtube.com/@jfversluis`.

Table of Contents

6

Working with Collections   123

Part 2: Building a .NET MAUI App Using MVVM

7

Dependency Injection, Services, and Messaging   153

8

Navigation in MVVM   179

9

Handling User Input and Validation   211

10

Working with Remote Data   235

Part 3: Mastering MVVM Development

11

12

13

14

Troubleshooting and Debugging Tips   343

Index   355

Other Books You May Enjoy   364

Preface

In an era where software design patterns and frameworks are at the heart of robust application development, mastering the **Model-View-ViewModel (MVVM)** pattern becomes crucial for developers stepping into the domain of .NET MAUI. *The MVVM Pattern in .NET MAUI*: A definitive guide to essential patterns, best practices, and techniques, has been meticulously crafted to serve as a guide for developers eager to embark on this journey.

What sets this book apart is its laser focus on .NET MAUI. We don't just talk about MVVM in general; we delve deep into its practical application within this specific framework. Even if you're new to MVVM or just starting with .NET MAUI, this guide is crafted to be both accessible and enriching.

Our journey begins with an in-depth exploration of the MVVM design pattern and the core components of the .NET MAUI framework. As we progress, we'll navigate through the intricacies of data binding, harnessing the power of community toolkits, and managing collections effectively. We'll dive deeper to understand dependency injection, service patterns, and messaging, and you will learn about different methods of navigation, understand user input and validation, and master the techniques of working with remote data. The latter chapters guide you through creating MVVM-friendly controls, localizing your applications, and the pivotal aspect of unit testing.

From these fundamentals to advanced techniques, by the end of this journey, you'll be fully equipped with the knowledge to integrate MVVM effectively into your .NET MAUI projects.

Welcome to your definitive guide!

Who this book is for

This book is tailored toward developers who aim to harness the power of the MVVM pattern within the context of .NET MAUI. Whether you're an enthusiast beginning your journey with .NET MAUI or a seasoned professional aiming to up their game in both .NET MAUI and MVVM, this guide has got you covered.

While prior experience with .NET MAUI or Xamarin.Forms aren't necessary, a foundational understanding of C# is essential. Developers familiar with C# will find the content approachable and structured to elevate their skills seamlessly to the wonderful worlds of .NET MAUI and MVVM.

From novices in the mobile application development arena to veterans seeking specialized knowledge in .NET MAUI's MVVM implementation, this book serves as a comprehensive guide for all.

What this book covers

Chapter 1, The MVVM Design Pattern, provides an overview of the core components of the MVVM pattern, showing their roles and interplay. It illustrates the value of separating UI from logic for better testability and maintenance. It addresses common MVVM misconceptions and offers a foundational grasp of MVVM, regardless of specific technology.

Chapter 2, What Is .NET MAUI?, gives an overview of the overarching landscape of .NET MAUI, its pivotal features and advantages, and its architecture. It provides insights into .NET MAUI's origins from Xamarin and Xamarin Forms, and its evolutionary journey.

Chapter 3, Data Binding Building Blocks in .NET MAUI, shows how data binding in .NET MAUI, a cornerstone for MVVM, is an essential part of .NET MAUI. This chapter unpacks the key principles, elements, and techniques underpinning this essential feature.

Chapter 4, Data Binding in .NET MAUI, builds upon the previous chapter but delves deeper into its intricacies and nuances, offering a comprehensive exploration of all the aspects of data binding in .NET MAUI.

Chapter 5, Community Toolkits, zeros in on two influential community toolkits: the MVVM Toolkit and the .NET MAUI Community Toolkit. It shows how these community-driven initiatives can amplify the effectiveness of MVVM in your .NET MAUI applications.

Chapter 6, Working with Collections, provides an overview of how to effectively display datasets using MVVM in .NET MAUI. From binding data and adapting to its changes to crafting data templates, this chapter offers an MVVM-centric guide to presenting data and facilitating user interactions with it.

Chapter 7, Dependency Injection, Services, and Messaging, illuminates the methods of aligning a ViewModel with a view via service registration and dependency injection. It highlights the nuances of injecting services into a ViewModel and facilitating seamless communication between ViewModels using messaging, all while upholding separation of concerns and enhancing testability.

Chapter 8, Navigation in .NET MAUI, is all about MVVM-based navigation. This chapter provides an overview of what .NET MAUI Shell is and its implications for navigation. It shows how to construct a navigation service tailored for both .NET MAUI apps that leverage Shell and apps that don't.

Chapter 9, Handling User Input and Validation, shows how to effectively handle user input, from validating data at the ViewModel level, standard and custom validation rules, to prompting the user for confirmations or cancellations in the presence of unsaved changes.

Chapter 10, Working with Remote Data, shows how to work with remote data, introduces repositories for maintaining separation of concerns, and utilizes dependency injection. It illustrates how to use Refit for streamlined API interactions, and how to handle asynchronous tasks and their UI implications.

Chapter 11, Creating MVVM-Friendly Controls, dives into the creation of custom controls that are tailored for MVVM, supporting data binding and interactivity through commands.

Chapter 12, Localization with MVVM, provides an overview of the techniques to localize hardcoded labels within the app, and how to effectively fetch language-specific data from APIs.

Chapter 13, Unit Testing, shows how easy and essential unit testing is. It guides you through setting up a unit test project, generating data, mocking dependencies, and testing MAUI code.

Chapter 14, Troubleshooting and Debugging Tips, highlights common hiccups and their solutions. It shows typical issues and pitfalls concerning data binding, dependency injection, and building custom controls and converters.

To get the most out of this book

You will need to be familiar with the basics of C#.

Early on in the book, we'll stipulate how to get your development environment up and running using Visual Studio 2022 or Visual Studio Code. The steps described in this book are based on Visual Studio, but everything that is explained and shown can also be done in any IDE that supports .NET MAUI.

If you are using the digital version of this book, we advise you to type the code yourself or access the code from the book's GitHub repository (a link is available in the next section). Doing so will help you avoid any potential errors related to the copying and pasting of code.

Download the example code files

You can download the example code files for this book from GitHub at `https://github.com/PacktPublishing/MVVM-pattern-.NET-MAUI`. If there's an update to the code, it will be updated in the GitHub repository.

We also have other code bundles from our rich catalog of books and videos available at `https://github.com/PacktPublishing/`. Check them out!

Conventions used

There are a number of text conventions used throughout this book.

`Code in text`: Indicates code words in text, database table names, folder names, filenames, file extensions, pathnames, dummy URLs, user input, and Twitter handles. Here is an example: "RecipeDetailViewModel represents the details of a recipe. For now, it only contains a `Title` property, which we now give a hardcoded value of `"Classic Caesar Salad"`."

A block of code is set as follows:

```
<Grid ColumnDefinitions="*, Auto">
    <Label
        FontAttributes="Bold" FontSize="22"
        Text="{Binding Path=Title, Mode=OneTime}"
```

```
            VerticalOptions="Center" />
    <Image
        x:Name="favoriteIcon"
        Grid.Column="1" Margin="5"
        HeightRequest="35" Source="favorite.png"
        VerticalOptions="Center" WidthRequest="35">
    </Image>
</Grid>
```

When we wish to draw your attention to a particular part of a code block, the relevant lines or items are set in bold:

```
private bool _hideAllergenInformation = true;
public bool HideAllergenInformation
{
    get => _hideAllergenInformation;
    set => SetProperty(ref _hideAllergenInformation, value);
}
```

Bold: Indicates a new term, an important word, or words that you see onscreen. For instance, words in menus or dialog boxes appear in **bold**. Here is an example: "Right-click the **Recipes.Client.Core** project and select **Add | New Folder** and name it Messages. "

> **Tips or important notes**
> Appear like this.

Get in touch

Feedback from our readers is always welcome.

General feedback: If you have questions about any aspect of this book, email us at customercare@ packtpub.com and mention the book title in the subject of your message.

Errata: Although we have taken every care to ensure the accuracy of our content, mistakes do happen. If you have found a mistake in this book, we would be grateful if you would report this to us. Please visit www.packtpub.com/support/errata and fill in the form.

Piracy: If you come across any illegal copies of our works in any form on the internet, we would be grateful if you would provide us with the location address or website name. Please contact us at copyright@packt.com with a link to the material.

If you are interested in becoming an author: If there is a topic that you have expertise in and you are interested in either writing or contributing to a book, please visit authors.packtpub.com.

Share Your Thoughts

Once you've read *The MVVM pattern in .NET MAUI*, we'd love to hear your thoughts! Scan the QR code below to go straight to the Amazon review page for this book and share your feedback.

https://packt.link/r/1805125001

Your review is important to us and the tech community and will help us make sure we're delivering excellent quality content.

Download a free PDF copy of this book

Thanks for purchasing this book!

Do you like to read on the go but are unable to carry your print books everywhere?

Is your eBook purchase not compatible with the device of your choice?

Don't worry, now with every Packt book you get a DRM-free PDF version of that book at no cost.

Read anywhere, any place, on any device. Search, copy, and paste code from your favorite technical books directly into your application.

The perks don't stop there, you can get exclusive access to discounts, newsletters, and great free content in your inbox daily

Follow these simple steps to get the benefits:

1. Scan the QR code or visit the link below

https://packt.link/free-ebook/9781805125006

2. Submit your proof of purchase

3. That's it! We'll send your free PDF and other benefits to your email directly

Part 1:
Key Concepts and Components

In this part, we start by discussing the Model-View-ViewModel design pattern without tying it to a specific platform. Next, we'll introduce the .NET MAUI framework and highlight why it works so well with MVVM. As we move forward, you'll learn about the benefits of community toolkits and get hands-on experience with collections. This foundation sets you up for more advanced topics later on.

This part has the following chapters:

- *Chapter 1, The MVVM Design Pattern*
- *Chapter 2, The .NET MAUI Framework*
- *Chapter 3, Data Binding Building Blocks in .NET MAUI*
- *Chapter 4, Data Binding in .NET MAUI*
- *Chapter 5, Community Toolkits*
- *Chapter 6, Working with Collections*

1

What Is the MVVM Design Pattern?

The **MVVM** or **Model-View-ViewModel** pattern is a very commonly used design pattern in the .NET ecosystem, where it has proven to be a good fit for front-end frameworks that utilize **XAML** to build graphical user interfaces. And it's not hard to see why.

This book will provide a good understanding of the MVVM design pattern and how to effectively apply it in **.NET MAUI** projects. It's important to note that while we will focus on applying MVVM in the context of .NET MAUI, the MVVM pattern itself is not exclusive to the .NET ecosystem. It is a widely used design pattern that has gained popularity across various software development ecosystems, including frameworks like WPF, WinUI, and others. We'll delve into various aspects of .NET MAUI to understand how it supports and enables the use of MVVM. Throughout the book, we'll be building the "*Recipes!*" app as a practical example, showcasing various aspects of the MVVM pattern applied in .NET MAUI.

In this chapter, we'll learn about the MVVM design pattern and its core components. We will look into what added value the pattern brings in terms of separation of concerns and why this is so important. A sample application will demonstrate the added value MVVM can bring to your code. Finally, we'll discuss some common misconceptions about MVVM.

By the end of this chapter, you will understand what MVVM is, what its main components are, and what each component's role is. You will also see what value MVVM adds in terms of the testability and maintainability of your code.

In this chapter, we are going to cover the following main topics:

- MVVM's core components
- Separation of concerns matters
- MVVM in action
- Common misconceptions about MVVM

Before diving into the details of MVVM in .NET MAUI, it's essential to familiarize ourselves with the core components of the MVVM pattern. In the following section, we'll define the key terminologies to ensure we have a solid foundation and a shared understanding moving forward.

Technical requirements

Although this chapter gives a theoretical overview of MVVM, later there is some code showing MVVM in action so you can start seeing the value this pattern brings. To implement this sample yourself, you'll need the following: *Visual Studio 2022 (17.3 or greater), or any IDE that allows you to create .NET MAUI apps.* Near the end of *Chapter 2, What Is .NET MAUI?*, we'll be looking at how to get your machine ready for developing .NET MAUI apps. The sample code can also be found on GitHub at `https://github.com/PacktPublishing/MVVM-pattern-.NET-MAUI`.

Looking at MVVM's core components

MVVM provides a very clear way to separate UI from business logic, promoting code reusability, maintainability, and testability while allowing flexible UI design and changes.

Having business logic living in the code-behind quickly becomes challenging as applications grow in size and complexity. Code-behind refers to the practice of placing the business logic within the same file as the user interface elements, often resulting in a significant amount of code being invoked through event handlers. This frequently results in a tight coupling between UI elements and the underlying business logic, as UI elements are directly referenced and manipulated within the code. As a result, making adjustments to the UI and performing unit testing can become more difficult. Later on in this chapter, in the *MVVM in action* section, we will see what it means to have business logic in the code-behind and how that complicates maintainability, testing, et cetera.

At first glance, MVVM might be slightly overwhelming or confusing. In order to fully understand what the pattern is all about and why it is so popular with XAML developers, we first need to dissect the MVVM pattern and look at its core components.

The name of the pattern already gives away three essential core components: the **Model**, the **View**, and the **ViewModel**. There are also two supporting elements that are crucial for efficiently using MVVM: **Commands** and **data binding**. Each of these elements has its own distinct role and responsibilities.

The following diagram shows MVVM's core components and how they interact with each other:

Figure 1.1 – Core components of MVVM

If you want to use the MVVM pattern effectively, it's important that you understand not only the responsibilities of each component but also how they interact with each other. At a high level, the View knows about the ViewModel, and the ViewModel knows about the Model, but the Model is unaware of the ViewModel. This separation prevents tight coupling between the UI and business logic.

In order to use the MVVM pattern efficiently and effectively, it is important that you understand how to organize your app code into suitable classes and how these classes interact with each other. Now, let's look into the core components.

Model

The Model is responsible for representing the data and business logic of the application. It encapsulates the data and provides a way to manipulate it. The Model can communicate with other components within the application, such as a database or a web service.

It is often implemented using classes that represent the objects in the application's domain, such as customers, orders, or products. These classes typically contain properties that represent the attributes of the objects and methods that define the behavior of the objects.

The Model is designed to be independent of the UI framework used in the application. As a result, it can be reused in other applications if needed. It can be maintained and tested in isolation, separately from the application's UI.

> **Note**
>
> Often, it's unclear to developers who are new to MVVM what type of object the Model can or should be: **Data Transfer Objects (DTOs)**, **Plain Old CLR Objects (POCOs)**, domain entities, proxy objects, services, and so on. All these types of objects can be seen as the Model.

Moreover, in most cases, the Model is a combination of different types of objects. Don't see the Model as a single thing. In fact, it's everything 'outside' the View and ViewModel – it's the application's domain and business logic. Ultimately, the choice of Model type will depend on the specific requirements, use case, and architecture of the application. Some developers may prefer to use DTOs for simplicity and ease of use, while others may prefer to use domain entities for better encapsulation and consistency with the domain model.

However, regardless of the specific type of Model being used, it's important to keep the business logic within the Model 'layer' and avoid it in the ViewModel. This helps to maintain separation of concerns and keeps the ViewModel focused on presentation logic, while the Model focuses on business logic.

View

The View is responsible for presenting the data to the user. It consists of (UI) elements, such as buttons, labels, collections, and inputs. The View receives input or actions from the user and communicates with the ViewModel so it can react to those interactions.

In .NET MAUI, the View is often implemented using XAML, which is a markup language used to define the UI elements and layouts. The XAML file defines the structure of the UI and its bindings to the ViewModel. It's important to note that while the MVVM pattern is often associated with XAML-based UIs, its principles are not limited to a specific UI framework. The MVVM pattern can be applied in other UI frameworks as well. In .NET MAUI, most apps use XAML for defining the UI, but it's also possible to create the UI entirely in C#. Even when taking this approach, developers can still effectively apply the MVVM pattern to separate the concerns of the View, ViewModel, and Model.

The most important aspect of the View is that it should be designed to be as simple as possible, without any business rules or logic. Its main purpose is to present data to the user and receive input from them. The View's focus should be on presentation logic, including formatting and layout, and it should not include any business logic or application logic to maintain proper separation of concerns in MVVM.

> **Tip**
> By keeping the View simple and focused on presentation logic, the code can be easier to maintain and test. It also enables the UI to be changed without affecting the underlying business logic, allowing for greater flexibility in adapting and evolving the application over time.

The View, whether it is implemented using XAML or C#, is the application's UI layer. Essentially, it is the collection of UI components, such as pages and controls, that make up the user interface.

ViewModel

The ViewModel sits in between the Model and the View. It's the "glue" between the UI and the business logic. Its responsibility is to expose data to the View for display and to handle any user input or UI events. It provides an interface for the View to interact with the Model, which contains the actual data and business logic of the application. Let's delve into what the ViewModel does, step by step:

1. **Exposing data**: The ViewModel retrieves data from the Model and exposes it to the View through public properties. These properties are usually bound to elements in the View, such as text boxes or labels. This way, the data from the Model gets displayed on the screen.

2. **Reflecting changes**: Now, you might be wondering what happens when the user changes something on the screen. That's where data binding comes in. Data binding is like a live channel of communication between the View and the ViewModel. When the user modifies data in the View, the ViewModel is instantly notified and updates its properties accordingly. Similarly, if something changes in the ViewModel, the View gets updated too.

3. **Handling user interactions**: The ViewModel doesn't just passively provide data; it's also responsible for dealing with user interactions, such as button clicks and text input. For example, if there's a **Save** button on the View, the ViewModel needs to know what to do when the user clicks on it.

4. **Updating the Model**: When the user interacts with the UI and makes changes, the ViewModel plays an essential role in updating the Model. The ViewModel takes the user's changes and translates them into actions that the Model can understand and process.

The ViewModel acts as an intermediary that handles the flow of data and actions between the View and the Model, ensuring that the user interface accurately represents the underlying data and responds correctly to user interactions. This modular approach, where it handles specific responsibilities separately from the View and Model, contributes to cleaner and more maintainable code. Finally, it's essential to understand that the ViewModel should not be tied to any specific UI framework. Being independent of a UI framework allows it to be shared across different applications and facilitates easier testing in isolation from the rest of the application.

Commands

Commands are an important concept used to represent actions that can be triggered by the UI. They are a way for the View to communicate user actions to the ViewModel. A Command is an object that implements the `ICommand` interface, which defines two methods: `Execute` and `CanExecute`. The `Execute` method is called when the Command is triggered, while the `CanExecute` method is used to determine whether the Command can be executed in its current state.

Commands can be seen as the equivalent of events in traditional event-driven programming. Both Commands and events serve as mechanisms to handle user actions or other triggers in an application. For instance, when the user clicks a button in the View, a Command in the ViewModel gets triggered, and the ViewModel takes appropriate actions such as saving data or fetching new information. Commands are highly versatile and are not limited to buttons. They can be associated with various UI elements such as menu items, toolbar buttons, or even gesture controls. Let's take a practical example: suppose you have a text editor application. You could have a Command associated with the **Save** button, another one for the **Copy** menu item, and yet another for a gesture control that triggers the **Paste** action. In each case, when the UI element is interacted with, the associated Command's `Execute` method is called and then performs the necessary action.

One of the key benefits of using Commands in the MVVM pattern is that they allow for better separation of concerns between the View and the ViewModel. By using Commands, the View can be designed without knowing anything about the underlying functionality that is associated with a particular UI element. This means that the ViewModel can handle the entire logic associated with the Command, without having to be tightly coupled to the UI.

In order to bind a Command to a UI element in the View, the Command needs to be exposed by the ViewModel as a public property. The View can then bind to this property using data binding. When a Command is bound to a UI element in the View, the UI element is listening for an event such as a button click to occur. When that event is triggered, the Command's `Execute` method, which contains the code that should be executed in response to the event, is called.

Overall, Commands are a powerful and flexible concept in the MVVM pattern, which enables better separation of concerns between the View and the ViewModel.

> **More about Commands**
> We'll dive into much more detail about Commands and how to use them in practice in *Chapter 3, Data Binding Building Blocks in .NET MAUI.*

Data binding

Data binding is a core feature of MVVM that enables the ViewModel to communicate with the View and the View with the ViewModel in a loosely coupled manner. Data binding allows you to bind data properties in the ViewModel to UI elements in the View, such as entry fields, labels, and list views. It is used to synchronize the data between the View and the ViewModel. When the data in the ViewModel changes, the data binding engine updates the View, and vice versa, depending on how the binding is configured. This allows the UI to reflect the current state of the application.

The binding process involves three components: a **source** object (the ViewModel), a **target** object (the UI element), and a **binding expression** that specifies how the two objects should be connected.

Data can flow in different directions: from the ViewModel to the View, the other way around, or both. Here are the ways data can flow:

- **One-way**: From the ViewModel to the View, this allows the values of the properties on the ViewModel to be displayed on the View. This type of binding is typically used when updates on the ViewModel should automatically update the value on the View.

- **One-way-to-source**: The exact opposite of one-way, the data only flows from the View to the ViewModel. Values entered in the View will automatically be reflected on the ViewModel.

- **One-time**: Like one-way, the data flows from the ViewModel to the View, but the data binding engine will not listen for any changes that occur on the bound property. Once the initial value is displayed on the UI, any subsequent changes to the property will not be reflected on the View. This can have a significant positive performance impact when doing a lot of data binding.

- **Two-way**: Data flows in two ways; from the View to the ViewModel and from the ViewModel to the View. Changes made to the data in the UI are automatically propagated back to the ViewModel. A common scenario for using two-way data binding is when displaying a property in the View that the user can modify. In this case, the property is typically bound to an input field using two-way data binding. This allows the initial value of the property to be displayed in the input field, and any changes made by the user to be automatically reflected to the ViewModel, without the need for additional event handling or manual updates.

Data binding is a very powerful concept and an essential component in the MVVM pattern. It allows the ViewModel to expose data and behavior as simple properties to the View, in a way that is independent of the UI framework. Through data binding, these properties can be bound to the UI in a loosely coupled manner. By using data binding, the View and ViewModel in MVVM can be synchronized seamlessly without the need for any manual code. The binding mode determines how changes in the data are propagated between the View and ViewModel. Additionally, data binding allows the View to communicate user input back to the ViewModel through Commands, which can then update the Model.

> **More about data binding**
>
> Everything you need to know about data binding and how to effectively use it in .NET MAUI is covered thoroughly in *Chapter 3, Data Binding Building Blocks in .NET MAUI*, and *Chapter 4, Data Binding in .NET MAUI*.

Now that we have a good understanding of MVVM's core components and have gained insights into each component's responsibility, let's discuss in a bit more detail why MVVM matters and what value it adds.

Separation of concerns matters

Separation of concerns is an important principle in software development that aims to divide software design and implementation into distinct parts, each with a specific and well-defined responsibility. This principle helps developers create more maintainable and flexible applications by reducing the complexity of each individual component and allowing for more modular and reusable code.

In practical terms, separation of concerns means that different aspects of a system are separated and dealt with independently, without overlapping concerns. This is achieved by creating distinct layers or modules, each with its own well-defined responsibilities and interfaces, and minimizing the dependencies between them.

Let's consider the example of a restaurant's management system. In such a system, there could be several concerns like table reservation, order taking, kitchen operations, and billing. According to the principle of separation of concerns, each of these areas should be handled by a separate module.

Each module has its own set of responsibilities and would communicate with others through well-defined interfaces. For example, when a customer orders a dish, the order-taking module communicates with the kitchen operations module so that the dish can be prepared.

This separation means that if you need to make changes to how table reservations work, you can do so without affecting kitchen operations or billing. This separation keeps the codebase more organized, easier to maintain, and allows for focused testing of individual modules.

Let's explore how separation of concerns enhances both maintainability and testability. These are the two crucial aspects that are vital to the long-term success of any software application.

Maintainability

By applying MVVM, we are separating the UI from the business logic and loosely coupling the ViewModel with the View. This improves maintainability greatly as each component has its distinct role and its distinct concern.

The View, for example, can be easily altered or updated. UI elements can be moved around or replaced with newer, more modern ones without requiring changes to the ViewModel, as long as no additional data needs to be displayed. This is because the only interface between the View and the ViewModel is through data binding. Therefore, updating the View should not affect the ViewModel unless additional or altered data needs to be displayed.

Additionally, when the View requires additional data to be displayed or a UI element is updated and requires further data, the ViewModel may need to be updated as well. However, if the required data is already available in the Model, the ViewModel can translate it between the Model and the View without affecting the Model itself. The ViewModel is responsible for managing data flow between the Model and the View, ensuring a clear separation of concerns between the different layers of the application.

In addition, any changes in the Model's business logic should not have a significant impact on the ViewModel or the View. Since the ViewModel acts as a mediator between the Model and the View, it's responsible for translating the data from the Model to be used by the View. Therefore, if any underlying business logic should change, the ViewModel can handle the translation without affecting the View, ensuring that any changes made to the Model are transparent to the user.

Even when an update to the Model or ViewModel is needed, thanks to the nature of the MVVM pattern, these changes can be easily tested in isolation from each other and, most importantly, independently of the UI. This separation enables efficient and focused testing.

Testability

Testability is a very important factor in software development. Not only do tests ensure that the tested code performs its intended function, but it also guarantees that it continues to operate as initially designed. When a successful set of tests is run, feedback is provided immediately after a code update inadvertently breaks the functionality. This is undoubtedly vital for maintaining the quality and stability of the codebase. In essence, comprehensive testing plays a crucial role in preserving the code's maintainability, allowing for efficient modifications and improvements over time.

> **Note**
> By designing an application with testability in mind, developers can create code that is more reliable, maintainable, and scalable.

Separation of concerns is crucial to achieving testability because it allows developers to isolate and test individual components of the application without worrying about dependencies on other parts of the system.

From the perspective of the MVVM design pattern, separation of concerns and testability are closely related. As the View, ViewModel, and Model are being treated as distinct components, each component is able to be written and tested independently of the others. Because the ViewModel is decoupled from the View and is agnostic of any specific UI framework, it is very easy to write automated unit tests for it. These automated tests are faster and more reliable than manual or automated UI testing, which allows developers to identify errors and regressions early in the development process before they become more difficult and expensive to fix. Similarly, the Model logic can also be effectively tested in isolation, independently of the ViewModel and the View.

That's the theory. Now, let's take a look at an MVVM example!

MVVM in action

Let's look at a very simple application that shows the user a quote of the day on the screen. When the user clicks a button on the screen, the application will fetch a quote of the day from an API and show it onscreen. Once the button is clicked, it should be hidden. The code-behind approach will show you how this app can be written without using the MVVM pattern, whereas the second example shows the same functionality implemented using MVVM with testability in mind.

The code-behind approach

In the following code snippet, there is no separation of concerns; all the code is handled in the code-behind of the XAML page. While this code seems to be doing what is expected, there is no easy, fast, or robust way to test whether it works. This is because all the logic is handled in the click event handler of the button.

In `MainPage.xaml`, we define a `Button` and a `Label`:

```
<Grid>
    <Button
        x:Name="GetQuoteButton"
        Clicked="Button_Clicked"
        Text="Get Quote of the day" />

    <Label
        x:Name="QuoteLabel"
```

```
                HorizontalOptions="Center"
                IsVisible="false"
                Style="{DynamicResource TitleStyle}"
                VerticalOptions="Center" />
    </Grid>
```

Both button and label controls have a `Name` so that they can be referenced from the code-behind. The label, is not visible by default.

In the code-behind (`MainPage.xaml.cs`), we handle the button click event as follows:

```
private async void Button_Clicked(
    object sender, EventArgs e)
{
    GetQuoteButton.IsVisible = false;

    try
    {
        var client = new HttpClient();
        var quote = await
            client.GetStringAsync(
            "https://my-quotes-api.com/quote-of-the-day");


        QuoteLabel.Text = quote;

        QuoteLabel.IsVisible = true;
    }
    catch (Exception)
    {
    }
}
```

On the button click, the `GetQuoteButton` is being hidden and a call to fetch a quote is being made. The `QuoteLabel`'s `Text` property is assigned the value of the retrieved quote.

Note that there's a subtle bug in this code: if the API call fails, the exception being thrown would be silently caught, but the `GetQuoteButton`'s visibility won't be restored to being visible, leaving the application unusable. But as there is no easy way to test this code, chances are high that this scenario is left unnoticed until the application gets to QA where, hopefully, a manual test might pick this issue up.

Using MVVM

Now, let's look at how we could transform this application using the MVVM pattern, keeping separation of concerns and testability in mind. It might be that not everything in this example is clear yet and that's perfectly fine. While going through this book, all of these aspects should become clear very rapidly.

Let's start off by looking at what the Model in this app would be.

The Model

In our sample application, the primary data we are working with is the quote that we fetch from an API. The logic that communicates with this API to fetch the data can be thought of as the Model. Instead of making the HTTP request directly in the code-behind as we previously did, we can encapsulate this logic into a separate class. This class will be responsible for fetching the quote and will act as our Model. Here's what that might look like:

```
public class QuoteService : IQuoteService
{
    private readonly HttpClient httpClient;

    public QuoteService()
    {
        httpClient = new HttpClient();
    }

    public async Task<string> GetQuote()
    {
        var response = await
        httpClient.GetAsync("https://my-quotes-api.com/
        quote-of-the-day");

        if (response.IsSuccessStatusCode)
        {
            return await
            response.Content.ReadAsStringAsync();
        }

        throw new Exception("Failed to retrieve quote.");
    }
}

public interface IQuoteService
{
```

```
    Task<string> GetQuote();
}
```

As you can see, we have created a `QuoteService` class, which contains the logic for fetching the quote from the API. This class implements an interface called `IQuoteService`. By defining an interface, we are making it easier to swap out the implementation or mock this service for testing purposes later.

By having this logic, which was previously in our code-behind, encapsulated in a dedicated class already gives us a cleaner separation of concerns.

This covers the Model part of the Model-View-ViewModel pattern. Let's see what the ViewModel could look like.

The ViewModel

The ViewModel acts as an intermediary between the View and the Model. It holds the data and the Commands that the View will bind to. For our simple application, we need the following things in our ViewModel:

- A property to hold the quote of the day once it is retrieved
- Two properties to control the visibility of the button and the label
- A Command that will be triggered when the button is clicked; this will be responsible for fetching the quote

We also need to have a constructor that takes a parameter of type `IQuoteService`. This is where dependency injection comes into play.

> **More about dependency injection**
>
> Dependency injection is key to making classes testable and modular, and is used very commonly in MVVM. *Chapter 7, Dependency Injection, Services, and Messaging*, covers this concept in depth.

Let's take a look at what this might look like in code:

```
public class MainPageViewModel : INotifyPropertyChanged
{
    private readonly IQuoteService quoteService;

    public MainPageViewModel(IQuoteService quoteService)
    {
        this.quoteService = quoteService;
    }
```

```
    public event PropertyChangedEventHandler
    PropertyChanged;
}
```

The constructor takes an instance of IQuoteService as a parameter. This instance is assigned to the quoteService field within the class. This way, the ViewModel has access to the quote-fetching service, allowing it to retrieve quotes when needed.

Also note that this class implements the INotifyPropertyChanged interface, and therefore needs to implement the PropertyChanged event. Its purpose is essentially to make sure the UI gets notified when data on the ViewModel changes so the View and ViewModel stay in sync. *Chapter 3, Data Binding Building Blocks in .NET MAUI,* covers this in much more depth!

QuoteOfTheDay is the property that holds the retrieved quote. This is just a simple property holding a string value. The only thing "special" about it is that it triggers the PropertyChanged event to inform the data binding engine about the updated value:

```
private string quoteOfTheDay;
public string QuoteOfTheDay
{
    get => quoteOfTheDay;
    set
    {
        quoteOfTheDay = value;
        PropertyChanged?.Invoke(this,
            new PropertyChangedEventArgs(
            nameof(QuoteOfTheDay)));
    }
}
```

The two properties that control the visibility of the button and the label are IsButtonVisible and IsLabelVisible, respectively. Again, these are simple public properties that trigger the PropertyChanged event:

```
private bool isButtonVisible = true;
public bool IsButtonVisible
{
    get => isButtonVisible;
    set
    {
        isButtonVisible = value;
        PropertyChanged?.Invoke(this,
            new PropertyChangedEventArgs(
            nameof(IsButtonVisible)));
    }
```

```
    }

bool isLabelVisible;
public bool IsLabelVisible
{
    get => isLabelVisible;
    set
    {
        isLabelVisible = value;
        PropertyChanged?.Invoke(this,
            new PropertyChangedEventArgs(
            nameof(IsLabelVisible)));
    }
}
```

Before we implement the Command that should be invoked when the user clicks the buttons, let's first implement the logic that needs to be executed by said Command:

```
private async Task GetQuote()
{
    IsButtonVisible = false;

    try
    {
        var quote = await quoteService.GetQuote();

        QuoteOfTheDay = quote;

        IsLabelVisible = true;
    }
    catch (Exception)
    {
    }
}
```

The GetQuote method is asynchronous, meaning it allows for non-blocking execution, which is especially important when fetching data from a network source. It starts by setting the IsButtonVisible property to false, which should hide the button on the screen. Next, we're calling the GetQuote method of the quoteService field, which will go out and fetch a quote. What this service actually does to retrieve the quote isn't important here, as that isn't the concern of our ViewModel. Once we receive a quote back from the GetQuote method of quoteService, we assign this value to the QuoteOfTheDay property. The IsLabelVisible property is set to true so that the label displaying the quote becomes visible.

Finally, we can create a Command that triggers this method:

```
public ICommand GetQuoteCommand => new Command(async _ => await
GetQuote());
```

Through `GetQuoteCommand`, we can now call the `GetQuote` method defined on the ViewModel.

With the Model and the ViewModel in place, let's finally have a look at the View.

The View

Essentially, not a lot of changes are needed to the UI: we still need a button that should trigger the retrieval of the `QuoteOfTheDay` and a label to show it. As we are no longer going to be accessing the label from the code-behind, there is no need to set the `x:Name` property:

```
<Grid>
    <Button
        Text="Get Quote of the day" />

    <Label
        HorizontalOptions="Center"
        IsVisible="false"
        Style="{DynamicResource TitleStyle}"
        VerticalOptions="Center" />
</Grid>
```

Also, the `Button_Clicked` event handler that we had earlier can be removed from the code-behind. And while we are there, we can also assign the `BindingContext` of the page to an instance of `MainPageViewModel`:

```
public partial class MainPage_MVVM : ContentPage
{
    public MainPage_MVVM()
    {
        InitializeComponent();
        BindingContext = new MainPageViewModel(
            new QuoteService());
    }
}
```

`BindingContext` is essentially the source that we are going to bind to. With this in place, we make some final adjustments to our XAML to include data-binding statements:

```
<Grid>
    <Button
        Command="{Binding GetQuoteCommand}"
```

```
    IsVisible="{Binding IsButtonVisible}"
    Text="Get Quote of the day" />

<Label
    HorizontalOptions="Center"
    IsVisible="{Binding IsLabelVisible}"
    Style="{DynamicResource TitleStyle}"
    Text="{Binding QuoteOfTheDay}"
    VerticalOptions="Center" />
</Grid>
```

These binding statements 'link' the public properties exposed on our ViewModel to the properties on the UI elements. When the user clicks the button, GetQuoteCommand on MainPageViewModel will be invoked, which in turn will execute the GetQuote method. While the GetQuote method is executed, the IsButtonVisible and IsLabelVisible properties are being updated, and a quote retrieved from QuoteService will be set as the value of the QuoteOfTheDay property. Through data binding, these changes will instantly and automatically be reflected on the View.

That's it! This is basically the same application as we had before. However, this time it is written using the MVVM pattern while keeping separation of concerns and testability in mind.

The first thing that immediately stands out is the fact that the MVVM example has more code to it. That's mostly because of the ViewModel. Luckily, ViewModels should be pretty simple. They should not contain any business logic. In this example, the business logic is inside the QuoteService class, which the ViewModel calls into to get the QuoteOfTheDay value. The properties on the ViewModel are there to represent the state of the View, such as for controlling the visibility of the button and the label, and for holding the Quote that QuoteService will return.

It should be clear by now that every piece in this example has its own responsibility:

- The View – MainPage_MVVM – is responsible for the UI layer. It contains the visual elements such as a Label and a Button and lays them out.

- The single responsibility of QuoteService – the Model in this scenario – is to fetch a Quote.

- MainPageViewModel glues it all together. It provides the properties and values that the View needs to display, as well as any Commands for handling interactions.

Every component has only one reason to change, which makes this code much more maintainable, compared to having everything in the code-behind. Not only maintainability, but also testability is improved a lot compared to the previous example. Don't take my word for it; let's explore how we can test the functionality of our app.

Testing your ViewModel

Finally, let's take a quick look at what this means for testability. The following code sample shows some unit tests for `MainPageViewModel`. Again, not everything in here might be clear, but everything will be covered thoroughly throughout this book. Moreover, *Chapter 13, Unit Testing*, is entirely dedicated to writing unit tests for your ViewModels. In these tests, we're using the **Moq** framework to create mock instances of the `IQuoteService` interface. Mocking is a technique used in unit testing to create a fake or simulated object that mimics the behavior of a real object. This is especially useful for isolating the code being tested and removing dependencies on external elements such as databases or APIs. In the constructor of our test class, which runs before each test, we create a new mock instance that returns an empty string as a result of the `GetQuote` method:

```
private Mock<IQuoteService> quoteServiceMock;

public MainPageViewModelTests()
{
    quoteServiceMock = new Mock<IQuoteService>();
    quoteServiceMock.Setup(m => m.GetQuote())
      .ReturnsAsync(string.Empty);
}
```

This mocked instance can be passed in as a parameter when creating a new instance of the `MainPageViewModel` class. This allows us to test the ViewModel without any external dependencies.

The first snippet shows two tests that test the value of the `IsButtonVisible` property:

```
[Fact]
public void ButtonShouldBeVisible()
{
    var sut = new
        MainPageViewModel(quoteServiceMock.Object);

    Assert.True(sut.IsButtonVisible);
}
[Fact]
public void GetQuoteCommand_ShouldSetButtonInvisible()
{
    var sut = new
        MainPageViewModel(quoteServiceMock.Object);

    sut.GetQuoteCommand.Execute(null);

    Assert.False(sut.IsButtonVisible);
}
```

The first of the preceding tests checks whether the initial value of the `IsButtonVisible` property is `true`. We create a new instance of `MainPageViewModel`, passing in the mocked `IQuoteService` instance. We can now use our `sut` variable (for system under test) to do assertions and see whether everything works as expected. The second test checks that as soon as `GetQuoteCommand` is invoked, the `IsButtonVisible` property is `false`.

The next test checks whether the `Quote` value returned by the injected `IQuoteService`'s `GetQuote` method is being set as the value of the `QuoteOfTheDay` property:

```
[Fact]
public void GetQuoteCommand_GotQuote_ShowQuote()
{
    var quote = "My quote of the day";
    quoteServiceMock.Setup(m =>
        m.GetQuote()).ReturnsAsync(quote);

    var sut = new
        MainPageViewModel(quoteServiceMock.Object);

    sut.GetQuoteCommand.Execute(null);

    Assert.Equal(quote, sut.QuoteOfTheDay);
}
```

In the preceding test, we define that the `GetQuote` method of the mocked `IQuoteSerivce` should return a particular value. After executing `GetQuoteCommand`, the `QuoteOfTheDay` property should have the same value.

And finally, we have a test that doesn't test the application's happy path. Instead, it tests whether the `IsButtonVisible` property is set to `true` after the `quoteService` failed to retrieve a quote, allowing the user to try again:

```
[Fact]
public void GetQuoteCommand_ServiceThrows_ShouldShowButton()
{
    quoteServiceMock.Setup(m =>
        m.GetQuote()).ThrowsAsync(new Exception());

    var sut = new
        MainPageViewModel(quoteServiceMock.Object);

    sut.GetQuoteCommand.Execute(null);

    Assert.True(sut.IsButtonVisible);
}
```

This test fails, revealing an issue in the implementation: the `GetQuote` method of the ViewModel handles any exception from `IQuoteService` silently, but fails to re-enable the button, leaving the app in a useless state. Without even running the app once, needing to deploy any other components, or needing to rely on the availability of the quote of the day API, the app's behavior is effectively being tested and a simple bug could already be identified very early on in the development process. These tests ensure that the application is behaving as it was intended to, but also that it keeps working like this in the future. If a change to the code would introduce different (unexpected) behavior, automated tests would fail, informing the developer that they have broken something and need to fix it before publishing the app. Unit tests like these are so valuable and very easy to write, as long as there is a clear separation of concerns and the application is written with testability in mind. The MVVM pattern is perfect for this! Like in this example, the ViewModel can be tested in complete isolation as it isn't tied to the View or any specific UI framework. This ViewModel will work in any kind of .NET application!

Compared to the previous example with code-behind implementation, testing becomes significantly more challenging: the app has to be deployed, and a UI testing framework must be used to launch the app, interact with the UI controls, and validate whether the UI shows what is expected. Automated UI tests can be time-consuming to write, run, and maintain. However, would you instead want to depend exclusively on manual testing and QA, rather than leveraging the benefits of automated testing to ensure the quality and reliability of your app's behavior?

When using the MVVM pattern, it becomes very easy to write unit tests that test different areas of the application, as it promotes separation of concerns and should be UI framework independent. Testing business logic through automated UI tests when everything is in the code-behind becomes very complex, hard to maintain, and error-prone very fast. UI tests have their purpose as they can test whether the user interface of an application behaves as expected. Both types of tests are important and serve different purposes in ensuring the quality of an application. But (automated) UI tests should just do that: test the UI. Your ViewModels and business logic should already be tested by other automated tests.

Common misconceptions about MVVM

There are several common misconceptions about MVVM that can lead to misunderstandings of its principles and best practices. Let's dispel some of these and provide clarity on the pattern.

There should be no code in the code-behind

While it is true that the main purpose of MVVM is to separate the presentation logic from the application logic, it is not necessarily the case that there should be *no* code in the code-behind. The code-behind can still be used to handle simple UI-related events or for any logic that is tightly coupled with the View.

In fact, there are scenarios where putting some code in the code-behind can be more efficient and maintainable than trying to move everything to the ViewModel. For example, handling UI animations, scrolling, and controlling focus or complex visual behaviors may be easier to implement in the code-behind rather than trying to do it through data binding.

To ensure proper separation of concerns in MVVM, it is imperative to avoid including business logic in the code-behind of the View. The code-behind should be kept to a minimum and remain as simple as possible to maintain the separation between the View and the ViewModel.

The Model should exclusively be a DTO, a domain entity, or a POCO

Although the type of object used for the Model in MVVM has been a topic of debate, in my opinion, it is not a critical factor. The main principle of MVVM is to keep the business logic out of the View and only have simple validation logic in the ViewModel. Thus, the Model can be any object type and is often a combination of different types of objects. The Model isn't a single type of thing; it is everything 'outside' the View and ViewModel that contains the application's entities, business logic, repositories, and so on. The important thing to remember is that the View and ViewModel should not contain any business or persistence logic.

The View and the ViewModel should not know each other

While the ViewModel should not have any knowledge of the View in order to maintain separation of concerns, the View can have a reference to the ViewModel. It is important to note that this does not violate the principles of MVVM, as long as the ViewModel is not dependent on the View. The use of 'compiled bindings' in platforms such as .NET MAUI can provide significant performance improvements, but in order for them to work, the View must have knowledge of the type it is binding to.

> **More about compiled bindings**
>
> Curious to find out more about compiled bindings? *Chapter 4, Data Binding in .NET MAUI,* has got you covered.

Also, there may be some situations where it's necessary for the View to directly invoke a method on the ViewModel from the code-behind. This can be necessary in cases where the UI is very complex, and the Command can't be easily bound.

MVVM is too complex and used only for large applications

MVVM itself is not necessarily complex, but it may require some learning and practice to become proficient with it. Understanding the concept of the separation of concerns and implementing it in MVVM can be a bit challenging for developers who are not used to working with this design pattern. Additionally, getting the bindings right can require some effort, especially when working with large and complex Views. However, once you understand it, you will notice that the development process becomes simpler and the code becomes more maintainable and testable. Even though there might be a learning curve, it is worthwhile to adopt MVVM in application development, even for small and simple applications. These kinds of apps need to be maintained and updated over time. In the course of time, their business logic would also benefit from unit testing, right?

That said, MVVM might be overkill for applications that have a very minimal UI, with only a handful of UI elements and little to no business logic being reflected on the UI. But then again, looking at the previous sample that only had two UI controls, we noticed that it benefited from being testable through applying the MVVM design pattern.

Summary

To summarize, the MVVM pattern separates the concerns of data, UI, and logic, which makes the application easier to test, modify, and extend. By using the Model to represent the data and business logic, the View to present the data to the user, and the ViewModel to mediate between the Model and the View, the MVVM pattern promotes a clear separation of responsibilities that makes it easier to develop and maintain complex applications. Additionally, the use of Commands and data binding provides a powerful way to handle user input and keep the UI in sync with the application's state. Understanding the components of MVVM is crucial for building successful .NET MAUI applications that are maintainable, scalable, and easy to test.

In *Chapter 2, What Is .NET MAUI?*, we'll dive into .NET MAUI so that you have a good understanding of this framework. If you already have a thorough knowledge of .NET MAUI, you can skip this chapter. If you know the basics of it, it should be a good refresher.

2

What is .NET MAUI?

Writing mobile applications for different platforms is hard, especially when it comes to creating cross-platform apps that run smoothly on different devices and operating systems. **.NET MAUI** (**Multi-platform App UI**) is a framework that aims to simplify this process by allowing developers to build native and performant cross-platform desktop and mobile apps for iOS, macOS, Android, and Windows – all from a single code base.

In this chapter, we'll take a look at the .NET MAUI framework. In order to thoroughly understand what this framework is and what it does, we'll discuss its core concept, how it works, its features, and its benefits. We will also look at what is needed to start building a .NET MAUI app, installing the necessary bits, and creating a new app.

After reading this chapter, you will have a solid understanding of what the .NET MAUI framework is and how it works. You will also know how to install the necessary tools to start building a .NET MAUI app and be able to create a new app from scratch. With this knowledge, you'll be well equipped to start developing cross-platform apps using the .NET MAUI framework.

In this chapter, we will go through the following main topics:

- .NET MAUI in a nutshell
- How does it work?
- Creating your first .NET MAUI app

Before we start applying MVVM to .NET MAUI, it is essential to know the framework itself.

Technical requirements

The final section of this chapter, *Creating your first .NET MAUI app*, guides you through everything you need to set up in order to create a .NET MAUI app.

The sample code can be found on GitHub at `https://github.com/PacktPublishing/MVVM-pattern-.NET-MAUI/tree/main/Chapter02`.

.NET MAUI in a nutshell

.NET MAUI is a framework from Microsoft for building native and performant cross-platform desktop and mobile apps for iOS, macOS, Android, and Windows, all from a single code base. Moreover, .NET MAUI's reach extends beyond these primary platforms, thanks to Samsung's efforts in adding support for Tizen OS. This additional support opens up possibilities for developers to target a wider variety of devices, such as smart TVs, wearables, and IoT devices that run on Tizen. However, for the purposes of this book, we'll focus on building apps for iOS, macOS, Android, and Windows. Using .NET MAUI, developers can create native cross-platform user interfaces using XAML or C#. The key idea is to share your code, both business logic and UI, across all the supported platforms (*Figure 2.1*).

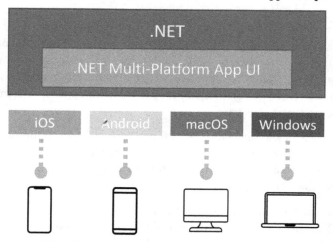

Figure 2.1: .NET MAUI high-level overview

It's important to notice that having this shared code base in .NET MAUI doesn't restrict you from accessing native platform-specific APIs using C#. In fact, .NET MAUI is designed to allow developers to access native features while maintaining a consolidated code base. .NET MAUI's rich library of cross-platform APIs forms an abstraction layer for common tasks that are typically platform-specific. Yet, when a certain feature requires a native platform API that is not available in .NET MAUI's cross-platform API, you still have the ability to directly use native platform APIs via C#. Through mechanisms such as partial classes, compiler directives, or dependency injection, .NET MAUI ensures that developers can achieve the optimal level of customization and functionality for their applications.

Reminiscent of Xamarin.Forms

This might sound familiar to developers who previously have heard of or have worked with **Xamarin.Forms**.

In fact, .NET MAUI is an evolution of Xamarin.Forms with many obvious and subtle differences. One of the significant differences is its integration into .NET starting with .NET 6. This integration means that developers no longer need to install additional NuGet packages or extensions for .NET MAUI, simplifying the setup process. Once the required **.NET workloads** for MAUI are installed, developers can start building applications right away.

Also, as a first-class citizen of .NET, MAUI benefits from improved tooling and developer experience in Visual Studio, making it more convenient and efficient to create mobile apps using the framework. This seamless integration and enhanced tooling help developers build cross-platform applications more easily and effectively.

But the main core idea remains the same: enabling developers to build native and performant cross-platform applications using .NET, with a single shared code base for both business logic and UI code. This approach simplifies the development process and promotes code reusability across different platforms, while providing the flexibility to access platform-specific APIs when needed, ensuring that developers can leverage native features and customize their applications as required.

.NET MAUI is built upon the same foundational principles as Xamarin.Forms, but additionally incorporates all the learnings from almost a decade of developer experience from its predecessor. By improving various aspects such as performance, project structure, and tooling, .NET MAUI aims to simplify the process of creating cross-platform applications while maintaining the core ideas of sharing business logic and UI code, and allowing easy access to platform-specific APIs.

Cross-platform UI and more

One of the things .NET MAUI does is, of course, allowing us to create a shared UI for mobile and desktop apps. The framework offers us concepts such as `Grid`, `VerticalStackLayout`, `AbsoluteLayout`, and so on, which gives us the ability to carry out layout controls in many different ways. As a developer, you get the choice of whether you want to define your layouts in XAML or in code. Whatever approach you choose, the same thing can be achieved with both. On top of that, we also get data binding, an essential concept for effectively doing MVVM, as we learned in the previous chapter. With built-in page types such as `FlyoutPage`, `TabbedPage`, `NavigationPage`, and others, we can create applications with advanced navigation patterns. And remember, all of this eventually gets transformed into a native app running a native UI!

Cross-platform APIs

But let's not forget that there is more to .NET MAUI than just the UI stuff. .NET MAUI provides cross-platform APIs that abstract away the platform-specific implementations for common tasks, enabling developers to access native device features using a single, unified API – accessing the device's compass, geolocation, filesystem, and so on – just to name a few. This allows us to write platform-agnostic code for such tasks, further simplifying the development process and promoting code reusability across different platforms. Some of the cross-platform APIs offered by .NET MAUI include the following:

- **Device Information**: Retrieve device-specific information, such as model, manufacturer, platform, and OS version.

- **Geolocation**: Access the device's location services to obtain GPS coordinates, perform geocoding and reverse geocoding, and track the device's movement.

- **Connectivity**: Determine the device's network connectivity status and monitor for changes.

- **Permissions**: Request and manage various runtime permissions required by your application, such as location, camera, and storage access.

- **Sensors**: Utilize device sensors such as the accelerometer, gyroscope, magnetometer, and barometer to gather data about the device's orientation, movement, and environment.

- **Preferences**: Store and retrieve simple key-value data for app settings and user preferences. Use the **Secure Storage** API to do this for sensitive data that needs to be secured.

- **Launcher**: Launch another app using that application's URI scheme. There is also the **Browser** API if you want to open a website using the OS default browser.

And there are many, many more!

> **What about Xamarin.Essentials?**
>
> Xamarin.Essentials is an open source library that was created to assemble cross-platform APIs for mobile applications, serving as an abstraction on top of common platform-specific tasks. With the evolution of Xamarin.Forms into .NET MAUI, these APIs are now more seamlessly integrated into the framework itself. This means the Xamarin.Essentials NuGet package is not needed in .NET MAUI applications.

Cross-platform life cycle events

.NET MAUI introduces a **uniform app life cycle**, which simplifies the management of application state across different platforms. In traditional Xamarin.Forms development, each platform had its own life cycle events and patterns, which sometimes led to inconsistencies and increased complexity when dealing with cross-platform scenarios.

Through the `Window` class, we can now react to the life cycle of our applications using a single set of events, regardless of the target platform.

The easiest way to subscribe to these events is by getting a reference to the application window via the `CreateMethod` in your `App` class and then subscribing to the events relevant to you.

These events allow us to handle a couple of life cycle events in a consistent manner across all supported platforms. Depending on our needs or our scenario, we can use these event handlers, for example, to stop long-running processes (in the `Stopped` event handler) or refresh the data on the current page (on the `Resumed` event). A pattern I often see in banking apps is that the app's UI gets obfuscated or blurred when it's put in the background or when it hasn't got focus. This could typically be handled in a cross-platform way with the help of the `Deactivated` and `Activated` events.

As always with .NET MAUI, abstractions such as these should not prevent you from accessing platform APIs or doing platform-specific things. If you need to react to a certain platform-specific life cycle event, you can still do that. Through the `ConfigureLifecycleEvents` extension method of `MauiAppBuilder`, we can define delegates that should be invoked on the life cycle events of the underlying platforms:

```
public static MauiApp CreateMauiApp()
{
    var builder = MauiApp.CreateBuilder();
    return builder
        .UseMauiApp<App>()
        .ConfigureLifecycleEvents(lifecycle =>
        {
        ...
        }).Build();
}
```

For example, if we want our app to be activated through a custom URI scheme, we might want to intercept the URL that triggered the app to open and react to that. Getting a hold on that URL can only be done on specific life cycle events on each platform: the `OnCreate` method on Android and `OpenUrl` on iOS. We can override these methods in `MainActivity` or `AppDelegate`, respectively, as we used to do with Xamarin.Forms. Alternatively, we can hook into these platform events with the earlier-mentioned `ConfigureLifecycleEvents`:

```
.ConfigureLifecycleEvents(lifecycle =>
{
#if ANDROID
    lifecycle.AddAndroid(android =>
    {
        android.OnCreate((activity, bundle) =>
        {
            //Get url activity.Intent.Data
        });
    });
#elif IOS
    lifecycle.AddiOS(ios =>
    {
        ios.OpenUrl((app, url, options) =>
        {
            return true;
        });
    });
#endif
})
```

Instead of having this kind of code scattered throughout your solution in platform-specific classes and files, I think the preceding solution is a lot more elegant as everything is in one place. I think this improves the readability and maintainability of your code a lot!

Single project structure (multi-targeting)

.NET MAUI also introduces a brand-new single project structure. Instead of having different projects per targeted platform and one project for the shared code, with .NET MAUI, we can build apps for different platforms from just one project. Not only the shared code, but also the platform-specific implementations, and resources, such as images, fonts, and app icons, are included directly within this one single project.

This is possible thanks to the **multi-targeting** capabilities of MSBuild, the build system used by .NET and .NET MAUI. With multi-targeting, we can basically put all our code in one project and define for what platforms the project should be built. These target platforms are defined in the project's csproj file. By default, in .NET MAUI, it looks like this:

```
<TargetFrameworks>net8.0-android;net8.0-ios;net8.0-
  maccatalyst</TargetFrameworks>
<TargetFrameworks Condition="$([MSBuild]::IsOSPlatform
  ('windows'))">$(TargetFrameworks);net8.0-
    windows10.0.19041.0</TargetFrameworks>
```

So, for a standard .NET MAUI project, this means we are targeting Android, iOS, Mac Catalyst, and Windows – the latter only when running on Windows.

When compiling, MSBuild will build for all the configured platforms, only taking the source files that are relevant to the platform it is compiling for and handling dependencies based on the specified target framework. In other words: one project results in multiple compiled libraries or apps, which on their own only contain the source code that is relevant for the platform it is compiled for. But how does MSBuild know which platform-specific files to take? There are a few ways of informing the build system which sources to take:

- **Preprocessor directives**: You can use preprocessor directives (#if, #elif, #else, and #endif) in your code to conditionally compile platform-specific code blocks. These directives enable you to include platform-specific code within a single source file, making it easier to share code across platforms and reducing the need for multiple files. For example, code surrounded by #if ANDROID and #endif will only be included and compiled when explicitly compiling for Android. The previous code sample about handling platform-specific life cycle events also contains these directives as the code they surround is only relevant to a particular platform and uses APIs specific to that platform.

- **Platform-specific folders**: You can use platform-specific folders to organize your platform-specific code and resources. By default, MSBuild will only include the contents of Platforms/Android, Platforms/iOS, Platforms/Windows, or Platforms/MacCatalyst when compiling for the corresponding platform. This allows us, without using preprocessor directives, to write platform-specific code in these folders that accesses native APIs. Proof of this is when looking at the default `Program` class in `Platforms/iOS`, there is a `UIKit.UIApplication` object being used, which is an object specific to iOS. To give an analogy, the `MainActivity` class in `Platforms/Android` uses `Android.App.ActivityAttribute`, something specifically for Android.

Not only do these platform-specific folders contain platform-specific code, but they also contain resources that are unique to the specific platform –`Package.appxmanifest` in `Platforms/Windows` or `Info.plist` in `Platforms/MacCatalyst`, for example.

- **File naming conventions**: You can also use file naming conventions to organize platform-specific code files. This approach is not supported by default; you need to add some additional configuration in the `csproj` file for this. This can be combined with platform-specific folders as well.

  Take a look at `https://learn.microsoft.com/dotnet/maui/platform-integration/configure-multi-targeting` to get a detailed approach on how to configure filename-based multi-targeting and how to combine it with platform-specific folders. Whatever approach you want to use is mostly personal preference and is completely up to you and your team to decide.

In Visual Studio, when inside a .NET MAUI project, there is an additional dropdown available, called the **Platform Selector**, which allows you to select one of the target platforms. By default, this dropdown can be found in the top left of your code editor when inside a C# code file (*Figure 2.2*):

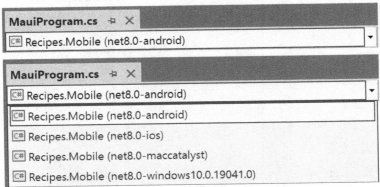

Figure 2.2: Platform Selector

Selecting an entry in this dropdown doesn't affect the compilation. The selected platform's purpose is to configure the development environment for that specific platform. That means, when working with preprocessor directives, it displays platform-specific code and makes sure IntelliSense and code navigation features are adjusted to work on the platform-specific code.

Figure 2.3 shows how the IDE grays out code that doesn't get compiled in the selected target platform (Android).

```
                    .ConfigureLifecycleEvents(lifecycle =>
                    {
#if ANDROID
                        lifecycle.AddAndroid(android =>
                        {
                            android.OnCreate((activity, bundle) =>
                            {
                                //Get url from activity.Intent.Data
                            });
                        });
#elif IOS
                        lifecycle.AddiOS(ios =>
                        {
                            ios.OpenUrls((app, url, options) =>
                            {
                                return true;
                            });
                        });
#endif
                    })
```

Figure 2.3: Android as the selected target platform

In the selected configuration, the code surrounded with #if ANDROID will get compiled; the iOS-specific code, however, will be ignored. Moreover, we don't get red squiggles in the IDE even though the iOS part has an error: the OpenUrls method doesn't exist, as OpenUrl is the correct name. This error only becomes visible when selecting iOS as the target platform in the **Platform Selector** dropdown (*Figure 2.4*).

```
                    .ConfigureLifecycleEvents(lifecycle =>
                    {
#if ANDROID
                        lifecycle.AddAndroid(android =>
                        {
                            android.OnCreate((activity, bundle) =>
                            {
                                //Get url from activity.Intent.Data
                            });
                        });
#elif IOS
                        lifecycle.AddiOS(ios =>
                        {
                            ios.OpenUrls((app, url, options) =>
                            {
                                return true;
                            });
                        });
#endif
                    })
```

Figure 2.4: iOS as the selected target platform

By selecting iOS as the build target, all the iOS-specific code lights up, while code specific to other platforms gets grayed out.

This dropdown helps tremendously when writing platform-specific code!

> **Note**
>
> To conclude, .NET MAUI is *a modern framework for building cross-platform native applications for mobile and desktop devices.* It supports Android, iOS, macOS, and Windows. It offers a shared UI layer with a rich set of controls, cross-platform APIs for common tasks, unified app life cycle events across different platforms, and a single project structure that simplifies development and deployment.

How does it work?

So now that we have a good understanding of .NET MAUI, you might wonder how this actually works. How does this .NET code eventually end up as a native app with a native UI on different platforms? It's not magic, but to understand how it works, we need to take a look under the hood.

Native apps with .NET

At compile time, native apps for each selected platform are being created. The necessary parts of the .NET **Base Class Library** (BCL), which contains the .NET datatypes, interfaces, and libraries, are embedded in the native app and tailored to the target platform. The BCL relies on the **.NET runtime** to create an execution environment for your application code. For Android, iOS, and macOS platforms, the **Mono runtime** serves as the .NET runtime implementation that powers the execution environment. Meanwhile, on Windows, **.NET CoreCLR** is responsible for providing the runtime environment for your application.

This mechanism isn't specific to .NET MAUI. This is actually the foundation for **.NET for Android**, **.NET for iOS**, **.NET for Mac**, and **WinUI**. These things might sound like something new, but in fact, these are the new names for the things that we previously might have known as **Xamarin.Android**, **Xamarin.iOS**, and **Xamarin.Mac**.

.NET for Android, .NET for iOS, and .NET for Mac provide bindings to platform-specific APIs, enabling developers to access specific features and controls using familiar .NET constructs. On Android, when the application is compiled, the .NET code is packaged with the Mono runtime, and the app is executed using **Just-in-Time** (JIT) compilation on Android devices. Due to Apple's restrictions on JIT compilation, .NET for iOS applications is compiled using **Ahead-of-Time** (AOT) compilation, which translates the .NET code into native ARM code that runs directly on iOS devices.

WinUI is a modern, native UI framework for building Windows applications using C# and XAML, using .NET. It is the latest version of **Windows UI Library**, which provides a set of UI controls, styles, and features for building fluent and high-performance Windows applications. Instead of the Mono runtime, it uses .NET CoreCLR as an execution environment.

Each of these frameworks can be used to create native applications with .NET, utilizing the UI patterns and paradigms specific to each platform to build the UI.

> **Tip**
>
> Even though .NET for Android and .NET for iOS offer a way to share a significant amount of code, creating and maintaining apps with a native UI for each platform can still be very challenging. Developers need to be proficient in the specifics of each platform and have a deep understanding of the differences between them. This can lead to higher development costs, longer time-to-market, and increased maintenance efforts.

.NET MAUI, another abstraction layer

This is where .NET MAUI comes in. It provides a convenient and efficient way to create truly native mobile apps for multiple platforms using a single code base. .NET MAUI adds an abstraction layer on top of the previously mentioned .NET platforms, allowing us to build a shared UI for all of them (*Figure 2.5*).

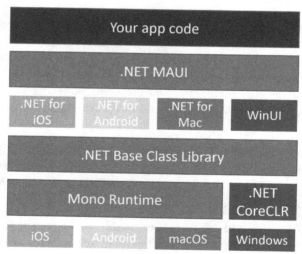

Figure 2.5: .NET MAUI architecture

The code in your .NET MAUI app primarily interacts with the .NET MAUI API, which in turn communicates with native platform APIs. Additionally, your .NET MAUI code can directly access platform-specific APIs to leverage unique platform features or customizations.

Let's explore the process of transforming a cross-platform-defined UI into a native UI specific to each platform.

From virtual to native view

When defining a UI in .NET MAUI, the platform-agnostic **controls** or **virtual views** are mapped to native UI elements or **native views** on each platform at runtime. The definition of .NET MAUI controls is often the most common denominator of the native controls it represents on all supported platforms. In some cases, platform-specific functionality is made available through platform-specific extensions.

But how do we go from a virtual view to a native view?

The **handlers** architecture, introduced in .NET MAUI, manages the mapping of the virtual views to the native UI elements for each supported platform. Handlers are lightweight and performant components that replace the traditional renderers used in Xamarin.Forms. Each MAUI control has corresponding handlers that are responsible for creating, updating, and managing the native UI element on a specific platform. Handlers handle property changes, events, and platform-specific customizations, translating the shared MAUI control code into platform-specific native controls and behaviors.

Figure 2.6 shows how an instance of `Microsoft.Maui.Controls.Button` (Virtual View) gets mapped to a specific Native View:

- On iOS, a handler maps the button to `UIKit.UIButton`. As .NET MAUI leverages Mac Catalyst to create native macOS applications, the same `UIKit.UIButton` is used for macOS. Mac Catalyst is a technology developed by Apple that allows developers to leverage the same project and source code to create native apps across iOS, iPadOS, and macOS.

- On Android, the button is being mapped by a handler to an instance of `AndroidX.AppCompat.Widget.AppCompatButton`.

- An instance of `Microsoft.UI.Xaml.Controls.Button` is created by a handler on Windows when mapping a .NET MAUI button.

As you can see in *Figure 2.6*, `ButtonHandlers` don't have a direct reference to the `Button` implementation; neither does the `Button` implementation have a reference to `ButtonHandlers`. Instead, every control implements an interface that abstracts the control. The handlers are accessed through the control-specific interface, such as `IButton` for `Button`.

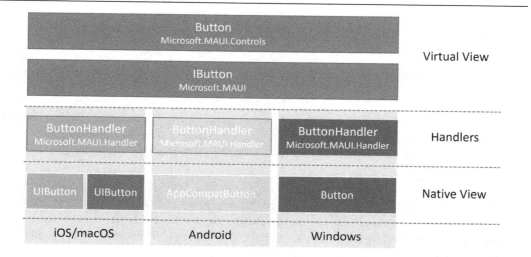

Figure 2.6: .NET MAUI's handlers architecture

We've talked a lot about *mapping* but that is, in essence, really what is happening in these handlers. It is not a coincidence that a handler has one or more **mappers**. A mapper is an object that defines what needs to happen when a property on the cross-platform control changes. It is a dictionary where the key value is the name of a property of the virtual view and the value is an action that needs to be executed whenever the property on the control changes. Per platform, the handler defines the actions that need to be executed on the native view to ensure that when a property is set on a cross-platform control, the corresponding native view updates accordingly. Aside from these **property mappers**, handlers often also have a **command mapper**, which is very similar to `PropertyMapper` but allows for an extra parameter to be passed. Handling cross-platform events such as `ScrollTo` on `ScrollView` is such an example. In order to make the native view scroll to the requested position, the position itself needs to be passed to the handler as an argument. This way, the handler can use this argument value to invoke the necessary action on the native view.

Compared to Xamarin.Forms' renderers implementation, the handlers' architecture offers several benefits: improved performance, easier customization, and better maintainability, making it a significant improvement point in transitioning from Xamarin.Forms to .NET MAUI.

Now that we've covered a substantial amount of theory and you understand how things work under the hood, it's time to roll up our sleeves and start creating something tangible. I know you're keen to dive in, so let's embark on building our very first .NET MAUI application!

Creating your first .NET MAUI app

Let's create our first .NET MAUI app! Before we can start writing any code, we need to set up our machine by installing some bits. So, let's walk through these initial setup steps together and see what options we have. Once we're set up, we'll move on to the exciting part: creating a .NET MAUI app from scratch, step by step.

Setting up your machine

Getting started with .NET MAUI development is pretty simple, especially if you are using Visual Studio as your IDE. But even if you don't want to use Visual Studio, the installation should be quite straightforward.

About .NET SDK versions and workloads

.NET MAUI is available from .NET 6, and at the time of writing the book, **.NET 8** is the most recent version. It is important to note that every version of .NET comes with a specific support policy: there are **Long-Term Support** (**LTS**) releases, which provide 3 years of free support and patches, and there are **Standard-Term Support** (**STS**) releases, which are good for 18 months of free support and patches. However, for .NET MAUI, this doesn't apply. Microsoft needs to make sure .NET MAUI supports the latest and greatest APIs on all of the supported platforms. New features and improvements will be mainly developed for the next version of .NET, and some may be backported to the current version. So, when it comes to .NET MAUI, the support policy is different than the general .NET support policy. It's best to use the latest available version of .NET so you have access to the newest platform APIs and the best-performing version of .NET MAUI, regardless of whether it's an LTS or STS release.

.NET 6 introduced the concept of **workloads**. A workload is a set of tools, templates, and libraries for a particular development scenario or target platform. When installing the .NET MAUI workload, we are installing everything that is needed to build cross-platform native apps with .NET. It will install the .NET MAUI class libraries, build and runtime components, platform-specific SDKs and tools, project templates, and so on.

The .NET MAUI workload can be installed and managed in two ways: using the Visual Studio Installer or via the command line if you choose not to work with Visual Studio.

> **Tip**
>
> In order for your .NET MAUI workload to remain in a stable state, it is important to stick with one and only one of the following options: you either install it with Visual Studio and manage it from there, or you do it from the command line. Don't mix the two!

Installing Visual Studio and the .NET MAUI workload

When working with Visual Studio (2022 17.3 or greater), we can use the Visual Studio Installer to install the .NET MAUI workload. This is by far the easiest way to install and manage your workloads. .NET MAUI development is supported on all versions of Visual Studio: from the free Community edition to the paid Enterprise edition.

If Visual Studio is not yet installed on your machine, you first need to download the Visual Studio Installer by going to `https://visualstudio.microsoft.com/downloads/`. Once the installer is downloaded, launch it, and choose **Install** (*Figure 2.7*)

Figure 2.7: Installing Visual Studio

Or, if you already have Visual Studio installed, you can launch the Visual Studio Installer and select **Modify** (*Figure 2.8*).

Figure 2.8: Modifying Visual Studio

Whether you are installing Visual Studio or modifying it, in the next dialog, you can choose the workloads you want to install. As shown in *Figure 2.9*, this is where we need to check **.NET Multi-platform App UI development**.

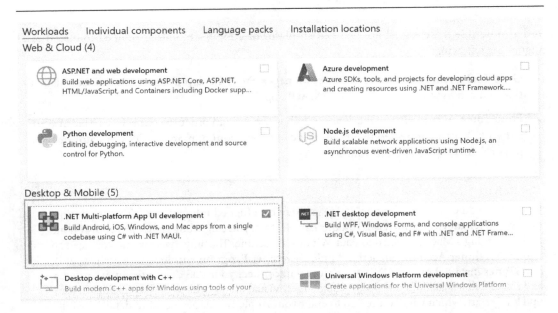

Figure 2.9: Installing the .NET MAUI workload

This will install all the bits and pieces in order for you to be able to build .NET MAUI apps.

Having Visual Studio freshly installed, launch it, and select **Continue without code** (*Figure 2.10*).

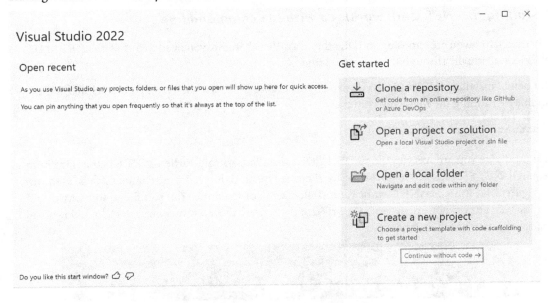

Figure 2.10: Starting Visual Studio without code

In order to be able to debug on an Android emulator or an iOS simulator, we need to install or configure the following:

- Go to **Tools | Android | Android Device Manager**. From there, you can add Android emulators that you can use to deploy your .NET MAUI app.

- From **Tools | iOS | Pair to Mac**, you can follow the steps in order to connect to a Mac in your network. When connected to a Mac, you can debug your app on an iOS simulator or on a physical device plugged into your Mac.

> **Hot Restart**
>
> Of course, you can also debug on a physical device, plugged into your PC. This is possible even on an iOS device! With Visual Studio **Hot Restart**, you can debug right onto your iPhone without having a Mac connected to your Windows machine. The only caveat is that you need an **Apple Developer Account**, an active **Apple Developer Program** enrollment (which is paid), and iTunes installed on your PC. As soon as you connect your iOS device to your computer and select it in Visual Studio as your debug target, Visual Studio will guide you through setting up Hot Restart, which will require you to enter your Apple Developer Account details. I would recommend heading over to `https://learn.microsoft.com/dotnet/maui/ios/hot-restart` to get step-by-step guidance on how to set up Hot Restart on iOS. While this is great for debugging, in order to release an iOS or macOS app, you still need a Mac to build and sign your app!

Installing the .NET MAUI workload with the command line

Alternatively, if you are choosing an IDE other than Visual Studio, you need to install the .NET MAUI workload manually through the command line.

But before installing .NET MAUI, you need to make sure .NET is installed on your machine. You can do this by running the following command:

```
dotnet --list-sdks
```

It should give you an overview of all .NET SDKs installed. As said earlier, .NET 6 is the minimum required .NET SDK needed to do .NET MAUI development. If the preceding command fails, as shown in *Figure 2.11*, it means .NET is not yet installed on your machine. You should go to `https://dotnet.microsoft.com/download/dotnet`, select the latest version of .NET, and download the appropriate installer or binaries.

```
C:\Users\pieter>dotnet --list-sdks
'dotnet' is not recognized as an internal or external command,
operable program or batch file.
```

Figure 2.11: 'dotnet' is not recognized

Once a recent version of .NET is installed on your machine, you can install the .NET MAUI workload via the command line by using the following command:

```
dotnet workload install maui
```

This will install everything that is needed to be able to build cross-platform apps with .NET MAUI using your favorite IDE.

Do note that this doesn't install any additional tools for managing Android emulators, for example, nor does it give you out-of-the-box tools that allow you to easily connect to a Mac or deploy to an iPhone.

Installing Visual Studio Code and the .NET MAUI extension

If you prefer working with **Visual Studio Code**, whether it is on Windows, macOS, or even Linux, there's some good news. The **.NET MAUI extension**, together with the **C# Dev Kit extension**, gives you everything you need to start creating MAUI apps with Visual Studio Code. The supported target platforms depend on the OS you are running. On Windows, you can create Windows and Android apps; on macOS, you are able to develop all but Windows apps; and on Linux, you can only create Android apps. Let's see how we can get Visual Studio Code up and running for creating .NET MAUI apps:

1. Install Visual Studio Code from `https://code.visualstudio.com/`. Install the .NET MAUI extension from the **EXTENSIONS** menu in Visual Studio Code. Find it by searching for `maui`, as shown in *Figure 2.12*:

Figure 2.12: .NET MAUI extension

2. Once the extension is installed, the **Welcome** page pops up in Visual Studio Code:

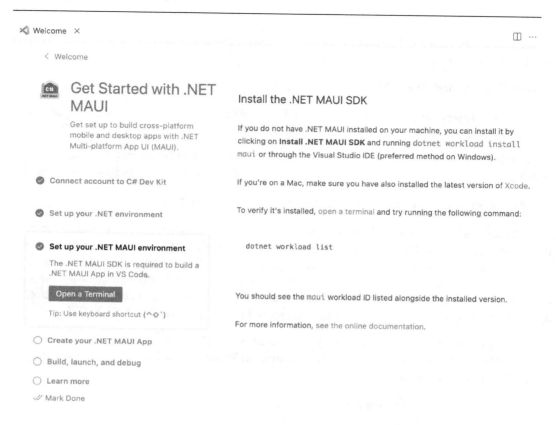

Figure 2.13: .NET MAUI extension Welcome page

This **Welcome** page guides you through every additional step you need to take to get your environment up and running. It covers everything from the installation of the .NET MAUI workload to downloading and installing Microsoft OpenJDK, which is essential for building and debugging Android apps. Additionally, it tells you to install Xcode and Xcode Command Line Tools on a Mac, which are needed for building and debugging iOS and macOS applications.

Now that we have got our preferred development environment all set up, let's create a .NET MAUI app! Note that throughout this book, the walk-throughs describe the workflow as in Visual Studio. However, it shouldn't be an issue to follow along in your IDE of choice.

Hello "Recipes!" app

Throughout this book, we will be working on the *Recipes!* app. With this app, users add their favorite recipes and share them with the world, allowing other users to rate and review them.

So, let's go ahead and create a .NET MAUI app that will serve as a starting point for our *Recipes!* app.

Creating a new project

With the excitement building, we're about to take our first steps toward developing our *Recipes!* app. To kick things off, we'll start by creating a new project in Visual Studio:

1. Fire up Visual Studio and select **Create a new project**, as shown in *Figure 2.14*:

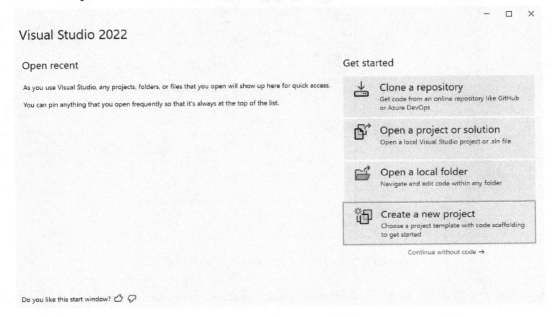

Figure 2.14: Create a new project

2. Next, select **.NET MAUI App** from the list of project templates. As this list can be quite long, you can type maui in the search bar at the top to query the list.

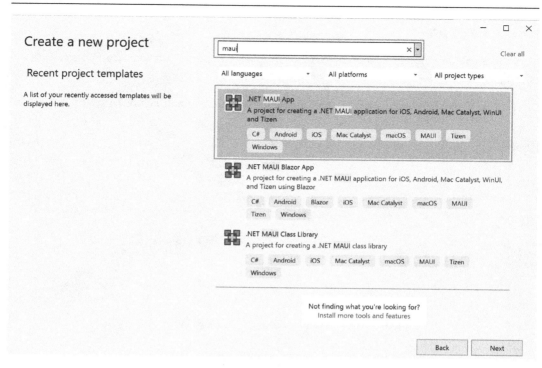

Figure 2.15: Choosing the .NET MAUI App template

3.   Next, enter the relevant details for **Project name**, **Location,** and **Solution name**.

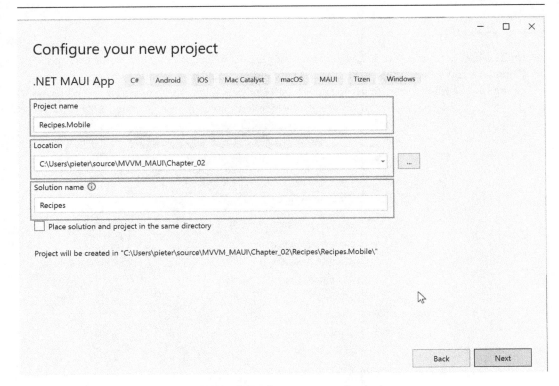

Figure 2.16: Configure your new project

4. On the final screen, select **.NET 8 (Long Term Support)** or any other .NET framework you want to target.

5. Hit the **Create** button.

This creates a solution containing a .NET MAUI project with the provided names at the given location, as shown in *Figure 2.17*:

Figure 2.17: Recipes! .NET MAUI project

Running your app

Right off the bat, you can run your brand-new cross-platform application on Windows by pressing *F5* or by clicking the **run** button in Visual Studio. The **run** button should have **Windows Machine** next to it, indicating you are going to run your app natively on Windows. If the button doesn't show **Windows Machine**, you can click the downward-pointing arrow for additional options, as shown in *Figure 2.18*:

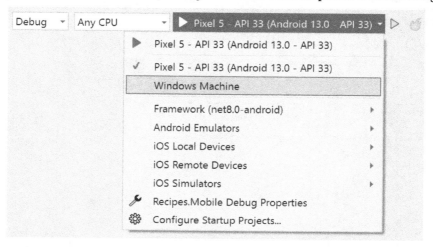

Figure 2.18: Choosing a Debug target

When debugging a Windows app for the first time, Visual Studio might prompt you to enable **Developer Mode** in Windows. After that, your shiny new app should be deployed and running on Windows!

We can also debug right away on Android: click the arrow next to **Windows Machine** that points downward, select **Android Emulators**, and select an emulator from the list. If this is your first time running an Android app, you will get an error message inside **Error List** in Visual Studio, prompting you to accept the Android SDK licenses. Double-clicking the message should open **Android SDK – License Agreement**, which you should accept in order to continue. Hit *F5* again, or click the **run** button – which should contain the name of your emulator – in Visual Studio. Starting the emulator for the first time and deploying it might take a while, but after some time, you will see an emulator popping up with your native Android app running on it.

In comparison, if you are connected to a Mac, you can select an iOS simulator as well and see your native iOS running on an iOS simulator! If you have an Android or iOS device connected to your PC, it should appear in the list as well. Selecting it and running the application should deploy your app onto your physical device.

.NET Hot Reload and XAML Hot Reload

With **.NET Hot Reload**, developers can make changes to their source code while the application is running, without the need to pause or rebuild the app. It enables faster iteration and real-time feedback on code modifications. Why don't we go ahead and make some changes to our code while the app is running?

1. Open the `MainPage.xaml.cs` file.

2. In the `OnCounterClicked` method, change `count++` to `count += 2`.

    Save your changes or manually hit **Hot Reload** (*Alt + F10*) in Visual Studio. In the drop-down menu of this button, you can also find a **Hot Reload on File Save** setting that you might want to check. Having this checked should automatically trigger **Hot Reload** when you save your changes.

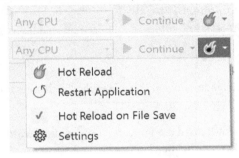

Figure 2.19: Hot Reload

3. Go back to the running app and click the button in the app and you should see that the counter is incremented by two every time you click it.

Additionally, with **XAML Hot Reload**, we can even update the XAML code while the app is running and immediately see the updated UI. So, while our app is running, let's update some things on the screen:

1. Run your app on your platform of choice.

2. While the app is running, go to Visual Studio and open `MainPage.xaml`.

3. Change the `Text` property of the first `Label` from `"Hello, World"` to `"Recipes!"`:

```
<Label
    FontSize="32"
    HorizontalOptions="Center"
    Text="Recipes!" />
```

Change the `Text` property of the second `Label` to `"Find your next favorite dish."`:

```
<Label
    FontSize="18"
    HorizontalOptions="Center"
    Text="Find your next favorite dish." />
```

4. Add a `BackgroundColor` property to `Button` and give it the value of `"#FCB64A"`, and set the `TextColor` property to `"white"`:

```
<Button
    x:Name="CounterBtn"
    BackgroundColor="#F8B146"
    Clicked="OnCounterClicked"
    HorizontalOptions="Center"
    Text="Click me"
    TextColor="white" />
```

5. Save the changes you have made, and you should see the UI changes immediately being reflected in your running app.

.NET Hot Reload and XAML Hot Reload are fantastic tools as they avoid needing to stop, rebuild, and redeploy your app for small, incremental changes.

Adding a splash screen and app icons

With .NET MAUI's single-project approach comes the ability to manage all of the app's resources (such as images, icons, fonts, and so on) in that single project. During compilation, all the resources inside the relevant `Platforms` folder are picked up together with everything inside the `Resources` folder. All of this is embedded in the resulting native app.

So, if you want, you can add a **splash screen** to your Android and iOS app by adding the file format required by the platform to the specific `Platforms` subfolder. The same goes for **app icons**: you can add them as resources in the required format and sizes to each of the `Platforms` subfolders. But, in MAUI, there is a much easier way: .NET MAUI can generate splash screens and app icons for us. Let's see how:

1. In the **Solution Explorer**, go to **Resources | Splash** and remove the existing `splash.svg` file.

2. Right-click the `Splash` folder, select **Add | Existing Item**, and browse to the file that you want to use as an image on the app's splash screen. Let's take the `Chapter 02/Assets/recipes-logo.svg` file, which can be found in the code repository shared at the start of this chapter.

3. Rename the file to `splash.svg` and set **Build Action** to **MauiSplashScreen**.

4. Open the project's `csproj` file by clicking on your MAUI project in the **Solution Explorer**. Inside the `csproj` file, find the `MauiSplashScreen` tag. You can add a `Color` property to define the background color that needs to be used for the splash screen. The given `svg` will be centered on the splash screen with the defined background color:

```
<MauiSplashScreen Include="Resources\Splash\splash.svg"
Color="#F8B146" />
```

5. Clean and rebuild your solution and run your app again. You should now see the updated splash screen, as shown in *Figure 2.20*:

Figure 2.20: The Recipes! app splash screen on iOS and Android

> **Note**
>
> When deploying on a physical iOS device from your Windows PC by using Hot Restart, your splash screen will not get updated and the standard .NET splash screen will remain. This is a limitation of Hot Restart, even though you have correctly configured your custom splash screen. In order to verify your splash screen, it's best to deploy it on a physical device that is connected to a Mac.

Not only is .NET MAUI capable of generating a splash screen for us, but .NET MAUI can also generate app icons for our app as well! Here's how:

1. In the **Solution Explorer**, go to **Resources | AppIcon** and delete the `appicon.svg` and `appiconfg.svg` files.

2. Right-click the `Resources` folder, select **Add | Existing Item**, and browse to the file that you want to use as the icon of your app. Let's take the `Chapter 02/Assets/recipes-appicon.svg` file.

3. Rename the file to `appicon.svg` and set **Build Action** to **MauiIcon**.

4. Look into the project's `csproj` file and look for the `MauiIcon` tag. Add a `Color` property:

```
<MauiIcon Include="Resources\AppIcon\appicon.svg"
Color="#F8B146" />
```

Clean and rebuild your solution to make sure your app icon gets shown on your device. You might want to delete the app from your device as well prior to deploying it. Once you have deployed your app, you should see your updated app icon:

Figure 2.21: The Recipes! app's icon on Android, Windows, and iOS

And there you have it! With very little effort, we've created a cross-platform app, complete with a splash screen and app icons.

Summary

In this chapter, we provided an overview of .NET MAUI: what it is, how it works, and how to get started with creating a cross-platform app using .NET MAUI. We walked through the process of creating an app, complete with a splash screen and app icons. Additionally, we examined .NET Hot Reload and XAML Hot Reload, features that enable us to update code while the app is running, dramatically increasing our efficiency. Now that you have a holistic understanding of .NET MAUI and the MVVM design pattern, we can continue our journey by exploring how to effectively apply this pattern within the .NET MAUI framework.

In *Chapter 3*, *Data Binding Building Blocks in .NET MAUI*, we'll explore the components available in .NET MAUI that enable us to build cross-platform apps using the MVVM pattern.

Further reading

To learn more about the topics that were covered in this chapter, take a look at the following resources:

- *Creating a splash screen in .NET MAUI*: `https://learn.microsoft.com/dotnet/maui/user-interface/images/splashscreen`

- *Working with app icons in .NET MAUI*: `https://learn.microsoft.com/dotnet/maui/user-interface/images/app-icons`

- *Configure multi-targeting*: `https://learn.microsoft.com/dotnet/maui/platform-integration/configure-multi-targeting`

- *.NET MAUI app lifecycle*: `https://learn.microsoft.com/dotnet/maui/fundamentals/app-lifecycle`

- *.NET MAUI installation*: `https://learn.microsoft.com/dotnet/maui/get-started/installation`

- *Pair to Mac*: `https://learn.microsoft.com/dotnet/maui/ios/pair-to-mac`

- *Android emulator*: `https://learn.microsoft.com/dotnet/maui/android/emulator/device-manager`

- *Setting up an Android device for debugging*: `https://learn.microsoft.com/dotnet/maui/android/device/setup`

- *.NET MAUI Support Policy*: `https://dotnet.microsoft.com/platform/support/policy/maui`

3

Data Binding Building Blocks in .NET MAUI

In the previous chapters, we familiarized ourselves with the core concepts of the MVVM pattern and explored the fundamentals of .NET MAUI. With the knowledge of MVVM principles and .NET MAUI's capabilities, we can now start looking at how to apply MVVM to .NET MAUI.

Data binding, a crucial component in .NET MAUI, is the key enabler of the MVVM pattern. In this chapter, we will focus on the fundamental concepts, components, and techniques that facilitate data binding in .NET MAUI. These critical elements link the View and ViewModel layers of your application, enabling efficient communication and ensuring a clean separation of concerns.

In the course of this chapter, we will cover the following topics:

- Key components for data binding
- Binding modes and the **INotifyPropertyChanged** interface
- Handling interactions with the **ICommand** interface

By the end of this chapter, you will have a solid understanding of the essential data-binding building blocks that come with .NET MAUI. This will help you understand the inner workings of data binding in .NET MAUI and what role each component plays. With this foundation in place, you will be well equipped to explore more advanced topics and techniques in the following chapters.

Technical requirements

Throughout this chapter, we will add functionality to the **Recipes!** app. All required assets needed to follow along, including all the code used in this chapter, can be found on GitHub at `https://github.com/PacktPublishing/MVVM-pattern-.NET-MAUI/tree/main/Chapter03`.

Key components for data binding

Let's first turn our attention to the core components that enable data binding in .NET MAUI: `BindableObject`, `BindableProperty`, and `BindingContext`. These components work in harmony to establish and manage the connections between your Views and ViewModels. Understanding the role and functionality of these elements is crucial, as they form the backbone of data binding in .NET MAUI.

Let's quickly discuss the elements that play a role in data binding.

Elements of data binding

Before we dive into the key components, let's go through the elements that we need to understand to effectively work with data binding in .NET MAUI applications. These elements play a vital role in facilitating communication between the View and ViewModel layers, enabling seamless synchronization of data and user interactions:

- **Binding source**: The binding source refers to the data being bound, typically originating from the ViewModel. It is often a property of an instance of a class that implements the `INotifyPropertyChanged` interface. This interface ensures that the View is notified whenever the data in the ViewModel changes, allowing the UI to update accordingly. It's essential to understand that implementing the `INotifyPropertyChanged` interface is not strictly required for a property to act as a binding source. In fact, any property, regardless of its enclosing class implementing `INotifyPropertyChanged` or not, can serve as a binding source.

- **Binding target**: The binding target is the `BindableProperty` on a UI element – or another `BindableObject` – that you may want to connect to the binding source. In .NET MAUI, most UI elements, such as labels, text boxes, and buttons, derive from the `Microsoft.Maui.Controls.BindableObject` class, which enables them to serve as a binding target. As opposed to the binding source, not every property can be a binding target, only properties of type `BindableProperty` on a class that inherits from a `BindableObject`.

- **Binding context**: The binding context establishes the relationship between the ViewModel and the View. It serves as a reference point for the data binding engine, providing a connection to the ViewModel instance. The binding context is usually set at the page level or on individual UI elements. By default, child elements inherit the context from their parent.

- **Binding path**: The binding path is an expression that specifies the property of the binding source that need to be bound to the binding target. In the simplest case, the binding path refers to a single property name in the ViewModel, but it can also include more complex expressions, such as property chains or indexers. The combination of the binding path and the binding context form the binding source.

- **Binding mode**: The binding mode determines the direction of data flow between the binding source and target, as we saw earlier in *Chapter 1, What Is the MVVM Design Pattern?*

- **ValueConverter**: A value converter modifies the data between the ViewModel and the View and vice versa. It allows us to convert the data value that is being bound and is particularly useful when the ViewModel's data type does not match the data type expected by the UI element in the View.

Throughout this and *Chapter 4, Data Binding in .NET MAUI*, all aspects of data binding will be thoroughly discussed.

Let's first take a look at the core component that makes data binding possible in .NET MAUI.

BindableObject

In .NET MAUI, the `Microsoft.Maui.Controls.BindableObject` class is the base class for objects that leverage data binding. It provides the foundation to enable data binding with UI elements and other objects by implementing essential properties, methods, and events related to the binding process. It is, in fact, the cornerstone of data-binding functionality in .NET MAUI, which is a crucial component of applying the MVVM pattern. It allows us to connect the View and the ViewModel, allowing them to communicate and stay in sync with each other without direct coupling.

Most UI elements in .NET MAUI, such as labels, buttons, and text boxes, are derived from the `BindableObject` class. This inheritance enables these elements to participate in data binding.

In essence, the `BindableObject` stores instances of `Microsoft.Maui.Controls.BindableProperty` and manages the `BindingContext`. These are crucial aspects to enable effective data binding, which in turn fosters seamless communication between the View and ViewModel, facilitating MVVM.

BindableProperty

`BindableProperty` is a special kind of property that can act as a binding target. It basically is an advanced CLR property, a property on steroids, if you will. Ultimately, a bindable property serves as a container for storing data related to the property, such as its default value and validation logic. It also provides a mechanism to enable data binding and property change notifications. It is associated with a public instance property, which serves as the interface for getting and setting the value of the bindable property. Many properties of UI elements in .NET MAUI are bindable properties, which allows us to set their values through data binding or using styles.

As an example, let's look at the `Text` property of `Label`:

```
public partial class Label : View ...
{
    ....
    public static readonly BindableProperty TextProperty =
        BindableProperty.Create(nameof(Text),
            typeof(string), typeof(Label), default(string),
```

```
                propertyChanged: OnTextPropertyChanged);
    ...

    public string Text
    {
        get { return (string)GetValue(TextProperty); }
        set { SetValue(TextProperty, value); }
    }

    static void OnTextPropertyChanged(
        BindableObject bindable,
        object oldvalue, object newvalue)
    {
        ...
    }
    ...
}
```

Let's start by looking at the Text property. This is just a CLR property, but instead of storing and retrieving the value from a backing field, it does the following:

- The getter retrieves the value by calling the GetValue method, passing in TextProperty. This GetValue method is a method on the BindableObject base class that Label inherits from.

- The setter calls the SetValue method of BindableObject, passing in TextProperty and the given value.

The TextProperty used in the GetValue and SetValue methods is a BindableProperty. It's static and belongs to the Label class. As mentioned earlier, BindableProperty is a sort of "container" that holds various bits of information about the property, including its value.

Let's break down this TextProperty. This property is defined as a public static field of type BindableProperty. It is instantiated by calling the BindableProperty.Create method, passing in the following values:

- **nameof(Text)**: The first parameter is the name of the public instance property associated with the static BindableProperty field. In this particular case, nameof(Text) is used to refer to the Text property of the Label class.

- **typeof(string)**: The second parameter is of type Type and defines the data type of the property that the bindable property is referring to. As the Text property is of type string, typeof(string) is passed in as a value.

- **typeof(Label)**: The third and final mandatory parameter is also of type `Type`. It refers to the owner type of the property, which is the class that the property belongs to. In this particular example, the `Text` property is defined in the `Label` class, so this type is passed as a value.

- **default(string)**: The next parameter in this example is the `defaultValue` parameter, which is of type `object`. This parameter is optional and allows us to provide a default value to the bindable property. In this case, `default(string)` is passed, which means NULL will be the default value.

- **OnTextpropertyChanged**: Optionally, we can provide a delegate that needs to be called when the value of the property changes.

The `BindableProperty.Create` method has a lot more optional parameters that you can provide if needed.

> **More about bindable properties**
>
> In *Chapter 11, Creating MVVM-Friendly Controls*, we will look at building our own controls. Understanding the concept of a `BindableProperty` is essential when it comes to creating MVVM-friendly controls. So, you can expect to dive deeper into this in that chapter.

The concept of a `BindableProperty` can be a little overwhelming or hard to understand to start with. For now, just remember that all of the UI elements inherit from `BindableObject` and that many of their properties are bindable properties, allowing us to use them as a binding target.

BindingContext

A `BindableObject` has a `BindingContext` property of type `object`, which acts as the glue between the binding source and the binding target. It points the data binding engine to an instance of a class that serves as the binding source. When you set the `BindingContext` property on a `BindableObject`, such as a .NET MAUI page or a UI element, you are specifying the source object for data binding expressions within that object's scope. Child elements within that scope will inherit the `BindingContext` by default unless a different `BindingContext` is explicitly set for them.

When the `BindingContext` is set on a `BindableObject`, the data-binding engine will resolve all bindings having their `Source` set to the `BindingContext`. Also, when the value of the `BindingContext` property changes, these bindings are reevaluated using the updated `BindingContext`.

Now that we've discussed all the core components that allow us to do data binding in .NET MAUI, let's see how to define and use them.

Data binding in practice

Before we can start writing our data binding, we first need to add our ViewModels to our solution. In order to fully embrace the separation of concerns, let's put them into a separate project:

1. In the **Solution Explorer**, right-click on your solution and select **Add | New Project…**.
2. Select **Class Library** from the list of project templates and click **Next**.
3. Enter `Recipes.Client.Core` under **Project name** and click **Next**.
4. Select `.NET 8.0` as **Framework** and click **Create**.

Once the project is created, let's delete `Class1.cs`, which was created by default. Next, we want to add our ViewModels to this project. In order to keep everything nice and organized, let's first create a `ViewModels` folder to put all of our ViewModels in:

1. Right-click on the `Recipes.Client.Core` project in the **Solution Explorer** and select **Add | New Folder** and enter the folder name `ViewModels`.
2. Right-click on the newly added folder and select **Add | Class…**, enter the name `RecipeDetailViewModel`, and add the following code:

```
namespace Recipes.Client.Core.ViewModels;

public class RecipeDetailViewModel
{
    public string Title { get; set; } = "Classic Caesar Salad";
}
```

`RecipeDetailViewModel` represents the details of a recipe. For now, it only contains a `Title` property, which we now give a hardcoded value of `"Classic Caesar Salad"`.

Next, we need to add a reference to this `Recipes.Client.Core` project from the `Recipes.Mobile` project. To do this, simply right-click on the `Recipes.Mobile` project, select **Add | Project Reference…**, and pick the `Recipes.Client.Core` project.

As a very last step, before we dive into data binding, we need to add a new page to our `Recipes.Mobile` project:

1. Right-click the project name and select **Add | New Item…**.
2. Select **.NET MAUI ContentPage (XAML)** and type in the name of the new page: `RecipeDetailPage.xaml`.
3. Open `App.xaml.cs` and, in the constructor, assign an instance of `RecipeDetailPage` to the `MainPage` property:

```
public App()
{
```

```
        InitializeComponent();

    MainPage = new RecipeDetailPage();
}
```

This ensures that on startup, the mobile app will show our newly created `RecipeDetailPage`.

4. Finally, in the code-behind of `RecipeDetailPage`, we need to assign its `BindingContext` property to an instance of `RecipeDetailViewModel`:

```
using Recipes.Client.Core.ViewModels;

namespace Recipes.Mobile;

public partial class RecipeDetailPage : ContentPage
{
    public RecipeDetailPage()
    {
        InitializeComponent();
        BindingContext = new RecipeDetailViewModel();
    }
}
```

Now, we can focus on `RecipeDetailPage` and start implementing some data bindings. Data bindings can be defined in code using C# and in XAML. Both have their cons and their pros, but essentially it comes down to preference. You can even mix and match both approaches if you want, although I wouldn't recommend doing that. Most commonly, data bindings are defined in XAML, minimizing the amount of code in the code-behind. Nevertheless, let's first see how we can define data bindings in C#.

Data binding in C#

Let's go to our new `RecipeDetailPage.xaml` file and start updating some XAML:

1. Remove any default XAML elements inside the `ContentPage` tag.

2. Add the following elements inside `ContentPage`:

```
<ScrollView>
    <VerticalStackLayout Padding="10">

    </VerticalStackLayout>
</ScrollView>
```

We are keeping the UI very simple and straightforward for now. That's why we are going to put everything in a `VerticalStackLayout`, which organizes child elements in a vertical stack. We're surrounding the `VerticalStackLayout` with a `ScrollView` in order to make sure we get scrollbars when not everything fits on the screen.

3. Add a `Label` to the `VerticalStackLayout` with the name `lblTitle`:

```
<Label x:Name="lblTitle"
    FontAttributes="Bold" FontSize="22" />
```

This label will be showing the recipe's title.

4. In the code-behind, within the constructor of `RecipeDetailPage`, we can now add data-binding code so that the value of the `Title` property of the `RecipeDetailViewModel` is shown in the `lblTitle` label:

```
lblTitle.SetBinding(
    Label.TextProperty,
    nameof(RecipeDetailViewModel.Title),
    BindingMode.OneWay);
```

Because we have given the `Label` the name `lblTitle`, a field with this name is generated, which allows us to access this label from the code-behind. By calling the `SetBinding` method, we can define and apply a binding.

5. Run the app and you should see the `Title` of `RecipeDetailViewModel`, which is currently hardcoded as `"Classic Caesar Salad"` on the screen.

By looking at the first data binding we've just implemented, you should be able to identify most of the data binding elements we've discussed earlier:

- **Binding target**: The `SetBinding` method is a method on the `BindableObject` class. The first parameter the `SetBinding` method needs is a `BindableProperty`. In this case, we are passing in the static `Label.TextProperty`, which corresponds to the `Text` instance property of a `Label`. The instance of the `BindableObject` we are calling the `SetBinding` method on, together with the `BindableProperty` we're specifying as the first parameter, form the binding target.

- **Binding source**: The second parameter the `SetBinding` method expects is the property path to bind to. This, together with the `BindingContext`, forms the binding source – but what is the `BindingContext` in this case? As we don't explicitly specify the `BindingContext` on the `Label`, the `BindingContext` is inherited from `lblTitle`'s parent, which is `RecipeDetailPage`. Therefore, the `BindingContext` of the label is also the instance of `RecipeDetailViewModel`.

- **Binding mode**: `BindingMode` is the third parameter in this example. This one, however, is optional. In this case, we are setting the `BindingMode` to `OneTime`. In *Chapter 1, What Is the MVVM Design Pattern?*, we briefly discussed different binding modes, and we will discuss binding modes in a bit more depth later on in this chapter.

Defining data binding in code is quite easy and straightforward. However, most of the time, data bindings are defined in XAML. Personally, I think defining them in XAML feels more natural and requires less context switching when creating your UI with XAML. So, let's have a look!

Data binding in XAML

As we are going to write our data binding in XAML, we can delete or comment out the binding code that we added to the constructor of `RecipeDetailPage` in *step 4* of the previous section.

We can now switch to `RecipeDetailPage.xaml` and update the label by removing the `x:Name` property and adding the `Text` property, which contains a **Binding markup extension**:

```
<Label
    FontAttributes="Bold"
    FontSize="22"
    Text="{Binding Path=Title, Mode=OneTime}" />
```

Because we are defining our data binding in XAML, we won't need a reference to the label in the code-behind. This is why we remove the `x:Name` property. Of course, if you need a reference to the label for any other reason (for example, you have some animation logic in the code-behind that animates the label), you need to keep the `x:Name` property.

But more importantly, let's take a look at the `Binding` markup extension that we've set to the `Text` property of the label.

XAML markup extensions

XAML markup extensions are a feature of XAML that allows you to provide values for properties during the parsing of the XAML markup more dynamically and flexibly. Markup extensions use curly braces ({ }) to enclose their syntax and enable you to add more complex logic or functionality to the XAML itself.

Markup extensions can be used to reference resources, create bindings, or even instantiate objects, among other things. They allow you to extend the capabilities of the XAML language.

A lot more about markup extensions can be found in the docs: `https://learn.microsoft.com/dotnet/maui/xaml/fundamentals/markup-extensions`.

The `Binding` markup extension is used to create a data binding between the `Text` property of the label and the `Title` property of the binding source. The binding source, in this case, is an instance of `RecipeDetailViewModel`, which is set as the `BindingContext` of the control's parent, `RecipeDetailPage`.

The `Path=Title` part of the binding expression specifies that the `Title` property from the binding source should be used as the source of the binding. In this scenario, you can omit `Path=` and simply use `Title`, as the binding expression is smart enough to recognize it as a property path. So, the binding expression can be written as follows:

```
<Label
    FontAttributes="Bold"
    FontSize="22"
    Text="{Binding Title, Mode=OneTime}" />
```

With `Mode=`, we can indicate the binding mode, just like we did in the previous example; we're setting it to `OneTime` in this example.

Apart from `Path` and `Mode`, there are more properties to the binding markup extension, such as `Source`, which allows us to point to another binding source, `Converter`, `TargetNullValue`, and others. *Chapter 4, Data Binding in .NET MAUI*, will cover all of this in much more detail.

Now, let's take a look at the different binding modes in more detail and how to reflect changes from the binding source automatically in the binding target.

Binding modes and the INotifyPropertyChanged interface

In *Chapter 1, What Is the MVVM Design Pattern*, we already discussed how data can flow:

- **One-way**: From ViewModel to View
- **One-way-to-source**: From View to ViewModel
- **One-time**: Only once from ViewModel to View
- **Two-way**: From ViewModel to View and from View to ViewModel

Now, let's take a look at how this is handled in .NET MAUI.

Binding modes in .NET MAUI

.NET MAUI supports all of these data flows, represented through the `Microsoft.Maui.Controls.BindingMode` enum: `OneWay`, `OneWayToSource`, `OneTime` and `TwoWay`. There is in fact a fifth value as well: `Default`. Remember when we talked about bindable properties earlier in this chapter? When creating a bindable property, there are some optional values we can set. One of those optional parameters is `defaultBindingMode`. This allows us to set a default binding mode on a bindable property. On `Entry`, for example, it makes sense to have the default binding mode on the `Text` property set to `TwoWay`, as it shows the value of the binding source, and the user is able to update the value as well. The `Text` property on a `Label`, on the other hand, is read-only, so the default binding mode there is OneWay. Now, going back to the BindingMode enum and more specifically, the Default value, when we don't specify a binding mode or use Default, the data-binding engine will use the binding mode that is specified as the default one on the bindable property of the binding target.

In the context of data binding and the various binding modes in .NET MAUI, it's crucial to have an efficient way to inform the UI about changes to the ViewModel's properties. The INotifyPropertyChanged interface addresses this need by providing a mechanism for your ViewModel to notify the UI when a property value has been updated.

INofityPropertyChanged

The INotifyPropertyChanged interface, part of the System.ComponentModel namespace, allows your binding source to communicate property changes to the binding target. This interface isn't specific to .NET MAUI; it's part of the .NET **Base Class Library** (**BCL**) and is used in other .NET UI frameworks such as WPF. When your ViewModel implements this interface, you can allow the data-binding engine to refresh the UI whenever the value of a data-bound property changes. This is simply done by the XAML engine, which automatically subscribes to the PropertyChanged event when the object that is being bound to implements the INotifyPropertyChanged interface. When the event is triggered, the engine will update the UI accordingly.

To implement the INotifyPropertyChanged interface, your ViewModel must include a PropertyChanged event, which can be triggered whenever a property's value changes. Furthermore, you typically create a method, usually called OnPropertyChanged, that triggers this event while providing the name of the altered property as a parameter. This method should be called within the property setter, immediately after the property value is updated:

```
public class SampleViewModel : INotifyPropertyChanged
{
    private string _title = string.Emtpty;
    public string Title
    {
        get => _title;
        set
        {
            if(_title != value)
            {
                _title = value;
                OnPropertyChanged(nameof(Title));
            }
        }
    }

    public void OnPropertyChanged(string propertyName)
```

```
    => PropertyChanged?.Invoke(this,
        new PropertyChangedEventArgs(propertyName));

    public event PropertyChangedEventHandler? PropertyChanged;
}
```

As you can see in the preceding sample, this `SampleViewModel` implements the `INotifyPropertyChanged` interface, which requires us to implement the `PropertyChanged` event of the `PropertyChangedEventHandler` type. The `PropertyChanged` event can easily be invoked by calling the `OnPropertyChanged` method and passing in the name of the property that has been changed. When looking at the code, in the setter of the `Title` property, the `OnPropertyChanged` method is called when a new value is assigned to the property's backing field, passing in the name of the property. When calling the `PropertyChanged` event, the current instance of the `SampleViewModel` is passed-in as the sender through the `this` keyword, followed by an instance of `PropertyChangedEventArgs`, which requires the name of the updated property. Through this event, the data-binding engine gets notified about the updated property and can, depending on the data-binding mode, update the binding target automatically.

`CallerMemberNameAttribute` is something that is very commonly used as an attribute on the `propertyName` parameter of the `OnPropertyChanged` method. This attribute automatically obtains the name of the method or property that calls the attributed method. This facilitates calling the `PropertyChanged` event from the property's setter even more, as the name of the property doesn't need to be explicitly passed as a parameter:

```
public class SampleViewModel : INotifyPropertyChanged
{
    ...
    public string Title
    {
        get => _title;
        set
        {
            if(_title != value)
            {
                _title = value;
                OnPropertyChanged();
            }
        }
    }

    public void OnPropertyChanged([CallerMemberName] string?
propertyName = null)
        => PropertyChanged?.Invoke(this,
            new PropertyChangedEventArgs(propertyName));
```

```
...
}
```

As the `Title` property calls the `OnPropertyChanged` method, without providing an explicit value as a parameter, the name of the caller – `Title` in this case – will be passed in as a value. In *Chapter 5*, *Community Toolkits*, we'll see how we can eliminate a lot of the ceremony here when triggering the `PropertyChanged` event.

Different binding modes in action

In the example earlier in this chapter, we bound the `Title` property of our `RecipeDetailViewModel` one time to the `Text` property of a `Label`. This means that the binding source is set only when the `BindingContext` of the binding target is set or when the `BindingContext` is assigned a new instance. In the context of our current setup, **one-time** data binding may not be the best choice because typically the data in the ViewModel is loaded asynchronously. This means that when we assign the ViewModel as the `BindingContext`, the initial value of the `Title` property is bound right away. However, any subsequent changes made to the `Title` property (such as updating it after the ViewModel loads data) won't be reflected in the UI due to the nature of one-time data binding. This won't be a problem for us right now since we're working with static data for demonstration purposes, but it's something to be aware of in a real-world application. As we progress through this book, we will revise this binding mode to handle such situations more effectively.

Let's add some more code and discuss the other binding modes. First, let's add an additional `IngredientsListViewModel` and extend our `RecipeDetailViewModel` with a property of that type:

1. In the **Solution Explorer**, right-click on the `ViewModels` folder in the `Recipes.Client.Core` project and select **Add | Class…**.

2. Enter `IngredientsListViewModel.cs` as name and click **Add**.

3. Let the class implement the `INotifyPropertyChanged` interface and add the `OnPropertyChanged` method. Add the following code to the newly created class:

    ```
    public class IngredientsListViewModel : INotifyPropertyChanged
    {
        public void OnPropertyChanged([CallerMemberName]
    string? propertyName = null)
            => PropertyChanged?.Invoke(this, new
    PropertyChangedEventArgs(propertyName));

        public event PropertyChangedEventHandler? PropertyChanged; }
    ```

    This is a typical implementation of the `INotifyPropertyChanged` interface with the `PropertyChangedEvent` and an `OnPropertyChanged` method that triggers the implemented `PropertyChhanged` event.

4. Next, we can add the `NumberOfServings` property, as shown in the following snippet. For brevity, the implementation of the `INotifyPropertyChanged` interface is left out:

```
public class IngredientsListViewModel : INotifyPropertyChanged
{
    private int _numberOfServings = 4;
    public int NumberOfServings
    {
        get => _numberOfServings;
        set
        {
            if(_numberOfServings != value)
            {
                _numberOfServings = value;
                OnPropertyChanged();
            }
        }
    }
    ...
    //ToDo: add list of Ingredients
}
```

`IngredientsListViewModel` contains a list of all ingredients and the quantities of them that are needed for a particular recipe. It also contains a `NumberOfServings` property, which indicates the number of servings for which the listed ingredients and their quantities are intended. The user should be able to adjust the number of servings in the UI and see how the quantity of the ingredients is being updated according to the selected amount. We will add the list of ingredients later.

5. Move over to `RecipeDetailViewModel` and add an `IngredientsList` property of type `IngredientsListViewModel` and assign it a new instance by default:

```
public IngredientsListViewModel
        IngredientsList { get; set; } = new ();
```

With this updated code in place, we can now go to `RecipeDetailPage` and focus on the XAML again. We want to update the UI to allow users to choose the desired number of servings. For this use case, we will create a `OneWay` and a `TwoWay` data binding.

Go to `RecipeDetail` and add the following XAML below the `Label` that shows the recipe's title:

```
<HorizontalStackLayout Padding="10">
    <Label Text="Number of servings:"
        VerticalOptions="Center" />
    <Label
        Margin="10,0" FontAttributes="Bold"
```

```
        Text="{Binding IngredientsList.NumberOfServings,
    Mode=OneWay}"
        VerticalOptions="Center" />

    <Stepper
        BackgroundColor="{OnPlatform WinUI={StaticResource
    Primary}}"
        Maximum="8" Minimum="1"
        Value="{Binding IngredientsList.NumberOfServings,
    Mode=TwoWay}" />
    </HorizontalStackLayout>
```

Let's have a look at the binding statements that we've added through this code:

- The Text property of the label is bound to the NumberOfServings property using the following binding statement: {Binding IngredientsList.NumberOfServings, Mode=OneWay}. The label displays the currently selected number of servings. The NumberOfServings property is part of the IngredientsList property on RecipeDetailViewModel, which is why the binding path is set to IngredientsList. NumberOfServings.

  Since the user can change the number of servings, we use the OneWay binding mode. This ensures that when the value of NumberOfServings is updated, the UI reflects the change accordingly.

- The Value property of the Stepper control is bound to the NumberOfServings property using the following binding statement: {Binding IngredientsList. NumberOfServings, Mode=TwoWay}. Stepper allows the user to adjust the currently selected number of servings.

  Since the user can change the number of servings and the ViewModel should update accordingly, we use the TwoWay binding mode. This ensures that not only the UI reflects the NumberOfServings property's value but also that the ViewModel is updated when the user modifies the number of servings via the Stepper control.

  Increments or decrements to the NumberOfServings property made using Stepper will be reflected in the previously discussed label due to OneWay binding, and the property triggers the PropertyChanged event.

In the XAML code, both bindings target properties within the IngredientsList property. In this example, all child elements of HorizontalStackLayout are bound to properties of the IngredientsList property in RecipeDetailViewModel. Since child elements inherit the binding context from their parent, it's possible to move the binding to the IngredientsList property one level up, if desired:

```
<HorizontalStackLayout Padding="10" BindingContext="{Binding
IngredientsList}">
    <Label Text="Number of servings:"
```

```
            VerticalOptions="Center" />

        <Label
            Margin="10,0" FontAttributes="Bold"
            Text="{Binding NumberOfServings, Mode=OneWay}"
            VerticalOptions="Center" />

        <Stepper
            BackgroundColor="{OnPlatform WinUI={StaticResource Primary}}"
            Maximum="8" Minimum="1"
            Value="{Binding NumberOfServings, Mode=TwoWay}"/>
    </HorizontalStackLayout>
```

In the preceding example, we are binding the BindingContext of HorizontalStackLayout to the IngredientsList property of RecipeDetailViewModel. This allows us to simplify the binding statements on the child elements. Of course, you can only do this when all the child elements have the same binding source.

As a final example, let's implement a OneWayToSource data binding in our **Recipes!** app. Here our aim is to show the allergen information for each recipe. As not everyone is interested in viewing this information, we will not show it by default. However, we want to allow the user to tick a box to get this information:

1. Go to RecipesDetailViewModel and let it implement INotifyPropertyChanged:

    ```
    public class RecipeDetailViewModel : INotifyPropertyChanged
    {
        ...
        public event PropertyChangedEventHandler? PropertyChanged;
    }
    ```

2. Create an OnPropertyChanged method that accepts propertyName as a parameter and calls the PropertyChanged event, just like we did in IngredientsListViewModel:

    ```
    public void OnPropertyChanged([CallerMemberName] string?
    propertyName = null)
                => PropertyChanged?.Invoke(this, new
    PropertyChangedEventArgs(propertyName));
    ```

3. Now, let's add a ShowAllergenInformation property of type bool. This property will be responsible for the visibility of the allergen information on RecipeDetailPage:

    ```
    private bool _showAllergenInformation;
    public bool ShowAllergenInformation
    {
        get => _showAllergenInformation;
    ```

```
    set
    {
        if (_showAllergenInformation != value)
        {
            _showAllergenInformation = value;
            OnPropertyChanged();
        }
    }
}
```

4. This property triggers the `PropertyChanged` event when its value changes. This allows us to bind it to the `IsVisible` property of a `VisualElement` so that whenever the value on the ViewModel changes, the UI element's visibility is updated automatically.

5. Finally, we can go to `RecipeDetailPage` and add the following XAML between the label that shows the recipe's title and the `HorizontalStackLayout` that is bound to `IngredientsList`:

```xml
<VerticalStackLayout Padding="10">
    <HorizontalStackLayout>
        <Label
            FontAttributes="Italic"
            Text="Show Allergen information"
            VerticalOptions="Center" />
        <CheckBox IsChecked="{Binding ShowAllergenInformation,
Mode=OneWayToSource}" />
    </HorizontalStackLayout>
    <Label IsVisible="{Binding ShowAllergenInformation,
Mode=OneWay}"
        Text="ToDo: add allergen information" />
</VerticalStackLayout>
```

This XAML code snippet displays a label, `"Show Allergen Information"`, followed by a checkbox that the user can toggle if they want to view the recipe's allergen information. The `IsChecked` property is bound using the `OneWayToSource` mode to the `ShowAllergenInformation` property in the ViewModel. This means that when the user checks the box, the property will update accordingly.

Additionally, we bind the same `ShowAllergenInformation` property using the `OneWay` mode to the `IsVisible` property of a label. This label will eventually display the allergen information. As a result, when the user toggles the checkbox, it updates the `ShowAllergenInformation` property in the ViewModel, which in turn triggers `PropertyChangedEvent`. This event will be picked up by the binding engine, which will update the `IsVisible` property of the label, allowing the allergen information to be displayed or hidden based on the user's preference.

> **INotifyPropertyChanged is not a requirement for the binding source**
>
> It is important to note that a binding target should always be a `BindableProperty` on a class that inherits from the `BindableObject`. The binding source, on the other hand, can be any property of any class. Most of the time, the binding source's class implements the `INotifyPropertyChanged` interface, but that's not a requirement. Only when using `OneWay` and `TwoWay` binding modes in scenarios where the values on the binding source can update and need to be reflected in the UI does the `INotifyPropertyChanged` interface need to be implemented. Alternatively, setting the `BindingContext` again would also update all the values, but that means everything needs to be reevaluated, which might not be a good idea.

Now that we've seen how .NET MAUI supports data binding and different binding modes, let's see how we can handle user interactions.

Handling interactions with the ICommand interface

In most applications, user interaction plays a vital role. Common interactions include clicking buttons, selecting items from a list, toggling switches, and more. To handle these interactions effectively while adhering to the MVVM pattern, it's essential to utilize a robust mechanism that encapsulates the necessary logic within the ViewModel. The `ICommand` interface is designed specifically for this purpose, enabling you to manage user interactions in a clean and maintainable way while ensuring a clear separation of concerns between the View and the ViewModel. In this section, we'll explore how to implement and use `ICommand` to handle user interactions in your .NET MAUI application.

The ICommand interface

The `ICommand` interface plays a crucial role in handling user interactions within the context of the MVVM pattern in .NET MAUI applications. `ICommand` is part of the `System.Windows.Input` namespace and allows you to encapsulate the logic for executing a specific action and determining whether that action can be executed in a ViewModel. Again, this interface isn't specific to .NET MAUI; it's an integral part of the .NET BCL.

`ICommand` has two main members: `Execute` and `CanExecute`:

- **Execute (object parameter)**: This method is what gets executed when the command is invoked. Through an optional parameter, additional data can be passed in if needed.

- **CanExecute (object parameter)**: This method indicates whether the command can be executed in its current state or not. Optionally, a parameter can be passed in if needed.

`ICommand` also exposes an event called **CanExecuteChanged**. This event is raised when the result of the `CanExecute` method changes, signaling the UI to re-evaluate whether the command can be executed. This enables automatic enabling/disabling of UI elements (such as buttons) based on the current state of the application.

To use ICommand in your ViewModel, you can create a custom command class that implements the ICommand interface or use a built-in command class such as Microsoft.Maui.Controls.Command. There are also third-party implementations available such as CommunityToolkit.Mvvm.Input.RelayCommand from the MVVM Toolkit, which we will dive into in more detail in *Chapter 5, Community Toolkits*. Typically, these implementations contain a method called ChangeCanExecute or NotifyCanExecuteChanged, which is called the CanExecuteChanged event.

Now that you're familiar with the ICommand interface and its role in a ViewModel, it's time to see it in action.

Putting it into action

As a simple demonstration, we want to allow users to add or remove a recipe as a favorite. For this, let's add two buttons to RecipeDetailPage, right below the VerticalStackLayout that contains the CheckBox element to display the allergen information:

```
<VerticalStackLayout>
    <Button Command="{Binding AddAsFavoriteCommand}" Text="Add as
favorite" />
    <Button Command="{Binding RemoveAsFavoriteCommand}" Text="Remove
as favorite" />
</VerticalStackLayout>
```

The first button's Command property binds to the AddAsFavoriteCommand property on our binding source, RecipeDetailViewModel. This button should allow a user to mark a recipe as a favorite when the recipe is not yet favorited. The second button does the exact opposite: it should allow a user to remove a recipe as a favorite. Let's take a look at the implementation of both commands:

1. In RecipeDetailViewModel, we can add an IsFavorite property:

    ```
    private bool _isFavorite = false;
    public bool IsFavorite
    {
        get => _isFavorite;
        private set
        {
            if (_isFavorite != value)
            {
                _isFavorite = value;
                OnPropertyChanged();
            }
        }
    }
    ```

    This property holds a bool value to indicate whether the user has marked this recipe as a favorite or not.

2. Next, we need to add the two commands, `AddAsFavoriteCommand` and `RemoveAsFavoriteCommand`:

    ```
    public ICommand AddAsFavoriteCommand
    {
        get;
    }

    public ICommand RemoveAsFavoriteCommand
    {
        get;
    }
    ```

    These are the two properties of type `ICommand` that the `Command` properties of the buttons bind to.

3. Now, we need to instantiate both commands. Whilst .NET contains an `ICommand` interface, it doesn't contain a concrete implementation. .NET MAUI, on the other hand, does have one! In order to access this implementation from the `Recipes.Client.Core` project, we need to configure the project to use the .NET MAUI framework.

    In the **Solution Explorer**, select the `Recipes.Client.Core` project. This should open up the associated `csproj` file, wherein you need to add `<UseMaui>true</UseMaui>`:

    ```
    <PropertyGroup>
      <TargetFramework>net8.0</TargetFramework>
      <ImplicitUsings>enable</ImplicitUsings>
      <UseMaui>true</UseMaui>
      <Nullable>enable</Nullable>
    </PropertyGroup>
    ```

    This allows us to access .NET MAUI-specific libraries from our `Core` project, such as `Microsoft.Maui.Controls.Command`, which implements `ICommand`.

4. In the constructor of `RecipeDetailViewModel`, we can now instantiate `AddAsFavoriteCommand` and `RemoveAsFavoriteCommand`:

    ```
    private void AddAsFavorite() => IsFavorite = true;
    private void RemoveAsFavorite() => IsFavorite = false;

    private bool CanAddAsFavorite()
        => !IsFavorite;
    private bool CanRemoveAsFavorite()
        => IsFavorite;

    public RecipeDetailViewModel()
    {
    ```

```
AddAsFavoriteCommand =
    new Command(AddAsFavorite, CanAddAsFavorite);
RemoveAsFavoriteCommand =
    new Command(RemoveAsFavorite, CanRemoveAsFavorite);
}
```

In this example, we have two commands on the ViewModel: AddAsFavoriteCommand and RemoveAsFavoriteCommand. Each command is created with an associated Action and a Func<bool> to determine its executability.

AddAsFavoriteCommand has an AddAsFavorite method as its action, which simply sets the IsFavorite property to true. Its CanExecute method is determined by the CanAddAsFavorite method, which returns true when the IsFavorite property has a value of false.

On the other hand, RemoveAsFavoriteCommand has a RemoveAsFavorite method as its action, which sets the IsFavorite property to false. The CanRemoveAsFavorite method is provided as the CanExecute check for this command, and it returns true when the IsFavorite property has a value of true.

> **Note**
>
> It's important to note that it is up to the control to check and adhere to the CanExecute method. It should not be a thing to blindly rely on, as it might not be implemented or work the way you expect. Make sure to read the control's documentation and test it thoroughly.

In summary, when the IsFavorite property is true, only RemoveAsFavoriteCommand can be executed, while AddAsFavoriteCommand cannot be. Conversely, when the IsFavorite property is false, AddAsFavoriteCommand can be executed, and RemoveAsFavoriteCommand cannot be. This ensures that the appropriate command is available for execution based on the current state of the IsFavorite property.

5. There is just one piece of the puzzle missing: whenever the IsFavorite property's value changes, the CanExecute method of both commands needs to be re-evaluated. In order to do that, we need to update the setter of the IsFavorite property:

```
if (_isFavorite != value)
{
    _isFavorite = value;
    OnPropertyChanged();
    ((Command)AddAsFavoriteCommand).ChangeCanExecute();
    ((Command)RemoveAsFavoriteCommand).ChangeCanExecute();
}
```

With all this code in place, we can run the app again. By default, only the first button (bound to AddAsFavoriteCommand) is enabled when the recipe is not a user favorite. Upon clicking this button, the IsFavorite property is updated, and the ChangeCanExecute method is called for both commands. As a result, the first button becomes disabled, while the second button (bound to RemoveAsFavoriteCommand) is automatically enabled. This ensures that the correct button is enabled or disabled based on the IsFavorite property.

Alternatively, we could also use a single command and use a CommandParameter to handle the toggling of the IsFavorite property:

1. For that, let's add a new SetFavoriteCommand property of type ICommand and initialize it in the constructor of RecipeDetailViewModel:

    ```
    public RecipeDetailViewModel()
    {
        ...
        SetFavoriteCommand =
            new Command<bool>(SetFavorite, CanSetFavorite);
    }
    private bool CanSetFavorite(bool isFavorite)
        => IsFavorite != isFavorite;

    private void SetFavorite(bool isFavorite)
        => IsFavorite = isFavorite;
    ```

    By assigning the command to an instance of Command<bool>, we are specifying that we expect a parameter of type bool in both the Execute and CanExecute methods.

2. In the setter of the IsFavorite property, we now need to call the CanExecuteChanged method of SetFavoriteCommand.

3. Finally, we can update the binding statements on both buttons:

    ```
    <Button
        Command="{Binding SetFavoriteCommand}"
        CommandParameter="{x:Boolean true}"
        Text="Add as favorite" />
    <Button
        Command="{Binding SetFavoriteCommand}"
        CommandParameter="{x:Boolean false}"
        Text="Remove as favorite" />
    ```

Both buttons call the same command, but they each pass in a different parameter, which gets passed to both the Execute and CanExecute methods.

UseMaui and MVVM best practices

In this chapter, we introduced the UseMaui property in our Core project, which may seem to contradict our previous statements about ViewModels being framework-agnostic. While adhering to the MVVM pattern, it is recommended to keep the ViewModels free from any framework-specific dependencies. However, in this specific case, we have opted for a more practical approach to demonstrate an implementation of ICommand through the Microsoft.Maui. Controls.Command class. In a strictly MVVM-compliant scenario, you would want to avoid such dependencies in your ViewModels to ensure maximum flexibility and maintainability.

In *Chapter 5, Community Toolkits*, we will take a look at the possibility of how to improve this code so that it follows these best practices more closely.

As a little extra, we also might want to display an icon indicating whether a recipe is a favorite or not. The visibility of this icon can be bound to the IsFavorite property. When toggling this property through the buttons and commands we've just created, the icon's visibility will be updated as well:

1. First, let's add the Chapter 03/Assets/favorite.png file to the Resources/ Images folder in the **Recipes.Mobile** project. Right-click on this folder in the **Solution Explorer**, select **Add | Existing Item…**, and select the favorite.png file. You might need to adjust the file type filter in the file picker popup to include **All Files** (*.*) in order to be able to see the .png file.

2. In RecipeDetailPage.xaml, add the following XAML directly below the Label displaying the recipe's title:

```
<Image
    Margin="5" HeightRequest="35"
    IsVisible="{Binding IsFavorite}"
    Source="favorite.png" WidthRequest="35" />
```

Now when we tap the **Add as favorite** or **Remove as favorite** button, you should see the favorite icon appearing or disappearing.

The ICommand interface plays a vital role in implementing the MVVM. By encapsulating user interactions within commands, it promotes a clean separation of concerns between the View and ViewModel. This allows for more maintainable, testable, and modular code. As demonstrated, ICommand, along with its CanExecute functionality, ensures that the appropriate actions are available to users based on the application's state, further enhancing the user experience. By leveraging ICommand, developers can effectively implement the MVVM pattern.

As we've explored the ICommand interface, you may be interested to know that there are additional tools and resources available for implementing MVVM in .NET MAUI. Thanks to the fantastic .NET and .NET MAUI community, various Community Toolkits provide even more support for the MVVM pattern in your projects.

Summary

In this chapter, we delved into the core components that enable the MVVM pattern in .NET MAUI. We discussed the essential building blocks, including `BindableObject`, `BindableProperty`, and `BindingContext`, and how they facilitate seamless communication between the View and ViewModel. Furthermore, we examined the importance of the `INotifyPropertyChanged` interface in notifying the UI of changes in ViewModel properties and demonstrated how the `ICommand` interface helps handle user interactions in a decoupled manner. By understanding these fundamental concepts, it becomes evident why .NET MAUI and the MVVM pattern are such a harmonious match.

As we move on to *Chapter 4, Data Binding in .NET MAUI*, we will take a closer look at data binding, diving deeper into topics such as value converters, fallback values, element and relative binding, multi-bindings, and compiled bindings. This will enable you to leverage the full power of data binding. Let's continue our journey!

Further reading

To learn more about the topics that were covered in this chapter, take a look at the following resources:

- Bindable properties: `https://learn.microsoft.com/dotnet/maui/fundamentals/bindable-properties`

- The `BindableObject` class: `https://learn.microsoft.com/dotnet/api/microsoft.maui.controls.bindableobject`

- The `INotifyPropertyChanged` interface: `https://learn.microsoft.com/dotnet/api/system.componentmodel.inotifypropertychanged`

Data Binding in .NET MAUI

In the previous chapter, we introduced the fundamentals of data binding in .NET MAUI. Data binding is not only a core feature of .NET MAUI but also a crucial component for effectively building applications using the MVVM design pattern. It creates a robust link between your View and ViewModel, facilitating efficient communication and synchronization between the two.

As we delve deeper into the realm of data binding, it's essential to grasp some advanced techniques and features. These are the building blocks that empower you to create dynamic user interfaces as efficiently as possible. They allow us to design user interfaces that are not only more interactive but also easier to manage and maintain.

This chapter will cover the following topics:

- ValueConverters and `StringFormat`
- Fallbacks
- Element and relative binding
- Multi-bindings
- Compiled bindings

By the end of this chapter, combined with what we've covered in the previous one, you will have a well-rounded and thorough understanding of data binding in .NET MAUI. This knowledge will enable you to effectively apply these techniques in your applications. Let's get started!

Technical requirements

Throughout this chapter, we will be adding functionality to the *Recipes!* app. All the required assets needed to follow along, including all the code used in this chapter, can be found on GitHub at `https://github.com/PacktPublishing/MVVM-pattern-.NET-MAUI/tree/main/Chapter04`.

ValueConverters and StringFormat

In many cases, the data in your ViewModel doesn't perfectly match the format expected by the UI. For example, you may have a `DateTime` object in your ViewModel that you want to display in a specific string format in your View, or an enumeration that should be represented as a more user-friendly string.

This is where **ValueConverters** and **StringFormat** come into play. Both of these techniques act as intermediaries, transforming and adapting your ViewModel data into a format suitable for display or interaction in the UI.

In this section, we'll delve into how to create and use ValueConverters to effectively manage these data transformations, and how formatting can further refine the presentation of your data, ensuring it is meaningful and user-friendly.

Creating and using ValueConverters

A ValueConverter acts as an intermediary between the source (typically the ViewModel) and the target (the View). It provides a way to transform or convert data as it passes from source to target or vice versa (*Figure 4.1*):

Figure 4.1: Usage of a converter

A common scenario might involve a ViewModel property that is a certain type, such as an enumeration or a complex object, which needs to be displayed differently in the UI. A ValueConverter can convert data from one type to another that is compatible and appropriate for the UI. Similarly, user input received in the UI may need to be converted back into a different format before being stored in the ViewModel.

ValueConverters are classes that implement the `Microsoft.Maui.Controls.IValueConverter` interface, which defines two methods – `Convert` and `ConvertBack`:

```
object Convert(object value, Type targetType, object
    parameter, CultureInfo culture);
object ConvertBack(object value, Type targetType, object
    parameter, CultureInfo culture);
```

The `Convert` method is responsible for transforming a value from the binding source to the binding target. It takes the original value, the target type, an optional parameter, and culture information as parameters. This method performs a conversion and returns an object that represents the transformed data. The transformed data is then used to update the property on the View. It is important to ensure that the returned object matches the expected type of the binding target property or a compatible type.

Let's take a look at the method's parameters:

- `value`: This is the source data that needs to be converted. This is usually data from your ViewModel that you want to display in your View. Because this can be anything, it is provided as `object`.

- `targetType`: This is the type of the binding target property. It's what the method should return the data as. For example, if you're binding to a property in your View that is of the `Microsoft.Maui.Graphics.Color` type, then `targetType` would be `Microsoft.Maui.Graphics.Color`.

- `parameter`: This is an optional `parameter` that can be used to pass additional information to the converter.

- `culture`: This is the `System.Globalization.CultureInfo` culture that should be used in the converter. This is especially important when dealing with dates, times, and numbers, as these can be represented differently in different cultures.

The `ConvertBack` method is used to reverse the conversion process, transforming data from the binding target back to the binding source. In many cases, the `ConvertBack` method is not implemented as it only has purpose on `TwoWay` and `OneWayToSource` data bindings, where the data on the View needs to be converted before it's passed to the ViewModel. The return value and parameters are analogous to the `Convert` method.

This might all be a little abstract at this point, so let's take a look at building and using a ValueConverter.

Creating a ValueConverter

To demonstrate the flexibility and power of ValueConverters, we're going to enhance our app by introducing a rating indicator for our recipes. Simply displaying a numeric value isn't the most appealing or intuitive way to represent a recipe's rating. Therefore, we'll utilize a ValueConverter to replace these numbers with star icons, creating a visually engaging and user-friendly rating representation. Our custom ValueConverter, `RatingToStarsConverter`, will convert a double value into a string. In conjunction with a specific font, this string will display as star icons. But before we can dive into building our converter, we need to take care of some preparatory steps first:

1. First, we are going to create `RecipeRatingsSummaryViewModel`. Right-click the `ViewModels` folder and select **Add | New Class...**; name the class `RecipeRatingsSummaryViewModel.cs`.

2. For now, we are only adding an `AverageRating` property of the `double` type to the class:

```
public class RecipeRatingsSummaryViewModel
{
    public double MaxRating { get; } = 4d;
    public double? AverageRating { get; set; } = 3.5d;
}
```

We are also including a value to indicate the maximum amount of stars that can be given by a user. Next, let's add an additional property called `RatingDetail` to `RecipeDetailViewModel` and assign it a new instance by default:

```
public RecipeRatingsSummaryViewModel RatingDetail {
    get; set; } = new ();
```

An efficient approach to displaying icons in an application is through the use of a specialized icon font. These fonts, which are readily available both for free and for purchase, allow you to easily incorporate various icons into your application. The principle is simple: incorporate the desired icon font into your app, then assign this font as `FontFamily` on the `Label` class where you wish to display the icon. From there, all that's left is to set the `Text` property on the `Label` class to the value that corresponds to the icon you wish to display.

Let's include Google's Material Design Icon font in our app so that we can use this font to display the recipe's rating later on. You can find the `MaterialIcons-Regular.ttf` font file in the `Chapter 04/Assets/Fonts` folder or you can download it from `https://github.com/google/material-design-icons/tree/master/font`:

1. In the Visual Studio **Solution Explorer** area, right-click the `Resources/Fonts` folder in the **Recipes.Mobile** project and select **Open Folder in File Explorer**.

2. Copy the `MaterialIcons-Regular.ttf` font file over to this folder.

3. Back in Visual Studio, you should see the newly added font file in the **Solution Explorer**. The file's **Build Action** should have automatically been set to **MauiFont**, as shown in *Figure 4.2*:

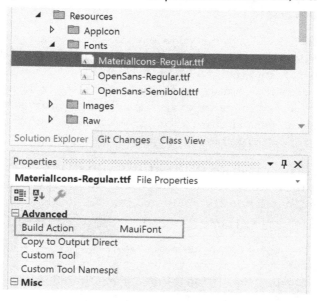

Figure 4.2: MaterialIcons-Regular.ttf file properties

4. Next, to be able to use this font in our MAUI app, we need to add it through `MauiAppBuilder`. Go to `MauiProgram.cs` and add it:

```
.ConfigureFonts(fonts =>
{
    ...

    fonts.AddFont("MaterialIcons-Regular.ttf",
      "MaterialIconsRegular");
});
```

The preceding code will allow us to use this font by setting the `FontFamily` property of a `Label` class or any control that displays text to `MaterialIconsRegular`.

Now that all of this is in place, we can finally start writing our first ValueConverter: `RatingToStarsConverter`. This converter should convert the rating of a recipe into little star icons.

RatingToStarsConverter

`RatingToStarsConverter` should convert any double value into a string value that represents stars. This is exactly what converters are for – taking in an object of a particular data type (double) and returning an object of another data type (string). For the visualization of the star icons, we can use the icon font we added earlier. `https://fonts.google.com/icons?icon.set=Material+Icons` provides an overview of all the available icons that exist in the font that we just added. By clicking an icon, you can see different ways to target it. We are interested in the code value. The star icon we want to use has a code of `e838` and the icon for a half star is identified by the `e839` code. Packed with this knowledge, let's see how we can create `RatingToStarsConverter`:

1. In the **Recipe.Mobile** project, add a new folder called `Converters`.

2. Right-click the `Converters` folder and select **Add | Class…**.

3. Enter the name of our converter, `RatingToStarsConverter`, and click **Add**.

4. Make the class implement the `Microsoft.Maui.Controls.IValueConverter` interface, as shown in the following code block:

```
public class RatingToStarsConverter : IValueConverter
{
    public object Convert(object value, Type
      targetType, object parameter, CultureInfo
        culture)
    {
        throw new NotImplementedException();
    }

    public object ConvertBack(object value, Type
      targetType, object parameter, CultureInfo
```

```
        culture)
    {
        throw new NotImplementedException();
    }
}
```

5. Now, we can start implementing the `Convert` method. As this converter could be used in any binding statement, the first thing that we need to do is check if the binding source is indeed a value of the `double` type:

```
public object Convert(object value, Type targetType,
    object parameter, CultureInfo culture)
{
    if (value is not double rating
        || rating < 0 || rating > 4)
    {
        return string.Empty;
    }
    ...
}
```

6. If the `value` parameter is not the type that we expect, or it doesn't fall within the expected range, we are returning a default value – in this case, `string.Empty`.

7. After we've validated the provided `value`, we can add the rest of the logic:

```
string fullStar = "\ue838";
string halfStar = "\ue839";

int fullStars = (int)rating;
bool hasHalfStar = rating % 1 >= 0.5;

return string.Concat(
    string.Join("", Enumerable.Repeat(fullStar,
    fullStars)), hasHalfStar ? halfStar : "");
```

Depending on the rating value we receive, we will return a string that contains icons defined in the `MaterialIcons` font we added to our project. For full stars, we must generate a collection of `fullStar` icons. The `string.Join` method then consolidates these individual icon strings into a single string. If the rating includes a decimal value of 0.5 or higher, we also append a `halfStar` icon to the string.

That's all we need to do in `RatingToStarsConverter`. We don't need to implement the `ConvertBack` method as this particular converter will not be used in `TwoWay` or `OneWayToSource` scenarios. When not implementing the `ConvertBack` method, it's good practice to add a comment indicating it's intentionally not implemented.

8. Next, we want to use our newly created converter, so we need to head over to `RecipeDetailPage`. The first thing we need to do there is add the namespace of the converter to our XAML, as shown in the following code snippet:

```
<ContentPage
    x:Class="Recipes.Mobile.RecipeDetailPage"
    xmlns="http://schemas.microsoft.com/dotnet/2021/maui"
    xmlns:x="http://schemas.microsoft.com/winfx/2009
      /xaml"
    xmlns:conv="clr-namespace:Recipes.Mobile
      .Converters"
    Title="RecipeDetailPage">
```

By declaring this XML namespace, we can reference anything within the `Recipes.Mobile.Converters` namespace directly in this XAML page using the `conv` prefix. The prefix can be anything you choose. To declare it, simply type `xmlns:` (XML namespace), followed by your chosen prefix, and then set it equal to the CLR namespace you wish to reference. This technique allows for cleaner and more organized code, as you can use this prefix to reference classes and components from the specified namespace.

9. Now, we need to add an instance of `RatingToStarsConverter` to our page so that we can use it later on in our binding statements. The following code block shows how we can add an instance of the converter as a resource to the page:

```
<ContentPage
    ...
    >
    <ContentPage.Resources>
        <conv:RatingToStarsConverter x:Key=
          "ratingToStarsConverter" />
    </ContentPage.Resources>
    ...
```

By giving the resource a Key value, we can reference it later on in our XAML.

10. Finally, we can now implement the binding of the `RatingDetail.AverageRating` property and use `RatingToStarsConverter` as the converter for this binding:

```
<Label
    FontFamily="MaterialIconsRegular"
    FontSize="18"
    Text="{Binding RatingDetail.AverageRating,
      Converter={StaticResource
        ratingToStarsConverter}}" />
```

In a `Binding Markup Extension`, we can define `Converter`. We can reference the instance we've declared on top of this page by using the `StaticResource Markup Extension` and passing in the key value of the converter instance. The converter will return a particular string value that, in combination with the label's `FontFamily` set to `MaterialIconsRegular`, will show icons on the screen.

About resources, StaticResource, and DynamicResource

The converter we've just added to the resources is now accessible on this particular page. It's important to note that the scope of this resource is local to this page only. That means if you want to use this converter on other pages, you would have to declare it in their resources too.

If you plan to use this converter across multiple pages, consider adding it to your `App.xaml` resources instead. By doing this, the converter becomes globally accessible throughout your app, eliminating the need to redeclare it on each page. This leads to cleaner and more maintainable code, especially for resources such as converters, which are often used throughout an application.

The `StaticResource Markup Extension` looks up a resource in a resource dictionary and assigns it to the property that it is set on. This resource lookup is performed only once when the page or control that uses `StaticResource` is loaded.

The `DynamicResource Markup Extension`, on the other hand, is used when the value can change and the UI needs to be updated to reflect this change. It maintains a link between the property and the resource, so when the resource changes, the property is updated too. `DynamicResource` is perfect for scenarios such as theme switching, where the values in the resource dictionary can be updated.

Alternatively, you can express the converter to use from the code if you define your data binding from code-behind. For this to work, you need to name the label you want to show the rating on `lblRating`, using the `x:Name` attribute:

```
lblRating.SetBinding(Label.TextProperty,
$"{nameof(RecipeDetailViewModel.RatingDetail)}.{nameof
  (RecipeRatingsSummaryViewModel.AverageRating)}",
    converter: new RatingToStarsConverter());
```

The `SetBinding` method accepts an optional converter parameter that allows you to specify the converter that should be used. When you run the app, you should see stars representing the recipe's rating, as shown in the following figure:

Classic Caesar Salad

Figure 4.3: RatingToStartsConverter in action

Let's enhance the user interface and user experience of our app a notch further. To achieve this, we'll assign unique colors to the rating indicator based on the average rating of a recipe.

RatingToColorConverter

With `RatingToColorConverter`, we should be able to give the stars that represent the recipe's rating a color depending on the average rating. Additionally, we want to display four stars consistently in the background, regardless of the recipe's average score. *Figure 4.4* shows exactly what we want to achieve:

Figure 4.4: Rating indicator using different colors

This visual cue serves as a rating scale that helps users immediately comprehend where a recipe stands in terms of rating. As the background stars need to be in a different color from the ones indicating the actual score, our new ValueConverter must accept a parameter to distinguish between foreground and background colors.

So, let's get started! Like we did before, we need to add a converter and implement the `IValueConverter` interface:

1. Right-click the **Converters** folder in the **Recipe.Mobile** project and select **Add | Class...**.

2. Enter `RatingToColorConverter` as the name and click **Add**.

3. Make the class implement the `IValueConverter` interface.

4. In the `Convert` method, we can check the parameter that is being passed in. When the `"background"` value is passed as a parameter to this converter, we want to return a slightly different color:

```
bool isBackground = parameter is string param
    && param.ToLower() == "background";
```

5. Once we have this information, we can go ahead and implement the rest of this method:

```
var hex = value switch
{
    double r when r > 0 && r < 1.4 => isBackground ?
      "#E0F7FA" : "#ADD8E6", //blue
    double r when r < 2.4 => isBackground ? "#F0C085"
      : "#CD7F32", //bronze
    double r when r < 3.5 => isBackground ? "#E5E5E5"
      : "#C0C0C0", //silver
    double r when r <= 4.0 => isBackground ? "#FFF9D6"
```

```
        : "#FFD700", //gold
    _ => null,
};
Return hex is null ? null : Color.FromArgb(hex);
```

Depending on the provided rating, this converter returns a particular color. On top of that, if the converter parameter is `"background"`, a slightly different color accent is returned that should serve as a background color.

6. The following code block shows how we can add this converter as a resource to `RecipeDetailPage`. This allows us to use the converter on the page:

```xml
<ContentPage.Resources>    ...
    <conv:RatingToColorConverter
        x:Key="ratingToColorConverter" />
</ContentPage.Resources>
```

With that in place, we can use the defined key, `"ratingToColorConverter"`, to reference this converter in our data binding statements.

7. Finally, replace the label we had previously showing the `Rating` property with the following code:

```xml
<Grid>
    <Label
        FontFamily="MaterialIconsRegular"
        FontSize="18"
        Text="{Binding RatingSummary.MaxRating,
        Converter={StaticResource
          ratingToStarsConverter}}"
        TextColor="{Binding
          RatingSummary.AverageRating,
        Converter={StaticResource
          ratingToColorConverter},
            ConverterParameter=background}" />

    <Label
        FontFamily="MaterialIconsRegular"
        FontSize="18"
        Text="{Binding RatingSummary.AverageRating,
        Converter={StaticResource
          ratingToStarsConverter}}"
        TextColor="{Binding
          RatingSummary.AverageRating,
        Converter={StaticResource
          ratingToColorConverter}}" />
</Grid>
```

By placing both labels in `Grid`, the labels will overlap and as a result, the first one will act as the backdrop for the rating indicator. This label's `Text` property is bound to the `RatingSummary.MaxRating` property and indicates the upper bound of the ratings. `RatingToStarsIconConverter` will transform this value into star icons. Additionally, its `TextColor` property is bound to the `RatingSummary.AverageRating` property of the ViewModel, using our newly created `RatingToColorConverter` to decide its color. Note that we've set the `ConverterParameter` property of the `Binding Markup Extension` to `"background"`. This parameter is forwarded to the converter, signaling that we need a color suitable for a background icon.

The second `Label` class's `Text` and `TextColor` properties are also bound to the `RatingSummary.AverageRating` property of `RecipeDetailViewModel`. `RatingToColorConverter` is used as the converter for the `TextColor` property, providing a color based on the recipe's rating. Because we didn't use `ConverterParameter` here, the converter understands that it needs to produce a color intended for the foreground.

These two simple ValueConverters provide a nice visualization for the recipe's rating. When running the app, we should see a nice colorful visualization of the recipe's rating, as shown in the following figure:

Classic Caesar Salad

★ ★ ★ ☆

Figure 4.5: Rating indicator using different colors

We haven't implemented the `ConvertBack` method of the ValueConverters in these examples as they only serve a purpose in `TwoWay` or `OneWayToSource` data bindings. Let's have a quick look at an example.

InverseBoolConverter

A very common and simple converter is `InverseBoolConverter`: it just takes a `bool` value and returns the inverse. An implementation of `InverseBoolConverter` typically also includes an implementation for its `ConvertBack` method. This is particularly relevant because, in the context of two-way data binding, an action on the UI can trigger an update to the bound bool value. By providing a `ConvertBack` implementation, we ensure that changes in the UI are correctly mirrored back to the ViewModel, keeping the data synchronized. Let's see how we can create a converter with an implemented `ConvertBack` method:

1. To create `InverseBoolConverter`, create a new class called `InverseBoolConverter` and let it implement the `IValueConverter` interface.

2. Let's write an `Inverse` method that returns a `bool` value and takes a `value` parameter of the `object` type:

```
private bool Inverse(object value)
    => value switch
    {
        bool b => !b,
        _ => false
    };
```

This method accepts a `value` parameter of the `object` type. Inside this method, we check if the provided value is a `bool` value. If it is, we return `inverse`; if it's not, we return `false`.

3. This method can now be used by both the `Convert` and `ConvertBack` methods as both methods should inverse the given `bool` value:

```
public object Convert(object value, Type targetType,
    object parameter, CultureInfo culture)
=> Inverse(value);

public object ConvertBack(object value, Type
    targetType, object parameter, CultureInfo culture)
=> Inverse(value);
```

4. To see this converter in action, we can go to `RecipeDetailViewModel`, update the `ShowAllergenInformation` property to `HideAllergenInformation`, and change its default value to `true`:

```
private bool _hideAllergenInformation = true;
public bool HideAllergenInformation
{
    get => _hideAllergenInformation;
    set
    {
        if (_hideAllergenInformation != value)
        {
            _hideAllergenInformation = value;
            OnPropertyChanged();
        }
    }
}
```

5. Because the meaning of this property is now the opposite of what it was, we need to update the bindings on our UI. This is exactly where our new `InverseBoolConverter` comes in. After we've added `InverseBoolConverter` to the resources of `RecipeDetailPage`, we can update the XAML to this:

```
<HorizontalStackLayout>
    <Label
        FontAttributes="Italic"
        Text="Show Allergen information"
        VerticalOptions="Center" />
    <CheckBox IsChecked="{Binding
      HideAllergenInformation, Mode=OneWayToSource,
        Converter={StaticResource
          inverseBoolConverter}}" />
</HorizontalStackLayout>
<Label IsVisible="{Binding HideAllergenInformation,
  Mode=OneWay, Converter={StaticResource
    inverseBoolConverter}}"
    Text="ToDo: add allergen information" />
```

`InverseBoolConverter` will inverse the `HideExtendedAllergenList` property's value. The `Convert` method will be invoked in the `OneWay` data binding scenario, whereas the `ConvertBack` method will be called when tapping `CheckBox`, triggering an update of `IsCheckedProperty`, which – through the `OneWayToSource` data binding – needs to update the property on the ViewModel.

ValueConverters are a powerful feature in data binding that enables seamless transformation of data between the ViewModel and the View. They provide a clean, maintainable way to control the display of data and handle discrepancies between the format of data in the ViewModel and how it needs to be displayed or inputted in the View.

Keep converters simple

Keep in mind that on screens with a lot of converters, these converters can be invoked a lot of times, especially in collections. As such, it is advised to keep converters as simple as possible and consider their performance.

As a developer, mastering ValueConverters will greatly enhance your ability to build dynamic, data-driven applications with .NET MAUI. In *Chapter 5*, *Community Toolkits*, we will see that the .NET MAUI Community Toolkit is packed with converters that are up for grabs for you to use in your projects.

An alternative approach to transform how data from the ViewModel needs to be displayed is by providing `StringFormat`.

StringFormat

Despite being less powerful than ValueConverters, providing `StringFormat` to your data binding offers a quick and straightforward way to modify the presentation of your data directly within your data binding expressions, saving you from the overhead of creating a separate converter for simple transformations. It leverages the standard .NET formatting conventions to shape the bound data into a specific string format. It's particularly useful when the bound data is of a primitive or built-in .NET data type, such as `DateTime`, `int`, `float`, `double`, and so on, and you want to format that data in a specific way for display.

As a first example, let's show the calories of the recipe on `RecipeDetailPage`, as shown in *Figure 4.6*:

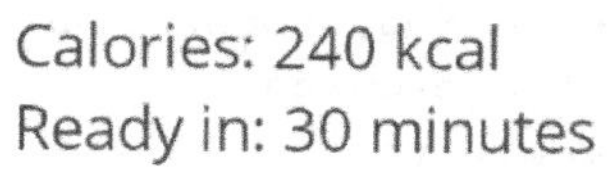

Calories: 240 kcal
Ready in: 30 minutes

Figure 4.6: Showing the calories and cooking time

Let's have a look at how simple this is to implement:

1. Add the optional `Calories` and `ReadyInMinutes` properties to `RecipeDetailViewModel`:

   ```
   public int? Calories { get; set; } = 240;
   public int? ReadyInMinutes { get; set; } = 35;
   ```

2. Now, as we want to show these properties on the screen, we need to indicate what this value means. We don't just want to show the raw values. For that, we could use multiple labels or a converter to enrich these raw values with additional context. Alternatively, we could use `StringFormat`, like this:

   ```
   <Label Text="{Binding Calories,
     StringFormat='Calories: {0} kcal'}" />
   <Label Text="{Binding ReadyInMinutes,
     StringFormat='Ready in: {0} minutes'}" />
   ```

Much like how we use the `string.Format` method in .NET, we can use the `StringFormat` property of `Binding Markup Extension`. In the format string, we can use a placeholder (`{0}`) to indicate where the bound value should be inserted. This approach provides a straightforward way to integrate bound values into formatted string expressions.

And the similarity with `string.Format` doesn't stop there. We can even use numeric, timespan, and date and time format strings.

To demonstrate this, let's add a `LastUpdated` timestamp to `RecipeDetailPage`. Let's look at the following steps:

1. First, we need to add a property called `LastUpdated` to `RecipeDetailViewModel`:

    ```
    public DateTime LastUpdated { get; set; }
        = new DateTime(2020, 7, 3);
    ```

2. Now, we can go to `RecipeDetailPage` and bind this value to a new label:

    ```
    <Label
        FontSize="8"
        HorizontalOptions="End"
        Text="{Binding LastUpdated, StringFormat='Last
            updated: {0:D}'}" />
    ```

    Just like with the `string.Format` method, we can add a format specifier to a placeholder. In this case, D is a standard `DateTime` format string representing the long date format specifier. It formats the bound `DateTime` value into a long date pattern. Of course, we could achieve the same result by creating a ValueConverter, but using the `StringFormat` property is a lot more concise and straightforward for such simple transformations. It saves us from the additional overhead of defining a separate converter class, thereby keeping our code cleaner and more maintainable.

3. Additionally, we might want to show the average ratings textually on the screen as well, limiting it to 1 decimal:

    ```
    <Label FontSize="8"
        Text="{Binding RatingDetail.AverageRating,
            StringFormat='{0:0.#} avg. rating'}" />
    ```

    This is all very intuitive as this follows the same format as the `string.Format` method.

Let's examine the app, specifically focusing on these two labels. Here is what they look like:

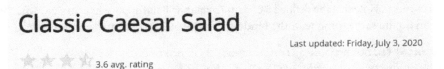

Figure 4.7: Leveraging StringFormat

ValueConverters and `StringFormat` not only facilitate the translation of data from the ViewModel into something more suitable for our UI, but also allow for the creation of more dynamic, responsive, and user-friendly applications. By using ValueConverters, we can handle complex conversions, while `StringFormat` helps us effortlessly format strings right in our bindings. Both of these mechanisms empower us to handle data transformations seamlessly, without overloading our ViewModel with UI-related concerns. Remember, effective data binding is not only about linking data; it's also about presenting data in the most intuitive way possible to our users.

But what about when things don't go exactly as planned? What if the data we're binding to is null? This is where **fallbacks** in data binding come into play. In the upcoming section, we'll explore the use of `TargetNullValue` and `FallbackValue` in our bindings to handle such cases and ensure a more robust, fail-safe user interface.

Fallbacks

There are occasions where data binding can fail; the binding source cannot be resolved (yet) or the returned value is null. Although ValueConverters and additional code could tackle many such situations, we can also enhance the resilience of our data bindings by setting fallback values. This can easily be done by setting the `TargetNullValue` or `FallbackValue` property in our binding expression.

TargetNullValue

The `TargetNullValue` property can be used in situations where we want to handle the situation where the resolved binding source target returns `null`. In other words, the binding engine can resolve the bound property, but this property returns a `null` value.

In our app, the `Calories` property on `RecipeDetailViewModel` is defined as a nullable `int`. This makes it essential for us to handle any potential null values in our data binding elegantly. If we leave the binding statement as-is, the label would show `"Calories:   kcal"` if the `Calories` property is `null`. Not very clean-looking, right? Let's fix this:

```
<Label Text="{Binding Calories, StringFormat='Calories: {0}
   kcal', TargetNullValue='No calories information
     available'}" />
```

By setting a value for the `TargetNullValue` property, we dictate what value should be used if the bound property returns `null`. Note that the defined `StringFormat` will not apply when `TargetNullValue` is used! We can do the same thing with the binding of the `ReadyInMinutes` property:

```
<Label Text="{Binding ReadyInMinutes, StringFormat='Ready
   in: {0} minutes', TargetNullValue='No cooking time
     specified'}" />
```

Let's spice up our UI a bit by adding an image to our `RecipeDetailPage`. And because there might not always be an image added to a recipe, we need to make sure we provide a `TargetNullValue` property so that a default image is shown. Let's take a look at how we could implement this:

1. First, we need to add the `Chapter 04/Assets/caesarsalad.png` and `Chapter 04/Assets/fallback.png` images to the `Resources/Images` folder of the `Recipes.Mobile` project. The easiest way to do this is by using your operating system's file manager to copy the files over.

2. Add an `Image` property to `RecipeDetailViewModel`:

```
public string Image { get; } = "caesarsalad.png";
```

3. Next, add the following XAML to `RecipeDetailPage.xaml`, just above the **Add/Remove as favorite** buttons:

```
<Image Margin="-10,10"
  Aspect="AspectFill" HeightRequest="200"
  HorizontalOptions="Fill"
  Source="{Binding Image, TargetNullValue=fallback.png}"
  />
```

Because the value on `RecipeDetailViewModel` is set to `caesarsalad.png`, the app will show this image on the screen. However, if you assign `null` to it, the `fallback.png` image will be shown as it is defined as `TargetNullValue`. *Figure 4.8* shows what this looks like:

Figure 4.8: Showing the recipe's image (left) or a fallback value (right)

Not too complex, right? It does get a little bit more complicated when a ValueConverter is involved. If the bound property is `null`, this `null` value will get passed into the ValueConverter. Only if said converter returns null will `TargetNullValue` be used. If the ValueConverter were to return a non-null value, `TargetNullValue` would not be used. While it is possible to define `TargetNullValue` as `StaticResource` or use the `x:Static Markup Extension` to assign it a static value, it is not possible to set its value with a binding expression.

Looking at the AverageRating property of RecipeRatingsSummaryViewModel, we could assign this a null value by default and update the TextColor binding statements to this:

```
TextColor="{Binding RatingDetail.AverageRating,
Converter={StaticResource ratingToColorConverter},
ConverterParameter=background, TargetNullValue={x:Static
Colors.HotPink}}"
```

The background stars are only displayed in HotPink because RatingToColorConverter returns null when the provided value is null. When we update RatingToColorConverter so that it returns a default color if the value doesn't fall within the expected range, the TargetNullValue will not be used:

```
public object Convert(object value, Type targetType, object
  parameter, CultureInfo culture)
{
    ...
    var hex = value switch
    {
        ...
        _ => "#EBEBEB"
    };
    return Color.FromArgb(hex);
}
```

TargetNullValue can be very useful for handling properties that might return a null value. However, it won't be helpful if the property or its source is inaccessible or doesn't exist since it isn't a null value issue but a problem with resolving the property itself. For example, in our app, it could be that the RatingDetail property of RecipeDetailViewModel is still null because it's not (yet) loaded. For that, we can use the FallBackValue property.

FallbackValue

FallbackValue is used when the binding engine is unable to retrieve a value due to an error or if the source itself is null, rather than when the resolved binding source returns null. As an example, we can set the RatingDetail property on RecipeDetailViewModel to null instead of assigning it a new instance and update the following data binding:

```
<Label FontSize="8"
Text="{Binding RatingDetail.AverageRating,
  StringFormat='{0:0.#} avg. rating',
    FallbackValue='Ratings not available'}"/>
```

This will result in the `Label` class displaying `"Ratings not available"` when the binding engine is unable to resolve the `RatingDetail.AverageRating` property. Just like with the `TargetNullValue` property, when `FallbackValue` is being used, the `StringFormat` property will be ignored. Additionally, a converter defined on this binding statement would also be ignored when using the `FallbackValue` value.

If we wish to combine the two, both `TargetNullValue` and `FallbackValue`, we could do the following:

```
<Label
    FontSize="8"
    Text="{Binding RatingDetail.AverageRating,
      StringFormat='{0:0.#} avg. rating',
        FallbackValue='Ratings not available',
          TargetNullValue='No ratings yet'}" />
```

`"No ratings yet"` will be displayed when the `AverageRating` property is set to `null`, whereas `"Ratings not available"` will be shown when the `AverageRating` property cannot be resolved due to the `RatingDetail` property being `null`.

Both `TargetNullValue` and `FallbackValue` are very valuable properties of the `Binding Markup Extension` and are very often overlooked. However, they can help tremendously in creating simple and easy-to-maintain UIs that make sense to the user. When both `FallbackValue` and `TargetNullValue` are defined in a binding, `TargetNullValue` takes precedence when the source property is null. `FallbackValue` is used when the binding system is unable to get a property value, such as when the path is incorrect or the source is not available. So, essentially, `TargetNullValue` is used for null values, while `FallbackValue` is used for binding errors.

Up until now, we've been binding to data on our ViewModel, but we can also bind to other elements in our visual tree. Let's have a look at element and relative data binding.

Element and relative binding

The versatility of data binding extends beyond linking our Views with ViewModel data. It's also possible to bind to different elements within our visual tree, opening up many new possibilities.

Both **element bindings** and **relative bindings** serve the purpose of allowing bindings to other elements. However, they differ in how they identify the source element:

- In an element binding, you specify the source element by its name, which is defined by using the `x:Name` attribute in XAML. The binding refers to this specific named element.

- In a relative binding, you refer to the source element concerning the position of the current element in the XAML tree. For example, you might bind to a property of the parent element or a property of the next sibling element, or you might even bind to a property of the element itself.

Let's have a look at both types of binding in more detail. First up: element binding.

Element binding

With element binding, we can bind to the property of another element by referencing that element by its name. For example, in our *Recipes!* app, we could remove the `HideExtendedAllergenList` property from the ViewModel and update our XAML to this:

```
<HorizontalStackLayout>
    <Label Text="Show extended allergen list?"
        VerticalOptions="Center" />
    <CheckBox x:Name="cbShowAllergens" IsChecked="False" />
</HorizontalStackLayout>
<VerticalStackLayout Margin="10,0,0,0" IsVisible="{Binding
    IsChecked, Source={Reference cbShowAllergens}}">
    <Label Text="ToDo, add extended allergen list" />
</VerticalStackLayout>
```

In the preceding example, we are binding the `IsVisible` property of `VerticalStackLayout` to the `IsChecked` property of the `cbShowAllergenList` CheckBox. This eliminates the need for an additional property on `RecipeDetailViewModel` and keeps the ViewModel clean and focused.

This direct connection between UI components streamlines the logic, reduces the ViewModel's responsibilities, and increases the maintainability of our code. It's a clear demonstration of how element binding can simplify interactions within the user interface.

Relative binding

Relative binding in XAML provides a way to set the source of a binding relative to the position of the binding target in the UI tree, and it can reference either the binding target itself or one of its ancestors.

The three main forms of relative binding are as follows:

- **Self**: This mode is used to bind a property to another property on the same element. It's useful when one property depends on the value of another.

- **FindAncestor**: This mode is used to bind a property to a property on an ancestor element in the visual tree. You can specify the type of the ancestor element and how far up the visual tree to search.

- **TemplatedParent**: This mode is used within a `ControlTemplate` to bind a property to a property on the control the template is applied to. It is particularly useful when creating custom templates for a control.

Let's have a look at these three forms of relative binding in more detail.

Self-relative binding mode

As an example of the self-relative binding mode, let's take a look at the two buttons in our app that allow the user to set or remove a recipe as a favorite. Wouldn't it be nice if we could hide the disabled button? We can easily achieve this by using the `Self` relative binding mode:

```
<Button
    Command="{Binding AddAsFavoriteCommand}"
    IsVisible="{Binding IsEnabled, Source={RelativeSource
      Self}}"
    Text="Add as favorite" />
```

`AddAsFavoriteCommand` is responsible for setting the button to enabled or disabled, depending on what the `CanExecute` method returns. With this relative binding, we are binding the `IsEnabled` property of the button itself to the `IsVisible` property. Now, when the button is disabled, it is not shown on the UI.

FindAncestor relative binding mode

In relative bindings, `AncestorType` is useful when you need to bind to a property of a parent element in the visual tree. It essentially "walks up" the tree of UI elements until it finds an instance of the specified type. By specifying `AncestorLevel`, we can define which ancestor to bind to. By default, `AncestorLevel` is 1, meaning it will bind to the nearest ancestor of the specified type. However, if you set `AncestorLevel` to 2, it will bind to the second nearest ancestor of the specified type, and so on. This offers a great deal of flexibility and control in choosing the specific ancestor in the visual tree that you want to bind to.

As a simple example, we can give the root `VerticalStackLayout` a `BackgroundColor` of `GhostWhite`. Now, if we want to bind the `TextColor` property of the two buttons on the bottom of the page to the `BackgroundColor` property of `VerticalStackLayout`, we could write the following:

```
<Button
    BackgroundColor="LightSlateGray"
    . . .
    TextColor="{Binding BackgroundColor,
      Source={RelativeSource AncestorLevel=2,
      AncestorType={x:Type VerticalStackLayout}}}" />
```

The `TextColor` property of the button is now bound to the `BackgroundColor` property of its second ancestor (`AncestorLevel=2`), which is of the `VerticalStackLayout` type (`AncestorType={x:Type VerticalStackLayout}`). Keep in mind that whenever the structure of the page changes, there might be no other ancestor of this type at the second level.

TemplatedParent relative binding mode

A `Control Template` is an XAML markup snippet that defines how a control should be rendered. When you're inside a control template, you can use `TemplatedParent` to bind to the properties of the control that's using the template. We will dive into this in more detail in *Chapter 11, Creating MVVM-Friendly Controls*.

Relative bindings in XAML offer a powerful way to connect properties of different elements within our user interface. One of its strongest aspects is its ability to traverse up the visual tree, enabling access to binding contexts of other elements. This feature becomes especially useful when the current element's binding context isn't sufficient or when we need to link a property to an element outside of its immediate scope.

In many UI scenarios, a certain state is defined by a combination of multiple properties. While it's certainly possible to create an additional property in the ViewModel that aggregates these properties for binding, there is a better, more elegant way to deal with this. Let's have a look at multi-bindings.

Multi-bindings

Multi-binding is a powerful feature in XAML data binding that allows you to bind a single target property to multiple source properties and then apply logic to produce one single value. This technique is particularly useful when a target property's value depends on more than one source property. The simplest example of this is using `StringFormat`.

Multi-binding StringFormat

A typical multi-binding scenario is where you would like to display multiple values in one label. We could, of course, create a property on the ViewModel that concatenates those values, or we could define this as a Multi-binding with `StringFormat`.

As an example, we want to show the author of the recipe next to the **Last updated** timestamp that we already have on our page (*Figure 4.9*):

Figure 4.9: Showing the author next to the Last updated timestamp

Here's how it's done:

1. First, let's add an `Author` property to our ViewModel:

    ```
    public string Author { get; set; } = "Sally Burton";
    ```

2. Next, replace the label that shows the `LastModified` timestamp with the following:

```
<Label FontSize="8" HorizontalOptions="End">
    <Label.Text>
        <MultiBinding StringFormat="Last updated:
         {0:D} | {1}">
            <Binding Path="LastUpdated" />
            <Binding Path="Author" />
        </MultiBinding>
    </Label.Text>
</Label>
```

The `MultiBinding` class allows us to set multiple bindings. The `StringFormat` property of `MultiBinding` allows us to construct a single string value from multiple bindings. This operates much like the `string.Format` method, utilizing different placeholders (`{0}`, `{1}`, `{2}`, and so on) that correspond to each binding. This makes it easier to construct complex string values from multiple data sources.

Binding properties

What you define as `Binding` inside `MultiBinding` is the same thing as `Binding Markup Extension`, which we used in our data bindings previously. It has properties such as `Converter`, `ConverterParameter`, `StringFormat`, `TargetNullValue`, `FallbackValue`, and others that can be individually configured for each `Binding` within `MultiBinding`, allowing for fine-grained control over each component of `MultiBinding`.

Multi-binding goes beyond just concatenating strings in a specific format. Let's have a look at the `Converter` property of `MultiBinding`.

IMultiValueConverter

The `MultiBinding` class has a property called `Converter` that's of the `Microsoft.Maui.Controls.IMultiValueConverter` type. This interface is similar to `IValueConverter` but with a significant distinction. The `Convert` method in `IMultiValueConverter` accepts an array of objects, representing all the individual bound values, rather than a single object as in `IValueConverter`. Likewise, the `ConvertBack` method of `IMultiValueConverter` returns an array of objects, not just one.

Let's update the `RatingIndicator` in `RecipeDetailView`. The colors of the stars should not only depend on the average rating but also the total of reviews. If the recipe has less than 15 reviews, we'll show a generic default color. Only when the recipes have more reviews will we use the color scale we used earlier. To make that work, we'll use `MultiBinding` to bind to both `AverageRating` and `TotalReviews` from `RecipeRatingsSummaryViewModel` and `IMultiValueConverter` to decide the color of the stars:

1. To start with, we need to add an additional property called `TotalReviews` to our RecipeRatingsSummaryViewModel:

```
public class RecipeRatingsSummaryviewModel
{
    public int TotalReviews { get; } = 15;
    public double MaxRating { get; } = 4d;
    public double? AverageRating { get; set; } =
        3.6d;}
```

2. Next, we can create the `RatingAndReviewsToColorConverter` class, which implements the `IMultiValueConverter` interface. For that, we need to right-click the `Converter` folder, select **Add | Class...**, and enter the name of the converter.

3. Make the class implement `IMultiValueConverter` and add the following code to the `Convert` method:

```
bool isBackground = parameter is string param
    && param.ToLower() == "background";

var hex = isBackground ? "#F2F2F2" : "#EBEBEB";

if (values.Count() == 2
    && values[0] is int reviewCount
    && values[1] is double rating)
{
    if (reviewCount >= 15)
    {
        hex = rating switch
        {
            ...
        };
    }
}
return hex is null ? null : Color.FromArgb(hex);
```

In this `Convert` method, we have access to the array of bound values. This allows us to write logic by taking every given value into account. In this scenario, we are expecting the total number of reviews to be the first value and the rating to be the second.

4. Now, we can add this converter as a resource to our `RecipeDetailPage`, just like we did before with other ValueConverters.

```
<conv:RatingAndReviewsToColorConverter
    x:Key="ratingAndReviewsToColorConverter" />
```

5. Finally, we can use `RatingAndReviewsToColorConverter` in a `MultiBinding` class on the `Label` class's `TextColor` property:

```xml
<Label.TextColor>
    <MultiBinding
        Converter="{StaticResource
          ratingAndReviewsToColorConverter}"
        ConverterParameter="background"
        TargetNullValue="{x:Static Colors.HotPink}">
        <Binding Path="RatingDetail.TotalReviews" />
        <Binding Path="RatingDetail.AverageRating" />
    </MultiBinding>
</Label.TextColor>
```

`IMultiValueConverter`, in conjunction with `MultiBinding`, offers a dynamic and flexible approach to dealing with complex binding scenarios. By accepting an array of inputs and processing them into a singular output, it allows us to handle multi-source dependencies in our UI.

The last thing we need to look into in the context of data binding is compiled bindings. This feature appears to be a little less known, despite it having a lot of advantages.

Compiled bindings

Compiled bindings are a more performant way of creating bindings and they are verified at compile-time instead of at runtime. Typically, the data binding engine uses reflection to get or set property values on the objects being bound. This approach is flexible and powerful because it allows the binding engine to interact with any object, regardless of its type. However, it also has some performance implications because reflection is slower than direct property access, and it can lead to errors that are only detectable at runtime if a property name is misspelled or if the property doesn't exist. In contrast, compiled bindings are checked at compile time, which means they can catch errors before the app is even run. Furthermore, because the bindings are compiled into the app, the runtime performance is improved as there's no need for the binding resolution process that takes place with traditional data binding.

Enabling compiled bindings is pretty simple: with the `x:DataType` attribute, we can specify the type of the object that the XAML element and its children will bind to. So, basically, on our `RecipeDetailPage`, we could add the following:

```xml
<ContentPage
    x:Class="Recipes.Mobile.RecipeDetailPage"
    ...
    xmlns:vms="clr-namespace:Recipes.Client.Core
      .ViewModels;assembly=Recipes.Client.Core"
    x:DataType="vms:RecipeDetailViewModel"
    Title="RecipeDetailPage">
```

With this, we indicate that the type of `BindingContext` will be `Recipes.Client.Core.ViewModels.RecipeDetailViewModel`, enabling the XAML compiler to validate bindings at compile time.

However, there is a caveat that will prevent us from compiling and running the application from the bat. In our existing XAML code, we've explicitly set `BindingContext` of `HorizontalStackLayout` to the `IngredientsList` property. This confuses the XAML compiler as it assumes elements inside `HorizontalStackLayout` are still bound to `RecipeDetailViewModel`, which isn't the case. This misunderstanding results in an error message in Visual Studio (*Figure 4.10*). This error message is evidence that, by adding the `x:DataType` attribute, bindings are now validated and compiled:

> ⊗ XFC0045 Binding: Property "NumberOfServings" not found on "Recipes.Client.Core.ViewModels.RecipeDetailViewModel".

Figure 4.10: Binding error

Sadly, fixing this error might not be as straightforward as you might think: it's not only adding setting the `x:DataType` attribute on `VerticalStackLayout` to `IngredientsListViewModel` – the binding itself also needs to be updated:

```
<HorizontalStackLayout
    x:DataType="vms:IngredientsListViewModel"
      BindingContext="{Binding IngredientsList,
        Source={RelativeSource AncestorType={x:Type
          vms:RecipeDetailViewModel}}}">
```

With these adjustments in place, we can build and run our app as before. But now, our app benefits from the performance improvements of compiled bindings. Need more proof that bindings are now compiled? Try misspelling the name of a bound property in a binding statement. As shown in *Figure 4.11*, Visual Studio will promptly alert you about the nonexistent property:

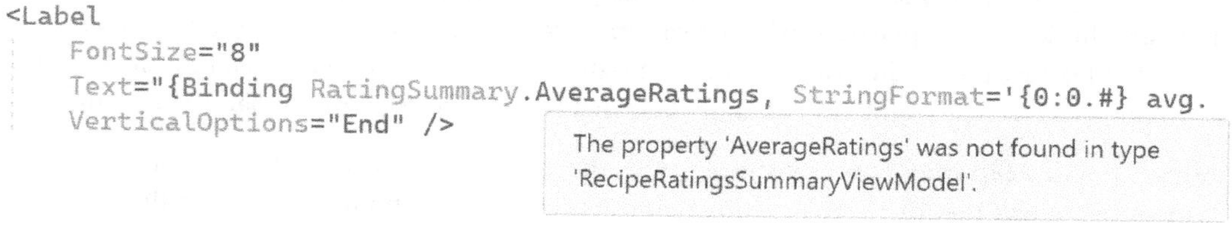

```
<Label
    FontSize="8"
    Text="{Binding RatingSummary.AverageRatings, StringFormat='{0:0.#} avg.
    VerticalOptions="End" />
```

> The property 'AverageRatings' was not found in type 'RecipeRatingsSummaryViewModel'.

Figure 4.11: Property not found on the specified type

Compiled bindings give you design-time checks and will even give you IntelliSense when writing binding statements. But most importantly, they also lead to faster page load times and better app performance overall.

Summary

Data binding is a powerful concept in XAML that makes it easier to separate our view logic from our business logic. It's a huge enabler for doing MVVM in .NET MAUI. It is a complex subject and it can be challenging to fully master every aspect of it. It involves understanding a variety of concepts and techniques, from simple data bindings to multi-bindings and converters, and from element and relative bindings to high-performance compiled bindings.

However, don't be overwhelmed. Like any complex subject, understanding data binding comes with time and practice. The more you work with it, the more comfortable you'll become, and many aspects of it will eventually become second nature.

Remember, the ultimate objective is to efficiently apply the MVVM pattern. In this context, data binding plays a crucial role in connecting your ViewModel's data and business logic with the UI. The knowledge you've gathered in this chapter has brought you one step closer to that goal.

In the next chapter, we'll be looking at community toolkits that can facilitate implementing the MVVM pattern in .NET MAUI.

Further reading

To learn more about the topics that were covered in this chapter, take a look at the following resources:

- *Multi-binding*: `https://learn.microsoft.com/dotnet/maui/fundamentals/data-binding/multibinding`

- *Relative bindings*: `https://learn.microsoft.com/dotnet/maui/fundamentals/data-binding/relative-bindings`

- *Compiled bindings*: `https://learn.microsoft.com/dotnet/maui/fundamentals/data-binding/compiled-bindings`

5

Community Toolkits

In this chapter, we will explore some of the popular **Community Toolkits** that have been developed to assist developers in using data binding and the MVVM pattern more efficiently and effectively in .NET MAUI. These toolkits offer valuable components and utilities that can greatly enhance your development experience and help you build robust and maintainable applications. There are numerous large and small frameworks or toolkits that facilitate data binding and the application of the MVVM pattern in your projects. Some of them have a significant overall impact on your code, while others are more focused on providing developers with a set of helpers or components that you typically rewrite for each new project.

Every existing toolkit or framework is the product of dedicated developers investing their time and expertise, and each one provides value to its users, whether or not it suits your particular coding style. In this book, I don't want to favor any specific framework or toolkit over others but rather showcase community-driven efforts that can be beneficial to developers. For this reason, we'll be exploring two Community Toolkits that provide some helpers and base classes that you can build upon but don't have a large impact on your code.

In this chapter, we will be discussing the following:

- The MVVM Toolkit
- The .NET MAUI Community Toolkit
- Other popular frameworks
- Contributing to the community

These toolkits were chosen as examples because they offer tools and components that can be integrated into your projects as needed, without imposing a specific architectural style or coding paradigm. This feature makes these toolkits particularly flexible and adaptable to a variety of coding styles and project requirements. Being part of the .NET Community Toolkits, they benefit from a wide community of contributors, including both Microsoft employees and independent developers. This collaboration ensures the toolkits remain up to date, reliable, and effective for developers across the board.

These toolkits aim to simplify many common tasks you will encounter when building .NET MAUI applications. The features they provide are often things we've covered in earlier chapters, but now, they've been conveniently implemented for you. It's important to understand that these toolkits are not magical entities; they encapsulate strategies and techniques that you could implement yourself. However, their true value lies in offering a ready-made, community-approved solution, saving you significant time and effort. By knowing what's available in these toolkits, you can make informed decisions about when to leverage them and when to customize your solutions. So, without further ado, let's dive in and see what they have to offer!

Technical requirements

Throughout this chapter, we will be updating some code from the *Recipes!* app. The updated code can be found on GitHub at `https://github.com/PacktPublishing/MVVM-pattern-.NET-MAUI/tree/main/Chapter05` for reference and comparison.

The MVVM Toolkit

The **MVVM Toolkit** (**CommunityToolkit.Mvvm**) is a comprehensive library that's designed to simplify and streamline the implementation of the MVVM pattern in your applications. Developed and maintained by the .NET community, this toolkit provides a robust set of framework-independent tools, components, and utilities that help you build applications using the MVVM pattern. It's important to note that this toolkit isn't .NET MAUI-specific; it's UI framework-agnostic.

Here are some of the key features of the MVVM Toolkit:

- **ObservableObject**: This class serves as a base class that implements the `INotifyPropertyChanged` interface, simplifying the process of raising the `PropertyChanged` event. Its `SetProperty` method streamlines setting property values and automatically raises the `PropertyChanged` event when needed. By using this class, developers can reduce the boilerplate code associated with checking for property updates and triggering the `PropertyChanged` event accordingly.

- **ObservableValidator**: `ObservableValidator` extends the `ObservableObject` class and includes built-in validation logic. This means that any object that inherits from `ObservableValidator` will have both observable and validating features.

- **RelayCommand** and **AsyncRelayCommand**: Both classes provide simple, lightweight, flexible, and framework-agnostic implementations of the `ICommand` interface. `RelayCommand` handles synchronous operations, while `AsyncRelayCommand` is designed for asynchronous tasks. Both support optional `CanExecute` logic.

- **WeakReferenceMessenger**: `WeakReferenceMessenger` is a messaging system that enables communication between loosely coupled components. It uses weak references to manage message subscriptions, which helps you avoid memory leaks and unintended strong dependencies between objects in your application. Messaging will be discussed in more depth in *Chapter 7, Dependency Injection, Services, and Messaging*.

- **Source Generators**: The toolkit includes some source generators that help automate the creation of boilerplate code, improving productivity and reducing the chance of errors. `ObservablePropertyAttribute` simplifies the implementation of properties that trigger the `PropertyChanged` event, and `RelayCommandAttribute` automates the creation of commands, respectively.

These are only a few examples of the components of an MVVM Toolkit. The idea here was to let you know what the MVVM library has to offer. Now, let's look into how to effectively use it in our project.

Adding the MVVM Toolkit to your project is very easy:

1. Right-click the `Recipes.Client.Core` project and select **Manage Nuget Packages**.

2. Search for `MVVM Toolkit` and select **CommunityToolkit.Mvvm** from the list. *Figure 5.1* shows the NuGet package we are searching for:

CommunityToolkit.Mvvm ✅ by Microsoft, **1,38M** downloads
This package includes a .NET MVVM library with helpers such as:
 - ObservableObject: a base class for objects implementing the INotifyPropertyChanged interface.

Figure 5.1: CommunityToolkit.Mvvm NuGet package

3. Hit **Install** to add the NuGet package to the `Recipes.Client.Core` project.

In the following example, we will be updating `RecipeDetailViewModel` and `IngredientsListViewModel` so that they use `ObservableObject` from the MVVM Toolkit.

ObservableObject

Implementing the `INotifyPropertyChanged` interface in each ViewModel can become tedious and repetitive. That's why developers often create a base class that takes care of this task. The MVVM Toolkit provides such a base class for free in the form of `ObservableObject`.

By inheriting from `ObservableObject`, your ViewModel classes can automatically notify the View of property changes, keeping the UI synchronized with the underlying data. `ObservableObject` also provides the `SetProperty` method, which allows developers to set a property's value. As a result, if the value has changed, it automatically triggers the `PropertyChanged` event to update the UI.

Let's update our code so that our ViewModels inherit from `ObservableObject` instead of each one having its own implementation of the `INotifyPropertyChanged` interface:

1. Head over to `IngredientsListViewModel` and let this class inherit from `ObservableObject` instead of implementing the `INotifyPropertyChanged` interface, as seen here:

    ```csharp
    using CommunityToolkit.Mvvm.ComponentModel;

    namespace Recipes.Client.Core.ViewModels;

    public class IngredientsListViewModel :
      ObservableObject
    {
        private int _numberOfServings = 4;
        public int NumberOfServings
        {
            ...
        }
        //ToDo: add list of Ingredients
    }
    ```

2. By inheriting `ObservableObject`, we can remove the `OnPropertyChanged` method and the `PropertyChanged` event that we had before.

3. Next, we can update the setter of the `NumberOfServings` property so that it uses the `SetProperty` method of `ObservableObject`:

    ```csharp
    public int NumberOfServings
    {
        get => _numberOfServings;
        set => SetProperty(ref _numberOfServings, value);
    }
    ```

The `SetProperty` method eases the implementation of calling the `PropertyChanged` event when the value is being updated. This method will update the provided backing field (`_numberOfServings`) and trigger the `PropertyChanged` event automatically when the value is being updated.

We can start doing the same thing for `RecipeDetailViewModel` as well:

1. Inherit from `ObservableObject`.

2. Remove the `OnPropertyChanged` method and the `PropertyChanged` event.

3. Update the setter of `HideAllergenInformation` so that it uses the `SetProperty` method, as shown in the following snippet:

```
private bool _hideAllergenInformation = true;
public bool HideAllergenInformation
{
    get => _hideAllergenInformation;
    set => SetProperty(ref _hideAllergenInformation, value);
}
```

By ensuring our ViewModels inherit from `ObservableObject` and utilize the `SetProperty` method, we can eliminate excessive boilerplate code. This would benefit us by reducing a significant amount of ceremony. This helps maintain the conciseness and clarity of our ViewModels, allowing them to stay focused on their core responsibilities. Unless you are being paid by lines of code, I think you would agree that these updated classes look a lot better with a lot less boilerplate code!

One of the most helpful features in the MVVM Toolkit is the different `ICommand` implementations. Let's take a look!

RelayCommand

The MVVM Toolkit provides several robust implementations of the `ICommand` interface. Each implementation serves a unique purpose, addressing varied needs for communication between the ViewModel and View in different scenarios. These implementations help streamline command operations:

- `RelayCommand`: This straightforward implementation of `ICommand` allows you to specify `Execute` and `CanExecute` methods using delegates, tailoring what the command does and whether it can be executed at a given time. This implementation is similar to `Microsoft.Maui.Controls.Command`, which we used earlier. However, the `Command` implementation had the `ChangeCanExecute` method, which we can call to trigger the re-evaluation of the `CanExecute` method. On the `RelayCommand` class, a method with this behavior is called `NotifyCanExecuteChanged`.

- `RelayCommand<T>`: This is a variant of `RelayCommand` that adds support for a parameter that can be passed to the `Execute` and `CanExecute` methods. The type of the parameter is determined by the generic type parameter. This implementation is similar to `Microsoft.Maui.Controls.Command<T>`.

- `AsyncRelayCommand`: An async variant of `ICommand`, `AsyncRelayCommand` returns a `Task`, making it ideal for managing asynchronous operations such as network data fetches.

- `AsyncRelayCommand<T>`: A parameter-supporting version of `AsyncRelayCommand`, this allows you to pass an argument to the asynchronous `Execute` and `CanExecute` methods, providing additional versatility for async operations.

Let's see how we can update our command so that it leverages the `RelayCommand` and `RelayCommand<T>` classes:

1. The following code block shows how we can initialize the commands in the constructor by updating their type from `Microsoft.Maui.Controls.Command` to `CommunityToolkit.Mvvm.Input.RelayCommand` and from `Microsoft.Maui.Controls.Command<T>` to `CommunityToolkit.Mvvm.Input.RelayCommand<T>`:

```
public RecipeDetailViewModel()
{
    AddAsFavoriteCommand =
        new RelayCommand(AddAsFavorite,
            CanAddAsFavorite);
    RemoveAsFavoriteCommand =
        new RelayCommand(RemoveAsFavorite,
            CanRemoveAsFavorite);
    SetFavoriteCommand =
            new RelayCommand<bool>(SetFavorite,
                CanSetFavorite);
}
```

This updated code will instantiate the three commands with a new `RelayCommand`, passing in the methods that should be triggered when calling the command's `Execute` and `CanExecute` methods.

2. While we are at it, we can also go ahead and update the types of the commands in this class. While `RelayCommand` implements the `ICommand` interface, it also implements the `IRelayCommand` interface:

```
public IRelayCommand AddAsFavoriteCommand
{
    get;
}
public IRelayCommand RemoveAsFavoriteCommand
{
    get;
}
public IRelayCommand SetFavoriteCommand
{
    get;
}
```

By updating the type of our commands, as shown in the preceding snippet, we can avoid additional castings later on.

3. The setter of `IsFavorite` can now be updated to this:

```
public bool? IsFavorite
{
    get => _isFavorite;
    private set
    {
        if(SetProperty(ref _isFavorite, value))
        {
            AddAsFavoriteCommand
                .NotifyCanExecuteChanged();
            RemoveAsFavoriteCommand
                .NotifyCanExecuteChanged();
            SetFavoriteCommand
                .NotifyCanExecuteChanged();
        }
    }
}
```

The `SetProperty` method returns `true` if the property was changed. This allows us to do additional things when the property is changed (or not). For example, in this case, we want to re-evaluate the `CanExecute` method of the commands when the `IsFavorite` property changes its value by calling each command's `NotifyCanExecuteChanged` method.

> **Adhering to the best practices of MVVM**
>
> Because we don't use `Microsoft.Maui.Control.Command` anymore, we can also remove the MAUI dependency that we currently have on this project. Click on the `Recipes.Client.Core` project so that the project's `.csproj` file opens and remove the `<UseMaui>` tag. Now, the ViewModels (and the `Recipes.Client.Core` project) are platform-agnostic again, adhering to the best practices of MVVM.

In *Chapter 1*, it was apparent that applying the MVVM pattern involves a lot more code compared to writing everything in code-behind. Mostly, that's because of all of the ceremony in the ViewModels. While classes such as `ObservableObject` already abstract away some of the boilerplate code, we could even go one step further and look at the Source Generators that are available in the MVVM Toolkit.

Source Generators

Source Generators are a compiler feature in .NET that allows developers to generate new code during the compilation process. This has the potential to greatly reduce manual coding and the likelihood of errors.

The MVVM Toolkit provides ObservablePropertyAttribute and RelayCommandAttribute, which are used by the Source Generators to create properties that notify the UI of changes and commands that handle user interactions, respectively. Additionally, other attributes such as NotifyPropertyChangedForAttribute and NotifyCanExecuteChangedForAttribute can be used in combination with ObservablePropertyAttribute to add even more functionality through code generation.

Given how Source Generators work, the class on which these attributes are applied must be declared as a partial class. In C#, partial classes allow you to split a class across multiple files using the partial keyword. At compile time, the different files are combined into one class. This feature is integral to source generators, which generate additional source code during compilation. Therefore, when you wish to use any of these attributes, remember to declare your ViewModel as partial:

```
public partial class RecipeDetailViewModel :
    ObservableObject
```

Now that the ViewModel has been declared as partial, we can begin to adapt our code to take advantage of these attributes. Let's see how this can be done.

Using the ObservableProperty attribute

Typically, we need to write some boilerplate code when implementing a property that triggers the PropertyChanged event. By using ObservablePropertyAttribute, we can let Source Generators generate this code for us.

This attribute can be applied to a field; at build time, a public property will be generated, with the annotated field as the backing field.

As an example, we can take a look at RecipeDetailViewModel. The HideExtendedAllergenList property can be deleted and ObservablePropertyAttribute can be added to the _hideExtendedAllergenList field:

```
[ObservableProperty]
private bool _hideExtendedAllergenList = true;
```

With this ObservableProperty attribute in place, a full-fledged public property named HideExtendedAllergenList will be generated at build time.

The generated property's set method will contain logic that checks whether the value is updated and triggers the PropertyChanged event accordingly. The setter will also call a handful of partial methods that are being generated, allowing us to add some custom code while the property value is being updated.

> **Note**
>
> It's very important to note that the `ObservableProperty` attribute generates a public property for us. When binding this value to the UI, make sure you bind to this generated property (`HideExtendedAllergenList`, in this case) and not try to bind to the field you've set the attribute on. Also, when assigning a value, always assign it to the generated property to make sure the `PropertyChanged` event gets triggered!

But what about the `IsFavorite` property of `RecipeDetailViewModel`?

In this setter, we call the `NotifyCanExecuteChanged` method of our commands. Can we make this work on a generated property as well? Yes; for those cases, we have the `NotifyCanExecuteChangedFor` attribute, which accepts the name of the command whose `NotifyCanExecuteChanged` method needs to be triggered when the value of the property is updated. This means that the entire `IsFavorite` property could be rewritten like this:

```
[ObservableProperty]
[NotifyCanExecuteChangedFor(nameof(AddAsFavoriteCommand))]
[NotifyCanExecuteChangedFor(nameof(RemoveAsFavoriteCommand))]
[NotifyCanExecuteChangedFor(nameof(SetFavoriteCommand))]
private bool? _isFavorite = false;
```

The first attribute, `ObservableProperty`, will generate a property that will trigger the `PropertyChanged` event when its value is being updated. The next three `NotifyCanExecuteChangedFor` attributes will make sure that the `NotifyCanExecuteChanged` method of the three commands of the `IRelayCommand` type will be invoked when the property updates.

Speaking of commands, there's a Source Generator for generating a `RelayCommand` as well. Let's take a look.

Using the RelayCommand attribute

You can apply the `RelayCommand` attribute to a method that you intend to use as the execution action for a command. At build time, this will generate a public `RelayCommand` property with the same name as the method, suffixed with "Command." When calling the `Execute` method of the generated `RelayCommand`, the method on which the attribute was applied will be invoked. This essentially simplifies the process of declaring a public `IRelayCommand` command, making a method to be invoked, and creating an instance of the command tied to that method, in the following simplified form:

```
[RelayCommand]
private void RemoveAsFavorite() => IsFavorite = false;
```

This will generate a `RemoveAsFavoriteCommand` public property of type `IRelayCommand` that will call the `RemoveAsFavorite` method when the command is being executed.

When applying this attribute to a method that accepts one parameter, the resulting command will be a generic RelayCommand<T>, where T corresponds to the type of the parameter.

Alternatively, we can also pass in a string parameter called CanExecute that points to a method, which should be invoked when calling the command's CanExecute method. This is essential if we want to update RecipeDetailViewModel and let AddAsFavoriteCommand, RemoveAsFavoriteCommand, and SetFavoriteCommand be generated by Source Generators. Let's see how we can achieve that:

1. Delete the public AddAsFavoriteCommand, RemoveAsFavoriteCommand, and SetFavoriteCommand properties of type IRelayCommand.

2. Delete the instantiation of these commands in the constructor of RecipeDetailViewModel.

3. Add the RelayCommand attribute to the AddAsFavorite, RemoveAsFavorite, and SetFavorite methods, as shown here:

```
[RelayCommand(CanExecute = nameof(CanSetFavorite))]
private void SetFavorite(bool isFavorite)
    => IsFavorite = isFavorite;


[RelayCommand(CanExecute = nameof(CanAddAsFavorite))]
private void AddAsFavorite() => IsFavorite = true;


[RelayCommand(CanExecute = nameof
    (CanRemoveAsFavorite))]
private void RemoveAsFavorite() => IsFavorite = false;
```

At build time, the public command will be generated thanks to the RelayCommand attributes. In this example, all of the attributes also point to a method that gets invoked when calling the generated command's CanExecute method.

While Source Generators can greatly simplify code bases and improve productivity by automating boilerplate code, I choose not to use them for a couple of reasons.

Firstly, they can obscure some of the underlying implementation details. This might make it challenging for newcomers or less experienced developers to fully understand the code and its intrinsic patterns.

Secondly, employing the MVVM Toolkit's Source Generators may require adjusting your coding style to match the "prescribed" style inherent to the toolkit. This may not appeal to all developers who prefer more flexibility in their coding approach.

However, it's essential to note that these are personal preferences, and many developers find great value in using Source Generators. They can significantly streamline your ViewModel development process, and if you find them beneficial and conducive to your coding style, I wholeheartedly recommend their usage!

At the end of the day, Source Generators are a tool. Like any tool, it's crucial to consider when and where they add the most value. Balancing the benefits of automation and simplicity with understanding, flexibility, and individual style in your code is always an important consideration in software development.

This covers most of the essentials of the MVVM Toolkit. Now, let's see how the .NET MAUI Community Toolkit can make our lives easier when applying the MVVM pattern.

The .NET MAUI Community Toolkit

The **.NET MAUI Community Toolkit** is a collection of useful components, controls, and utilities designed to enhance the development experience with .NET MAUI. Although its primary focus is not on enabling or facilitating MVVM, the toolkit does provide features that can greatly assist developers in implementing the MVVM pattern in their .NET MAUI projects:

- **Behaviors**: These are reusable pieces of functionality that can be attached to certain types of controls. By encapsulating code in behaviors, you can keep your views clean and easy to understand.

- **Converters**: As we've seen before, converters help transform data from one type into another, making it easier to bind data from your ViewModel to your View. The toolkit has a lot of converters for a huge range of common scenarios.

There is much more to the .NET MAUI Community Toolkit, but in the context of MVVM, these are the relevant bits. Please note that this is a toolkit that should only be added to MAUI projects and not to the core project that houses your ViewModels, for example. Why? Because the .NET MAUI Community is .NET MAUI-dependent and therefore it should not be referenced to projects that are agnostic of UI frameworks.

By offering these additional features and helpers, the .NET MAUI Community Toolkit contributes to a more efficient and streamlined development process when working with MVVM in .NET MAUI.

Installing the .NET MAUI Community Toolkit is just like installing any other NuGet package:

1. Right-click the `Recipes.Mobile` project and select **Manage NuGet Packages**.

2. Search for `Maui Community` and select **CommunityToolkit.Maui** from the list. *Figure 5.2* shows the NuGet package we should download:

 CommunityToolkit.Maui ✅ by Microsoft, **414K** downloads
The .NET MAUI Community Toolkit is a collection of Animations, Behaviors, Converters, and Custom Views for development with .NET MAUI. It simplifies and demonstrates common developer tasks building iOS, Android, macOS and Windows apps with .NET MAUI.

Figure 5.2: CommunityToolkit.Maui NuGet package

3. Hit **Install** to add the NuGet package to the `Recipes.Mobile` project.

4. Once installed, head over to `MauiProgram.cs` and make sure you call `UseMauiCommunityToolkit` on `MauiAppBuilder`:

```
builder.UseMauiCommunityToolkit();
```

5. To use components from the toolkit in XAML, you will need to add the namespace to the XAML pages where you want to use the toolkit:

```
xmlns:toolkit="http://schemas.microsoft.com/dotnet/2022/maui/toolkit"
```

Once all of this is in place, we can start using the .NET MAUI Community Toolkit.

Converters

In *Chapter 4, Data Binding in .NET MAUI*, we discussed what value converters are and how to create them. The .NET MAUI Community Toolkit comes packed with a whole lot of ready-to-use value converters. One such converter is `ListToStringConverter`, which can be very handy for displaying a list of items as a single string. Let's use it to display the allergen information of the recipe:

1. To start, let's add an array of strings called `Allergens` to `RecipeDetailViewModel`:

```
public string[] Allergens { get; }
    = new string[]{ "Milk", "Eggs", "Nuts", "Sesame" };
```

This property holds a list of all allergens that the recipe contains. For now, we're hardcoding some values here.

2. On `RecipeDetailPage`, add the toolkit's namespace:

```
xmlns:toolkit=
http://schemas.microsoft.com/dotnet/2022
    /maui/toolkit
```

This will allow us to access the Community Toolkit library in XAML using the `toolkit` prefix.

3. Add an instance of `ListToStringConverter` to the page's `Resources`:

```
<ContentPage.Resources>

    ...

    <toolkit:ListToStringConverter
      x:Key="listToStringConverter" Separator=", " />
</ContentPage.Resources>
```

`ListToStringConverter` has a property called `Separator` that we set to ",".

4. Finally, we can update the label that should display the allergen information:

```
<Label IsVisible="{Binding HideAllergenInformation,
  Mode=OneWay, Converter={StaticResource
```

```
        inverseBoolConverter}}"
    Text="{Binding Allergens, Converter={StaticResource
        listToStringConverter}}" />
```

By using `ListToStringConverter`, we can bind the `Allergens` property of the ViewModel to the `Text` property of the label. This converter will take the items from the `Allergens` array and concatenate them to show them as one string value.

This value converter and some other converters in the toolkit aren't exactly rocket science. It's something you could write yourself. However, in my opinion, why reinvent the wheel when someone has already done the hard work for you? Utilizing these ready-made tools can certainly make your coding life easier!

Behaviors

Behaviors allow you to add functionality to UI controls without the need to build custom controls from scratch. This greatly helps in constructing rich and intuitive user interfaces tailored to your specific requirements. By encapsulating UI-specific actions within the View layer, behaviors help reduce the complexity of ViewModels, adhering to the separation of concerns principle central to MVVM. The .NET MAUI Community Toolkit comes with a variety of ready-to-use behaviors, saving you time and effort in enhancing your UI.

One of the behaviors provided by the .NET MAUI Community Toolkit is `EventToCommand`, which allows you to map events to commands. This allows you to further enhance the decoupling of your UI and business logic. This behavior is particularly useful when dealing with events that do not directly support binding to commands.

As a very simple example, let's imagine that we want to collect some user behavior throughout the app. One of the things we might be interested in is whether the user scrolls on a recipe page or not, as that might indicate some level of interest in that particular recipe. `ScrollView` has a `Scrolled` event, but no corresponding command. In such a use case, `EventToCommandBehavior` can be very helpful, as I will show you in the next steps:

1. Create a `RelayCommand` on `RecipeDetailViewModel`, which needs to be invoked when the user scrolls on the page:

    ```
    [RelayCommand]
    private void UserIsBrowsing()
    {
        //Do Logging
    }
    ```

    In the preceding snippet, the `RelayCommand` attribute is used to generate `UserIsBrowsingCommand`, but you could write a `RelayCommand` yourself as well, of course.

2. Next, we can add `EventToCommandBehavior` to `ScrollView`:

```
<ScrollView>
    <ScrollView.Behaviors>
        <toolkit:EventToCommandBehavior
            Command="{Binding UserIsBrowsingCommand}"
            EventName="Scrolled" />
    </ScrollView.Behaviors>
    ...
</ScrollView>
```

The `Command` property of `EventToCommandBehavior` is bound to the `UserIsBrowsingCommand` property that we just created on the ViewModel. By setting the `EventName` property to `"Scrolled"`, we define that we want this command to be invoked on the `Scrolled` event of `ScrollView`.

As a final example to demonstrate how helpful this toolkit can be by combining behaviors and converters, imagine the following: a heart icon should always be shown on the screen, but only when the user has marked the recipe as a favorite, and it should be red. We can write this without adding a single line of C# code and without working with multiple icons! Let's see how this is done:

1. Until now, in our *Recipes!* app, the favorite icon was a little misplaced. Let's start by placing the favorite icon next to the recipe title. You can accomplish this by replacing the label that displays the recipe's title with the following XAML code:

```
<Grid ColumnDefinitions="*, Auto">
    <Label
        FontAttributes="Bold" FontSize="22"
        Text="{Binding Path=Title, Mode=OneTime}"
        VerticalOptions="Center" />
    <Image
        x:Name="favoriteIcon"
        Grid.Column="1" Margin="5"
        HeightRequest="35" Source="favorite.png"
        VerticalOptions="Center" WidthRequest="35">
    </Image>
</Grid>
```

Now, the favorite icon will permanently appear right next to the recipe's title.

2. The .NET MAUI Community Toolkit offers `IconTintColorBehavior`, which we can apply to change the color of `favoriteIcon`. We can add this behavior to our image:

```
<Image
    x:Name="favoriteIcon"
    ...>
```

```
    <Image.Behaviors>
        <toolkit:IconTintColorBehavior
            TintColor="#E9E9E9E9" />
    </Image.Behaviors>
</Image>
```

After adding this behavior, the icon will take on the specified `TintColor`.

3. Now, we need to set the `TintColor` value based on the `IsFavorite` property of `RecipeDetailViewModel`. Conveniently, the toolkit provides `BoolToObjectConverter`, which we can utilize to convert a `boolean` value into another value. We can add an instance of it to `RecipeDetailPage`:

```
<toolkit:BoolToObjectConverter
    x:Key="isFavoriteToColorConverter"
    x:TypeArguments="Color"
    FalseObject="#E9E9E9E9"
    TrueObject="#FF0000" />
```

4. By setting this instance's `TypeArguments` to `"Color"`, we specify that we want to convert a `bool` value into a `Color` value. The `FalseObject` and `TrueObject` properties set the values that the converter should return for false and true, respectively.

5. The last step is to update `IconTintColorBehavior` on the image. The challenge is binding the `TintColor` property of the behavior to the `IsFavorite` property of `RecipeDetailViewModel`. Since behaviors do not inherit their `BindingContext` from the controls they're defined on, we'll use `ElementBinding` to access `RecipeDetailViewModel` through the `BindingContext` of the `favoriteIcon`:

```
<toolkit:IconTintColorBehavior TintColor="{Binding
    Source={x:Reference favoriteIcon},
        Path=BindingContext.IsFavorite,
            Converter={StaticResource
                isFavoriteToColorConverter}}" />
```

Now, `TintColor` is effectively bound to the `IsFavorite` property on the ViewModel and `isFavoriteToColorConverter` determines the color to use.

The .NET MAUI Community Toolkit is an invaluable resource that streamlines the development process. It offers a wide variety of reusable building blocks, reducing the necessity for duplicative work and allowing you to focus on creating unique application features. With components such as behaviors, converters, and more, the toolkit empowers developers to build rich and interactive user experiences with less effort and complexity. Although the toolkit isn't focused on MVVM, it helps in implementing the MVVM pattern by offering handy features such as behaviors, converters, and more.

Other popular frameworks

As mentioned earlier, there are numerous MVVM frameworks available, each with its unique characteristics and advantages. Throughout this chapter, we've explored the MVVM Toolkit and .NET MAUI Community Toolkit. These toolkits, being community-driven and highly accessible, offer a variety of useful tools to simplify your MVVM code.

However, the landscape of MVVM frameworks is vast, so it might be worth seeing what other frameworks can provide. Here's a list of some of the most popular third-party MVVM frameworks that are compatible with .NET MAUI:

- ReactiveUI: `https://www.reactiveui.net/`
- Prism Library: `https://prismlibrary.com/`
- TinyMvvm: `https://github.com/dhindrik/TinyMvvm`
- FreshMvvm: `https://github.com/XAM-Consulting/FreshMvvm.Maui`

Whether you are seeking a simple toolkit for the basics or a comprehensive framework with advanced capabilities, you will soon discover a framework that would best suit your specific needs and align with your coding style. However, it's important to remember that using an MVVM framework is not a prerequisite for effective MVVM. It is entirely possible to implement the MVVM pattern effectively without a dedicated framework. Ultimately, the choice of whether to use a framework – and if so, which one – should depend on your project's requirements, your team's familiarity with the framework, and your personal coding preferences. *Remember, tools are there to assist you, not dictate how you code.*

Contributing to the community

As we wrap up this chapter, it's important to recognize that these third-party toolkits and frameworks are, at their core, community contributions. They're the result of someone else's hard work, thought, and passion. All this code is accessible to you on platforms such as GitHub, and it's maintained by community-minded individuals who are always open to suggestions, improvements, and bug reports.

Remember, contributing to the community isn't limited to creating a new project or toolkit of your own. It can be as simple as reporting a bug, suggesting a feature, or even making a small code improvement on an open source project. This open source ethos is one of the key strengths of the .NET ecosystem.

So, if you're using these frameworks and see something that can be improved or a bug that needs fixing, don't hesitate to contribute. By doing so, you'll not only improve the tool for yourself but also for other developers who use it. This way, you can give back to the community and maybe learn a thing or two in the process.

In conclusion, never forget that these open source MVVM frameworks are not just tools for you to use, but they're also opportunities for you to grow as a developer and contribute to the broader .NET community.

Summary

To summarize, both the MVVM Toolkit and .NET MAUI Community Toolkit offer a comprehensive collection of components that facilitate the implementation of the MVVM pattern in your applications. By using these toolkits, you can avoid the need to build everything from scratch or reinvent existing solutions, ultimately saving time and effort, and allowing you to focus on building your application.

Throughout the rest of the code samples in this book, we'll be using the MVVM Toolkit and make use of classes such as `ObservableObject` and `RelayCommand`. These classes are quite straightforward to understand. Even if you choose not to use this toolkit, you should still find the code samples clear and comprehensible as the underlying concepts are not overly complex.

Further reading

To learn more about the topics that were covered in this chapter, take a look at the following resources:

- Introduction to the MVVM Toolkit: `https://learn.microsoft.com/dotnet/communitytoolkit/mvvm/`

- .NET MAUI Community Toolkit documentation: `https://learn.microsoft.com/dotnet/communitytoolkit/maui/`

- .NET MAUI Community Toolkit converters: `https://learn.microsoft.com/dotnet/communitytoolkit/maui/converters/`

- .NET MAUI Community Toolkit behaviors: `https://learn.microsoft.com/dotnet/communitytoolkit/maui/behaviors/`

- `ObservablePropertyAttribute`: `https://learn.microsoft.com/dotnet/communitytoolkit/mvvm/generators/observableproperty`

- `RelayCommandAttribute`: `https://learn.microsoft.com/dotnet/communitytoolkit/mvvm/generators/relaycommand`

Working with Collections

Collections are a fundamental part of nearly every application, allowing us to manage and organize groups of related objects. In this chapter, we'll explore the power of collections in the context of the MVVM design pattern, offering you the tools and knowledge to efficiently work with data in your .NET MAUI applications.

Up until now, our focus has primarily been on binding single values, such as titles, ratings, and commands. However, with the introduction of collections, we can take our applications to the next level. Collections empower us to represent groups of items, whether it be a collection of recipes, lists of ingredients, or arrays of user ratings. By harnessing the capabilities of collections, we can create dynamic, data-driven UIs that provide enhanced user experiences.

This chapter is structured into three key sections:

- Using `BindableLayout`
- The `ICollectionChanged` interface
- Working with `CollectionView`

By the end of this chapter, you will have a strong understanding of working with collections in .NET MAUI, significantly expanding your capabilities in building rich, data-centric applications such as our *Recipes!* app. Let's dive in!

Technical requirements

Throughout this chapter, we will be enhancing the functionality of the *Recipes!* app. The code base for this chapter and all the assets, including the additional classes and code required to cover the topics in this chapter effectively, can be found on GitHub at https://github.com/PacktPublishing/MVVM-pattern-.NET-MAUI/tree/main/Chapter06. The starting point for this chapter is provided in the Start folder, which includes the necessary classes and code that have been added specifically for this chapter. The code in the Start folder serves as the starting point to follow along with this chapter's content, building upon the foundation we established in the previous chapters. The completed code, which includes all the code we have written throughout this chapter, can be found in the `Finish` folder for reference and comparison.

Using BindableLayout

The `BindableLayout` class is a static class that provides *attached properties* for binding collections to layout containers. An attached property is a concept that allows you to attach additional properties to existing elements or controls. These properties are not defined within the element itself but are provided by an external class. They enable you to extend the behavior and functionality of elements without modifying their underlying code. `Grid.Row` is probably one of the most commonly used attached properties in .NET MAUI. It can be applied to any UI element, allowing you to define the row position within a `Grid` layout. It is not a property of the UI element itself; instead, it is an attached property that enhances the flexibility and power of the `Grid` layout. As such, `BindableLayout` provides a set of attached properties that can be used to bind collections of data to layout containers, such as `VerticalStackLayout` or `Grid`. You can leverage its attached properties to effortlessly bind and display dynamic collections of data.

Although the `BindableLayout` class's attached properties can be added to any layout that derives from the `Layout` class, it is commonly used with layouts such as `VerticalStackLayout` and `HorizontalStackLayout`.

> **Note**
>
> `BindableLayout` is a lightweight and straightforward solution for displaying collections of data. It works great for scenarios with a limited number of items, offering simplicity and ease of use.
>
> However, it's important to consider that `BindableLayout` generates UI elements for each item in the collection without built-in features such as virtualization or view recycling. This means that for large collections with many items, there may be performance implications and increased memory usage.

Let's have a look at how we can use `BindableLayout` to show a collection of data inside a `VerticalStackLayout`.

What to show and how to show it

Two essential attached properties of `BindableLayout` are `ItemsSource` and `ItemTemplate`. These two properties play a crucial role in defining what collection of data needs to be shown and how each data item should be visualized. The `ItemsSource` property is used to bind a collection of data, while the `ItemTemplate` property is used to define the `DataTemplate` for each item in the collection.

Since a recipe is nothing without its list of ingredients, in the first example, we are going to display the list of ingredients on `RecipeDetailPage`. However, before we dive into how to effectively use `BindableLayout`, let's first discuss `RecipeIngredientViewModel`, which is used to hold the information of ingredients.

Defining ingredients

The `RecipeIngredientViewModel` class represents an ingredient within a recipe.

It contains the name of the ingredient and information about the required quantity of the ingredient for a specific number of servings. The purpose of the `DisplayAmount` property is to dynamically adjust and display the appropriate quantity of ingredients for the desired number of servings. It allows the user to see the adjusted amount that aligns with their selected serving size, providing accurate ingredient measurements for their recipe preparation. Let's have a look at its `UpdateServings` method:

```
public void UpdateServings(int servings)
{
    var factor = servings / (double)baseServings;
    DisplayAmount = factor * baseAmount;
}
```

This method updates the `DisplayAmount` property based on the desired number of servings, allowing the user to see the appropriate quantity of the ingredient for their selected serving size. As the setter of the `DisplayAmount` property calls the `PropertyChanged` event when its value changes, we can bind this property to a UI element in our view to dynamically display the adjusted ingredient amount based on the selected number of servings.

We can extend `IngredientsListViewModel` with an additional property: `Ingredients`. This property is a list of `RecipeIngredientViewModel` objects that, for demo purposes, is assigned a hard-coded list of ingredients needed for making a Caesar salad.

Finally, the `NumberOfServings` property is updated. The following code block shows how the `UpdateServings` method on each of the ingredients is called when the value of the `NumberOfServings` property is changed:

```
public int NumberOfServings
{
    get => _numberOfServings;
    set
    {
        if (SetProperty(ref _numberOfServings, value))
        {
            Ingredients.ForEach(
                i => i.UpdateServings(value));
        }
```

```
    }
  }
```

When updating `NumberOfServings`, the `DisplayAmount` property of each ingredient is updated as well, by calling the `UpdateServings` method.

With all of this in place, we can finally move over to XAML and see how we can bind this collection of `RecipeIngredientViewModels` to a `VerticalStackLayout` while using the attached properties of `BindableLayout`.

Showing ingredients on the screen

In the following steps, we'll go through the process of setting up the XAML code to display the ingredients in a visually appealing manner. Note that everything we are about to do in XAML can also be done in code:

1. On `RecipeDetailPage`, right below the `HorizontalStackLayout`, which holds the `Stepper` property that controls the number of servings, we can add a new `VerticalStackLayout`. As shown in the following code block, we can use the `ItemsSource` property of the `BindableLayout` class to bind to the list of ingredients:

```xml
<VerticalStackLayout
    Margin="0,10" Spacing="10"
    BindableLayout.ItemsSource="{Binding
      IngredientsList.Ingredients}">
</VerticalStackLayout>
```

2. Now, we need to define the UI elements that need to be rendered for each of the items in the bound collection. We can define this using the `ItemTemplate` property. This property needs a value of the `DataTemplate` class. It can be defined like this:

```xml
<VerticalStackLayout ... >
    <BindableLayout.ItemTemplate>
        <DataTemplate x:DataType=
          "vms:RecipeIngredientViewModel" >

        </DataTemplate>
    </BindableLayout.ItemTemplate>
</VerticalStackLayout>
```

Notice that on a `DataTemplate`, we can define `x:DataType` if we want to leverage compiled bindings, as we saw in *Chapter 4, Data Binding in .NET MAUI*.

> **Note**
>
> It's very important to realize that the `BindingContext` of a `DataTemplate` is set to an individual item of the bound collection. Because the template is repeated for each item in the collection, UI elements named with `x:Name` in `DataTemplate` are inaccessible in the code behind. Their name is confined to that template's scope. However, the name can still be used for element binding within the same `DataTemplate`.

3. The following code snippet shows how we can define a `DataTemplate` for the ingredients. This is how we define how each of the ingredients needs to be visualized:

```
<DataTemplate x:DataType=
  "vms:RecipeIngredientViewModel">
    <HorizontalStackLayout Spacing="5">
        <Label
            FontAttributes="Bold" FontSize="16"
            Text="{Binding IngredientName,
              StringFormat='{0}:', Mode=OneTime}"
            VerticalOptions="Center" />
        <Label Text="{Binding DisplayAmount,
          Mode=OneWay}" VerticalOptions="Center" />
        <Label
            Text="{Binding Measurement, Mode=OneTime}"
            VerticalOptions="Center" />
    </HorizontalStackLayout>
</DataTemplate>
```

For each ingredient, we want to render a `HorizontalStackLayout` containing a label showing the ingredient's name, a label showing the `DisplayAmount`, and finally, a label showing the `Measurement`. *Figure 6.1* shows what it looks like:

Figure 6.1: The Ingredients list

Notice that `DisplayAmount` is bound `OneWay`, meaning that when the `PropertyChanged` event for this property is triggered, the label's `Text` property is updated accordingly. All the other properties can be bound `OneTime` as their values won't change once they're displayed.

> **Tip**
>
> In terms of performance, it's worth noting that `OneTime` binding mode is generally more efficient than `OneWay` data binding. This is especially important when binding collections of data! `OneTime` binding establishes the binding once and does not track subsequent changes to the source property. Therefore, it's advisable to use `OneTime` binding wherever possible to optimize performance and reduce unnecessary UI updates.

A `DataTemplate` can also be defined in a resource dictionary. This allows `DataTemplates` to be reused, which can be especially convenient when showing the same kind of data in different parts of your app. By defining the template once in `Application.Resources` (in `App.xaml`), for example, it can be reused throughout the app. Then, we can use the `StaticResource` markup extension to bind a particular `DataTemplate` to the `BindableLayout ItemTemplate` property using the key that was defined in the resource dictionary. The following code block shows how to add a `DataTemplate` to the page's resources and use it later on as the `ItemTemplate` of the `VerticalStackLayout` showing the ingredients:

```
<ContentPage.Resources>
    <DataTemplate x:Key="recipeIngredientTemplate"
            x:DataType="vms:RecipeIngredientViewModel">
        ...
```

```
    </DataTemplate>
</ContentPage.Resources>
...
    <VerticalStackLayout
        Margin="0,10"
        BindableLayout.ItemsSource="{Binding IngredientsList.
Ingredients}"
        BindableLayout.ItemTemplate="{StaticResource
            recipeIngredientTemplate}"
        Spacing="10"/>
```

In the previous code snippet, a `DataTemplate` is defined within the `ContentPage.Resources` section and is assigned the `"recipeIngredientTemplate"` key. Later, this template is used in the `VerticalStackLayout` by us referencing it through the `StaticResource` markup extension, using the `"recipeIngredientTemplate"` key.

Note

In .NET MAUI, if you bind a collection without assigning a specific `DataTemplate`, the framework automatically invokes the `ToString` method of each object in the collection. The returned string value is what will be displayed on the screen.

With all of this in place, our app now shows a list of ingredients on the recipe's detail page, where each ingredient is rendered using the defined `ItemTemplate`.

But what if not all items in a particular collection should be rendered the same way? Let's see how we can choose a `DataTemplate` dynamically at runtime.

Dynamically choosing a DataTemplate at runtime

While ingredients are essential to a recipe app, not much can be done with the ingredients without a comprehensive set of cooking instructions. So, let's bring these instructions to life within our app! In addition to the essential steps, a list of instructions may also include valuable cooking tips and additional information to enhance the cooking experience. Let's explore how we can incorporate these cooking instructions, along with any accompanying notes, into our *Recipes!* app.

Defining cooking instructions and notes

In our app, we use `InstructionViewModel` and `NoteViewModel` for cooking instructions and notes, respectively. `InstructionViewModel` has `Index` and `Description` properties, while `NoteViewModel` has just a `Note` property. Both are grouped under a common parent, `InstructionBaseViewModel`, and stored in a list called `Instructions` in `RecipeDetailViewModel`.

For now, this list is initialized with some cooking instructions and a tip for creating a Caesar salad.

If we want to show this list, which contains both instructions and notes, on the screen, we would need a mechanism that would allow us to use a different `ItemTemplate`, depending on the type. Let's see how a `DataTemplateSelector` can achieve this!

Creating a DataTemplateSelector

With a `DataTemplateSelector`, we can write code that determines what `DataTemplate` to use at runtime. Writing a `DataTemplateSelector` is pretty straightforward. Let's have a look at how we can build one:

1. In the **Solution Explorer**, add a folder called `TemplateSelectors` by right-clicking the **Recipes.Mobile** project and selecting **Add | New Folder**.

2. Next, right-click this newly added folder, select **Add | Class...**, and enter `InstructionsDataTemplateSelector` as the name.

3. For our class to function as a `DataTemplateSelector`, it needs to inherit from `Microsoft.Maui.Controls.DataTemplateSelector`, as shown in the following snippet:

    ```
    public class InstructionsDataTemplateSelector :
      DataTemplateSelector
    {
        protected override DataTemplate
          OnSelectTemplate(object item, BindableObject
            container) { }
    }
    ```

Inheriting from the `DataTemplateSelector` class requires overriding the abstract `OnSelectTemplate` method. This method is invoked at runtime to select the appropriate `DataTemplate` and takes two parameters:

*   `item` (of type `object`) is the object we want to display, such as a `NoteViewModel` or `InstructionViewModel` item in our app

*   `container` (of type `BindableObject`) refers to the layout element that holds the collection, such as `VerticalStackLayout` in our example

Using these parameters, the `OnSelectTemplate` method in a `DataTemplateSelector` assists you in selecting the appropriate `DataTemplate` for a given item. In our specific scenario, the method will determine the template based solely on the type of the passed-in item.

Let's introduce two properties to `InstructionsDataTemplateSelector`. These two properties, `NoteTemplate` and `InstructionTemplate`, dictate which `DataTemplate` the `DataTemplateSelector` should return based on the type of the passed-in item parameter. Specifically, if it is a `NoteViewModel`, the `OnSelectTemplate` method should return `NoteTemplate`.

Conversely, if it's an `InstructionViewModel`, `InstructionTemplate` will be returned. Let's explore how to accomplish this:

1. Add the following properties to `InstructionsDataTemplateSelector`:

    ```
    public DataTemplate NoteTemplate { get; set; }
    public DataTemplate InstructionTemplate { get; set; }
    ```

2. The following code block shows how we can implement the `OnSelectTemplate` method so that it checks the type of the given item and returns the appropriate `DataTemplate`:

    ```
    protected override DataTemplate OnSelectTemplate
      (object item, BindableObject container)
    {
        if (item is InstructionViewModel)
            return InstructionTemplate;
        else if(item is NoteViewModel)
            return NoteTemplate;

        return null;
    }
    ```

    If the given item isn't an `InstructionViewModel` or `NoteViewModel` item, `null` is returned. As a result, the value returned by the object's `ToString` method will be rendered, which is the same behavior when not providing a `DataTemplateSelector`.

That's it for `InstructionsDataTemplateSelector`. Let's see how we can use this `DataTemplateSelector` to show both instructions and notes in the app.

Showing instructions and notes on the screen

Now that the data is in place as well as the `DataTemplateSelector` that we want to use, we need to do a few things in XAML to display the recipe's instructions and notes:

1. Let's start by thinking about how we want to represent a `InstructionViewModel` in the app. Here's a template that we could add to the `RecipeDetailPage`'s resources for that data type:

    ```
    <ContentPage.Resources>
    ...
        <DataTemplate x:Key="instructionTemplate"
          x:DataType="vms:InstructionViewModel">
            <VerticalStackLayout Spacing="10">
                <Label FontSize="20" Text="{Binding Index,
                  StringFormat='{0:D2}.', Mode=OneTime}" />
                <Label Margin="10,0" Text="{Binding
                  Description, Mode=OneTime}" />
    ```

```
            </VerticalStackLayout>
        </DataTemplate>
    </ContentPage.Resources>
```

The `DataTemplate` for an `InstructionViewModel` defines how we want to visualize this type of item: showing the `Index` property with the `Description` below it.

Note that we've given the `DataTemplate` a key (`instructionTemplate`) that we can use later on to reference this specific template.

2. Let's add a `DataTemplate` for the `NoteViewModel` items as well. The following code block shows a `DataTemplate` for visualizing such items:

```
<DataTemplate x:Key="noteTemplate" x:DataType=
  "vms:NoteViewModel">
    <Grid Margin="20,0" ColumnDefinitions="35,*">
        <Label
            FontFamily="MaterialIconsRegular"
            FontSize="20" Text="&#xe873;"
            TextColor="LightSlateGray" />
        <Label
            Grid.Column="1" FontAttributes="Italic"
            Text="{Binding Note, Mode=OneTime}"
            TextColor="LightSlateGray" />
    </Grid>
</DataTemplate>
```

By using this `DataTemplate`, we can visualize notes by showing an icon – for which we use the `MaterialIconsRegular` font – followed by the note itself. Both are in a specific color so that there is a clear distinction between notes and instructions. As before, we've given the `DataTemplate` a specific key (`noteTemplate`) so that we can reference it later on.

3. Next, let's add an `InstructionsDataTemplateSelector` to `RecipeDetailPage`. Start by adding said `DataTemplateSelector`'s namespace as an XML namespace to the page, as shown here:

```
xmlns:selectors="clr-namespace:Recipes
  .Mobile.TemplateSelectors"
```

Once this is in place, we can add an instance of the `InstructionsDataTemplateSelector` class to the page's `Resources`, as shown in the following snippet:

```
<selectors:InstructionsDataTemplateSelector
    x:Key="instructionDataTemplateSelector"
    InstructionTemplate="{StaticResource
      instructionTemplate}"
    NoteTemplate="{StaticResource noteTemplate}" />
```

The `StaticResource` markup extension is used to reference the two `DataTemplates` that we created earlier to assign them to the respective properties of this `InstructionsDataTemplateSelector`. Just like we did with the individual `DataTemplate`, we've given this instance of the `InstructionsDataTemplateSelector` a key (`instructionDataTemplateSelector`) that we can use later on to reference it.

4. To display the list of instructions, we can add a `VerticalStackLayout` near the bottom of `RecipeDetailPage`. The following code snippet demonstrates this setup:

```
<VerticalStackLayout Padding="10">
    <Label FontAttributes="Italic,Bold"
        FontSize="16" Text="Instructions" />
    <VerticalStackLayout
        Margin="0,10" Spacing="10"
        BindableLayout.ItemsSource="{Binding
            Instructions}"
        BindableLayout.ItemTemplateSelector=
            "{StaticResource instruction
                DataTemplateSelector}"/>
</VerticalStackLayout>
```

In this code snippet, we bound the `Instructions` property of our ViewModel to the `BindableLayout ItemsSource` property. Additionally, by using the `StaticResource` markup extension and the key we used in the resource dictionary for our `DataTemplateSelector`, we set the `ItemTemplateSelector` property. The result is shown in *Figure 6.2*:

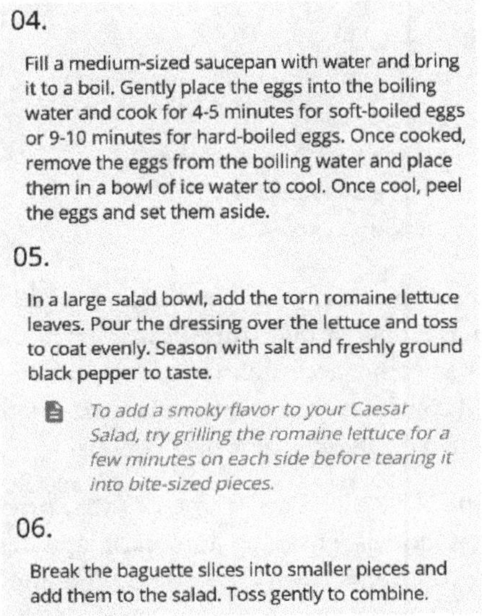

04.

Fill a medium-sized saucepan with water and bring it to a boil. Gently place the eggs into the boiling water and cook for 4-5 minutes for soft-boiled eggs or 9-10 minutes for hard-boiled eggs. Once cooked, remove the eggs from the boiling water and place them in a bowl of ice water to cool. Once cool, peel the eggs and set them aside.

05.

In a large salad bowl, add the torn romaine lettuce leaves. Pour the dressing over the lettuce and toss to coat evenly. Season with salt and freshly ground black pepper to taste.

To add a smoky flavor to your Caesar Salad, try grilling the romaine lettuce for a few minutes on each side before tearing it into bite-sized pieces.

06.

Break the baguette slices into smaller pieces and add them to the salad. Toss gently to combine.

Figure 6.2: Showing instructions and notes

With that, we've explored how to leverage `DataTemplates` and a `DataTemplateSelector` to visualize instructions and notes within our *Recipes!* app. By defining separate `DataTemplates` and using a `DataTemplateSelector`, we can dynamically choose the appropriate template for each item in the collection, providing a customized and intuitive display of cooking instructions and additional notes.

Now that we have successfully implemented the visualization of instructions and notes, let's move on to handling empty collections.

Handling empty collections

Besides the `ItemsSource` and `ItemTemplate` properties, `BindableLayout` also has `EmptyView` and `EmptyViewTemplate` properties. These properties allow us to define what to show if the provided `ItemsSource` is empty or null.

The `EmptyView` property can be a string value or a `View`. So, in its simplest form, we could add the following to a `VerticalStackLayout` to show the shopping list:

```
<VerticalStackLayout
    BindableLayout.EmptyView="Nothing to see here"
    ... >
```

"`Nothing to see here`" is shown on the screen when the bound `ItemSource` contains no items.

Or, if we want to have more control over the appearance of what is shown when the collection is empty, we could also do the following:

```
<VerticalStackLayout
    ...>
        <BindableLayout.EmptyView>
            <Label Text="Nothing to see here"
                FontAttributes="Bold" />
        </BindableLayout.EmptyView>
```

Alternatively, with `EmptyViewTemplate`, we can specify a `DataTemplate` that needs to be shown when the bound collection is empty or null. This means that in this template, you can bind to values on the parent UI element or any other accessible context within the UI hierarchy. This flexibility enables you to create dynamic and context-aware empty views that can display relevant information or provide interactive elements based on the available data context.

As we saw earlier, data binding and the `INotifyPropertyChanged` interface allow the UI to stay in sync with the data on ViewModels, ensuring automatic updates. However, when it comes to dynamically adding or removing items from collections, the binding engine alone will not automatically reflect these changes in the UI. To achieve this kind of behavior, we need to explore the `ICollectionChanged` interface.

The ICollectionChanged interface

The ICollectionChanged interface provides a powerful mechanism for notifying the UI about changes in a collection itself, rather than on individual items within the collection. By implementing this interface, a collection can raise events that inform the binding engine and UI elements about structural changes, such as additions, removals, or modifications to the collection itself.

While it is possible to assign an updated list of items to a property on your ViewModel and trigger the PropertyChanged event, dynamically changing a collection requires a more optimal approach. By utilizing a collection that implements the INotifyCollectionChanged interface, we can achieve more efficient rendering of the UI. Instead of needing to re-render the entire collection on the UI, the binding engine can perform updates in a more optimized manner, resulting in improved performance and responsiveness.

The ICollectionChanged interface defines the CollectionChanged event, which is raised whenever the collection undergoes a structural change. This event provides detailed information about the type of change that occurred, such as whether an item was added, removed, or modified, and the position at which the change occurred. Let's see what this means in terms of binding modes.

The ICollectionChanged interface and binding modes

To use this interface as efficiently as possible, it's very important to understand how different binding modes affect this behavior.

OneTime binding

When using OneTime binding, the UI will perfectly update when items inside the collection change. However, there's a caveat: if a new instance is assigned to the property holding the collection, this change won't reflect in the UI. In such cases, instead of assigning a new instance, we need to clear the existing collection and add the new items to it. Importantly, the property setter should not trigger the NotifyPropertyChanged event as it's unnecessary for OneTime binding.

OneWay binding

OneWay binding might offer more flexibility, allowing you to replace the collection with a new instance and reflect this in the UI. In this mode, make sure the property setter calls the NotifyPropertyChanged event to update the UI. While OneWay binding allows for greater flexibility, replacing an entire collection can be resource-intensive, requiring the UI to re-render the collection. This is especially important to consider when dealing with large datasets. If only a few items change, modifying the existing collection is often more efficient than replacing it.

By understanding these subtleties, you can make more informed decisions on what data binding mode to use.

Let's put this into action and add some functionality to the *Recipes!* app by leveraging the ObservableCollection class.

Using the ObservableCollection

The `ObservableCollection` class is a specialized collection class provided by .NET that implements the `ICollectionChanged` interface out of the box.

Let's enhance the functionality of our *Recipes!* app by introducing a `Shopping List` feature. We want to provide users with the ability to add ingredients from the list of recipe ingredients to a separate `Shopping List`. To achieve this, we will associate a button with each ingredient in the list. When the user taps the button, the corresponding ingredient will be added to an `ObservableCollection` named `ShoppingList`. As a result, the UI will be automatically updated each time an ingredient is added or removed from the list:

1. Let's start by adding an additional property, `ShoppingList`, of type `Observable Collection<RecipeIngredientViewModel>` to `RecipeDetailViewModel`:

    ```
    public ObservableCollection<RecipeIngredientViewModel>
    ShoppingList { get; } = new();
    ```

    We are automatically assigning a new instance to this property, which makes perfect sense: the instance of this property will not change as we will be adding and removing items from the collection. As `ObservableCollection` implements the `IObservableCollection` interface, the UI will remain in sync as the `CollectionChanged` event will be triggered when we manipulate the collection.

2. Currently, we don't have functionality for managing items in the `ShoppingList` collection. So, let's add the following to `RecipeDetailViewModel`:

    ```
    public IRelayCommand AddToShoppingListCommand { get; }
    public IRelayCommand RemoveFromShoppingListCommand
    { get; }

    private void AddToShoppingList(
      RecipeIngredientViewModel viewModel)
    {
        if (ShoppingList.Contains(viewModel))
            return;
        ShoppingList.Add(viewModel);
    }

    private void RemoveFromShoppingList
      (RecipeIngredientViewModel viewModel)
    {
    ```

```
        if (ShoppingList.Contains(viewModel))
            ShoppingList.Remove(viewModel);
}
```

The `AddToShoppingList` method will be responsible for adding an instance of `RecipeIngredientViewModel` to the `ShoppingList` collection if the given ViewModel isn't already in there. The `RemoveFromShoppingList` method, on the other hand, will remove the item from `ShoppingList`.

For both methods, we've also created two corresponding commands, which we need to instantiate in the constructor of `RecipeDetailViewModel`, as shown here:

```
public RecipeDetailViewModel()
{
    ...

    AddToShoppingListCommand = new RelayCommand
        <RecipeIngredientViewModel>(AddToShoppingList);
    RemoveFromShoppingListCommand = new RelayCommand
        <RecipeIngredientViewModel>
            (RemoveFromShoppingList);
}
```

3. Next, add the following XAML to the `VerticalStackLayout` that shows the ingredients of the recipe:

```
<VerticalStackLayout Padding="10">
    <Label ...
        Text="Ingredients list" />
    ...
    <VerticalStackLayout Margin="10,0" Padding="10">
        <Label
            FontAttributes="Italic,Bold"
            FontSize="16" Text="Shopping list" />
        <VerticalStackLayout
            Margin="0,10" Spacing="10"
            BindableLayout.ItemsSource="{Binding
                ShoppingList, Mode=OneTime}"
            BindableLayout.EmptyView="Nothing added">
        </VerticalStackLayout>
    </VerticalStackLayout>
</VerticalStackLayout>
```

Below the list of ingredients, we've added a label with the text `"Shopping list"`, followed by another `VerticalStackLayout`. The `ShoppingList` property is bound to the `BindableLayout.ItemsSource` property. We've added an `EmptyView` property that will be shown when no items are on the list.

The `ItemTemplate`, which will be rendered for each item in `ShoppingList`, will be added in a few steps.

4. Let's add a `Button` to the `ItemTemplate` of the `VerticalStackLayout` showing the ingredients. The `Button`'s Command should be bound to the `AddToShoppingListCommand` on the `RecipeDetailViewModel` as shown here:

```
<HorizontalStackLayout Spacing="5">
    <Button
        Command="{Binding AddToShoppingListCommand,
            Source={RelativeSource AncestorType={x:Type
                vms:RecipeDetailViewModel}}}"
        CommandParameter="{Binding}"
        FontFamily="MaterialIconsRegular"
        Text="&#xe854;" />
    <Label
        FontAttributes="Bold"
        FontSize="16" VerticalOptions="Center"
        Text="{Binding IngredientName,
            StringFormat='{0}:'}" />
    ...
</HorizontalStackLayout>
```

The `Button`'s Command property is bound to the `AddToShoppingListCommand` on the `RecipeDetailViewModel`. As the `Button`'s `BindingContext` is the current `RecipeIngredientViewModel`, we need to use relative binding to point to the `RecipeDetailViewModel`. `CommandParameter` is data bound by just defining `{ Binding }`. This will bind it to the binding context of the UI element itself, which is the current `RecipeIngredientViewModel`. As a result, the `RecipeIngredientViewModel` instance is passed to the `AddShoppingList` method, allowing us to add it to the `ShoppingList` collection.

5. Finally, we can define the `ItemTemplate` of the `ShoppingList` items. We can copy the `DataTemplate` of the `"Ingredients list"`. However, we need to update the `Button` to this:

```
<Button
    Command="{Binding RemoveFromShoppingListCommand,
        Source={RelativeSource AncestorType={x:Type
            vms:RecipeDetailViewModel}}}"
    CommandParameter="{Binding}"
    FontFamily="MaterialIconsRegular"
    Text="&#xe928;" />
```

This B u t t o n has a different icon and has its C o m m a n d bound to RemoveFromShoppingListCommand, allowing the user to remove an ingredient again from the list.

With everything in place, users can now add ingredients from "Ingredients list" to "Shopping list", from which items can also be removed again. Here's what it looks like:

Figure 6.3: Shopping list

By using ObservableCollection – or any collection that implements IObservableCollection – it becomes very easy and efficient to keep a list of objects in sync with the UI.

> **Don't overuse ObservableCollection**
>
> It is important to use ObservableCollection judiciously in your application. This specialized collection should be utilized when the collection itself dynamically changes, such as when items are added or removed, and the UI needs to reflect those changes. However, if the collection is fixed or assigned to a property in its entirety, there is no need to use ObservableCollection.

As we mentioned earlier, using BindableLayout is very easy to use and is perfect for showing small collections. For more advanced scenarios, there is CollectionView. Let's have a look at it!

Working with CollectionView

CollectionView is an advanced control specifically designed for efficiently displaying large amounts of data. It offers all the properties available in BindableLayout, such as ItemsSource, ItemTemplate, ItemTemplateSelector, EmptyView, and EmptyViewTemplate. Additionally, CollectionView provides a wealth of powerful features, including item grouping, header and footer support, item selection and highlighting, item virtualization, and incremental loading of data as the user scrolls. These features enable you to create highly interactive and engaging user interfaces while efficiently managing and presenting your data. Item virtualization ensures that only the visible items are rendered, optimizing performance and memory usage, especially for large collections.

Other specialized controls

Aside from `CollectionView`, there are other specialized controls, such as `CarouselView` and `ListView`, for displaying collections in .NET MAUI. These controls also support `ItemsSource` binding and allow you to define an `ItemTemplate` or `DataTemplateSelector`. Each comes with a unique set of features and use cases, but the basic principles of data binding remain similar.

Now, let's explore a simple example of using `CollectionView`. In our `RecipesOverviewViewModel`, we expose an `ObservableCollection` of `RecipeListItemViewModels` called `Recipes`. Each `RecipeListItemViewModel` represents a recipe and contains a subset of properties relevant to displaying it on an overview page, such as the recipe's ID, title, image, and favorite status. While the recipe's ID may not be necessary for direct display on the screen, it is valuable for identifying the selected item for navigation purposes or implementing features such as "favoriting" an item from the list. For our app to start on `RecipesOverviewPage`, we need to update the `AppShell.xaml` file, as shown in the following snippet:

```
<ShellContent ContentTemplate="{DataTemplate
local:RecipesOverviewPage}" />
```

We haven't touched on navigation just yet; that's still to come in *Chapter 8, Navigation in MVVM*. So, for now, just update the `AppShell.xaml` file, as shown earlier, and don't worry about it.

To display the recipes in `RecipesOverviewPage`, we can use `CollectionView`. The `ItemsSource` property of `CollectionView` is bound to the `Recipes` property of the `RecipesOverviewViewModel` class, which serves as the page's `BindingContext`. Similar to `BindableLayout`, we define the `ItemTemplate` property to specify how each item in the collection should be rendered. The following code snippet demonstrates this setup:

```
<CollectionView
    ItemsSource="{Binding Recipes}">
    <CollectionView.ItemTemplate>
        <DataTemplate>

            ...

        </DataTemplate>
    </CollectionView.ItemTemplate>
</CollectionView>
```

The usage of `CollectionView` should feel familiar if you have worked with `BindableLayout` before. You can copy the `DataTemplate` class from `BindableLayout` and it will show up the same.

Now, let's leverage one of the more powerful features of `CollectionView`: data grouping. Let's explore how to effectively display grouped data.

Displaying grouped data

Grouping data in a collection is a powerful way to organize and present information in a meaningful and structured manner. By grouping related items, you can provide intuitive navigation and enhance the user experience. `CollectionView` allows us to easily display grouped data and provides both `GroupHeaderTemplate` and `GroupFooterTemplate` properties. These templates allow us to define what's being displayed above and below a group of items. *Figure 6.4* illustrates how a list of grouped items is rendered with group headers and footers:

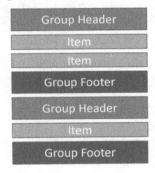

Figure 6.4: Group headers and footers

`RecipeRatingDetailPage`, which can be accessed by tapping on the rating information on `RecipeDetailPage`, should show all the ratings of a recipe grouped by the number of stars. Let's walk through the steps needed to set this up:

1. While `RecipeRatingsDetailViewModel` already contains a list of all the reviews of a recipe, it doesn't group the data yet. First, let's create a class for holding a group of ratings. In the **Solution Explorer**, right-click the **ViewModels** folder in the **Recipes.Client.Core** project and select **Add | Class...**. Enter `RatingGroup` as its name.

2. The `RatingGroup` class inherits from `List<UserReviewModel>` and has an additional property called `Key`. Here's what it looks like:

```
public class RatingGroup : List<UserReviewViewModel>
{
    public string Key { get; private set; }

    public RatingGroup(string key,
        List<UserReviewViewModel> reviews) :
        base(reviews)
    {
```

```
            Key = key;
        }
    }
```

This class serves as a specialized list for holding `UserReviewViewModel` objects. It inherits from `List<UserReviewViewModel>`, meaning it can do anything a regular list can do, such as holding multiple `UserReviewViewModel` items. In addition to that, the class includes an extra property called Key. This property is used to group the user reviews by some criteria, such as a rating or a category.

3. Next, add a `GroupedReviews` property to `RecipeRatingsDetailViewModel`. This property is of type `List<RatingGroup>`. It holds groups of reviews that are organized based on the number of stars. Each `RatingGroup` in the list will contain reviews that share the same number of stars, which is represented by the Key property. The following snippet shows this newly added property and how it gets initialized in the constructor:

```
List<RatingGroup> _groupedReviews = new();
public List<RatingGroup> GroupedReviews
{
    get => _groupedReviews;
    private set => SetProperty(ref _groupedReviews,
      value);
}


public RecipeRatingsDetailViewModel(...)
{
    ...

    Reviews = new() { ... };

    GroupedReviews = Reviews.GroupBy(r =>
      Math.Round(r.Rating / .5) * .5)
        .OrderByDescending(g => g.Key)
        .Select(g => new RatingGroup(g.Key.ToString(),
          g.ToList()))
        .ToList();
}
```

In the constructor, we have grouped all the reviews by their rating, rounded to 0.5. We use this grouping to create a list of `RatingGroups` items that we assign to the `GroupedReviews` property.

4. Now, we can bind the `GroupedReviews` property to the `CollectionView` on `RecipeRatingDetailPage`. When binding a grouped collection, we also need to make sure the `IsGrouped` property of `CollectionView` is set to true, as the following snippet shows:

```
<CollectionView
        IsGrouped="True"
        ItemsSource="{Binding GroupedReviews}">
...
</CollectionView>
```

5. As we did previously, we should be defining an `ItemTemplate` to declare how each item should be rendered. Once that is in place, `CollectionView` renders all the items but there isn't a clear distinction between the different groups yet.

6. So, let's add `GroupHeaderTemplate` and `GroupFooterTemplate` to clearly distinguish the different groups. The following code block demonstrates how this can be done:

```
<CollectionView.GroupHeaderTemplate>
    <DataTemplate x:DataType="{x:Type
      vms:RatingGroup}">
        <Label
            Margin="0,25,0,0" FontSize="16"
            Text="{Binding Key, StringFormat='{0}
              stars Reviews'}" />
    </DataTemplate>
</CollectionView.GroupHeaderTemplate>
<CollectionView.GroupFooterTemplate>
    <DataTemplate x:DataType="{x:Type
      vms:RatingGroup}">
        <Label FontSize="12" Text="{Binding Count,
          StringFormat='{0} reviews'}" />
    </DataTemplate>
</CollectionView.GroupFooterTemplate>
```

The `BindingContext` of these templates is an instance of `RatingGroup`, allowing us to bind to its properties, such as `Key` and `Count`. With this, we can make the groupings visually clear to the user.

Grouping data in `CollectionView` allows for a more organized and structured presentation of information, as shown in *Figure 6.5*:

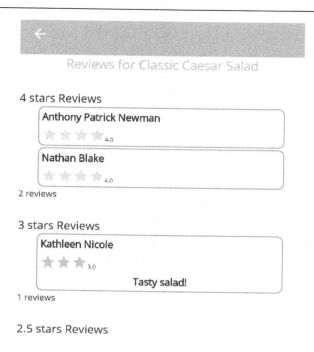

Figure 6.5: Grouping data

By leveraging the GroupHeaderTemplate and GroupFooterTemplate properties, you can enhance the user experience and provide intuitive navigation within your app.

Not only can CollectionView render your data, it also offers various interactive features to engage users with your app. From selecting items to incrementally loading data and other common functionalities, let's discover how to get the most out of this powerful control, by keeping MVVM principles in mind.

Selecting items

When working with CollectionView, you have various options for selecting items and managing the selection state. By binding the SelectedItem property, you can easily track the currently selected item in your ViewModel. Additionally, you can bind the SelectedItems property to a collection in your ViewModel to track multiple selected items. The SelectionMode property allows you to define whether single or multiple items can be selected or whether or not selecting items is disabled. You can use the SelectionChangedCommand property to bind a command in your ViewModel that will be executed when the selection changes or handle the SelectionChanged event, allowing you to implement flexible and interactive item selection behavior in your app.

Let's see how we can allow the user to select one or more reviews, allowing the user to report inappropriate reviews, for example:

1. Add the following property to `RecipeRatingsDetailViewModel`:

    ```
    public ObservableCollection<object> SelectedReviews
    { get; } = new();
    ```

    This property will hold the items that the user has selected on the `CollectionView`. Note that this `ObservableCollection` uses `object` as its type parameter, rather than a more specific type. Though it's not explicitly documented, using `object` appears to be the only way to successfully bind multiple selections in `CollectionView`.

2. Now, let's add a command called `ReportReviewsCommand` that can only be executed when one or more reviews are selected, as shown here:

    ```
    public RelayCommand ReportReviewsCommand { get; }

    public RecipeRatingsDetailViewModel()
    {
        ...
        ReportReviewsCommand = new
            RelayCommand(ReportReviews,
            () => SelectedReviews.Any());
    }

    private void ReportReviews()
    {
        var selectedReviews = SelectedReviews
            .Cast<UserReviewViewModel>().ToList();
        //do reporting
        SelectedReviews.Clear();
    }
    ```

3. As the `SelectedReviews` property is an `ObservableCollection`, we can listen to the `CollectionChangedEvent` and call the `ReportReviewsCommand`'s `NotifyCanExecuteChanged` method. That way the `ReportReviewsCommand`'s `CanExecute` method gets re-evaluated. The following snippet shows how to implement this:

    ```
    public RecipeRatingsDetailViewModel()
    {
        ...
        SelectedReviews.CollectionChanged +=
            SelectedReviews_CollectionChanged;
    }
    ```

```
private void SelectedReviews_CollectionChanged(object?
  sender, NotifyCollectionChangedEventArgs e)
=> ReportReviewsCommand.NotifyCanExecuteChanged();
```

4. Update the `CollectionView` on `RecipeRatingDetailPage` so that its `SelectedItems` property is bound to the `SelectedReviews` property. We also need to set the appropriate `SelectionMode`, as shown here:

```
<CollectionView
    IsGrouped="True"
    ItemsSource="{Binding GroupedReviews}"
    SelectedItems="{Binding SelectedReviews}"
    SelectionMode="Multiple">
```

By adding this code, the items the user selects on the UI will be added to the `SelectedReviews` list, while selected items that the user de-selects will be removed from it. The **Report review(s)** button is enabled as soon as the user selects one or more reviews from the list. In the `ReportReviews` method, we can easily access the `SelectedReviews` property to see what items have been selected.

As a final example, let's look at how we can bind the `SelectedItem` and `SelectionChangedCommand` properties to trigger something such as navigation. Let's take a look at how to implement this on `RecipesOverviewPage`:

1. On `RecipesOverviewPage`, update the `CollectionView` and bind its `SelectedItem` and `SelectionChangedCommand` properties, like this:

```
<CollectionView
    ...
    SelectedItem="{Binding SelectedRecipe,
      Mode=TwoWay}"
    SelectionChangedCommand="{Binding
      NavigateToSelectedDetailCommand}"
    SelectionMode="Single">
```

The `SelectedItem` property is bound `TwoWay` to the `SelectedRecipe` property and `SelectionChangedCommand` is bound to `NavigateToSelectedDetailCommand`. Both properties will be added shortly. Also, the `SelectionMode` property is set to `"Single"`, allowing the user to select one item in the list.

2. Now, let's add the two properties mentioned earlier to `RecipeOverviewViewModel`. Here's what they look like:

```
RecipeListItemViewModel? _selectedRecipe;
public RecipeListItemViewModel? SelectedRecipe
{
    get => _selectedRecipe;
```

```
        set => SetProperty(ref _selectedRecipe, value);
    }

    public AsyncRelayCommand NavigateTo
        SelectedDetailCommand { get; }
```

3. The following snippet shows how the command is instantiated in the constructor of the ViewModel:

```
    public RecipesOverviewViewModel()
    {
    ...
        NavigateToSelectedDetailCommand = new
            AsyncRelayCommand(NavigateToSelectedDetail);
    }
```

Because this command is bound to the `SelectionChangedCommand` of the `CollectionView`, it will get triggered when an item is selected or de-selected.

4. The following code block shows the `NavigateToSelectedDetail` method:

```
    private Task NavigateToSelectedDetail()
    {
        if (SelectedRecipe is not null)
        {
            //ToDo navigate to selected item
            SelectedRecipe = null;
        }
        return Task.CompletedTask;
    }
```

When the user selects an item in `CollectionView`, the `SelectedRecipe` property on the ViewModel will be updated. Next, `NavigateToSelectedDetailCommand` will be executed, which will call the `NavigateToSelectedDetail` method. In this method, we can access the `SelectedRecipe` property and act upon it, such as navigating to its detail page, for example. Finally, we set the `SelectedRecipe` property to null. As this property is bound `TwoWay`, the item will get de-selected in `CollectionView`. As a result, if we navigate back from `RecipeDetailPage`, no item will be selected on the overview and then we can immediately select another one.

Now, let's have a look at how we can load data incrementally while the user scrolls through a large dataset.

Incrementally loading data

As the user scrolls through large datasets in `CollectionView`, providing a seamless and interactive user experience is crucial. The `RemainingItemsThreshold` and `RemainingItemsThresholdReachedCommand` properties allow you to effortlessly load additional items. By specifying a threshold value for the remaining items, new data is dynamically fetched and seamlessly loaded, ensuring a smooth and continuous experience. Let's explore how to implement this interactive functionality in just a few simple steps:

1. Add the following method to `RecipesOverviewViewModel`:

    ```
    private async Task TryLoadMoreItems()
    {
        //Dummy implementation
        if (Recipes.Count < TotalNumberOfRecipes)
        {
            await Task.Delay(250);
            foreach (var item in items)
            {
                Recipes.Add(item);
            }
        }
    }
    ```

    This method adds items to the `Recipes ObservableCollection` class as it has fewer items than what's defined in the `TotalNumberOfRecipes` property. It's a pretty dumb implementation, but it should get the point across. In a real-life scenario, we would fetch this data from an API or something. We'll look at this in *Chapter 10, Working with Remote Data*.

2. Next, let's add a command called `TryLoadMoreItemsCommand`. This is the command that should be invoked when we want to load more items. We want to instantiate it in the constructor of `RecipesOverviewViewModel`, as shown here:

    ```
    public AsyncRelayCommand TryLoadMoreItemsCommand
    { get; }

    public RecipesOverviewViewModel()
    {
        Recipes = new ObservableCollection
          <RecipeListItemViewModel>(items);
        TryLoadMoreItemsCommand = new AsyncRelayCommand
          (TryLoadMoreItems);
    }
    ```

3. Now, we can update the `CollectionView` and add both `RemainingItemsThreshold` and `RemainingItemsThresholdReachedCommand`, as shown in the following code block:

```
<CollectionView
    ItemsSource="{Binding Recipes}"
    RemainingItemsThreshold="5"
    RemainingItemsThresholdReachedCommand="{Binding
      TryLoadMoreItemsCommand}"
    ...>
```

With this code in place, `TryLoadMoreItemsCommand` will be invoked as soon as the user scrolls and the number of remaining items reaches the specified threshold of five or less. The `TryLoadMoreItems` method will then add items to the `Recipes ObservableCollection`. Because this method implements the `ICollectionChanged` interface, the added items will be automatically added to `CollectionView`.

Incrementally loading data is a good idea when dealing with very large datasets and `CollectionView` makes it extremely convenient to implement using the `RemainingItemsThreshold` and `RemainingItemsThresholdReachedCommand` properties.

Other common interactions

In addition to the features we've discussed, it's worth mentioning that common interactions such as pull-to-refresh and item context menus are also available in .NET MAUI. These interactions allow users to refresh the data that's displayed in the collection and access additional actions or information specific to each item. While they are used on collections very often, it's important to note that these features are not exclusive to `CollectionView` and can be implemented anywhere in your application.

`SwipeView` is a versatile control that allows you to add swipe gestures to individual items in a collection. It enables users to perform actions by swiping horizontally or vertically on an item, such as deleting an item or revealing additional options.

`RefreshView`, on the other hand, is a control that provides a standard pull-to-refresh functionality. It allows users to refresh the data that's displayed in a collection by pulling down on the screen. When triggered, `RefreshView` executes a command to update the collection with fresh data.

Summary

In this chapter, we explored the powerful features and capabilities of collections in .NET MAUI. We learned how to effectively bind collections to UI elements using `BindableLayout` and `CollectionView`, enabling dynamic and efficient rendering of data. We covered topics such as data templating, item selection, grouping, and incremental loading. `CollectionView` proved to be a versatile control, offering advanced functionality such as item virtualization and seamless data loading.

As we continue our journey in building robust and scalable apps, in the next chapter, we will delve into the important concepts of dependency injection, services, and messaging. These fundamental aspects of app development will empower us to create modular and maintainable code, enhance code reusability, and enable effective communication between different parts of our application.

Further reading

To learn more about the topics that were covered in this chapter, take a look at the following resources:

- `BindableLayout`: `https://learn.microsoft.com/en-us/dotnet/maui/user-interface/layouts/bindablelayout`
- `CollectionView`: `https://learn.microsoft.com/dotnet/maui/user-interface/controls/collectionview`
- `ListView`: `https://learn.microsoft.com/dotnet/maui/user-interface/controls/listview`
- `CarouselView`: `https://learn.microsoft.com/dotnet/maui/user-interface/controls/carouselview`
- `SwipeView`: `https://learn.microsoft.com/dotnet/maui/user-interface/controls/swipeview`
- `RefreshView`: `https://learn.microsoft.com/dotnet/maui/user-interface/controls/refreshview`

Part 2:
Building a .NET MAUI App
Using MVVM

In this part, we focus on equipping you with the essential tools and techniques needed to craft a genuine .NET MAUI application that leverages the MVVM pattern. We will dive into the core mechanisms such as dependency injection, services, and messaging, which form the backbone of any robust app. We will help you master MVVM-based navigation in .NET MAUI with or without Shell, refine user interactions with precise input and validation, and connect seamlessly with remote data sources.

This part has the following chapters:

- *Chapter 7, Dependency Injection, Services, and Messaging*
- *Chapter 8, .NET MAUI Shell and Navigation*
- *Chapter 9, Handling User Input and Validation*
- *Chapter 10, Working with Remote Data*

Dependency Injection, Services, and Messaging

As we continue building our *Recipes!* app using .NET MAUI, we want to make the most of the MVVM design pattern. MVVM is great for keeping our code organized and also promotes industry-standard practices that make our code base more maintainable and testable. In this chapter, we will focus on two critical concepts that are central to a solid MVVM architecture: **Dependency Injection** (**DI**) and **messaging**. DI promotes separation of concerns and allows our code to be much more testable. Messaging helps us keep different parts of our code from getting tangled up with each other. It allows different areas of our app to talk to each other in a loosely coupled way. Both concepts are extremely important to ensure that our MVVM architecture truly stands out.

Let's take a look at what this chapter covers:

- Inversion of Control through Dependency Injection
- Registering, resolving, and injecting services
- Messaging

By the end of this chapter, you'll have a good understanding of these concepts as we implement them in our *Recipes!* app. So, let's go ahead and get into it.

Technical requirements

Throughout this chapter, we will be enhancing the functionality of the *Recipes!* app. All the resources, including additional classes and code required for the topics covered in this chapter, are available on GitHub at `https://github.com/PacktPublishing/MVVM-pattern-.NET-MAUI/tree/main/Chapter07`. To follow along with this chapter's content, you can start with the provided `Start` folder. It contains the initial code and necessary classes specific to this chapter. This code serves as the foundation, building upon what we have learned in the previous chapters. If you want to reference or compare the completed code, including all the code written throughout this chapter, you can find it in the `Finish` folder.

Inversion of Control through Dependency Injection

Inversion of Control (IoC) is a programming principle where the control over certain aspects of a program's flow is handed over from the main code to a framework or a container. In simple terms, instead of a component being responsible for managing its dependencies and life cycle, these responsibilities are inverted or delegated to an external controller. This approach is particularly useful for creating modular and flexible systems.

In a typical software design without IoC, a class that requires certain functionalities from other classes would create or manage these dependent objects within itself. With IoC, this creation and management is handled by an external component, hence inverting the control.

IoC can be achieved through various methods such as DI, Factory Pattern, Service Locator, and more. Among these, DI is the most commonly used method in the context of MVVM.

Dependency Injection

DI, a specific form of IoC, involves injecting the dependencies of an object (such as services or components) into the object by an external entity rather than having the object create them. This is typically done through the constructor.

Using DI brings a lot of advantages. Let's take a look:

- **Separation of concerns**: Each component or class focuses on its core responsibility. The creation and life cycle management of its dependencies are handled externally.

- **Testability**: DI makes it much easier to test components by allowing mock dependencies to be injected. This is crucial because, in unit testing, you want to isolate the component being tested and not have to worry about the dependencies. For example, if a ViewModel depends on a service that fetches data, you can inject a mock data service that simulates data retrieval without actually hitting a database or API. This makes tests faster, repeatable, and more reliable.

- **Reusability and maintainability**: Components become more reusable and maintainable because they are not tightly coupled with their dependencies.

- **Flexibility**: It becomes easier to change or swap implementations of dependencies without altering the dependent class.

By allowing dependencies to be injected from the outside, DI supports the creation of more loosely coupled code. This not only results in a more maintainable and scalable system but is also highly advantageous for testing. Through the injection of mock or stub implementations during testing, you can focus on testing the functionality of individual components in isolation, without the complexity and unpredictability of the entire system.

The ability to inject different implementations is one of the powerful aspects of DI and is central to creating robust and flexible architectures.

Remember, back in *Chapter 1, What Is the MVVM Design Pattern?*, where we had a `MainPageViewModel` and its constructor accepted an interface called `IQuoteService`? Let's have a look:

```
public class MainPageViewModel : INotifyPropertyChanged
{
    private readonly IQuoteService quoteService;

    public MainPageViewModel(IQuoteService quoteService)
    {
        this.quoteService = quoteService;
    }
...
}
```

This is a textbook example of DI. `MainPageViewModel` should not be responsible for retrieving the "quote of the day." Instead, this should be the responsibility of another class. `MainPageViewModel` is dependent on an instance of a class that implements `IQuoteService` for that functionality. However, instead of directly creating or managing an instance of this service, it receives the instance through its constructor. This is what's known as **constructor injection**. By accepting the `IQuoteService` dependency through its constructor, `MainPageViewModel` adheres to the principle of **separation of concerns**. This principle asserts that a class should only be concerned with its core responsibility and not the responsibilities of its dependencies. In this case, the `MainPageViewModel` class's responsibility is to provide data for the view, while the responsibility to fetch the actual data is delegated to `IQuoteService`.

Here, `MainPageViewModel` has no knowledge about where the class implementing the `IQuoteService` interface comes from, how it's instantiated, or how its life cycle is managed. It simply receives an instance and uses it. This makes the ViewModel independent from the concrete implementation of the `IQuoteService` interface and it can be any class that implements this interface.

This **decoupling** opens up a lot of flexibility. Say, for instance, that the way we retrieve quotes changes in the future. Maybe we initially fetch the quotes from a static file, but later decide to retrieve them from a remote API instead. Because our ViewModel isn't directly tied to a specific implementation of the `IQuoteService` interface, we can just create a new class that implements it and fetch data from the API. We can then inject this new class into our ViewModel without having to change any code inside `MainPageViewModel` itself. The ViewModel is only concerned with the fact it has a class implementing the `IQuoteService` interface to work with, not the details of how it accomplishes its tasks.

> **Note**
>
> While it's common to see DI used with interfaces, it's not a strict requirement. Interfaces are popular in DI because they promote loose coupling. However, abstract classes or even concrete classes can be injected as well. The choice depends on the specific needs of your application and your design goals.

The advantage of this decoupling becomes even more evident when it comes to testing. Let's say we want to write unit tests for `MainPageViewModel`. To make these tests reliable, we need to ensure they're not affected by the unpredictability of external dependencies. With DI, we can easily achieve this by creating a mock implementation of `IQuoteService` that returns controlled data, perfect for testing scenarios. This way, we can test all aspects of `MainPageViewModel` in isolation, without any unpredictable behavior from external dependencies.

Let's see DI in action and have a look at how we can register, resolve, and inject dependencies.

Registering, resolving, and injecting services

.NET MAUI comes with built-in support for DI. It has been designed with DI in mind, which allows for easier configuration and management of services that your application relies on. By providing out-of-the-box support for DI, .NET MAUI enables developers to leverage the concept of DI and IoC to make their code more maintainable and more loosely coupled. As the MVVM pattern benefits tremendously from DI and IoC, it shows again that MVVM and .NET MAUI are a perfect match!

The `Microsoft.Extensions.DependencyInjection` namespace is where .NET MAUI gets its default implementation for DI. However, it's important to note that .NET MAUI is DI container agnostic, which means you're not limited to the default. If you prefer a third-party DI container, you're free to replace the default with your preferred choice. Let's see how we can register services using .NET MAUI's default DI implementation.

Registering services

.NET MAUI hosts a DI container and makes it accessible throughout your application. When your application starts, you have the opportunity to configure the services that will be available for injection. This is done using the `Services` property of the `MauiAppBuilder` instance. If you have worked with ASP.NET before, then you already know how this works. Through the `Services` property, we can set up services for use throughout your application.

The `Services` property on `MauiAppBuilder` is of type `IServiceCollection`, which is a framework-provided interface for a collection of service descriptors. It provides methods to register services in the container. In the following example, the `AddSingleton` method is used to register `QuoteService` as a Singleton service for the `IQuoteService` interface:

```
public static MauiApp CreateMauiApp()
```

```
{
    var builder = MauiApp.CreateBuilder();
    ...
    builder.Services.AddTransient<IQuoteService,
      QuoteService>();
    ...
    return builder.Build();
}
```

The preceding code shows how we can associate a concrete implementation (QuoteService) with an interface (IQuoteService). As a consequence, when the app's IServiceProvider needs to resolve an instance of a class that implements the IQuoteService, it will create (or reuse) an instance of the QuoteService class. IServiceProvider represents a service container, which is a collection of service registrations. It's essentially the object that is responsible for resolving and providing instances of services, which were registered through the associated IServiceCollection, when they are needed. Registering a concrete implementation for a particular interface allows us to decouple the implementation from the actual usage in our code. It's good practice to code against interfaces and not against implementations and this is exactly what we can achieve here.

However, in the case of ViewModels or other classes that don't necessarily have an associated interface, we can register them directly, as the following snippet shows:

```
builder.Services.AddTransient<MainPageViewModel>();
```

When we do this, every time an instance of MainPageViewModel is requested from the DI container, it will provide an instance of the class and manage its life cycle.

Services can be registered in different ways, depending on their intended lifetimes:

- **Transient**: Transient services are created each time they're requested from the container. This lifetime works best for lightweight, stateless services. In theory, Transient services take up more memory because a new instance is created every time the service is requested. However, because each instance can be garbage-collected as soon as it's no longer in use, this memory can be reclaimed quickly.

- **Singleton**: Singleton services are created once, and the same instance is used throughout the application's lifetime. This works best for stateful services that need to maintain consistency across the app, or for heavy services that would be expensive to create multiple times. Singleton services take up the least amount of memory because only one instance is ever created. However, because the same instance is used throughout the entire application, it stays in memory for as long as the application is running.

- **Scoped**: Scoped services are created once per scope. However, in a .NET MAUI application, this is similar to Singleton since there is generally only one scope.

Choosing between these lifetimes depends entirely on the specific needs of the service. If your service is stateless and lightweight, a Transient lifetime might be appropriate. If your service needs to maintain state across the entire application, or if it's expensive to create, a Singleton lifetime might be the best option. Choosing the right lifetime for your services is important. It can affect how your app behaves and performs, so think about it carefully. In my experience, I usually choose Transient as much as possible for my services. I do this because I aim to keep my services simple and without state. This way, they use memory more efficiently since they're removed as soon as they're not needed. Also, it helps to avoid problems that can come up when a shared state is changed in different places, especially in multi-threaded situations. But remember, there's no one-size-fits-all solution here. Each service is unique and so is your app. Depending on what your service does and what your app needs, you might have to choose a different lifetime. That's why it's key to understand these concepts and make smart choices for your specific app.

Let's see how we can resolve and inject these registered services.

Resolving and injecting services

DI containers, such as the one built into .NET MAUI, are capable of resolving not only direct dependencies but also nested dependencies.

In essence, when an instance of a class or service is being resolved by the container, all of its dependencies, and the dependencies of those dependencies, are automatically resolved and injected as well. This forms a complete object graph where every class has its dependencies satisfied.

If a particular class has a dependency that needs to be injected, it is as simple as defining the dependency as a parameter of the class's constructor. That's exactly what we did with `MainPageViewModel`: it has a constructor that requires an instance of a class implementing the `IQuoteService` interface.

> **Which constructor does the DI container use?**
>
> As the DI container can instantiate classes for us, you might wonder which constructor it uses when the class has multiple constructors. The answer is pretty simple: it uses the constructor with the most parameters that it can resolve. If there are two or more constructors with the same number of parameters the DI container can resolve, or when no constructor is found for which all dependencies could be resolved, an exception will be thrown.

We are also able to resolve services on the fly, so long as we get a hold of the app's `IServiceProvider` container. This interface exposes a `GetService<T>` method that we can call to get an instance of a class that was associated with the provided generic type parameter. The following code block shows how we can create a static `ServiceProvider` class that we could use to access the services container from anywhere in our app:

```
public static class ServiceProvider
{
    public static TService GetService<TService>()
```

```
        => Current.GetService<TService>();

    public static IServiceProvider Current
        =>
#if WINDOWS10_0_17763_0_OR_GREATER
        MauiWinUIApplication.Current.Services;
#elif ANDROID
        MauiApplication.Current.Services;
#elif IOS || MACCATALYST
        MauiUIApplicationDelegate.Current.Services;
#else
        null;
#endif
}
```

So, instead of instantiating a `MainPageViewModel` in the code behind the `MainPage_MVVM` class, and needing to manually provide an instance of a class that implements IQuoteService, we can do the following:

```
public MainPage_MVVM()
{
    InitializeComponent();
    BindingContext = ServiceProvider
        .GetService<MainPageViewModel>();
}
```

Because we have registered `MainPageViewModel` as a service and `QuoteService`, which we associated with the `IQuoteService` interface, the `GetService` method will return an instance of `MainPageViewModel`, which is instantiated by injecting an instance of the `QuoteService` class through its constructor. This `ServiceProvider` class can be very helpful to resolve instances of classes on the fly from the DI container. However, for this particular example, we could take this a step further and avoid the need to manually resolve an instance of `MainPageViewModel`. We can achieve this by adding an instance of `MainPageViewModel` as a dependency to the `MainPage_MVVM` class, as shown here:

```
public MainPage_MVVM(MainPageViewModel vm)
{
    InitializeComponent();
    BindingContext = vm;
}
```

The following code snippet shows how we can register the `MainPage_MVVM` class as well:

```
builder.Services.AddTransient<MainPage_MVVM>();
```

In this sample app, we're using .NET MAUI Shell for navigation. This allows an instance of a page to be dynamically resolved during the navigation process. So, when we navigate to the `MainPage_MVVM` page, the DI container springs into action. It resolves an instance of the `MainPage_MVVM` page and all of its dependencies.

> **What is .NET MAUI Shell?**
>
> In *Chapter 8, Navigation in MVVM*, we will dive much deeper into the aspects of navigation and .NET MAUI Shell.

Now that we've got a taste of DI with the *Quote of the Day* app, let's take things up a notch by applying what we've learned to our feature-rich *Recipes!* app. This will allow us to delve deeper into DI and see how it can be skillfully utilized in a more complex project. So, roll up your sleeves, and let's get cooking with DI in the *Recipes!* app.

Applying Dependency Injection

So far, in the ViewModels in our *Recipes!* app we have been working with hard-coded data. Now, it's time to breathe more life into our application by introducing services that can fetch and manage data dynamically. The `Begin` directory in the GitHub repository for this chapter presents some updates and additional code that includes new service interfaces such as `IRecipeService`, `IFavoritesService`, and `IRatingsService`, along with their respective implementations. These services will play crucial roles in our application: the `IRecipeService` interface defines a contract for a service that will load and manage recipe data. Similarly, `IFavoritesService` outlines the rules for a service that will handle the user's favorite recipes, and the `IRatingsService` interface does the same for a service managing recipe ratings. As we move forward, we'll explore how to use these services within the MVVM architecture and how DI brings it all together in a clean, manageable manner.

To introduce DI in our *Recipes!* app, we need to make sure that, unlike what we have been doing up until now, we don't initialize ViewModels in the code-behind ourselves. Instead, these ViewModels need to be injected and assigned to the page's `BindingContext`. Let's have a look at this before we update the ViewModels.

Adding dependencies to pages

To add the dependency of a particular ViewModel to a page, we simply need to add the type of ViewModel as a parameter to the constructor. Also, we need to make sure that both the page and the ViewModel are registered in the DI container:

1. Head over to the code-behind of `RecipesOverviewPage` and add a parameter of type `RecipeOverviewViewModel` to the page's constructor, as shown in the following snippet:

    ```
    public RecipesOverviewPage(RecipesOverviewViewModel
    ```

```
    viewModel)
{
    InitializeComponent();
    BindingContext = viewModel;
}
```

2. Next, we need to make sure the RecipesOverviewPage and RecipeOverviewViewModel classes are registered with the DI container. Only then can the DI container resolve RecipesOverviewPage and resolve its dependency, an instance of RecipesOverviewViewModel. Head over to MauiProgram and add the following lines of code:

```
public static MauiApp CreateMauiApp()
{
    var builder = MauiApp.CreateBuilder();
    builder
        .UseMauiApp<App>()
    ...
    builder.Services
        .AddTransient<RecipesOverviewPage>();
    builder.Services
        .AddTransient<RecipesOverviewViewModel>();
    ...
}
```

3. Similarly, we need to do the same for RecipeDetailPage and RecipeRatingDetailPage: add their respective ViewModels as dependencies by including them as parameters. This is what it looks like for RecipesOverviewPage:

```
public RecipesOverviewPage(
    RecipesOverviewViewModel viewModel)
{
    InitializeComponent();
    BindingContext = viewModel;
}
```

And likewise, for RecipeRatingDetailPage, we must do the following, where we want to inject RecipeRatingsDetailViewModel:

```
public RecipeRatingDetailPage(
    RecipeRatingsDetailViewModel viewModel)
{
    InitializeComponent();
    BindingContext = viewModel;
}
```

4. Now, just like we did before, let's register these additional pages and their ViewModels in the DI container within the `MauiProgram` class:

```
public static MauiApp CreateMauiApp()
{
    var builder = MauiApp.CreateBuilder();
    builder
        .UseMauiApp<App>()
    ...
    builder.Services
        .AddTransient<RecipesOverviewPage>();
    builder.Services
        .AddTransient<RecipesOverviewViewModel>();
    builder.Services
        .AddTransient<RecipeDetailPage>();
    builder.Services
        .AddTransient<RecipeDetailViewModel>();
    builder.Services
        .AddTransient<RecipeRatingDetailPage>();
    builder.Services
        .AddTransient<RecipeRatingsDetailViewModel>();
    ...
}
```

With these modifications in place, we've successfully implemented the foundational elements of DI in our *Recipes!* app. By registering the pages and their corresponding ViewModels with the DI container, we've ensured that whenever these components are needed, they can be easily resolved and provided by the DI container. Moreover, by injecting the ViewModels into our pages through their constructors, we've shifted the responsibility of creating and managing ViewModel instances away from the pages themselves and toward the DI container. This sets up a more flexible and maintainable structure for our application, paving the way for us to further enhance it with additional services and functionality.

Now, let's take a closer look at the specific changes we need to make to our ViewModels to fully incorporate DI.

Adding dependencies to ViewModels

We no longer want our ViewModels to contain hard-coded data, nor do we want them to be responsible for retrieving data. So, let's introduce some dependencies to our ViewModels:

1. At the very top of the `RecipesOverviewViewModel` class, we can start by removing the `items` field. We're moving away from hard-coded data and will use services to fetch data instead.

2. The following code snippet shows how we introduce two fields to this class: `recipeService`, which is of type `IRecipeService`, and `favoritesService`, which is of type `IFavoritesService`:

```
private readonly IRecipeService recipeService;
private readonly IFavoritesService favoritesService;
```

These services will take responsibility for loading the recipes on this page and displaying whether they are favorited by the user or not. Both of these services are dependencies that will be injected into the ViewModel.

3. This code block shows exactly how these dependencies can get injected through the constructor of the ViewModel:

```
public RecipesOverviewViewModel(
    IRecipeService recipeService,
    IFavoritesService favoritesService)
{
    this.recipeService = recipeService;
    this.favoritesService = favoritesService;

    Recipes = new ();
    TryLoadMoreItemsCommand =
        new AsyncRelayCommand(TryLoadMoreItems);
    NavigateToSelectedDetailCommand =
        new AsyncRelayCommand
            (NavigateToSelectedDetail);

    LoadRecipes(7, 0);
}
```

By defining these two parameters in the constructor for `RecipesOverviewViewModel`, the DI container will attempt to resolve instances for both when creating a `RecipesOverviewViewModel`. The resolved instances are then passed as parameters to the constructor, where we can assign them to the fields we created earlier.

4. When we examine the `LoadRecipes` method, we can see how we utilize these services to load the data we need:

```
private async Task LoadRecipes(int pageSize, int page)
{
    var loadRecipesTask =
        recipeService.LoadRecipes(pageSize, page);
    var loadFavoritesTask =
        favoritesService.LoadFavorites();

    ...
}
```

The ViewModel doesn't concern itself with where these recipes or favorites are coming from. It only trusts that the injected services – recipeService and favoritesService – adhere to the specified interfaces and deliver the required functionality. The exact implementation is abstracted away from the ViewModel, highlighting one of the main benefits of DI.

5. Head over to RecipeDetailViewModel. In this class, we also want to remove all hard-coded data: Title, Allergens, Calories, and so on. And while we are at it, we should update the properties to "full" properties that trigger the PropertyChanged event. This is needed because the data on the ViewModel will be loaded asynchronously, so it won't be there when the page is being rendered. As a result, the PropertyChanged event for each property needs to be triggered when the data is loaded to reflect the loaded values on the UI. The following snippet shows some of the updated properties:

```
string _title;
public string Title
{
    get => _title;
    set => SetProperty(ref _title, value);
}


string[] _allergens = new string[0];
public string[] Allergens
{
    get => _allergens;
    set => SetProperty(ref _allergens, value);
}


int? _calories;
public int? Calories
{
    get => _calories;
    set => SetProperty(ref _calories, value);
}
```

6. Now is also the time to update the binding mode on the label, which shows the recipe's title. Up until now, this was defined as a OneTime binding, but as we now load the data of the recipe after the ViewModel is set as the BindingContext of the RecipeDetailPage, we need to make sure the updated value is shown on the screen as well. Let's update the binding mode to OneWay so that when the PropertyChanged event is triggered after the value of the Title property is set, the binding engine updates the value on the UI. The following snippet shows the updated label:

```
<Label
    FontAttributes="Bold"
    FontSize="22"
```

```
        Text="{Binding Path=Title, Mode=OneWay}"
        VerticalOptions="Center" />
```

7. Let's update the constructor of `RecipeDetailViewModel` so that it accepts an instance of `IRecipeService`, `IFavoritesService`, and `IRatingsService`, as shown here:

```
public RecipeDetailViewModel(
    IRecipeService recipeService,
    IFavoritesService favoritesService,
    IRatingsService ratingsService)
{
    this.recipeService = recipeService;
    this.favoritesService  = favoritesService;
    this.ratingsService = ratingsService;

    ...
}
```

8. These services (`recipeService`, `favoritesService`, and `ratingsService`) are `readonly` fields that we should define in the ViewModel, as demonstrated in the following snippet:

```
private readonly IRecipeService recipeService;
private readonly IFavoritesService favoritesService;
private readonly IRatingsService ratingsService;
```

9. The following code block shows `LoadRecipe`, which accepts the ID of the recipe to load as a parameter. This method uses the injected services to load all relevant data for this ViewModel:

```
private async Task LoadRecipe(string recipeId)
{
    var loadRecipeTask =
        recipeService.LoadRecipe(recipeId);
    var loadIsFavoriteTask =
        favoritesService.IsFavorite(recipeId);
    var loadRatingsTask =
        ratingsService.LoadRatingsSummary(recipeId);

    await Task.WhenAll(loadRecipeTask,
        loadRecipeTask, loadRatingsTask);

    if(loadRecipeTask.Result is not null)
        MapRecipeData(
            loadRecipeTask.Result,
            loadRatingsTask.Result,
            loadIsFavoriteTask.Result);
}
```

The three async tasks that retrieve `RecipeDetailDto`, `RatingsSummaryDto`, and the `bool` value indicating whether the recipe is a favorite or not are launched in parallel. Through the `Task.WhenAll` method, we wait for all three to complete. Beyond this point, the `Result` property of the tasks holds the retrieved data. This data is then mapped to the ViewModel through the `MapRecipeData` method.

10. In the next chapter, *Chapter 8, Navigation in MVVM*, we'll have a look at how we can pass the ID of the selected recipe from `RecipesOverviewViewModel` to `RecipeDetailViewModel` to load the recipe details of the chosen recipe. For now, let's add the following snippet at the end of the ViewModel's constructor to load the details of the recipe with an ID of 3:

```
LoadRecipe("3");
```

11. Finally, we also need to update `RecipeRatingsDetailViewModel`. As before, we want to remove all hard-coded data and update the constructor so that it accepts an instance of a class that implements `IRecipeService` and one that implements the `IRatingsService` interface. The following snippet shows the updated constructor, where we also deleted the initialization of both the `Reviews` and `GroupedReviews` properties:

```
public RecipeRatingsDetailViewModel(
    IRecipeService recipeService,
    IRatingsService ratingsService)
{
    this.recipeService = recipeService;
    this.ratingsService = ratingsService;
    ...
}
```

12. The `Reviews` property can be removed and we should make sure the `RecipeTitle` property calls the `PropertyChanged` event when it is being updated. Again, like we did previously, we must do this because the data is loaded asynchronously and we must notify the UI about the updated values. The following code block shows the updated `RecipeTitle` property, which uses the `SetProperty` method of the `ObservableObject` class to assign the value and trigger the `PropertyChanged` event. It also shows the fields that we added, to which we assign the injected dependencies in the constructor:

```
public class RecipeRatingsDetailViewModel :
  ObservableObject
{
    private readonly IRatingsService ratingsService;
    private readonly IRecipeService recipeService;

    string _recipeTitle = string.Empty;
    public string RecipeTitle
    {
```

```
            get => _recipeTitle;
            set => SetProperty(ref _recipeTitle, value);
        }
        ...
    }
```

13. Let's also add the LoadData method, which accepts the ID of the recipe we want to load the rating for. It uses the injected services to dynamically load the data needed in this ViewModel. Let's take a look:

```
private async Task LoadData(string recipeId)
{
    var recipeTask =
        recipeService.LoadRecipe(recipeId);
    var ratingsTask =
        ratingsService.LoadRatings(recipeId);

    await Task.WhenAll(recipeTask, ratingsTask);

    RecipeTitle =
        recipeTask.Result?.Name ?? string.Empty;

    GroupedReviews = ratingsTask.Result
        ...
        .ToList();
}
```

14. For now, let's call the LoadData method from the constructor so that it loads some data when we initialize the ViewModel:

```
LoadData("3");
```

With all the updates done on the ViewModels, let's finish up by registering the services that our updated ViewModels now have as dependencies.

Registering services

Now that our ViewModels have some dependencies, we have to make sure these dependencies get registered so that the DI container can resolve them.

Registering the required dependencies is done again in the MauiProgram class. The following snippet shows how we register FavoritesService, which is very straightforward:

```
builder.Services.AddSingleton<IFavoritesService,
    FavoritesService>();
```

We intentionally register `FavoritesService` as a Singleton because this particular implementation stores the user's favorites in memory. If we were to register it as Transient, a new instance would be created each time it's injected as a dependency, which would result in the favorites not persisting between page navigations. It's worth noting, however, that keeping favorites in memory isn't ideal, but for the sake of this example, it will serve our purpose. In a real-life scenario, we would want the favorites to be persisted in an (online) data store.

Registering `RecipeService` involves a slightly more complex process. The reason for this is that the constructor of `RecipeService` requires a `Task` property that returns a stream to a JSON file that holds all the recipe information. This is shown in the constructor of `RecipeService`:

```
public RecipeService(Task<Stream> recipesJsonStreamTask)
{
    this.recipesJsonStreamTask = recipesJsonStreamTask;
}
```

We can't register `RecipeService` in the same way we did with `FavoritesService` or other services we registered in earlier examples. This is because the DI container needs to know what parameter to pass to the constructor. In previous examples, it was straightforward: we just specified the concrete type that we wanted to associate with an interface or base class, or with the type itself. The container could then create an instance of the concrete class by invoking its default constructor or injecting other resolved dependencies.

However, in the case of `RecipeService`, the required parameter for creating an instance isn't something we plan to register, meaning it cannot be resolved by the DI container. To tackle scenarios like this, the `AddTransient`, `AddSingleton`, and `AddScoped` methods provide an overload. This overload lets us pass in a function that returns an instance of the type we want to associate with the given base type. This function is invoked every time the associated type needs to be resolved. What's more, the function's parameter is `IServiceProvider` itself, allowing us to resolve any additional dependencies if necessary. The following code block shows how we can register `RecipeService`, using the overloaded function, while passing in a function that creates an instance of this class:

```
builder.Services.AddTransient<IRecipeService>(
    serviceProvider => new RecipeService( FileSystem.
        OpenAppPackageFileAsync("recipedetails.json")));
```

The passed-in function will be invoked every time an object of `IRecipeService` needs to be resolved by the DI container. However, as the `AddSingleton` method was used, the function would be invoked only once. This means that in this specific use case, registering the service as a Singleton could be a sensible decision as it would ensure that the JSON file only gets read once, keeping the recipes in memory, and thereby optimizing the application's performance.

The same thing goes for the registration of `RatingsService`. Just like `RecipeService`, this class will also read from a local file to get the ratings. So, as before, we want to register this service using the overloaded `AddTransient` method, as shown here:

```
builder.Services.AddSingleton<IRatingsService>(
    serviceProvider => new RatingsService( FileSystem.
        OpenAppPackageFileAsync("ratings.json")));
```

Once all these services have been registered, we can go ahead and run the *Recipes!* app. Our code now leverages DI, a practice that greatly enhances the modularity and testability of our application. By injecting dependencies, we decouple concrete classes with interfaces or base classes, allowing us to change or swap underlying implementations without affecting dependent classes. In the context of the MVVM pattern, DI allows us to provide ViewModels with the necessary services to handle their tasks, such as data fetching or business logic, without hard-coding these dependencies, promoting a clean separation of concerns. Moreover, we have even taken this concept a step further by using DI to inject ViewModels directly into our views, further emphasizing the flexibility and versatility this practice provides in our app development process.

> **Note**
> While we've primarily discussed constructor-based DI in .NET MAUI, it's worth mentioning that in broader contexts, dependencies can also be injected via properties or methods. However, such methods are not natively supported in .NET MAUI. The essence of DI is providing the class with its dependencies, irrespective of the method. Constructor injection is often preferred for clarity, but the technique that's used might vary based on the platform and the design goals.

DI plays a crucial role in keeping our application's components decoupled. Next, we'll delve into another mechanism that promotes decoupling in our application.

Messaging

Messaging is a software architectural pattern that facilitates communication between different parts of an application. In the context of .NET MAUI and MVVM architecture, messaging is typically used to send notifications between loosely coupled components, such as between ViewModels, or from a Model to a ViewModel. This decouples the components and promotes a more modular and maintainable code base.

The concept of messaging is especially useful when data needs to be passed or events need to be communicated between parts of your application that do not have a direct relationship. Instead of tightly coupling these parts by having them directly call each other, you can use a messaging system where one part sends a message that any interested part of your application can receive and react to.

This pattern is a form of the **Observer** pattern, where an object, named the **Subject**, maintains a list of its dependents, called **Observers**, and notifies them automatically of any state changes, typically by calling one of their methods. Similarly, in MVVM, messaging is used to communicate between decoupled components of the application: any object in your application, including a ViewModel, a service, or a model class or service can send a message, and any other class that is subscribed to that particular type of message will be notified and can react accordingly.

> **About MessagingCenter**
>
> MessagingCenter, originally introduced in Xamarin.Forms as a mechanism for loosely-coupled communication between components, is present but marked as obsolete in .NET MAUI. While it's retained in .NET 8 for transition scenarios, its use is discouraged!

Typically, in the context of MVVM, as shown in the following figure, the messaging system itself maintains a list of observers and handles passing messages from senders to appropriate receivers:

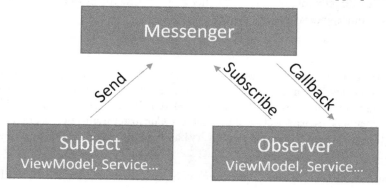

Figure 7.1: Messaging overview

One notable challenge with the messaging pattern is its inherent opacity: it can be difficult to determine which parts of the application are subscribing to a particular message. This lack of transparency can lead to unforeseen side effects when altering the code and makes the code base more challenging to navigate and debug. When I do use messaging, I use it with caution. Keeping messages minimal and focused on a specific task can help mitigate this challenge. Another potential risk of using messaging is inadvertently causing memory leaks. This can occur when an object subscribes to a message but never unsubscribes. If this happens, the messaging system continues to hold a reference to the subscriber object, preventing it from being garbage collected even if there are no other references to it in the application. Over time, this can lead to increased memory usage and can eventually degrade the performance of the application.

This issue is particularly important in the context of MVVM, where ViewModels might subscribe to messages during their initialization and then get replaced by new ViewModels as the user navigates through the application. If these ViewModels don't unsubscribe from the messages when they're no longer in use, they will stay in memory indefinitely.

That's where `WeakReferenceMessenger` comes in.

WeakReferenceMessenger

The MVVM Toolkit, which we discussed earlier, provides us with a robust messenger implementation called `WeakReferenceMessenger`. Designed with MVVM applications in mind, this messenger ensures we can enjoy the benefits of messaging without worrying about potential memory leaks.

Unlike a traditional messenger, which holds strong references to its subscribers, `WeakReferenceMessenger` holds weak references. This means it doesn't prevent its subscribers from being garbage collected. So, even if you forget to unsubscribe, the garbage collector can still clean up your ViewModel when it's no longer in use, preventing memory leaks.

> **Note**
>
> In this section, we'll be using `WeakReferenceMessenger` from the MVVM Toolkit as our messaging system. However, it's important to note that other messaging systems are available as well. While we're focusing on `WeakReferenceMessenger`, the core concepts we'll be discussing here – such as sending and receiving messages – apply to most messaging systems. Always remember to study and understand the specific messaging system you're working with to make the most of its features and avoid potential pitfalls.

`WeakReferenceMessenger` uses a type-based messaging system. This means that when you send a message, you specify a message type and only the recipients that have subscribed to that specific type will receive the message. The message type is typically defined as a class, and the message data is stored as properties of that class.

To send a message, you must use the `Send` method, passing in the message object and, optionally, a sender and target. The messenger will then deliver the message to all the registered recipients for the specified message type. To receive messages, a class needs to register with the messenger by calling the `Register` method, specifying the message type it wishes to receive, and providing a callback method that will be invoked when a message of that type is sent.

Let's take a look at how we can update our code and make it more loosely coupled by using `WeakReferenceMessenger`.

Updating the number of servings

Through messaging, ViewModels can communicate with each other in a loosely coupled manner. As an example, let's take a look at `IngredientsListViewModel`. When updating the value of the `NumberOfServings` property, we loop through all elements in the `Ingredients` collection (which are `RecipeIngredientViewModel` objects) and call their `UpdateServings` method, passing in the updated value:

```
public int NumberOfServings
{
    get => _numberOfServings;
    set
    {
        if (SetProperty(ref _numberOfServings, value))
        {
            Ingredients
                .ForEach(i => i.UpdateServings(value));
        }
    }
}
```

This approach is tightly coupled since the property knows about the implementation details of other objects, specifically `RecipeIngredientViewModel`. Also, it doesn't adhere well to the **Single Responsibility Principle**: *the property doesn't only concern itself; it is also responsible for updating the values of other properties.*

So, let's introduce messaging here!

- As `WeakReferenceMessenger` is a type-based messaging system, we must create a new type that we can send and subscribe to whenever the number of servings is being updated by the user. Right-click the **Recipes.Client.Core** project, select **Add | New Folder**, and name it `Messages`.

- Right-click the **Messages** folder, select **Add | Class...**, and name it `ServingsChangedMessage`.

Although `WeakReferenceMessenger` can send messages of any type, there are some base message classes you might want to inherit from. In this case, we could inherit from the generic `CommunityToolkit.Mvvm.Messaging.Messages.ValueChanged` class because that is exactly what `ServingsChangedMessage` is for.

The following code block shows the implementation of this class:

```
using CommunityToolkit.Mvvm.Messaging.Messages;

namespace Recipes.Client.Core.Messages;
```

```
public class ServingsChangedMessage :
    ValueChangedMessage<int>
{
    public ServingsChangedMessage(int value)
        : base(value)
    { }
}
```

We can now go ahead and update the `NumberOfServings` method on the `IngredientsListViewModel` class. Instead of looping over every item in the ingredients list and calling its `UpdateServings` method, we can now send `ServingsChangedMessage`, as shown here:

```
public int NumberOfServings
{
    get => _numberOfServings;
    set
    {
        if (SetProperty(ref _numberOfServings, value))
        {
            WeakReferenceMessenger.Default.Send(
                new ServingsChangedMessage(value));
        }
    }
}
```

Sending a message is as easy as calling the `Send` method on an instance of `WeakReferenceMessenger`, passing the message you want to send.

Finally, we need to update `RecipeIngredientViewModel`. This class will need to subscribe to `ServingsChangedMessage` so that it can react to it. Registering to a type of message is done by calling the generic `Register` method on `WeakReferenceMessenger`. As a type parameter, you need to pass in the type of message you want to listen to. Here is one way to register to the `ServingsChangedMessage`:

```
public RecipeIngredientViewModel(...)
{
...
    WeakReferenceMessenger.Default
    .Register<ServingsChangedMessage>(this, (r, m) =>
    ((RecipeIngredientViewModel)r)
    .UpdateServings(m.Value));
}
```

The first parameter of the `Register` method is the recipient of the message, which in our case will be the class itself. The second parameter is the handler that gets invoked when the message is received. The first parameter of the handler is the receiver and the second one is the message itself. The passed-in receiver allows the Lambda expression to not capture `this`, which improves performance. It might also be a good idea to update the access modifier of the `UpdateServings` method to `private` as no public access to this method is needed anymore.

With this updated implementation, the `NumberOfServings` property in `IngredientsListViewModel` no longer needs to know about the `RecipeIngredientViewModel` objects. Instead, it simply sends a message when its value changes. The `RecipeIngredientViewModel` objects, which are subscribed to these messages, can update their state accordingly. This decouples the two classes and ensures that each is only responsible for managing its own state, adhering to the single responsibility principle and separation of concerns.

In the following example, we'll have a look at the fact that messaging isn't only valuable between ViewModels. A service might also send messages that ViewModels can respond to.

Keeping favorites in sync

In the *Recipes!* app, the `RecipesOverviewPage` displays all recipes, and users can mark favorites on the `RecipeDetailPage`. However, without reloading `RecipesOverviewPage`, newly favorited recipes aren't highlighted. Given that the recipes database isn't frequently updated, constant page reloads would be overkill and could be bad for the user experience.

A more efficient strategy involves using messaging. When a recipe is favorited, a message is dispatched. The individual `RecipeListItemViewModels` contained within `RecipesOverviewViewModel` subscribe to this message, and upon receiving it, they update their favorite status in real time. This approach prevents unnecessary data fetches, thereby enhancing the app's performance and responsiveness. Let's see what we need to do to make this work:

1. First, let's add a new message type. Right-click the **Messages** folder in the **Recipes.Client.Core** project, select **Add | Class...**, and enter `FavoriteUpdateMessage` as the class name.

2. Add the following code to the `FavoriteUpdateMessage` class:

```
public class FavoriteUpdateMessage
{
    public string RecipeId { get; }
    public bool IsFavorite { get; }

    public FavoriteUpdateMessage(string recipeId,
        bool isFavorite)
    {
        RecipeId = recipeId;
        IsFavorite = isFavorite;
```

```
        }
    }
```

This class holds two properties, `RecipeId` and `IsFavorite`, so that with this message, we can signal which recipe has been marked or removed as a favorite.

3. The following code block shows how we can send this `FavoriteUpdateMessage` from the `FavoritesService` whenever a recipe is added as a favorite:

```
public Task Add(string id)
{
    if(!favorites.Contains(id))
    {
        favorites.Add(id);
        WeakReferenceMessenger.Default.Send(
            new FavoriteUpdateMessage(id, true));
    }
    return Task.CompletedTask;
}
```

4. Similarly, when a recipe is removed as a favorite, a `FavoriteUpdateMessage` can be sent, as shown here:

```
public Task Remove(string id)
{
    if (favorites.Contains(id))
    {
        favorites.Remove(id);
        WeakReferenceMessenger.Default.Send(
            new FavoriteUpdateMessage(id, false));
    }
    return Task.CompletedTask;
}
```

5. The final step involves subscribing to this message in `RecipeListItemViewModel`. This ensures that when a `FavoriteUpdateMessage` arrives, the `IsFavorite` property can be updated accordingly. Unlike the previous example, where we defined a message handler using the `Register` method, we'll use a different approach this time by implementing the `IRecipient` interface. Here's how we can do this:

```
public class RecipeListItemViewModel :
    ObservableObject,
    IRecipient<FavoriteUpdateMessage>
{
    ...
```

```
public RecipeListItemViewModel(...)
{
    ...

    WeakReferenceMessenger.Default.Register(this);
}

void IRecipient<FavoriteUpdateMessage>
    .Receive(FavoriteUpdateMessage message)
{
    if (message.RecipeId == Id)
    {
        IsFavorite = message.IsFavorite;
    }
}
}
```

By implementing the CommunityToolkit.Mvvm.Messaging.IRecipient<TMessage> interface, where TMessage is FavoriteUpdateMessage in this case, we're specifying the type of message we want to handle. Implementing this interface allows us to call the Register method of WeakReferenceMessenger and pass the class itself as the only parameter. The interface requires us to implement the Receive method, which is invoked when a message of the specified type is received.

Through the updated code, a message is dispatched whenever a user adds or removes a recipe as a favorite. Instances of RecipeListItemViewModel are set to listen for this message and update their IsFavorite property accordingly. As a result, when the user navigates back from a detail page, where the favorite status was updated, the refreshed status is immediately visible on the overview page – all without reloading any data.

> **Note**
>
> While WeakReferenceMessenger provides a robust solution for many messaging scenarios, it's important to use it with caution when dealing with a large number of listeners. Always monitor the performance and behavior of your application, especially when dispatching messages to thousands of listeners, and consider optimizing or reevaluating your design if necessary.

Summary

In this chapter, we delved into two pivotal topics in the architecture of modern applications: DI and messaging. First, we explored DI, a technique for achieving loose coupling between objects and their dependencies. In the context of the MVVM pattern, we utilized this technique to inject services and other dependencies into our ViewModels, enhancing their testability and maintainability.

The latter part of this chapter focused on messaging, another integral component in MVVM applications for promoting decoupled communication between components. We examined `WeakReferenceMessenger` provided by the MVVM Toolkit, which facilitates loose coupling in the application.

In essence, this chapter aimed to reinforce the importance of loose coupling in software design, showcasing how both DI and messaging contribute significantly to the creation of maintainable and testable applications.

In the upcoming chapter, we'll delve deep into the intricacies of navigation in .NET MAUI and how we can integrate navigation into our MVVM architecture.

Further reading

To learn more about the topics that were covered in this chapter, take a look at the following resources:

- Dependency injection: `https://learn.microsoft.com/dotnet/architecture/maui/dependency-injection`

- MVVM Toolkit messenger: `https://learn.microsoft.com/dotnet/communitytoolkit/mvvm/messenger`

Navigation in MVVM

So far in our journey of building the *Recipes!* app, we have laid a robust foundation using the MVVM design pattern. Now, there's one important part missing: navigation – that is, moving between different pages of the app. This chapter will focus on the practical side of navigation within .NET MAUI. We'll break down our discussion into four key areas:

- About .NET MAUI Shell
- Setting up navigation in a .NET MAUI Shell app
- Setting up navigation without .NET MAUI Shell
- Passing results back

MVVM largely focuses on the separation of concerns, decoupling the logic from the presentation layer. When we integrate navigation within the MVVM architecture, we're essentially extending the principle of "separation of concerns" to the navigation logic. To implement this effectively, it's essential to grasp key principles of navigation.

By the end of this chapter, you'll have a solid grasp of .NET MAUI's navigation capabilities. Whether you opt to utilize .NET MAUI Shell or stick with traditional navigation methods, you'll be equipped to make your app's navigation seamless and user-friendly. It's time to dive in!

Technical requirements

We will continue to add functionality to the *Recipes!* app throughout this chapter. As always, everything can be found on GitHub at `https://github.com/PacktPublishing/MVVM-pattern-.NET-MAUI/tree/main/Chapter08`. You can start from the code provided in the `Start` folder to follow along with this chapter. The `Finish` folder contains the completed code, which you can consult for reference.

About .NET MAUI Shell

.NET MAUI Shell is an opinionated way to create the structure of a .NET MAUI app. It introduces a more simplified approach to building mobile applications, which can be quite complex when it comes to structuring and navigation. Shell streamlines these aspects by providing a unified, declarative syntax for expressing the structure and navigation pattern of an application.

Being opinionated, .NET MAUI Shell has specific guidelines and conventions it expects developers to follow, with the benefit of reducing boilerplate code and effort. It brings a variety of features to the table, aiming to reduce the complexity of mobile application development:

- **URI-based navigation**: Shell supports a URI-based navigation scheme, similar to web development models. Developers can define a **route** to a particular page. These routes allow for easy and loosely coupled navigation around the app, making the navigation code more straightforward and less error-prone.

- **Simplifying complex app structures**: Shell offers out-of-the-box support for common UI elements such as flyout menus, tabs, and navigation bars, and all of them combined. Developers can easily add these structures to their apps and have Shell manage the rendering on different platforms.

- **Performance**: Shell also aims to improve performance by handling the life cycle of its components more efficiently, offering faster rendering times.

However, the opinionated nature of Shell means it might not be suitable for every application scenario or developer. It provides a predefined structure and expects developers to adhere to it, which can be beneficial for simpler apps but might limit flexibility for more complex scenarios.

> .NET MAUI Shell
>
> .NET MAUI Shell is a powerful tool in any mobile developer's toolbox. It provides a high level of abstraction to simplify app development, but developers should evaluate whether its opinionated approach aligns with their project requirements and constraints.

Let's have a look at how to leverage Shell in a .NET MAUI app.

Setting up Shell

By default, when creating a new .NET MAUI app, `Shell` is already wired up automatically. An `AppShell` class, which inherits from `Microsoft.Maui.Controls.Shell`, is generated and an instance of this `AppShell` class is assigned to the `MainPage` property of the `App` class:

```
public App()
{
    InitializeComponent();
```

```
    MainPage = new AppShell();
}
```

The value of the `MainPage` property specifies the first page that will be displayed when the application is launched. In other words, it's the entry point into your application's UI. This can be a single content page, a navigation page, a tabbed page, or even a master-detail page. Or, as shown here, when leveraging `Shell`, it can also be a `Shell` object. `Shell` acts as a container for your application's structure and navigation, defining the initial layout and flow of your application.

Though `MainPage` is the initial page that's displayed, it is technically possible to change it at any point in the app's life cycle to accommodate the needs of your application. For instance, you may initially set `MainPage` to `LoginPage`, and once the user successfully logs in, you could then change `MainPage` to your `AppShell`.

Within the `AppShell` class, you define the major structural elements of your application. For instance, if your app includes a flyout menu and several tabbed pages, you can define these elements in your `AppShell`. Here's a basic example of what that might look like:

```
<Shell.FlyoutHeader>
    . . .
</Shell.FlyoutHeader>
<FlyoutItem Title="Quotes" Icon="badge.png">
    <Tab Title="MVVM">
        <ShellContent
            Title="Quote of the Day"
            ContentTemplate="{DataTemplate
              local:MainPage_MVVM}"
            Icon="badge.png" />
    </Tab>
    <Tab Title="Not MVVM">
        <ShellContent
            Title="Quote of the Day"
            ContentTemplate="{DataTemplate local:MainPage}"
            Icon="badge.png" />
    </Tab>
</FlyoutItem>
<FlyoutItem Title="Settings" Icon="settings.png">
    <ShellContent Title="Settings"
                  ContentTemplate="{DataTemplate
                    local:SettingsPage}" />
</FlyoutItem>
```

The code shown here will render a shell containing a flyout menu with two items: **Quotes** and **Settings**, both accompanied by a relevant icon. Each `FlyoutItem` represents a distinct section of the app. The `Quotes` section is defined to contain two tabs, each with its title. The content of each tab is defined by a `ShellContent` object that references the page to be displayed when the tab is selected. The `Settings` section only contains a `ShellContent` item, which refers to `SettingsPage`. Without .NET MAUI Shell, creating a complex layout with a flyout menu, tabs, and separate sections, while managing the navigation between them, could be quite complex and require a lot of boilerplate code. But with Shell, you can define this structure in a simple, declarative way right in your `AppShell`, making it easier to manage and update. *Figure 8.1* shows what the layout shown here, defined in XAML using Shell, looks like:

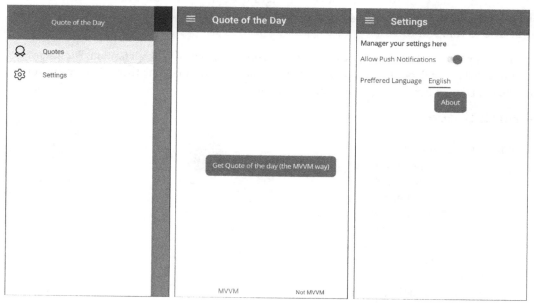

Figure 8.1: Flyout items and tabs when using Shell

Not only does Shell allow us to define the main structure of our app, but it also gives us the ability to define routes. Let's have a look at that.

Routing

.NET MAUI Shell's routing system is based on the concept of named routes, which are essentially unique identifiers, or routes, for pages within your application. This simplifies the process of navigating among pages and introduces a way to loosely couple your navigation logic from your page types. Rather than directly referencing page types, you navigate to registered routes. This enables a level of abstraction as you're navigating to "a page" registered with a specific name, not directly to a specific page. This allows your concrete page associated with a particular route to be changed without requiring changes in your navigation logic.

We can register a route using the `RegisterRoute` method on the static `Microsoft.Maui.Controls.Routing` class. Often, routes are registered in the `AppShell` class's constructor, but it can be done anywhere in the app, so long as it happens early on in the application's life cycle. So, the `CreateMauiApp` method in the `MauiProgram` class is also a good candidate. In the *Quote Of The Day* app, the registration of routes is done in the latter. Whatever location you choose to register your app's routes, here's how it's done:

```
Routing.RegisterRoute("about", typeof(AboutPage));
```

Once registered, you can navigate to the route like so:

```
await Shell.Current.GoToAsync("about");
```

In addition, Shell supports both absolute and relative navigation. An absolute URI, starting with a slash (/), resets the navigation stack before navigation, whereas a relative URI, not starting with a slash, pushes the navigation operation onto the navigation stack. For clarity, the navigation stack is essentially a history of pages the user has navigated through, allowing for forward and backward navigation in the app.

This named-route-based navigation also supports passing parameters between pages:

```
await Shell.Current.GoToAsync("about?foo=bar");
```

I'm not a big fan of using query string parameters for navigation, as shown here. Instead, I prefer the following approach, which allows us to pass parameters in a dictionary of type `IDictionary<string, object>`:

```
await Shell.Current.GoToAsync("about",
    new Dictionary<string, object>()
    {
        {"foo", "bar" }
    });
```

The reason I prefer this approach is the fact that this allows for passing complex objects, whereas the query string approach only allows for primitive types. And because I like consistency, I prefer to always use the dictionary.

These parameters, which we pass from one page to another, can be retrieved in different ways. One of them is to let the target page inherit the `Microsoft.Maui.Controls.IQueryAttributable` interface. As shown here, this interface defines just one method, `ApplyQueryAttributes`, that needs to be implemented:

```
public partial class AboutPage : ContentPage,
    IQueryAttributable
{
...
    public void ApplyQueryAttributes(
    IDictionary<string, object> query)
    {
        lblParameter.Text = $"Parameter {query
            .First().Key}: {query.First().Value}";
    }
}
```

Moreover, if an instance of a class that implements the `IQueryAttributable` interface is assigned as the target page's `BindingContext` (such as a ViewModel), that `ApplyQueryAttributes` method would also be invoked.

Adhering to MVVM best practices

I've often seen ViewModels inheriting the `IQueryAttributable` interface to receive navigation parameters. Although that works perfectly well, it goes against one of MVVM's best practices, which says that ViewModels should be framework agnostic. This interface is .NET MAUI and Shell-specific, so it requires a dependency on these frameworks. Later in this chapter, I'll show you how to not rely on the `IQueryAttributable` interface and still be able to receive navigation parameters.

As we mentioned previously, there are also other ways to receive parameters on the navigation target. I'm not going to dive deeper into that as we won't be relying on that when we implement navigation in MVVM.

Let's have a look at one final aspect I want to highlight about Shell before we go further: Shell's support for DI.

Supporting Dependency Injection

In the previous chapter, we discussed DI and briefly touched on the fact that Shell allows pages to be resolved dynamically. This allowed us to define the ViewModel as a dependency of a page, which gets injected through the page's constructor, as shown here:

```
public AboutPage(AboutPageViewModel vm)
{
    InitializeComponent();
    BindingContext = vm;
}
```

The only caveat here is that the page itself needs to be registered in the `IServiceCollection`, alongside its dependencies of course. With the following in place, we can navigate to `"about"` and Shell will resolve `AboutPage` and its dependencies – in this case, `AboutPageViewModel` – and inject them:

```
Routing.RegisterRoute("about", typeof(AboutPage));
builder.Services.AddTransient<AboutPage>();
builder.Services.AddTransient<AboutPageViewModel>();
```

There is even a convenient extension method in the .NET MAUI Community Toolkit that does all of this at once. Take a look:

```
builder.Services.AddTransientWithShellRoute<AboutPage,
    AboutPageViewModel>("about");
```

The same method also exists for adding the types as scoped or singleton, of course.

In this section, we merely scratched the surface of .NET MAUI Shell, exploring its routing system and support for DI. We saw how it provides a robust, flexible, and intuitive approach to structuring your application and managing navigation.

However, remember that .NET MAUI Shell has a lot more to offer, including advanced features such as flyout customization, search handling, and life cycle events, among others. For deeper insights into these aspects of .NET MAUI Shell, be sure to visit the *Further reading* section at the end of this chapter.

Now that we've established a solid understanding of .NET MAUI Shell, it's time to see how we can leverage it within MVVM. In the next section, we'll focus on setting up navigation in our *Recipes!* app while adhering to the MVVM pattern. So, let's dive right in!

Setting up navigation in a .NET MAUI Shell app

Effective navigation within the MVVM pattern begins with an integral component: a `NavigationService`. This service is the driving force behind MVVM navigation. In essence, a `NavigationService` is a class that implements an `INavigationService` interface. The `INavigationService` interface provides the contract for navigating between pages, defining the various methods needed for such operations. These methods could include operations such as `GoToDetailPage()`, `GoBack()`, and others, depending on your specific requirements.

Here's the beauty of this setup: during the app's startup, we register a framework-specific implementation of the `INavigationService` interface with the DI container. It's a perfect illustration of the power of DI, where we program to an interface, not an implementation. This allows our ViewModels to be completely platform-agnostic. This not only promotes code flexibility and testability but also allows us to replace or modify our `NavigationService` implementation without affecting the rest of our app.

Before we dive deeper into the setup of an `INavigationService` and explore how it operates within our *Recipes!* app, notice that the UI of the app has changed a little bit. The main UI now shows two tabs: **Recipes**, which shows `RecipesOverviewPage`, and **Settings**, which holds a new `SettingsPage`. Let's have a look at implementing a `NavigationService` interface that leverages .NET MAUI Shell.

Creating an INavigationService interface

It all starts with this interface, which will get injected into the ViewModels that want to navigate. And this is where developers tend to have different opinions. Some developers prefer to have a very slimmed-down interface only containing methods such as `GoTo(string name)`, `GoTo(string name, IDictionary<string, object> parameters)`, and `GoBack()`. This allows for a very generic interface and implementation that can easily be reused. I prefer a more per-app approach where I have methods such as `GoToOverview()`, `GoToDetail(string id)`, and others. The big advantage I find in this approach is the fact that when I want to navigate to a certain page, I know exactly what parameters are required to navigate to that page. I also find it easier to unit test and it makes it easier to implement app-specific edge cases. I've also seen and used generic implementations over the years, containing methods such as `GoTo<TViewModel>()` for example. It pretty much comes down to personal preference, use case requirements, and the specific needs of the project. I'll be demonstrating the approach I typically use and have used successfully over the years. Once you understand the main concept of a `NavigationService`, please use whatever approach you prefer! Let's create the `INavigationService` interface for our *Recipes!* app:

1. In the `Recipes.Client.Core` project, add a new folder by right-clicking the project in the **Solution Explorer**, selecting **Add | New Folder**, and naming the folder `Navigation`.

2. Next, right-click the newly created folder and select **Add | New Item…**. Select **Interface** from the list of templates and enter `INavigationService` as the name for the new interface.

3. As the *Recipes!* app doesn't have a lot of navigation going on, we can keep the interface pretty simple, as shown here:

```
public interface INavigationService
{
    Task GoToRecipeDetail(string recipeId);
```

```
        Task GoToRecipeRatingDetail(RecipeDetailDto
          recipe);
        Task GoBack();
    }
```

The interface currently holds three methods. The `GoToRecipeDetail` method should navigate to the detail page. It accepts a string parameter representing the ID of the recipe we want to load on that page. The `GoToRecipeRatingDetail` method should load the ratings overview page of the given `RecipeDetailDto` object. Finally, there is the `GoBack` method, which should allow us to programmatically navigate back into the app.

> **Note**
>
> This `INavigationService` interface holds no reference to .NET MAUI or Shell. It's just a contract for triggering navigations. The fact the interface is part of the `Recipes.Client.Core` project already gives away that it is framework agnostic. So, whether you want to leverage Shell or not, this interface probably won't change.

Now that we have this interface in place, let's see how we can implement a `NavigationService` interface that leverages Shell.

Creating and using a NavigationService

Because the implementation of `NavigationService` is specific to a framework, we are going to add it to the `Recipes.Mobile` project:

1. Let's add a `Navigation` folder to the **Recipes.Mobile** project by right-clicking the project in the **Solution Explorer** and selecting **Add | New Folder**.
2. Now, right-click the **Navigation** folder, select **Add | Class…**, and name it `NavigationService`.
3. This class needs to implement `INavigationService`, as shown here:

    ```
    public class NavigationService : INavigationService
    {
        ...
    }
    ```

4. Now, this is where Shell comes in! Earlier in this chapter, we saw how easy it is to use Shell for navigation: just call `Shell.Current.GoToAsync` and pass in the name of the page you want to navigate to. Let's add the following method, which wraps around this `GoToAsync` method, to our new `NavigationService` class:

    ```
    private async Task Navigate(string pageName,
        Dictionary<string, object> parameters)
    {
    ```

```
        await Shell.Current.GoToAsync(pageName);
    }
```

This `Navigate` method just calls the `GoToAsync` method of `Shell`, passing in the given `pageName` parameter. We'll look at the `parameters` parameter later.

5. What remains for `NavigationService` is implementing the `INavigationService` interface's methods, which is now pretty easy to do, as shown here:

```
public Task GoToRecipeDetail(string recipeId)
    => Navigate("RecipeDetail",
        new () { { "id", recipeId } });

public Task GoToRecipeRatingDetail(RecipeDetailDto
  recipe)
    =>  Navigate("RecipeRating",
        new () { { "recipe", recipe } });

public Task GoBack()
    =>  Shell.Current.GoToAsync("..");
```

The first two methods call the `Navigate` method we created earlier, passing in the name of the page that needs to be loaded, as well as a dictionary containing the `recipeId` parameter. The `GoBack` method calls the `GoToAsync` method of `Shell`, passing in "..", signaling we want to navigate up the navigation stack.

6. Next, we can go ahead and register this `NavigationService` in the DI container. Open `MauiProgram.cs` and add the following:

```
builder.Services.AddSingleton<INavigationService,
  NavigationService>();
```

And with that in place, it's time to update our ViewModels and add `INavigationService` as a dependency:

1. Head over to `RecipesOverviewViewModel` and update its constructor so that it accepts an `INavigationService`. As before, we should also create a `readonly` field to hold the injected value:

```
public class RecipesOverviewViewModel :
  ObservableObject
{
    private readonly INavigationService
      navigationService;
...
    public RecipesOverviewViewModel(
        IRecipeService recipeService,
```

```
        IFavoritesService favoritesService,
        INavigationService navigationService)
    {

        this.navigationService = navigationService;
    ...
    }
}
```

2. Further down this class, we can now update the `NavigateToSelectedDetail` method to the following:

```
private async Task NavigateToSelectedDetail()
{
    if (SelectedRecipe is not null)
    {
        await navigationService.GoToRecipeDetail
          (SelectedRecipe.Id);
        SelectedRecipe = null;
    }
}
```

3. In `RecipesOverviewPage.xaml`, the following can be removed:

```
SelectionChanged="CollectionView_SelectionChanged"
```

In the `RecipesOverviewPage.xaml.cs` file, the `CollectionView_SelectionChanged` method can be removed as well. Up until now, this is what triggered the navigation from the overview page to the detail page.

Now, we need to give `RecipeDetailViewModel` the same treatment: inject `INavigationService` and use it to execute navigation to the `RecipeRatingsDetailPage`:

1. As before, add an additional parameter to the class's constructor and keep a reference to it in a `readonly` field:

```
public partial class RecipeDetailViewModel :
  ObservableObject
{

    private readonly INavigationService
      navigationService;

    ...

    public RecipeDetailViewModel(
        IRecipeService recipeService,
        IFavoritesService favoritesService,
```

```
                IRatingsService ratingsService,
                INavigationService navigationService)
            {
                this.navigationService = navigationService;
                ...
            }
            ...
        }
```

2. The following snippet shows how we can update the `NavigateToRatings` method:

```
        private Task NavigateToRatings()
            => navigationService
                .GoToRecipeRatingDetail(recipeDto);
        }
```

This method gets called when `NavigateToRatingsCommand` is invoked.

3. Finally, we need to head over to the `RecipeDetailPage.xaml` file and update the `TapGestureRecognizer` on the `HorizontalStackLayout`, which shows the rating, to the following:

```
        <HorizontalStackLayout.GestureRecognizers>
            <TapGestureRecognizer Command="{Binding
                NavigateToRatingsCommand}" />
        </HorizontalStackLayout.GestureRecognizers>
```

Tapping this control will now trigger `NavigateToRatingsCommand`, which we just created, which will call the `NavigationService` to initiate navigation to the `RatingsDetailPage`.

4. The `Ratings_Tapped` method in the code-behind of `RecipeDetailPage` can be deleted as it is no longer of any use.

The pages, their ViewModels, and their routes, are already registered in `MauiProgram`'s `CreateMauiApp` method, as shown here:

```
...
builder.Services.AddTransient<RecipesOverviewPage>();
builder.Services.AddTransient<RecipesOverviewViewModel>();
builder.Services.AddTransient<RecipeDetailPage>();
builder.Services.AddTransient<RecipeDetailViewModel>();
builder.Services.AddTransient<RecipeRatingsDetailPage>();
builder.Services.AddTransient<RecipeRatingsDetailViewModel>
();
builder.Services.AddTransient<SettingsPage>();
builder.Services.AddTransient<SettingsViewModel>();
```

```
Routing.RegisterRoute("MainPage",
    typeof (RecipesOverviewPage));
Routing.RegisterRoute("RecipeDetail",
    typeof (RecipeDetailPage));
Routing.RegisterRoute("RecipeRating",
    typeof (RecipeRatingsDetailPage));
```

With all of these changes in place, we can now effectively navigate from one page to another. The injected instance of `NavigationService` in the ViewModels leverages Shell to navigate between pages. But there is still one thing missing: passing parameters from one page to another. Let's see how to add this!

Passing parameters

As mentioned earlier, although .NET MAUI Shell has a baked-in way of passing parameters, I'm not fond of using that in my ViewModels as it would require my ViewModels to depend on MAUI and Shell. Luckily, a solution to that is not that complex. Moreover, it fits nicely in the broader setup of our `NavigationService`, as we will discuss later in this chapter.

Let's introduce a new interface: `INavigationParameterReceiver`. This interface exposes one method called `OnNavigatedTo` that receives a dictionary of type `Dictionary<string, object>` as a single parameter. This interface can be implemented by ViewModels that want to accept navigation parameters. When navigated to a page, the `NavigationService` can check whether the `BindingContext` of the new page implements this interface and then call the `OnNavigatedTo` method, passing in the parameters. Let's see how we can implement this:

1. First, let's add the `INavigationParameterReceiver` interface. Right-click the `Navigation` folder in the `Recipes.Client.Core` project and select **Add | New Item...** in the list of templates. Then, select **Interface** and enter `INavigationParameterReceiver` as the name of the interface.

2. As we mentioned previously, this interface should expose the `OnNavigatedTo` method. Let's add this:

   ```
   public interface INavigationParameterReceiver
   {
       Task OnNavigatedTo(Dictionary<string, object>
           parameters);
   }
   ```

3. Head over to the `Navigate` method of the `NavigationService` class and update it to the following:

   ```
   private async Task Navigate(string pageName,
       Dictionary<string, object> parameters)
   ```

```
{
    await Shell.Current.GoToAsync(pageName);
    if (Shell.Current.CurrentPage.BindingContext
        is INavigationParameterReceiver receiver)
    {
        await receiver.OnNavigatedTo(parameters);
    }
}
```

The preceding code will pass the provided parameters to the ViewModel once Shell has navigated to the new page. We can retrieve the current page by calling `Shell.Current.CurrentPage`. Once we have the current page, we can check whether the page's `BindingContext` implements the `INavigationParameterReceiver` interface. If it does, we can call the `OnNavigatedTo` method to pass the provided parameters.

4. `RecipeDetailViewModel` can now implement the `INavigationParameterReceiver` interface, as shown here:

```
public partial class RecipeDetailViewModel :
  ObservableObject, INavigationParameterReceiver
{
...
    public Task OnNavigatedTo(
        Dictionary<string, object> parameters)
        => LoadRecipe(parameters["id"].ToString());
}
```

When the `OnNavigatedTo` method is called, the `id` parameter is retrieved from the dictionary and passed to the `LoadRecipe` method.

5. Up until now, the constructor of `RecipeDetailViewModel` called the `LoadRecipe` method with a hard-coded ID. This call can now be removed.

6. `RecipeRatingsDetailViewModel` also needs to be updated for it to be able to receive parameters. The following code block shows how it can implement `INavigationParameterReceiver`:

```
public class RecipeRatingsDetailViewModel :
  ObservableObject, INavigationParameterReceiver
{
...
    public Task OnNavigatedTo(
        Dictionary<string, object> parameters)
        => LoadData(parameters["recipe"]
            as RecipeDetailDto);
}
```

Please note that there has been a slight change in the `LoadData` method signature since the previous chapter. Rather than accepting a string, it now takes a `RecipeDetailDto` object as its parameter. This is an optimization strategy that aims to avoid over-fetching. When we navigate from `RecipeDetailPage`, we have already loaded the details of a recipe. Therefore, it's not needed to reload these same details when we move to `RecipeRatingDetailPage`. By passing in a `RecipeDetailDto`, we effectively utilize the data we've already fetched.

With `INavigationParameterReceiver` in place, we can effectively pass navigation parameters from one page to another. Let's see how we can extend our navigation infrastructure even more to allow us to hook into and manage important parts of the ViewModel's life cycle: specifically, the moments of navigation to and from a ViewModel.

Avoid "magic strings"

The code samples in this chapter use a lot of "magic strings": specific routes are registered for pages, parameters are passed using exact keys, and navigation requires correct input of these routes and keys. While this makes the code samples simple and clear, it's risky in practice. A single spelling error can lead to runtime errors that aren't immediately apparent. To prevent such issues, it's advisable to use string constants for route names and parameters stored in designated classes. We didn't follow this best practice here for the sake of simplicity, but keep it in mind when you're writing your code.

Hooking into navigation

Often, we want to hook into the navigation process to effectively manage ViewModel states during transitions. This allows us to handle setup and cleanup operations, as well as manage state changes when a ViewModel becomes active or inactive in the application. This strategy is particularly useful for tasks such as subscribing to or unsubscribing from services, loading or saving states, and initiating or canceling network requests.

For that purpose, let's introduce two new interfaces: `INavigatedFrom` and `INavigatedTo`. Just like `INavigationParameterReceiver`, ViewModels can choose to implement these interfaces if they want to react to certain navigation events. Let's see what they look like:

```
public interface INavigatedFrom
{
    Task OnNavigatedFrom(NavigationType navigationType);
}

public interface INavigatedTo
{
    Task OnNavigatedTo(NavigationType navigationType);
}
```

Both the `OnNavigatedFrom` and `OnNavigatedTo` methods accept one parameter of type `NavigationType`, which is an enum. This enum has the following implementation:

```
public enum NavigationType
{
    Unknown,
    Forward,
    Back,
    SectionChange,
}
```

With this `enum` type, we want to give context to the type of navigation that occurred. The `SectionChanged` value can be used when the user opens another tab for example or selects another item from `FlyoutMenu`. As you might expect, the `Forward` and `Back` values are used when navigating hierarchically from one page to another.

These methods and values of the `NavigationType` enum enable nuanced reactions to a wide variety of navigation scenarios. Let's consider some examples:

- When the `OnNavigatedFrom` method of a ViewModel is called with `Back` as the parameter, we can infer that we're navigating backward away from this ViewModel. In this context, you should consider stopping any ongoing tasks or network requests related to that ViewModel. The page no longer exists on the `NavigationStack`, so unsubscribing from messages or events may be wise, allowing any unneeded resources to be reclaimed via garbage collection.

- If the `OnNavigatedFrom` method is invoked with `Forward` as the parameter, we know the page and its ViewModel remain on the `NavigationStack`. Therefore, the user can easily navigate back to this page. In this situation, we may also want to clean up specific processes or running tasks, but it's important to ensure they can be quickly reinstated. When the user navigates back to the ViewModel, the `OnNavigatedTo` method will be triggered with `Back` as the parameter, signaling a need to restart previously paused processes.

Let's see how we can add these additional interfaces to our ViewModels and hook up the necessary code to call the methods these interfaces expose:

1. Add the interfaces (`INavigatedFrom` and `INavigatedTo`) and the `NavigationType` enum, as shown in the earlier code blocks, to the `Navigation` folder of the `Recipes.Client.Core` project.

2. When inheriting from the `AppShell` class, we can override the `OnNavigated` method. This method is invoked when a navigation is executed by the Shell framework. This is the ideal place to call into the methods of the interfaces that we've introduced. Go ahead to the `AppShell` class and override this method, as shown here:

```
protected override async void OnNavigated
    (ShellNavigatedEventArgs args)
```

```
{
    var navigationType =
        GetNavigationType(args.Source);

    base.OnNavigated(args);
}
```

The `ShellNavigatedEventArgs` parameter that's passed into this method has a `Source` property. This `Source` property is of type `ShellNavigationSource` and indicates how the navigation occurred: Push, Pop, PopToRoot, and so on. We want to translate this to the `NavigationType` enum we introduced earlier, allowing it to be framework-independent from here on.

3. To translate `ShellNavigationSource` to `NavigationType`, create the following `GetNavigationType` method in the `AppShell` class:

```
private NavigationType GetNavigationType
    (ShellNavigationSource source) =>
      source switch
      {
          ShellNavigationSource.Push or
          ShellNavigationSource.Insert
              => NavigationType.Forward,
          ShellNavigationSource.Pop or
          ShellNavigationSource.PopToRoot or
          ShellNavigationSource.Remove
              => NavigationType.Back,
          ShellNavigationSource.ShellItemChanged or
          ShellNavigationSource.ShellSectionChanged or
          ShellNavigationSource.ShellContentChanged
              => NavigationType.SectionChange,
          _ => NavigationType.Unknown
      };
```

4. Now, we need to find a way to access the ViewModels of the current and previous page, from within the overridden `OnNavigated` method. Once we get a hold of them, we can call `OnNavigatedFrom` and `OnNavigatedTo` when the ViewModel implements the corresponding interfaces. For that purpose, let's introduce a new interface: `INavigationInterceptor`. Here's what it looks like:

```
public interface INavigationInterceptor
{
    Task OnNavigatedTo(object bindingContext,
        NavigationType navigationType);
}
```

For now, this interface only exposes one method: OnNavigatedTo. It accepts a parameter of the object type that represents the BindingContext of the current page. It also accepts a parameter of type NavigationType.

5. Add this interface as a constructor parameter to AppShell and call its OnNavigatedTo method from the OnNavigated method of Shell, which we've just overridden. The following code block shows how to add this:

```
public partial class AppShell : Shell
{
    readonly INavigationInterceptor interceptor;

    public AppShell(INavigationInterceptor
      interceptor)
    {
        this.interceptor = interceptor;
        InitializeComponent();
    }

    protected override async void OnNavigated
      (ShellNavigatedEventArgs args)
    {
        var navigationType =
            GetNavigationType(args.Source);

        base.OnNavigated(args);

        await interceptor.OnNavigatedTo(
            CurrentPage?.BindingContext,
              navigationType);
    }
    ...
}
```

6. Because the AppShell class now lacks its default constructor and requires a parameter of type INavigationInterceptor, we need to update our code in the App.xaml.cs file, as shown here:

```
public App(INavigationInterceptor interceptor)
{
    ...
    MainPage = new AppShell(interceptor);
}
```

The constructor of the App class has been updated so that it accepts a parameter of the INavigationInterceptor type.

7. What remains is implementing INavigationInterceptor and registering it in the DI container. This interface can be implemented by our existing NavigationService. Let's see how:

```
Public class NavigationService : INavigationService,
  INavigationInterceptor
{
...
    WeakReference<INavigatedFrom> previousFrom;
    public async Task OnNavigatedTo(object
      bindingContext, NavigationType navigationType)
    {
        if(previousFrom is not null && previousFrom
            .TryGetTarget(out INavigatedFrom from))
        {
            await from.OnNavigatedFrom
              (navigationType);
        }

        if (bindingContext
            is INavigatedTo to)
        {
            await to.OnNavigatedTo(navigationType);
        }

        if(bindingContext is INavigatedFrom
          navigatedFrom)
            previousFrom = new (navigatedFrom);
        else
            previousFrom = null;
    }
}
```

A lot is going on here, so let's discuss what happens. Remember that the OnNavigatedTo method is called when we have already navigated. So, we must keep a reference to the previous page's BindingContext if we want to call a method on that later on. This reference is kept as WeakReference because we don't want this reference to cause the object not to be garbage collected and causing memory leaks. First, we check whether the previousFrom field is not null and whether it still holds a reference to a value that implements the INavigatedFrom interface. If we get back a value, the OnNavigatedFrom method is called on the BindingContext of the page we've navigated from.

Next, we check whether the passed-in `bindingContext` parameter implements the `INavigatedTo` interface. If that's the case, the `OnNavigatedTo` method is called.

In the end, we check whether the given `bindingContext` implements the `INavigatedFrom` interface. If so, we store it in the `previousFrom` field. If not, the `previousFrom` field is assigned null.

8.   It's important to notice that we've introduced state to our `NavigationService` by keeping track of the `BindingContext` of the previous page through the `previousFrom` field. As a result, `NavigationService` should be registered as Singleton so that throughout the app, the same instance of `NavigationService` is being used. Moreover, the `NavigationService` should be resolvable as `INavigationService` in the ViewModels and as `INavigationInterceptor` for instantiating the `AppShell` class. To accommodate this, we can update the registration, as follows:

```
builder.Services.AddSingleton<NavigationService>();

builder.Services.AddSingleton<INavigationService>(
    c => c.GetRequiredService<NavigationService>());

builder.Services.AddSingleton<INavigationInterceptor>(
    c => c.GetRequiredService<NavigationService>());
```

`NavigationService` itself is registered as a singleton. We also added singleton registrations for `INavigationService` and `INavigationIntercepter`, both returning the registration of `NavigationService`. This allows us to register one type for multiple interfaces, all pointing to the same instance.

Go ahead and implement the `INavigatedTo` and `INavigatedFrom` interfaces in some ViewModels. Add a breakpoint to the implemented methods, run the app, and see what happens by inspecting the parameter values. For our little *Recipes!* app, there is no need to add an implementation to said methods, but as managing ViewModel states during transitions is something developers tend to struggle with in larger apps, I wanted to share how I handle these kinds of scenarios.

Setting up navigation without .NET MAUI Shell

As I mentioned earlier, Shell is an opinionated way to create the structure of a .NET MAUI app. This might not work for you or your particular project. Not using Shell complicates the implementation of a `NavigationService` a lot, especially when your app has a complex structure such as tabs or a flyout menu. Let's focus on a simple hierarchical navigation and see what is needed to implement a `NavigationService` without relying on another framework.

Luckily, the interfaces we created earlier (INavigationService, INavigatedTo, INavigatedFrom, and INavigationParameterReceiver) are framework-independent and can still be used as the backbone of this implementation:

1. No Shell means no routing. However, I do like the concept of having keys associated with a particular view as it allows for a loosely coupled way of navigating. That's why we're creating a static Routes class in the Navigation folder of the Recipes.Mobile project, as shown here:

```
public static class Routes
{
    static Dictionary<string, Type> routes
        = new Dictionary<string, Type>();

    public static void Register<T>(string key)
        where T : Page
        => routes.Add(key, typeof(T));

    public static Type GetType(string key)
        => routes[key];
}
```

This class allows us to map keys to types that inherit from Page.

2. Next, instead of using the static Routing.RegisterRoute method to register routes in the MauiProgram class, we can now use our own Routes class, like this:

```
Routes.Register<RecipesOverviewPage>("MainPage");
Routes.Register<RecipeDetailPage>("RecipeDetail");
Routes.Register<RecipeRatingsDetailPage>
    ("RecipeRating");
```

The Routes.GetType method will allow us to retrieve a key's Type later.

3. Before diving into the implementation of the non-Shell NavigationService, let's add the following code to the INavigationService interface:

```
Task GoToOverview();
```

4. In App.xaml.cs, update the App's constructor as shown here:

```
public App(INavigationService navigationService)
{
    Application.Current.UserAppTheme = AppTheme.Light;
    InitializeComponent();

    MainPage = new NavigationPage();
```

```
navigationService.GoToOverview();
}
```

With the updated code, a class implementing the INavigationService interface will be injected. After assigning a new NavigationPage to the MainPage property, we can call the newly added GoToOverview method on the injected INavigationService for it to navigate to the OverviewPage.

5. Now, we can go and start implementing the non-Shell NavigationService. Create a new class called NonShellNavigationService in the Navigation folder of the Recipes.Mobile project. As you might expect, this class needs to implement the INavigationService interface, as shown here:

```
public class NonShellNavigationService :
INavigationService
```

6. The first thing we want to add is the Navigation property, which is of type Microsoft.Maui.Controls.INavigation. Through this property, we want to effectively route our navigation. The INavigation interface defines navigation-related methods and properties. Let's see what that property looks like:

```
protected INavigation Navigation
{
    get
    {
        INavigation? navigation =
            Application.Current?.MainPage?.Navigation;
        if (navigation is not null)
            return navigation;
        else
        {
            throw new Exception();
        }
    }
}
```

Through the static Current property of the Application class, we can get to the instance of the application, allowing us to access its MainPage property. The MainPage property, which is of type Page, has a Navigation property of type INavigation, which is exactly what we need.

7. Like on `NavigationService`, which used `Shell`, we also want to add a private `Navigate` method that other methods in this class can use. Here's what this looks like:

```
private async Task Navigate(string key,
    Dictionary<string, object> parameters)
{
    var type = Routes.GetType(key);
    var page = ServiceProvider.Current
        .GetService(type) as Page;

    page.NavigatedFrom += Page_NavigatedFrom;

    await Navigation.PushAsync(page);

    if (page.BindingContext
        is INavigationParameterReceiver receiver)
    {
        await receiver.OnNavigatedTo(parameters);
    }

    if (Navigation.NavigationStack.Count == 1)
    {
        if (page.BindingContext
        is INavigatedTo to)
            await to.OnNavigatedTo(NavigationType
                .SectionChange);
    }
}
```

With the given key, we can resolve the type we want to navigate to. Using the `ServiceProvider`, we can retrieve an instance of the given type, satisfying all of its dependencies. Next, an event handler for the resolved page's `NavigatedFrom` event is added before we access our `Navigation` property and push this page onto the navigation stack with the `PushAsync` method. This is what executes the effective navigation to the requested page. After the page is pushed, its `BindingContext` is checked to see whether it implements the `INavigationParameterReceiver` interface. If that's the case, its `OnNavigatedTo` method is called, passing in the navigation parameters. The final thing that happens in this method is that it checks whether the size of `NavigationStack` is 1. This means that we navigated to a page and that there's only one item on the stack, or in other words, this is the first page we're navigating to. If that is the case, we want to call the `OnNavigatedTo` method on the page's `BindingContext` if said `BindingContext` implements the `INavigatedTo` interface and pass in `NavigationType.SectionChange`. With this in place, the `OnNavigatedTo` method is called on initial navigation.

8. In the previous method, we added a handler to the page's `NavigatedFrom` event. The following code block shows its implementation:

```
private async void Page_NavigatedFrom(object sender,
  NavigatedFromEventArgs e)
{
    bool isForwardNavigation =
        Navigation.NavigationStack.Count > 1
        && Navigation.NavigationStack[^2] == sender;
    if (sender is Page page)
    {
        if (!isForwardNavigation)
        {
            page.NavigatedFrom -= Page_NavigatedFrom;
        }
        await OnNavigatedTo(Navigation.NavigationStack
          .Last().BindingContext,
            isForwardNavigation ? NavigationType
              .Forward : NavigationType.Back);
    }
}
```

As we are focusing on hierarchical navigation, navigation from a page can happen for two reasons: we're navigating forward to another page or we're navigating back to the previous page. This is what is determined at the beginning of this method. As this event is handled after the navigation occurred, we can determine forward navigation by looking at the second-to-last item on the `NavigationStack`: if that entry equals the sender, it means we navigated forward from the sender to another page. If it wasn't forward navigation, meaning we've navigated back from the page to the previous page, we need to remove the event handler from the page's `NavigateFrom` event. We need to do this so that the page has no references and can be garbage collected, avoiding potential memory leaks. Finally, we call the `OnNavigated` method, passing in the `BindingContext` of the current page (which is the last item in `NavigationStack`). Depending on whether it is forward navigation or not, we pass in `NavigationType.Forward` or `NavigationType.Backward`.

9. The `OnNavigatedTo` method that is being called in the previous code block might look familiar. That's because it is completely identical to the `OnNavigatedTo` method we had in our previous implementation of the `NavigationService`:

```
WeakReference<INavigatedFrom> previousFrom;
private async Task OnNavigatedTo(object
  bindingContext,
    NavigationType navigationType)
{
    if (previousFrom is not null && previousFrom
```

```
            .TryGetTarget(out INavigatedFrom from))
    {
        await from.OnNavigatedFrom(navigationType);
    }

    if (bindingContext
        is INavigatedTo to)
    {
        await to.OnNavigatedTo(navigationType);
    }

    if (bindingContext is INavigatedFrom
      navigatedFrom)
        previousFrom = new(navigatedFrom);
    else
        previousFrom = null;
}
```

10. Finally, let's have a look at the implemented methods of the `INavigationService` interface:

```
public Task GoBack()
    => Navigation.PopAsync();

public Task GoToRecipeDetail(string recipeId)
=> Navigate("RecipeDetail",
    new() { { "id", recipeId } });

public Task GoToRecipeRatingDetail(RecipeDetailDto
  recipe)
=> Navigate("RecipeRating",
    new() { { "recipe", recipe } });

public Task GoToOverview()
=> Navigate("Overview", null);
```

They also look very much like they did in the previous implementation because the `Navigate` method accepts the same parameters as in the previous sample.

11. The only thing that's left to do is register this `NonShellNavigationService`:

```
builder.Services.AddSingleton<INavigationService ,
  NonShellNavigationService>();
```

In this setup, we're not using `INavigationInterceptor`, so there's no need to register that.

With that in place, we've successfully created a simple `NavigationService` that does not leverage .NET MAUI Shell. Many of the core concepts were reused in this example, demonstrating that they are a good level of abstraction. That said, this implementation is very simple and naïve. It lacks the support for modal navigation and navigation inside tabs and doesn't have anything for handling a flyout menu. This example might give you some ideas and insights, but building a `NavigationService` from scratch, without leveraging Shell, is quite daunting. In many cases, when Shell is not an option for you or your specific project, I think relying on other third-party frameworks might be the way to go. Libraries such as *FreshMvvm* and especially *Prism Library* are worth checking out!

Before concluding this chapter, it's important to address a potentially unclear aspect: how can we effectively return a result from a child page to its parent?

Passing results back

In this chapter, we've explored passing parameters from one page to another during forward navigation. But what if we need to take an object, use it as a parameter to navigate to another page, manipulate it there, and then retrieve the updated result?

There are various approaches to achieve this, but the most straightforward method is to add a little extension to our navigation framework and allow parameters to be passed when navigating back. For example, on the `SettingsPage` of the *Recipes!* app, we show the user's current language. There's a button that navigates to the `PickLanguagePage`, where the user can select a different language. The current language needs to be passed from the `SettingsPage` to the `PickLanguage` page so that the latter can show the current value. When the user selects a new language, the `PickLanguagePage` should navigate back to the `SettingsPage` and pass the selected language as a parameter. *Figure 8.2* shows how this looks schematically:

Figure 8.2: Passing values back

Let's explore how to implement this scenario:

1. First, add the `GoBackAndReturn` method to `INavigationService`:

    ```
    Task GoBackAndReturn(Dictionary<string, object>
    parameters);
    ```

By introducing this method, we want to allow a ViewModel to trigger back navigation and pass parameters to the ViewModel of the previous page.

2. This method is very easy to implement in both `NavigationService` and `NonShellNavigationService`. First, let's take a look at the implementation in `NavigationService`:

```
public async Task GoBackAndReturn(
    Dictionary<string, object> parameters)
{
    await GoBack();

    if (Shell.Current.CurrentPage.BindingContext
        is INavigationParameterReceiver receiver)
    {
        await receiver.OnNavigatedTo(parameters);
    }
}
```

In this method, we first call the `GoBack` method. Once the back navigation is executed, we check whether `BindingContext` of the current page implements the `INavigationParameterReceiver` interface. If that's the case, we call its `OnNavigatedTo` method, passing in the parameters.

3. On `NonShellNavigationService`, this method looks very similar:

```
public async Task GoBackAndReturn(
    Dictionary<string, object> parameters)
{
    await GoBack();
    if(Navigation.NavigationStack.Last()
        .BindingContext
        is INavigationParameterReceiver receiver)
    {
        await receiver.OnNavigatedTo(parameters);
    }
}
```

We are doing the same thing here as in the `NavigationService`, except we're not using the Shell APIs to retrieve the current page. Instead, we're getting the current page from `NavigationStack`.

4. Next, let's add the method that should navigate to `PickLanguagePage`. Add the `GoToChooseLanguage` method to the `INavigationService` interface:

```
Task GoToChooseLanguage(string currentLanguage);
```

5. In both `ShellNavigationService` and `NonShellNavigationService`, implement the `GoToChooseLanguage` method, like this:

```
public Task GoToChooseLanguage(string currentLanguage)
    => Navigate("PickLanguagePage",
    new() { { "language", currentLanguage } });
```

The registration of `PickLanguagePage`, its route, and its ViewModel is already done in the `CreateMauiApp` method of the `MauiProgram` class, as shown here:

```
...
builder.Services.AddTransient<PickLanguagePage>();
builder.Services.AddTransient<PickLanguageViewModel>
    ();
...
Routing.RegisterRoute("PickLanguagePage",
    typeof (PickLanguagePage));
...
//Non-Shell
//Routes.Register<PickLanguagePage>
//("PickLanguagePage");
//Non-Shell
...
```

6. Update `PickLanguageViewModel` as it needs to implement the `INavigationParameterReceiver` interface and needs to get a dependency on the `INavigationService` interface. Here's how it looks:

```
public class PickLanguageViewModel : ObservableObject,
    INavigationParameterReceiver
{
    readonly INavigationService _navigationService;
    ...
    public PickLanguageViewModel(I
        NavigationService navigationService)
    {
        _navigationService = navigationService;
    }

    public async Task OnNavigatedTo(
        Dictionary<string, object> parameters)
    {
        _selectedLanguage =
            parameters["language"] as string;
        OnPropertyChanged(nameof(SelectedLanguage));
```

```
    }
}
```

Note that in the OnNavigatedTo method, we're assigning the _selectedLanguage field rather than the SelectedLanguage property. This is intentional because updating the property will immediately invoke the LanguagePicked method. We don't want to trigger this when we set the initial value of this property. Because of that, we need to call OnPropertyChanged manually, passing the name of the SelectedLanguage property.

7. The LanguagePicked method is called when the user selects a new language from the dropdown. This should be where we utilize our new GoBackAndReturn method to navigate back and return the selected language. Let's take a look:

```
private Task LanguagePicked()
{
    return _navigationService.GoBackAndReturn(
        new Dictionary<string, object> {
            { "SelectedLanguage", SelectedLanguage }
        });
}
```

8. Go to SettingsViewModel and make it implement the INavigationParameterReceiver interface:

```
public class SettingsViewModel :
    ObservableObject, INavigationParameterReceiver
```

Here's what the implemented OnNavigatedTo method looks like:

```
public Task OnNavigatedTo(
    Dictionary<string, object> parameters)
{
    if(parameters is not null &&
        parameters.ContainsKey("SelectedLanguage"))
    {
        CurrentLanguage =
            parameters["SelectedLanguage"] as string;
    }
    return Task.CompletedTask;
}
```

This OnNavigatedTo method will be called both when navigating "forward" to this ViewModel as well as when navigating "back" to it. The SelectedLanguage parameter that's sent by PickLanguageViewModel can be picked up here.

9. `SettingsPageViewModel` also needs to get the `INavigationService` interface injected. Here's how:

```
Readonly INavigationService _navigationService;
...
public SettingsViewModel(INavigationService service)
{
    _navigationService = service;
...
}
```

10. Finally, the `ChooseLanguage` method, which gets triggered when the user taps **Select Language**, needs to trigger navigation to `PickLanguagePage`, as shown here:

```
private async Task ChooseLanguage()
{
    await _navigationService
        .GoToChooseLanguage(CurrentLanguage);
}
```

With this update, moving data between pages is easier and more flexible. Our app now offers smoother user experiences, all thanks to our navigation framework.

Summary

The fundamental picture of navigation is quite straightforward: a navigation service, which is injected into ViewModels, is utilized to handle navigation. ViewModels can implement specific interfaces, enabling them to receive parameters or be notified about navigation activities, be it from or to them.

While the overall idea seems simple, the implementation can be complex, and this is where developers often become puzzled. Fortunately, .NET MAUI Shell streamlines the navigation process in complex UIs, providing a level of ease in the implementation. But as with anything, Shell's opinionated nature may not suit every application or developer's preferences. Therefore, we didn't stop at exploring Shell navigation but also dove into building a navigation service that is not reliant on Shell.

Toward the end of this chapter, we looked a bit deeper into passing parameters and results between pages. We demonstrated that by efficiently combining navigation services and ViewModel coordination, we can create a seamless user experience.

Navigating through the complexities of .NET MAUI navigation can be a challenge, but with a good understanding of the underlying principles and implementation details, we're better equipped to handle it. As we move forward, we'll explore handling user input and validation, diving into how to make our applications more interactive.

Further reading

To learn more about the topics that were covered in this chapter, take a look at the following resources:

- *.NET MAUI Shell*: `https://learn.microsoft.com/dotnet/maui/fundamentals/shell/`

- *Prism Library*: `https://prismlibrary.com/`

- *FreshMvvm*: `https://github.com/XAM-Consulting/FreshMvvm.Maui`

Handling User Input and Validation

User input forms the core of any interactive application. The way we manage this input, validate it, and respond to it directly influences the user experience of our application. While backend validation of user input is indispensable to maintaining data integrity, providing immediate and useful feedback on the frontend is equally important for a good user experience. In this chapter, we're going to dig into the crucial topic of managing user input and validation within a .NET MAUI application utilizing the MVVM design pattern.

This chapter is organized into the following sections:

- Implementing input validation on ViewModels
- Visualizing validation errors with triggers
- Prompts and alerts
- Confirming or canceling navigation

With the aim of making our application more dynamic and interactive, this chapter will focus on handling user input effectively – ensuring a smooth and seamless user experience. Let's dive in!

Technical requirements

In this chapter, we'll further enrich the *Recipes!* app with more features. To stay in sync, all the resources and code snippets are available on GitHub: `https://github.com/PacktPublishing/MVVM-pattern-.NET-MAUI/tree/main/Chapter09`. If you're looking to actively code alongside the chapter, it's best to kick off from the `Start` folder. The finalized version can be found in the `Finish` folder.

Implementing input validation on ViewModels

Input validation can be implemented in various ways and at different points within the life cycle of user interaction. It could happen as soon as a user changes a property, providing immediate feedback on the validity of the data entered. On the other hand, it might be performed only when the user initiates a certain action, such as clicking a button, thereby offering a more cumulative validation experience. Deciding on when and how to implement validation often depends on the specific requirements of your project. It's a balance between the need for immediate feedback and maintaining a smooth, uninterrupted user flow. There's no one-size-fits-all solution, and the strategy can vary based on the complexity of the data, the form of user interaction, and the overall design of your application.

Implementing validation on the frontend offers several advantages: it provides users with immediate feedback, ensuring a more responsive and intuitive experience. Moreover, by catching and rectifying issues right at the source, we can reduce the risk of sending incorrect data to the backend. However, it's essential to note that frontend validation should complement, not replace, backend validation. The ViewModel is the ideal location for frontend validation as it serves as our first line of defense against potential data inconsistencies or errors before they reach backend systems.

In this section, we'll be focusing on the implementation of input validation in ViewModels. We'll specifically delve into the use of the `ObservableValidator`, a powerful tool that's part of the MVVM Community Toolkit. This feature makes handling validation responses and displaying meaningful feedback to the user a breeze. Let's move on to explore the `ObservableValidator` in detail, and how it can enhance our approach to input validation.

Using the ObservableValidator

Validating user input is a cornerstone of robust applications. While it's entirely possible to write our own validation logic – checking properties as they update or when commands are invoked and then populating validation properties that can be bound to the UI – it often involves reinventing common patterns. Instead of starting from scratch, why not leverage existing tools designed for this exact purpose? One of the best practices for user input validation in the MVVM pattern is the use of the `ObservableValidator`. This class, a part of the MVVM Community Toolkit, inherits from the `ObservableObject` class and implements the `System.ComponentModel.INotifyDataErrorInfo` interface. This interface, which isn't specific to .NET MAUI, provides a robust system for reporting and managing errors in objects. It includes an `ErrorsChanged` event that you can subscribe to in order to be notified of changes in validation status and a `GetErrors` method that retrieves validation errors for a specified property or the entire object.

When a property value is updated, the `ObservableValidator` has the ability to automatically validate it using its `SetProperty` method overloads. It also offers `TrySetProperty` overloads that update a property value only when validation is successful and can return any generated errors. For scenarios that require manual control over validation, the `ObservableValidator` provides `ValidateProperty` and `ValidateAllProperties` methods, which can be used to manually trigger validation for specific properties or all properties, respectively. Additionally, it offers a `ClearAllErrors` method, ideal for resetting a form for reuse.

The flexibility of `ObservableValidator` extends to compatibility with the wide range of validation attributes provided by the `System.ComponentModel.DataAnnotations` namespace. This means you can leverage a set of common validation rules that are essential in many scenarios, such as `[Required]`, `[StringLength]`, `[Range]`, `[Compare]`, `[RegularExpression]`, and many more. These attributes allow for an expressive way to define validation rules directly on your ViewModel's properties, leading to a highly readable and maintainable code base. The `ObservableValidator` will pick up these attributes when validating a property, making the validation process seamless and straightforward. You can also define your own specific validation rules by encapsulating complex validation logic into dedicated validation methods or even in custom `ValidationAttribute` classes, which can be reused across your application.

Let's go ahead and see how we can add validation to `AddRatingViewModel` using the `ObservableValidator`.

Pre-configured validation rules

As previously mentioned, the `ObservableValidator` class leverages the power of the validation attributes found within the `System.ComponentModel.DataAnnotations` namespace. These attributes can be easily applied to your properties and the `ObservableValidator` class will use them for validating the corresponding property values. This relationship between the `ObservableValidator` and the `DataAnnotations` namespace offers an array of pre-configured validation rules, simplifying the process of implementing input validation in your ViewModel. Let's start by marking some properties as required:

1. Head over to `AddRatingViewModel` and instead of inheriting the `ObservableObject` class, make it inherit the `ObservableValidator` class, as shown here:

    ```
    public class AddRatingViewModel : ObservableValidator,
    INavigationParameterReceiver, INavigatedFrom
    ```

2. Next, we can add the `Required` attribute to the `EmailAddress`, `DisplayName`, and `RatingInput` properties:

    ```
    [Required]
    public string EmailAddress { … }

    [Required]
    public string DisplayName { ... }

    [Required]
    public string RatingInput { ... }
    ```

3. The `AddRatingViewModel` class contains a `SubmitCommand`, which calls the `OnSubmit` method. Let's update this method so it validates all the properties and writes the validation messages to the debug window:

```
private Task OnSubmit()
{
    ValidateAllProperties();

    if(HasErrors)
    {
        var errors = GetErrors();
        Debug.WriteLine( string.Join("\n",
            errors.Select(e => e.ErrorMessage)));
    }
    else
    {
        Debug.WriteLine("All OK");
    }
    return Task.CompletedTask;
}
```

With the `ValidateAllProperties` method, all properties of the current class are validated. After calling this method, we can check the `HasErrors` property to see if there are any violations. If so, the `GetErrors` method allows us to retrieve a list of `ValidationResult` objects. A `ValidationResult` object contains a list of member names affected by this result and an `ErrorMessage`.

Go ahead and debug the app! If you go to the `AddRatingPage`, leave everything empty and click the **Submit** button. You'll see the error messages printed in the **Output** window in Visual Studio.

> **Validating and errors**
>
> The `ValidateAllProperties` method validates all properties in the ViewModel. The `ValidateProperty` method, which accepts a value and property name will check whether the given value is valid for the given property. This is an easy way to validate a single property. The `HasErrors` property will be set according to the properties that have been validated. The same thing goes for the `GetErrors` method: it returns `ValidationResult` objects for the properties that have been validated. This method also has an overload where you can pass in a property name to get back the errors for that specific property. The `GetErrors` method won't do any validation by itself, trying to get the errors of a property that hasn't been validated will yield no results. The `ClearErrors` method allows for removing all errors or only those of a particular property when a property name is provided.

Let's enhance our validation by adding more validation rules and disabling the **Submit** button until all input is valid.

On the `EmailAddress` property, we should add an additional validation attribute. We can use the `RegularExpressionAttribute` to check whether a value matches a given regex expression:

1. The following snippet shows how we can add an extra validation attribute to the `EmailAddress` property using the `RegularExpressionAttribute` to ensure the value matches a specified regex pattern. This pattern will be used to validate whether the given value is an email address:

    ```
    public const string EmailValidationRegex =
     "^[aA-zZ0-9]+@[aA-zZ]+\.[aA-zZ]{2, 3}$";
    ...
    [Required]
    [RegularExpression(EmailValidationRegex)]
    public string EmailAddress { ... }
    ```

2. To ensure the `DisplayName` property has a minimum and maximum length, we can use the `MinLength` and `MaxLength` attributes. Let's add them:

    ```
    public const int DisplayNameMinLength = 5;
    public const int DisplayNameMaxLength = 25;

    ...
    [Required]
    [MinLength(DisplayNameMinLength)]
    [MaxLength(DisplayNameMaxLength)]
    public string DisplayName { ... }
    ```

3. To constrain the `RatingInput` property to a value between 0 and 4 with zero or one decimal point, we can use the `RangeAttribute` for the range constraint and `RegularExpressionAttribute` for the decimal limit:

    ```
    public const string RangeDecimalRegex = @"^\d+(\.\d{1,1})?$";
    public const double RatingMinVal = 0d;
    public const double RatingMaxVal = 4d;

    ...
    [Required]
    [RegularExpression(RangeDecimalRegex)]
    [Range(RatingMinVal, RatingMaxVal)]
    public string RatingInput { ... }
    ```

4. And finally, we want to validate each property when its value gets updated. The `ObservableValidator` class has an overloaded `SetProperty` method, which accepts a `bool` value indicating whether the provided value needs to be validated. This is how it looks for the `EmailAddress` property:

    ```
    SetProperty(ref _emailAddress, value, true);
    ```

We can go ahead and update the `DisplayName`, `RatingInput`, and `Review` properties on this ViewModel as well, to use this overloaded `SetProperty` method, passing in `true` in order to trigger validation when the value is set. If we were to pass in `false` as the last parameter, the validation would not be triggered.

> **SetProperty and TrySetProperty**
>
> Note that this overloaded `SetProperty` will set the value of the backing field and trigger the `PropertyChanged` event, no matter whether the provided value is valid or not. There is also a `TrySetProperty` on the `ObservableValidator` class, which will not set the value on the property when it is invalid. It returns a `bool` value indicating whether the value was set or not and has an `out` parameter, which returns a collection of errors.

5. The `AddRatingViewModel` class contains a command `SubmitCommand`. This command should only be executable when the provided values of the properties are considered valid. For that, we can point the `canExecute` function of the `SubmitCommand` to the `HasErrors` property, as shown here:

    ```
    SubmitCommand =
        new AsyncRelayCommand(OnSubmit, () => !HasErrors);
    ```

6. Finally, we need a place to call the `NotifyCanExecuteChanged` method of the `SubmitCommand`, so the `canExecute` function can be re-evaluated. The `ObservableValidator` class exposes an event called `ErrorsChanged`, which gets triggered whenever there is a change in validation errors. That's the ideal moment to call the `NotifyCanExecuteChanged` method of the `SubmitCommand`. Let's subscribe to this event and implement this:

    ```
    public AddRatingViewModel(
        INavigationService navigationService)
    {
        ...

        ErrorsChanged += AddRatingViewModel_ErrorsChanged;
    }

    private void AddRatingViewModel_ErrorsChanged(
        object? sender, DataErrorsChangedEventArgs e)
    {
        SubmitCommand.NotifyCanExecuteChanged();
    }
    ```

Now, if you run the app and navigate to `AddRatingPage`, you'll find the **Submit** button is initially disabled. It will only be enabled when all required fields have valid input. This is all thanks to the automatic evaluation of property values when they change and the result of the `CanExecute` method of `SubmitCommand` being based on the absence of validation errors. *Figure 9.1* shows what this looks like:

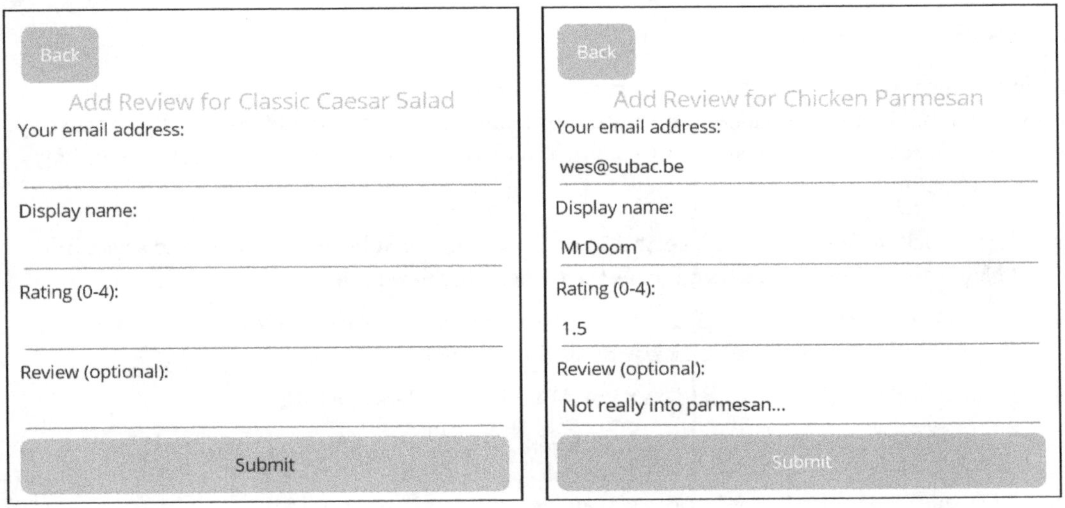

Figure 9.1: Enabled Submit button when there are no errors (right)

The pre-configured validation attributes we've discussed so far can simplify the process of adding validation to your ViewModels. However, there will be scenarios where these built-in rules don't meet your specific requirements, and you'll need to create your own custom validation logic. Let's explore how to implement that next.

Creating custom validation rules

Often, the pre-configured validation rules just won't cut it and you'll need to add your own custom validation logic. When working with the `ObservableValidator` class, there are two options for implementing custom validation rules:

- The first approach involves creating a completely new validation attribute by extending the base `ValidationAttribute` class. This allows you to encapsulate your own validation logic in a reusable component, keeping your ViewModel cleaner and more focused on its primary responsibility. You can then apply this custom attribute to any property in the same way you'd apply the built-in attributes.

- The second option involves using the `CustomValidation` attribute, which enables you to specify a static method to handle the validation right at the point of declaration. This method allows for more localized, context-specific validation scenarios where creating a separate attribute class might be overkill.

Let's examine both methods in more detail to see how they can be used to address custom validation requirements.

Create a custom attribute

Let's add a validation rule that we want to use on the `Review` property. Although a review is optional, if provided, it must fall within a certain length range. Since such a rule could potentially be reused across different scenarios, it makes sense to put this validation logic in a custom attribute. Here's how we can go about it:

1. Right-click the `Recipes.Client.Core` project in the **Solution Explorer** and select **Add | New Folder**. Enter `Validation` as the name of the new folder.

2. Right-click the `Validation` folder, select **Add | Class...**, and enter `EmptyOrWithinRangeAttribute` as the class name.

3. Make this class inherit the `ValidationAttribute` class like this:

    ```
    public class EmptyOrWithinRangeAttribute : ValidationAttribute
    ```

4. Next, add two properties, `MinLength` and `MaxLength`, of type `int`:

    ```
    public int MinLength { get; set; }
    public int MaxLength { get; set; }
    ```

    These properties allow an even wider usage of this attribute. They allow developers to customize the length constraints each time they apply this attribute to a property. This way, the exact minimum and maximum lengths required for validation can be tailored to fit each individual property's needs as the developer can declare the desired minimum and maximum length.

5. The next step is to override the `IsValid` method. This method gets invoked when the validation process begins for the property where the attribute is applied. Let's see how we can implement it:

    ```
    protected override ValidationResult IsValid(object? value,
    ValidationContext validationContext)
    {
        if (value is string valueAsString && (
            string.IsNullOrEmpty(valueAsString) ||
            (valueAsString.Length >= MinLength
            && valueAsString.Length <= MaxLength)))
        {
            return ValidationResult.Success;
        }
        else
        {
            return new ValidationResult($"The value should be
    between {MinLength} and {MaxLength} characters long, or
    empty.");
    ```

```
        }
    }
```

The value parameter, of type `object`, represents the property value that needs to be validated. The second parameter, of type `ValidationContext`, provides further context, including the instance of the object being validated and the property. Returning `ValidationResult.Success` indicates that the given value is valid, else we return a descriptive error message.

6. Finally, we can use this attribute on the `Review` property of the `AddRatingViewModel` like this:

```
[EmptyOrWithinRange(MinLength = 10, MaxLength = 250)]
public string Review
{
    get => _review;
    set => SetProperty(ref _review, value, true);
}
```

With our custom validation attribute in place, the `Review` property can be validated so that it is empty or falls within the given length range. This attribute can easily be reused across the entire app.

Using the CustomValidation attribute

The **CustomValidation** attribute is typically used for very specific validation that is reused less throughout the app. This attribute points to a static method with a specific signature: it must return a `ValidationResult` object and take a parameter matching the type of the property being validated, along with a `ValidationContext` object. This is similar to the `IsValid` method we override when implementing our own `ValidationAttribute`. Let's add an additional validation to the `Review` property so that it is required when the given rating is less than or equal to 2:

1. In the `AddRatingViewModel`, add a new static method called `ValidateReview` with the following implementation:

```
public static ValidationResult ValidateReview(string review,
ValidationContext context)
{
    AddRatingViewModel instance =
        (AddRatingViewModel)context.ObjectInstance;

    if (double.TryParse(instance.RatingInput,
        out var rating))
    {
        if (rating <= 2 &&
            string.IsNullOrEmpty(review))
        {
```

```
            return new("A review is mandatory when rating the
    recipe 2 or less.");
        }
    }
    return ValidationResult.Success;
}
```

This method accepts a parameter of type `string`, matching the type of the property we want to validate. The second parameter is of type `ValidationContext`, which we can use to access the instance of the object the property is defined on. This allows us to access other properties on the object that is being validated, such as the `RatingInput` property in our case. When we can parse the `RatingInput` value to `double`, we can check whether it is less than or equal to 2. If that is the case and the given review value is empty, we return a validation error. Otherwise, `Success` is returned.

2. Now, we need to add a `CustomValidation` attribute to the `Review` property and point this to the static `ValidateReview` method that we just created. Let's see how that's done:

```
[CustomValidation(
    typeof(AddRatingViewModel),
    nameof(ValidateReview))]
[EmptyOrWithinRange(MinLength = 2, MaxLength = 250)]
public string Review
{
    get => _review;
    set => SetProperty(ref _review, value, true);
}
```

The first parameter the `CustomValidation` attribute requires is the type the static validation method is defined on. In our case, we defined it on `AddRatingViewModel` itself, so we pass that in as the type. This means it is possible to define your validation methods elsewhere, bundling them in separate classes, for example. The second parameter is the name of the validation method. We use the `nameof` keyword to avoid magic strings and add compile-time error checking.

3. As the validation of the `Review` property is also dependent on the entered `RatingInput` property, we must make sure the `Review` property is also validated when the `RatingInput` property changes. As the following snippet shows, we can easily do this by calling the `ValidateProperty` method for the `Review` property when the value on the `RatingInput` property is updated:

```
[Required]
[RegularExpression(RangeDecimalRegex)]
[Range(RatingMinVal, RatingMaxVal)]
public string RatingInput
{
```

```
    get => _ratingInput;
    set
    {
        SetProperty(ref _ratingInput, value, true);
        ValidateProperty(Review, nameof(Review));
    }
}
```

That's it! That is all that's needed to add custom validation, leveraging the `CustomValidation` attribute. This approach typically is for validation checking that is to be reused on different objects less. In this particular case, we access the `ValidationContext ObjectInstance` and cast it to a certain type, which naturally makes it unusable on different types.

Run your application and notice how the **Submit** button gets disabled when a rating of less than 3 is given and the review is left empty. Our validation logic is operating as expected! However, the current implementation lacks user-friendliness because it does not provide any feedback regarding invalid entries. Let's see how to display these validation errors to the user.

Showing errors onscreen

There are basically two approaches to show validation errors to the user. The first method usually provides an overview of all issues at once, typically at the top or bottom of a form. The second approach gives feedback right on the input field where the error occurred. This can often help users to correct the error more directly and quickly. Both methods have their uses and are often combined in applications for the best user experience.

Showing all errors

While `ObservableValidator` doesn't provide a property that lists all validation errors directly, it does offer a `GetErrors` method to fetch them. Sadly, data binding to methods isn't possible. To align better with MVVM practices and facilitate data binding, it would be beneficial to introduce an `Errors` property of type `ObservableCollection<ValidationResult>`. This way, we can bind to our validation errors in the UI.

Let's see how we can achieve this:

1. Add a property called `Errors` of type `ObservableCollection<ValidationResult>` to `AddRatingViewModel`:

   ```
   public ObservableCollection<ValidationResult> Errors { get; } =
   new();
   ```

2. The `AddRatingViewModel_ErrorsChanged` method on `AddRatingViewModel` is invoked when the `ErrorsChanged` event of `ObservableValidator` is triggered. Currently, this calls the `NotifyCanExecuteChanged` method on the `SubmitCommand`,

but let's update it so that it also (re-)populates the `Errors` collection that we just defined. The following code block shows how we can do this:

```
private void AddRatingViewModel_ErrorsChanged(object? sender,
DataErrorsChangedEventArgs e)
{
    Errors.Clear();
    GetErrors().ToList().ForEach(Errors.Add);
    SubmitCommand.NotifyCanExecuteChanged();
}
```

The preceding code first clears the `Errors` collection. Next, it calls the `GetErrors` method of `ObservableValidator` to get all the errors. With the `ForEach` method, we can loop over all the items and call the `Errors.Add` method to add the current item to the `Errors` collection.

3. The preceding code should add all the current validation errors to the `Errors` property. The only thing that is left to do is to bind this collection to our view, as shown here:

```
<VerticalStackLayout BindableLayout.ItemsSource="{Binding
Errors}">
    <BindableLayout.ItemTemplate>
        <DataTemplate x:DataType="annotations:ValidationResult">
            <Label Text="{Binding ErrorMessage}"
                FontSize="12" TextColor="Red"/>
        </DataTemplate>
    </BindableLayout.ItemTemplate>
</VerticalStackLayout>
```

At this point, you should find the XAML code familiar and straightforward: the `Errors` collection is bound to the `BindableLayout ItemsSource` property on a `VerticalStackLayout`. The `ItemTemplate` stipulates that for each item we want to render a `Label` that shows its `ErrorMessage` property. The `DataType` of the `DataTemplate` is a `ValidationResult`. The `annotations` XML namespace is defined at the top of the page: `xmlns:annotations="clr-namespace:System.ComponentModel.DataAnnotations;assembly=System.ComponentModel.DataAnnotations"`.

The preceding code will result in showing a list of all the validation errors onscreen. Run the application and you should see the validation errors appearing and disappearing as you enter values, as *Figure 9.2* demonstrates.

Figure 9.2: Showing up-to-date validation errors

Although this already should improve the user experience a lot, we can take this a step further. Let's enhance the UX by showing error messages inline, directly adjacent to the relevant input fields.

Showing inline errors

The main challenge when it comes to displaying individual errors is developing a mechanism that enables us to retrieve and display validation errors related to a single property, rather than all validation errors at once. There is a very simple approach to this: for each property, expose an additional property containing a collection of errors for that property. Take a look at the following example:

```
public List<ValidationResult> EmailValidationErrors
{
    get => GetErrors(nameof(EmailAddress)).ToList();
}
```

This `EmailValidationErrors` property gives a list of only the validation errors related to the `EmailAddress` property. This `EmailValidationErrors` property can be bound to the UI so that we can display the errors only relevant to the `EmailAddress` property on the screen. In order to keep this bound list up-to-date, we need to make sure we trigger the `PropertyChanged` event of the `EmailValidationErrors` property each time the `EmailAddress` property is updated, as shown here:

```
public string EmailAddress
{
```

```
    get => _emailAddress;
    set
    {
        SetProperty(ref _emailAddress, value, true);
        OnPropertyChanged(nameof(EmailValidationErrors));
    }
}
```

By creating a dedicated property for each input's validation errors and ensuring it's updated whenever the input value changes, we can effectively isolate and display validation errors for individual fields. However, it does come with a caveat: for forms with numerous input fields, this method can be somewhat labor-intensive and repetitive. Let me show you an alternative that automates this process and saves us some manual work. The end result will be that we are going to bind to a particular property called ErrorExposer. Then, using its **indexer**, we will specify which property's validation errors we want to retrieve and display, something like this:

```
<VerticalStackLayout BindableLayout.ItemsSource="{Binding
ErrorExposer[EmailAddress]}">
```

Let's see how we can implement this mechanism:

1. In the **Solution Explorer**, right-click the Validation folder that we created earlier, select **Add | Class…**, and enter ValidationErrorExposer as the class name.

2. The ValidationErrorExposer class should implement two interfaces: INotifyPropertyChanged and IDisposable, as shown in the following snippet:

    ```
    public class ValidationErrorExposer : INotifyPropertyChanged,
    IDisposable
    {
        public event PropertyChangedEventHandler? PropertyChanged;

        public void Dispose()
        {
        }
    }
    ```

3. Next, let's introduce a readonly field validator of type ObservableValidator. The value for this field should be passed in through the class constructor, as shown here:

    ```
    readonly ObservableValidator validator;

    public ValidationErrorExposer(
            ObservableValidator observableValidator)
    {
    ```

```
        validator = observableValidator;
    }
```

The passed-in `observableValidator` is the instance that we want to automatically expose per-property validation errors.

4. It's time to add the `ValidationErrorExposer` indexer. An indexer in .NET allows an instance of a class to be accessed using an index, similar to an array or dictionary. This index can be of any type, such as a string or an int, and it lets you retrieve or set values without explicitly calling a method or property. In this case, we set the index to be a string as it represents the name of the property we want to get the validation errors of. This is how we can do this:

```
public List<ValidationResult> this[string property]
    => validator.GetErrors(property).ToList();
```

The indexer on `ValidationErrorExposer` accepts a string value as the index and returns a list of `ValidationResult` objects. This value, which represents the name of the property we want to get the errors of, is passed into the `ObservableValidator` `GetErrors` method. The result is returned as a `List`.

5. In the constructor of the `ValidationErrorExposer` class, we should also subscribe to the `ErrorsChanged` event of the `ObservableValidator` that is being passed in, like this:

```
public ValidationErrorExposer(ObservableValidator
observableValidator)
{
    validator = observableValidator;
    validator.ErrorsChanged +=
ObservableValidator_ErrorsChanged;
}

private void ObservableValidator_ErrorsChanged(object? sender,
DataErrorsChangedEventArgs e)
    => PropertyChanged?.Invoke(this, new
PropertyChangedEventArgs($"Item[{e.PropertyName}]"));
```

While it might seem like there's some magic happening, the concept is fairly straightforward. In .NET MAUI, if an object has an indexer, you can bind to that indexer property as demonstrated by `{Binding ErrorExposer[EmailAddress]}`, where `ErrorExposer` is an instance of a type that contains an indexer. To notify the UI of an updated value, we can invoke the `PropertyChanged` event from the `ErrorExposer` and pass `Item[EmailAddress]` as the property name. Doing so will prompt all bindings tied to `ErrorExposer[EmailAddress]` to re-evaluate. Alternatively, invoking the `PropertyChanged` event with `PropertyChangedEventArgs` having `Item` as the property name will trigger a re-evaluation of all bindings associated with the indexer.

6. Finally, in `ValidationErrorExposer`, we should update the `Dispose` method to the following:

```
public void Dispose()
    => _validator.ErrorsChanged -=
       ObservableValidator_ErrorsChanged;
```

Because we have subscribed to the `ObservableValidator ErrorsChanged` method, we need to provide a mechanism to unhook from this event, preventing any memory leaks. For that, we can use the `Dispose` method.

7. Let's head back to `AddRatingViewModel` and add a property of type `ValidationErrorExposer`, as shown here:

```
public ValidationErrorExposer ErrorExposer { get; }
```

8. In the constructor of `AddRatingViewModel`, assign a new instance to this property:

```
public AddRatingViewModel(INavigationService navigationService)
{
...

    ErrorExposer = new (this);
...
}
```

We pass in `this` to the constructor of the `ValidationErrorExposer` class because it is the instance of the `AddRatingViewModel` itself that inherits from `ObservableValidator` and thus holds all validation errors.

9. In XAML, we can now bind to a list of validation errors, specific to a particular property using the indexer on the `ValidationErrorExposer` class. This allows us to show these errors close to the relevant input fields themselves, as shown in the following snippet:

```
<Editor Text="{Binding Review, Mode=TwoWay}" />
<VerticalStackLayout BindableLayout.ItemsSource="{Binding
ErrorExposer[Review]}">
    <BindableLayout.ItemTemplate>
        ...
    </BindableLayout.ItemTemplate>
</VerticalStackLayout>
```

`ValidationErrorExposer` allows us to easily get validation errors from a specific property, without needing to do any manual work: once this is in place, we can bind to the errors of any specific property using its indexer property.

Displaying validation errors near user input further improves the user experience. Let's explore how to visually indicate the validity of entered values, improving the experience even more.

Visualizing validation errors with triggers

Triggers help us customize how UI elements work and look without building new controls from scratch.

While there are different types of triggers, we'll focus on **data triggers**. These kick in when a property (on the ViewModel) changes, allowing us to adjust elements of a UI control dynamically, based on what the user does.

Types of triggers

There are different types of triggers in .NET MAUI: PropertyTrigger, DataTrigger, EventTrigger, and so on… They all allow you to change the appearance of a UI control declaratively in XAML based upon a trigger. They only differ in what triggers the change: a property value, a bound value, an event. You can learn more about them at `https://learn.microsoft.com/dotnet/maui/fundamentals/triggers`.

In essence, a DataTrigger provides a way to declaratively set up UI changes in response to data changes, directly within your XAML, without having to write procedural code in your code-behind, a custom ValueConverter, or ViewModel.

DataTriggers are a fairly easy-to-understand concept. So, let's just dive in and add a visual indicator right next to the different `Entry` controls, indicating with a symbol and a particular color whether the entered value is valid or not, as *Figure 9.3* shows:

Figure 9.3: Indicating input is valid (right) or not (left)

What about ValueConverters?

In *Chapter 4, Databinding in .NET MAUI*, we discussed the usage of value converters. The things that you can do with DataTriggers are also achievable with value converters and vice versa. But, with a DataTrigger, it is very easy to implement these visual effects declaratively, without a single line of C# code, also making the XAML more readable.

Let's have a look at how we can implement these visual cues using DataTriggers:

1. First, add a `Grid` around the `Entry` for the `EmailAddress` property:

```
<Grid ColumnDefinitions="*, Auto" HeightRequest="45">
    <Entry
        Keyboard="Email"
        Text="{Binding EmailAddress, Mode=TwoWay}"
```

```
                    VerticalOptions="End" />
    </Grid>
```

This `Grid` has two columns, with the `Entry` in the first one, and we will be adding the validity indicator in the second one.

2. Inside this `Grid`, below the `Entry`, add the following `Label`, which will serve as the validity indicator:

```
<Label
    Grid.Column="1" FontFamily="MaterialIconsRegular"
    FontSize="20" Text="&#xe000;" TextColor="Red"
    VerticalOptions="Center">
</Label>
```

By default, this `Label` shows the invalid state: red text and an exclamation mark icon.

3. Now, we can add the `DataTrigger` and define that the `Label` needs to show a blue checkmark when the provided email address is valid. The following snippet shows how we can do that:

```
<Label ... >
    <Label.Triggers>
        <DataTrigger
            TargetType="Label"
            Binding="{Binding ErrorExposer[EmailAddress].Count}"
            Value="0">
            <Setter Property="Text"
                Value="&#xe86c;" />
            <Setter Property="TextColor"
                Value="Blue" />
        </DataTrigger>
    </Label.Triggers>
</Label>
```

A `DataTrigger` has a `Binding` property that allows us to bind to a certain value. In this case, we bind to the `Count` property of the list of validation errors related to the `EmailAddress` property. With the `Value` property, we can set a condition for this bound property. We set the value to `"0"`, meaning that there are no validation errors associated with the `EmailAddress` property. When the value of the property meets this condition, the trigger activates. Once activated, the trigger can change one or more properties of the UI control. In this particular case, we're updating the `Text` and `TextColor` properties by specifying a `Setter` for these properties and providing a certain `Value`.

As said, this can also be achieved with custom `ValueConverters`, but this declarative way of defining it in XAML is very readable, maintainable, and easy to use.

> **Behaviors**
>
> Another way to give the user visual cues about the validity of entered values is by using **Behaviors**. Behaviors are like little plugins you can add to your UI elements, enhancing their default behavior without having to subclass them. They're particularly useful because they encapsulate logic in reusable pieces, allowing developers to apply the same functionality across different controls. For example, a Behavior might allow a text input field to only accept numerical input or change its color when certain conditions are met. The .NET MAUI Community Toolkit comes with a set of ready-to-use Behaviors! You can learn more about them at `https://learn. microsoft.com/dotnet/maui/fundamentals/behaviors`.

In the next section, we'll have a look at how to display prompts and alerts, essential parts for providing user feedback and gathering input.

Prompts and alerts

Direct feedback and clear communication are paramount when it comes to a solid user experience. As users navigate your application and interact with various inputs, there are moments where a subtle notification or a direct prompt can make all the difference. Prompts and alerts serve as these essential tools, guiding users through their journey, ensuring they're informed and make intentional decisions.

Showing prompts and alerts is something that is platform-specific. Luckily .NET MAUI has got us covered as they provide simple and intuitive APIs for this. On the other hand, in an MVVM scenario, displaying a prompt or alert is mostly triggered from a ViewModel, which should be framework-independent. The solution, of course, is creating an interface for this functionality that a ViewModel can talk to. On the MAUI side of things, we can easily implement this interface and register it in our DI container so the implementation gets injected into the ViewModels. Let's go ahead and set this up!

1. To begin with, let's add an interface that defines some methods for displaying prompts and alerts. Right-click the `Recipes.Client.Core` project in the **Solution Explorer** and select **Add | New Folder**. Give it the name `Services`.

2. Add a new interface to this folder and call it `IDialogService`.

3. The methods defined in an `IDialogService` can defer from project to project. The following code block shows some method declarations that are often present in an `IDialogService` interface:

```
public interface IDialogService
{
    Task Notify(string title, string message,
        string buttonText = "OK");
    Task<bool> AskYesNo(string title, string message,
        string trueButtonText = "Yes",
        string falseButtonText = "No");
    Task<string?> Ask(string title, string message,
```

```
        string acceptButtonText = "OK",
        string cancelButtonText = "Cancel");
}
```

As said, depending on your specific use case, this interface might be extended with some other concrete method definitions.

4. Next, we need to add an implementation for this interface. Add a new folder called `Services` to the `Recipes.Mobile` project.

5. Right-click the new `Services` folder and select **Add | Class...**. Enter `DialogService` as the name of the new class and add the following code:

```
public class DialogService : IDialogService
{
    public Task Notify(string title, string message,
        string buttonText = "OK")
    => Application.Current.MainPage
        .DisplayAlert(title, message, buttonText);

    public Task<bool> AskYesNo(string title,
        string message,
        string trueButtonText = "Yes",
        string falseButtonText = "No")
    => Application.Current.MainPage
        .DisplayAlert(title, message,
            trueButtonText, falseButtonText);

    public Task<string?> Ask(string title,
        string message,
        string acceptButtonText = "OK",
        string cancelButtonText = "Cancel")
    => Application.Current.MainPage
        .DisplayPromptAsync(title, message,
            acceptButtonText, cancelButtonText);
}
```

In .NET MAUI, the `Page` class provides various methods for displaying alerts, prompts, and action sheets. Within the `DialogService` class, we can access these methods by referencing `MainPage` through the static `Current` property of the `Application` class.

6. The next thing we need to do is register `DialogService` in our DI container. Move over to `MauiProgram.cs` and add the following:

```
builder.Services.AddSingleton<IDialogService, DialogService>();
```

7. Finally, we can add the `IDialogService` as a dependency to our ViewModels. Let's add it to `AddRatingViewModel` as shown here:

```
readonly IDialogService dialogService;
...
public AddRatingViewModel(INavigationService navigationSerivce,
IDialogService dialogService)
{
...
    this.dialogService = dialogService;
...
}
```

8. Move over to the `OnSubmit` method and update it as shown here:

```
private async Task OnSubmit()
{
    var result = await _dialogService.AskYesNo(
        "Are you sure?",
        "Are you sure you want to add this rating?");
    if (result)
    {
        //ToDo: Submit data
        await _dialogService.Notify("Rating sent",
            "Thank you for your feedback!");
        GoBackCommand.Execute(null);
    }
}
```

In the updated `OnSubmit` method, we first ask for confirmation. If the user confirms, an alert will be shown saying the rating was sent (*Figure 9.3*). After the user closes the alert, `GoBackCommand` is invoked, closing the `AddRatingPage`.

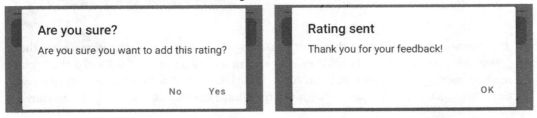

Figure 9.3: Showing alerts and prompts

With the `IDialogService` and its `DialogService` implementation in place, we have laid the foundation for basic popup interactions in our application. Next, we'll explore how to leverage this to prompt users for confirmation when they attempt to leave a specific page.

Confirming or canceling navigation

As users interact with our application, there may be moments when they're about to navigate away from a page containing unsaved changes or important input. To prevent potential data loss, it's essential to prompt for confirmation before allowing such navigation. Let's see how we could build this by leveraging the `NavigationService` that we built in the previous chapter:

1. Let's start by adding the following interface called `INavigatable` to the `Navigation` folder of the `Recipes.Client.Core` project:

```
public interface INavigatable
{
    Task<bool> CanNavigateFrom(NavigationType navigationType);
}
```

ViewModels that want to control whether the user is able to navigate can implement this interface. This is analogous to the other interfaces we introduced in the context of navigation, such as the `INavigatedFrom`, `INavigatedTo`, and `INavigationParameterReceiver` interfaces.

2. Extend the `INavigationInterceptor` interface with the following method definition:

```
Task<bool> CanNavigate(object bindingContext, NavigationType type);
```

3. The `NavigationService` class, which implements the `INavigationInterceptor` interface, now needs to implement this method. Here's what it looks like:

```
public Task<bool> CanNavigate(object bindingContext,
NavigationType type)
{
    if(bindingContext is INavigatable navigatable)
        return navigatable.CanNavigateFrom(type);

    return Task.FromResult(true);
}
```

This method checks whether the given `bindingContext` parameter implements the `INavigatable` interface. If that's the case, it returns the result from its `CanNavigateFrom` method, passing in the `NavigationType`. If the `bindingContext` doesn't implement the `INavigatable` interface, `true` is returned, indicating the navigation can be executed.

4. In the `AppShell` class, we must now override the `OnNavigating` method. In this method, we can retrieve a `ShellNavigatingDeferral` from the passed-in `ShellNavigatingEventArgs`. This deferral token can be used to complete the navigation. Or, if the navigation should be canceled, the `Cancel` method on the `ShellNavigatingEventArgs` can be called. The next code block shows the overridden method:

```
protected override async void
OnNavigating(ShellNavigatingEventArgs args)
{
    base.OnNavigating(args);

    var token = args.GetDeferral();

    if(token is not null)
    {
        var canNavigate = await interceptor
        .CanNavigate(CurrentPage?.BindingContext,
GetNavigationType(args.Source));

        if (canNavigate)
            token.Complete();
        else
            args.Cancel();
    }
}
```

By calling the interceptor's `CanNavigate` method, we can determine whether we must complete the navigation or not. Depending on the outcome, we can call the `Complete` method on the deferral token and complete the navigation or call the `Cancel` method on the passed-in `args` to cancel it.

5. Finally, we can go to `AddRatingViewModel`, make it implement the `INavigatable` interface, and add the following:

```
public class AddRatingViewModel : ObservableValidator,
INavigationParameterReceiver, INavigatedFrom, INavigatable
{
...
    public Task<bool> CanNavigateFrom(
        NavigationType navigationType) =>
        _dialogService.AskYesNo(
        "Leaving this page...",
        "Are you sure you want to leave this page?");
}
```

As a result, when navigating from the AddRatingView, the OnNavigating method on the Shell class will get called, which – via the NavigationService – will call the CanNavigateFrom method on the AddRatingViewModel. The ViewModel will present a dialog to the user and return the response. Depending on the response given by the user, the navigation will be completed or canceled. The INavigatable interface can be implemented by any ViewModel and can contain any business logic to determine whether navigation is allowed or not.

Summary

In this chapter, we delved deep into enhancing user experience through effective validation, prompts, and alerts. We explored the power of ObservableValidator for validation logic and learned the nuances of showing errors both as a collective list and inline, right next to input fields. With triggers, we learned how to customize UI elements without reinventing the wheel. We also explored using an IDialogService leveraging alerts and prompts, which is essential in contexts where user feedback or confirmations, such as during critical actions or navigations, are required. As we move forward, we'll pivot to a vital aspect of many modern apps: making remote API calls.

Further reading

To learn more about the topics that were covered in this chapter, take a look at the following resources:

- ObservableValidator: https://learn.microsoft.com/dotnet/communitytoolkit/mvvm/observablevalidator
- Triggers: https://learn.microsoft.com/dotnet/maui/fundamentals/triggers
- Behaviors: https://learn.microsoft.com/dotnet/maui/fundamentals/behaviors
- .NET MAUI Community Toolkit Behaviors: https://learn.microsoft.com/dotnet/communitytoolkit/maui/behaviors/
- .NET MAUI popups: https://learn.microsoft.com/dotnet/maui/user-interface/pop-ups

Working with Remote Data

So far, we've dug deep into MVVM and .NET MAUI, covering everything from the basics of the MVVM design, from data binding and Dependency Injection to navigation and handling user input. But there's one big piece of the puzzle we haven't tackled yet: getting data from the internet.

It's hard to imagine an app these days that doesn't talk to an online service to grab fresh data. Adding backend communications also means we need to tackle some architectural challenges such as maintaining separation of concerns, building your app with maintainability in mind, and so on.

Here's what we'll dive into in this chapter:

- Revisiting the model architecture
- API communication with Refit
- API communication from ViewModels

By the end of this chapter, our *Recipes!* app will be more than just a standalone thing. It'll communicate with a backend service to fetch fresh data and push updates. We're going to equip it with the essential tools and skills needed for solid MVVM apps.

Technical requirements

In this chapter, we update the general architecture of the *Recipes!* app to better facilitate communication with remote APIs. To ensure you're on the same page, all resources and code snippets are available on GitHub: `https://github.com/PacktPublishing/MVVM-pattern-.NET-MAUI/tree/main/Chapter10`. If you wish to code along, start with the code in the `Start` folder, which has been refactored to serve as the foundation for this chapter. Upon completion, you can compare your work with the `Finish` folder to see the finalized version.

Revisiting the model architecture

In our journey so far, our model has been straightforward. We simply used services that read local JSON files and fed **Data Transfer Objects (DTOs)** directly to our ViewModels. But as we introduce remote data, this simplistic model won't suffice.

A straightforward approach would be to make an API call directly within our service and pass the resulting DTOs to our ViewModels. However, leaning on the principle of SoC, I believe services shouldn't be making API calls. Moreover, using API-specific DTOs directly within our ViewModels is a slippery slope. It tightly couples our application with the external API, which can lead to maintenance nightmares, especially if the API changes often or isn't under our control.

Instead, I advocate for mapping these DTOs to **Plain Old CLR Objects (POCOs)**, or entities or domain models – whatever you prefer to name them. The core idea? Work with types we own and control.

> **Tip**
>
> By keeping the interaction points between our app and the API to a minimum, our code will be less impacted by potential API changes, enhancing maintainability.

To realize this, we'll introduce the concept of **repositories** in our architecture. These repositories will interface with the API (or any data source), fetch the DTOs, map them to our domain models, and then supply them to our services and ViewModels. The following diagram captures this envisioned architecture:

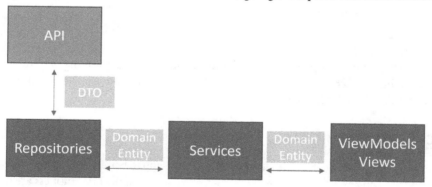

Figure 10.1: Architectural overview

Now, one might ask: is this really needed? Can't we just directly call an API from a service while using DTOs in our ViewModels? The answer is no, it is not needed; you can perfectly well call an API from a service if you want. This can definitely work for smaller "dumb" apps where all the business logic is done on the server. But as we scale or tackle more complex scenarios, thoughtful architecture becomes crucial for several reasons:

- **Separation of concerns**: By introducing repositories, we distinctly segregate the roles within our system. Repositories are primarily concerned with fetching data from a data source – be it an API or another data store – and then translating it into a format our services can readily use. Positioning the repository layer outside of the core project not only emphasizes its distinct responsibility but also ensures that changes or expansions to data sources don't interfere with the core business logic. This separation enhances the system's adaptability and maintainability. It becomes clear that the repository's sole purpose is data retrieval, acting as a thin layer that fetches data from various sources and feeds it to the core services. With repositories acting as intermediaries, changes to the data source or alterations to the data structure are centralized, streamlining modifications.

- **Improved testability**: By introducing a repository layer, we enhance our app's testability. With repositories in place, we can effortlessly mock the data layer in our tests. This abstraction ensures our tests focus on the logic within our services, free from dependencies on external data sources. In *Chapter 13*, *Unit Testing*, we will be looking at this in much more detail.

- **Augmented services**: The service layer remains free to introduce additional features such as caching, business logic, or data aggregation from multiple repositories. This decoupling means services aren't tied directly to specific data sources and can evolve independently.

Before we dive deep into the concepts of repositories and other details, let's explore the solution found in the `Start` folder of this chapter's accompanying code base to understand the changes that have been made.

Updates to the codebase

As we journey deeper into creating a robust MVVM architecture, it's crucial to familiarize ourselves with changes and additions that have been made to the code base. If you take a look at the `Start` folder of the accompanying repository for this chapter, you'll notice some changes. Here are notable updates:

- A `Recipes.Web.Api` API project has been added. At its core, it still reads from local JSON files, reminiscent of our earlier services. The implementation of the API is pretty bare-bones and only for demo purposes.

- The new `Recipes.Shared` project holds the DTOs that the API returns and accepts.

- In the `Features` folder of the `Recipes.Client.Core` project, we've added new POCO or domain entities. These are reflections of our DTOs but designed to be entirely under our control, ensuring a smoother integration with the rest of our app's infrastructure.

- A new `Recipes.Client.Repositories` project has been created. This project will hold the implementations of the repositories that we will be creating. The idea is to keep them separate from the `Recipes.Client.Core` project so that the core project is completely isolated from the API and its DTOs. This project also contains mappers that map the DTOs returned by the API to POCO entities that we will be using throughout the app.

- The services and ViewModels no longer depend upon DTOs. Now, they interact solely with our own POCOs, ensuring a clean and maintainable architecture.

- The `ratings.json` and `recipedetails.json` files have been removed from the `Recipes.Mobile` project as we are going to fetch our data from the API.

- The registrations of `IRecipeService` and `IRatingsService` in the `MauiProgram` class have been updated to the following:

```
builder.Services.AddTransient<IRatingsService,
    RatingsService>();
builder.Services.AddTransient<IRecipeService,
    RecipeService>();
```

These changes set the stage for the introduction of repositories and interactions with the API.

Always return a result

In conventional coding, exceptions are commonly used to indicate failure. While they're useful for *exceptional* cases, they might not be the best choice for regular, expected error scenarios. Using exceptions for expected errors can clutter the code and make it harder to follow.

That's why I tend to use a `Result<TSuccess>` object to handle such cases. This object acts as a wrapper around the data we expect on success (`TSuccess`) and provides fields for an error code, error data, and an `Exception` error in the case of failure. It's a very simple and convenient wrapper, as you can see here:

```
public sealed class Result<TSuccess>
{
    ...
    public bool IsSuccess { get; }
    public TSuccess? Data { get; }
    public string? ErrorCode { get; }
    public string? ErrorData { get; }
    public Exception? Exception { get; }

    private Result(TSuccess? data,
        string? errorCode, string? errorData,
        Exception? exception, bool isSuccess)
    {
        Data = data;
        ErrorCode = errorCode;
        ErrorData = errorData;
        Exception = exception;
```

```
        IsSuccess = isSuccess;
    }
}
```

As the following code block shows, this class also contains some static methods that instantiate a `Success` or `Fail` `Result` object, facilitating the usage of this object:

```
public static Result<TSuccess> Success(TSuccess data)
    => new Result<TSuccess>(data, null, null, null, true);

public static Result<TSuccess> Success()
    => new Result<TSuccess>(default, null, null,
        null, true);

public static Result<TSuccess> Fail(string errorCode,
    string? errorData = null, Exception? exception = null)
    => new Result<TSuccess>(default, errorCode,
        errorData, exception, false);

public static Result<TSuccess> Fail(Exception exception)
    => new Result<TSuccess>(default, nameof(exception),
        exception.Message, exception, false);
```

By using the `Result` object, we can easily distinguish between two types of errors:

- **Unexpected errors**: These are real "exceptions" that we can't predict and don't know how to handle. They are still best managed by throwing exceptions.

- **Expected errors**: These include scenarios such as validation failures or transient network issues. For these, we use our `Result` object.

For example, a mobile app unable to retrieve data isn't an exceptional case; it's a scenario we should plan for. The `Result` object allows us to handle such situations gracefully without resorting to exceptions. It offers a richer context than simply returning `null` or `false`, letting us understand why an operation failed. This even works when we talk to an API that we don't control: this is just a simple wrapper around an object.

The `Result` object brings clarity and consistency to our code. It removes uncertainties such as *"Can this method throw an exception? If so, what type? Is it the same exception type thrown in similar scenarios?"*

Errors versus exceptions

By segregating expected errors from true exceptions, we make the code more readable and maintainable. It lets exceptions be what they should be: indicators of critical, unexpected failures.

As we extend our *Recipes!* app to communicate with a backend API, the chances for various types of errors increase significantly. To prepare for this complexity, we'll be wrapping the return values of our services and repositories in a `Result` object. This approach not only helps us deal effectively with expected errors but also brings a level of standardization and clarity to our error-handling strategy. Let's see how this `Result` object brings elegance and robustness to the ViewModels.

Putting the Result object to work

The following code snippet shows how the `Result` object can gracefully handle both successful and unsuccessful outcomes in the `RecipeRatingsDetailViewModel`:

```
private async Task LoadData(RecipeDetail recipe)
{
...

    var loadRatings = await
        ratingsService.LoadRatings(recipe.Id);

    if(loadRatings.IsSuccess)
    {
        GroupedReviews = loadRatings.Data
        ...
        .ToList();
    }
    else
    {
        var shouldRetry = await dialogService.AskYesNo(
            "Failed to load", "Retry?");
        if (shouldRetry)
            await LoadData(recipe);
        else
            await navigationService.GoBack();
    }
}
```

This example underscores the elegance and robustness the `Result` object brings to our ViewModels. By using the `IsSuccess` property, we can immediately determine the success of the operation. If it's successful, we proceed to work with the data we've received. If not, we offer the user a chance to retry or go back. Additionally, the `Result` object also contains valuable error information in `ErrorMessage`, `ErrorCode`, and `Exception`, allowing us to tailor our error-handling strategy, such as displaying specific error messages to the user. This approach removes the necessity of adding exception-handling sections across our ViewModels, leading to a cleaner, easier-to-read, and more maintainable code structure.

If we would like to leverage C# **pattern matching** abilities, we could make the preceding code even more elegant, like so:

```
if (loadRatings is { IsSuccess: true, Data: var ratings })
{
    GroupedReviews = ratings
    ...
    .ToList();
}
else
{
    ...
}
```

By using pattern matching, we could check for the `Result` object's `IsSuccess` property to be `true`, and in the same statement, assign the `Result` object's `Data` property to the `ratings` variable. This allows us to access the `Data` property more easily through the `ratings` variable inside that `if` block. Now that we have a good understanding of the `Result` object, we can start adding repositories to our architecture.

Adding repository interfaces

Let's start adding repositories, the pieces of code that will directly interact with our API:

1. In the `Recipes.Client.Core` project, add an interface called `IRecipeRepository` to the `Features/Recipes` folder. Here's what this interface looks like:

    ```
    public interface IRecipeRepository
    {
        Task<Result<LoadRecipesResponse>> LoadRecipes(
            int pageSize = 7, int page = 0);
        Task<Result<RecipeDetail>> LoadRecipe(string id);
    }
    ```

    This interface defines the contract that any class needs to implement in order to be able to fetch recipes from a data source. There are two methods defined in this interface: `LoadRecipes` and `LoadRecipe`. The first method returns a `LoadRecipesResponse` object, which is a response containing a paged collection of recipes. The second method returns a `RecipeDetail` object for a recipe identified by its ID. The return value of both of these methods is wrapped in a `Result` object, allowing us to deal with the fact that the requested data (temporarily) couldn't be retrieved, for example.

2. Head over to the `RecipeService` class and add a parameter of type `IRecipeRepository` to its constructor. A field is also added to keep a reference to this instance, as shown in the following snippet:

```
public class RecipeService : IRecipeService
{
    readonly IRecipeRepository _recipeRepository;
...
    public RecipeService(
        IRecipeRepository recipeRepository)
    {
        _recipeRepository = recipeRepository;
    }
}
```

3. As there isn't much "business logic" going on in the `RecipeService` class, its methods should just call the injected repository's methods and return their result. Have a look:

```
public Task<Result<RecipeDetail>> LoadRecipe(
    string id) => _recipeRepository.LoadRecipe(id);

public Task<Result<LoadRecipesResponse>> LoadRecipes(
    int pageSize = 7, int page = 0)
    => _recipeRepository.LoadRecipes(pageSize, page);
```

We can add the same treatment to the `RatingsService` class: create a repository interface, add it as a dependency to the service, and call the interface's methods from the `RatingsService` class's methods. We'll proceed as follows:

1. Let's create an `IRatingsRepository` interface for the `Features/Ratings` folder and add the following definitions to the newly created interface:

```
Task<Result<IReadOnlyCollection<Rating>>>
    GetRatings(string recipeId);
Task<Result<RatingsSummary>> GetRatingsSummary(
    string recipeId);
```

There are two methods defined in this interface: `GetRatings` and `GetRatingsSummary`. The first method returns a collection of `Rating` objects associated with the specified recipe ID. The second method returns a `RatingsSummary` for a recipe identified by its ID. As noted earlier, the return values are wrapped in a `Result` object.

2. Next, we add `IRatingsRepository` as a dependency of the `RatingsService` class, by defining it as a constructor parameter:

```
public class RatingsService : IRatingsService
{
```

```
        readonly IRatingsRepository _ratingsRepository;
...
        public RatingsService(
            IRatingsRepository ratingsRepository)
        {
            _ratingsRepository = ratingsRepository;
        }
    }
```

3. Finally, as the `RatingsService` class doesn't contain any additional logic, this class will just call the repository's methods, as you can see here:

```
public Task<Result<RatingsSummary>>
    LoadRatingsSummary(string recipeId)
    => _ratingsRepository.GetRatingsSummary(recipeId);
public Task<<Result<IReadOnlyCollection<Rating>>>
    LoadRatings(string recipeId)
    => _ratingsRepository.GetRatings(recipeId);
```

That leaves us with one service left to update: `FavoritesService`. Unlike the previous services that we've been updating, `FavoritesService` does contain some additional logic. But let's first take a look at what the `IFavoritesRepository` interface looks like:

```
public interface IFavoritesRepository
{
    Task<Result<IReadonlyCollection<string>>>
        LoadFavorites(string userId);
    Task<Result<Nothing>> Add(string userId, string id);
    Task<Result<Nothing>> Remove(string userId, string id);
}
```

This interface defines three methods: `LoadFavorites`, `Add`, and `Remove`. Since our favorites are stored on a centralized server, it's essential to pass the user's identifier (or `userId`) to the API. This ensures that favorites fetched, added, or removed are specific to that user. Neither the `Add` method nor the `Remove` method has an intrinsic return value. To be consistent with the rest of our APIs, we want to return a value wrapped in a `Result` object. That's why a custom `Nothing` type is returned. This is just an empty struct, as you can see here:

```
public struct Nothing
{
}
```

Let's update the `FavoritesService` so that it leverages the `IFavoritesRepository` interface:

1. Go ahead and add the `IFavoritesRepository` interface to the `Features/Favorites` folder.

2. Update `FavoritesService` so that its constructor accepts a parameter of type `IFavoritesRepository`:

```
public class FavoritesService : IFavoritesService
{
    readonly IFavoritesRepository
        _favoritesRepository;
...
    public FavoritesService(
        IFavoritesRepository favoritesRepository)
    {
        _favoritesRepository = favoritesRepository;
    }
}
```

3. `FavoritesService` keeps a list of the user's favorites in memory. This in-memory list can easily be used in the `IsFavorite` method to rapidly check whether the given `recipeId` exists in the list. Here's how we can load this list in memory:

```
List<string> favorites = null;

private async ValueTask LoadList()
{
    if (favorites is null)
    {
        var loadResult = await _favoritesRepository
            .LoadFavorites(GetCurrentUserId());
        if (loadResult.IsSuccess)
        {
            favorites = loadResult.Data.ToList();
        }
    }
}

//Dummy implementation,
//could be retrieved via injected service
private string GetCurrentUserId()
    => "3";
```

The `LoadList` method calls the `LoadFavorites` method on the `IFavoritesRepository` when the favorites list is `null`. The "dummy" `GetCurrentUserId` method provides a fake identifier for the given user of the app. In a real-life scenario, this could be retrieved from an injected service.

4. As said before, this in-memory list facilitates the implementation of the IsFavorite method, as shown in the next code block:

```
public async Task<bool> IsFavorite(string id)
{
    await LoadList();
    return favorites is not null
        && favorites.Contains(id);
}
```

This method calls the LoadList method, which will retrieve the favorites from the API if the in-memory list is null. When favorites have been loaded, we can check whether the list contains the given ID.

In contrast to the earlier services we discussed, where each method simply invoked a corresponding method in the injected repository, things are slightly more complex here due to the presence of an in-memory list. Also, because both the Add and Remove methods send a FavoriteUpdateMessage instance, they require some extra logic for implementation. Here's how it's done:

1. The first thing to do in FavoritesService's Add method is to call the repository's Add method, passing in the (fake) userId value, as shown here:

```
public async Task<Result<Nothing>> Add(string id)
{
    var result = await _favoritesRepository
        .Add(GetCurrentUserId(), id);
}
```

2. The Add method of the IFavoritesRepository returns a Nothing object wrapped in a Result object. Thanks to the Result object, we can check if the API call was successful or not. If that's the case, we add the ID of the favorited recipe to the in-memory list of favorites and send the FavoriteUpdateMessage as shown here:

```
if (result.IsSuccess)
{
    if (favorites is not null
        && !favorites.Contains(id))
        favorites.Add(id);

    WeakReferenceMessenger.Default
        .Send(new FavoriteUpdateMessage(id, true));
}
return result;
```

3. The Remove method is very similar:

```
public async Task<Result<Nothing>> Remove(string id)
{
    var result = await _favoritesRepository
        .Remove(GetCurrentUserId(), id);

    if (result.IsSuccess)
    {
        if (favorites is not null
            && favorites.Contains(id))
            favorites.Remove(id);

        WeakReferenceMessenger.Default
            .Send(
            new FavoriteUpdateMessage(id, false));
    }
    return result;
}
```

With all of our code in place, it's time to add implementations for these repositories and make sure they get registered in the DI container.

Adding and registering repository implementations

There's a dedicated project in which we can place the implementations of the repository interfaces. As these repositories will communicate to our API, I tend to use ApiGateway as the naming. Personally, I think this name perfectly illustrates its functionality. In the Recipes.Client.Repositories project, we can add three classes: FavoritesApiGateway, RatingsApiGateway, and RecipeApiGateway. These classes should implement the IFavoritesRepository, IRatingsRepository, and IRecipeRepository interfaces respectively. In the next section, we will be discussing how to effectively activate API communication using Refit.

Now, let's turn our attention to registering these repositories in the DI container. Instead of handling each registration in the MauiProgram class, we'll delegate this task entirely to the code in the Recipes.Client.Repositories project:

1. Add the Microsoft.Extensions.DependencyInjection.Abstractions NuGet package to the Recipes.Client.Repositories project.

2. In the Recipes.Client.Repositories project, add a ServiceCollectionExtension class. Here's what this static class looks like:

```
public static class ServiceCollectionExtension
{
    public static IServiceCollection
```

```
    RegisterRepositories(
    this IServiceCollection services)
{
    services.AddTransient<IRatingsRepository,
        RatingsApiGateway>();
    services.AddTransient<IRecipeRepository,
        RecipeApiGateway>();
    services.AddTransient<IFavoritesRepository,
        FavoritesApiGateway>();

    return services;
}
}
```

This class contains one method: `RegisterRepositories`. This method is an extension method that extends the `IServiceCollection` interface. To use `IServiceCollection`, ensure you've included the `Microsoft.Extensions.DependencyInjection` namespace, which is part of the NuGet package we added in the first step. This method is all about registering the repositories. Ending the method by returning the `services` instance allows us to adopt a builder pattern, enabling the chaining of additional extension methods.

3. Now, we can head over to the `MauiProgram.cs` file and add the following to the `CreateMauiApp` method:

    ```
    builder.Services.RegisterRepositories();
    ```

    The `RegisterRepositories` extension method can only be resolved when the `Recipes.Client.Repositories` namespace is added.

With all of this in place, the services of our app now depend on repositories that will eventually communicate to the app's API. The implementation of those repository interfaces and their registration is done in the dedicated `Recipes.Client.Repositories` project. This keeps everything organized and modular and ensures a clear separation of concerns, making our codebase more maintainable.

Although we now have repositories that are being registered, they still lack communication with our API. Moreover, we registered the `RatingsApiGateway`, `RecipeApiGateway`, and `FavoritesApiGateway` classes, which don't exist yet. Let's see how we can add these and leverage Refit to make API requests and receive strongly typed responses, making it easier to handle errors and parse data.

API communication with Refit

Up to this point, we've set up a neat architecture for our repositories, but they're still missing the ability to talk to our API. To add this functionality, we could use `HttpClient` manually to make API calls and deserialize the response. While that's entirely possible, it's also cumbersome and prone to errors, not to mention it takes a lot of boilerplate code to get it right.

This is where Refit comes into the picture. Refit is a powerful library that simplifies API calls by providing a more declarative and less error-prone approach. Instead of writing tedious HTTP requests and responses, you just define a C# interface that maps to the API's endpoints. Refit takes care of the underlying `HttpClient` calls, serialization, and deserialization for you, letting you focus on what matters – the logic of your application.

In this section, we'll see how Refit can make our life easier by reducing code complexity and increasing readability, while still offering customization options for more complex scenarios. So, let's get our repositories talking to our API the smart way.

Getting started with Refit

Refit is a type-safe REST client for .NET that allows you to easily make API calls by defining an interface. You annotate the interface methods with HTTP attributes such as `[Get]`, `[Post]`, and so on, specifying the API endpoints. Refit is then able to generate the implementation for you, turning those interface methods into API calls. Let's take a look at an example:

1. First, we need to define the API endpoints we'll be interacting with by declaring an interface:

```
public interface IRecipeApi
{
    [Get("/recipe/{recipeId}")]
    Task<ApiResponse<RecipeDto>>
        GetRecipe(string recipeId);
}
```

   Here, the `IRecipeApi` interface defines an API call for fetching a single recipe by its ID. The `Refit.Get` attribute is used to define an HTTP GET method for a specific endpoint. The `{recipeId}` portion of the endpoint specifies a path parameter that is used to pass the `recipeId` parameter to the method. When the `GetRecipe` method is called with a recipe ID, we want the Refit library to send an HTTP GET request to the specified endpoint, replacing the `{recipeId}` portion of the endpoint with the specified ID.

2. Secondly, we use `RestService.For` to generate an implementation of your interface, as shown here:

```
var api = RestService.For<IRecipeApi>(
        "https://api.yourservice.com");
```

This single line of code creates an object that knows how to make the API calls defined in `IRecipeApi`. This `RestService.For` method accepts a string parameter that defines the base URL of the API. Alternatively, an instance of `HttpClient` can be passed as a parameter, instead of the string value. Refit will use the given `HttpClient` to communicate with the API. Later on in the chapter, we'll see why passing in an `HttpClient` can be useful.

3. Finally, we can use the generated object to make API calls and handle the responses, as the following code snippet demonstrates:

```
var recipeResponse = await api.GetRecipe("1");
if (recipeResponse.IsSuccessStatusCode)
{
    RecipeDto recipe = recipeResponse.Content;
}
```

`recipeResponse` is an object of type `ApiResponse<RecipeDto>` that gives you both the deserialized content and additional HTTP response details.

Alternatively, you could also define a `GetRecipe` method in the `IRecipeApi` interface as follows:

```
Task<RecipeDto> GetRecipe(string recipeId);
```

This would just return the deserialized object. I prefer the approach that returns `ApiResponse<T>` because it provides a fuller picture of what's happening during the API interaction, which is crucial for robust error handling and insightful logging.

And there you have it: three simple steps to replace what would have otherwise been much more boilerplate code. Now, let's get back to our *Recipes!* app and put this into practice.

Creating API interfaces

Let's add API interfaces to the `Recipes.Client.Repositories` project. Later on, we will be using them together with Refit to generate the required code to effectively communicate to the API:

1. In the **Solution Explorer**, right-click the `Recipes.Client.Repositories` project and select **Add | New Folder**. Name the folder `Api`.

2. Add an interface called `IFavoritesApi` to the newly created folder. The following code snippet shows what this interface looks like:

```
public interface IFavoritesApi
{
    [Get("/users/{userId}/favorites")]
    Task<string[]> GetFavorites(string userId);

    [Post("/users/{userId}/favorites")]
    Task AddFavorite(string userId,
```

```
                    FavoriteDto favorite);

        [Delete("/users/{userId}/favorites/{recipeId}")]
        Task DeleteFavorite(string userId,
            string recipeId);
    }
```

This interface maps directly to the API endpoints responsible for managing user favorites. The Get, Post and Delete attributes specify the HTTP methods that should be used for each API call. Parameters such as userId that appear in the URL are automatically populated from the method arguments. Notice the favorite parameter in the AddFavorite method. This parameter is not part of the defined endpoint URL; instead, it gets serialized and sent as the request body. Alternatively, it's also possible to explicitly indicate that the favorite parameter needs to be sent in the message's body by using the Body attribute. This is what that looks like:

```
    [Post("/users/{userId}/favorites")]
        Task AddFavorite(string userId,
            [Body] FavoriteDto favorite);
```

3. Next, we can add the IRatingsApi interface, which looks like this:

    ```
    public interface IRatingsApi
    {
        [Get("/recipe/{recipeId}/ratings")]
        Task<ApiResponse<RatingDto[]>> GetRatings(
            string recipeId);

        [Get("/recipe/{recipeId}/ratingssummary")]
        Task<ApiResponse<RatingsSummaryDto>>
            GetRatingsSummary(string recipeId);
    }
    ```

    Again, these methods and their attributes correspond with the endpoints that allow us to retrieve ratings and a ratings summary for a given recipe ID.

4. Finally, let's define the IRecipeApi interface:

    ```
    public interface IRecipeApi
    {
        [Get("/recipe/{recipeId}")]
        Task<ApiResponse<RecipeDetailDto>>
          GetRecipe(string recipeId);

        [Get("/recipes")]
        Task<ApiResponse<RecipeOverviewItemsDto>>
          GetRecipes(int pageSize = 7, int pageIndex = 0);
    }
    ```

As you probably know by now, as with the previous ones, this interface also maps to certain API endpoints. The `pageSize` and `pageIndex` parameters of the `GetRecipes` method don't appear in the endpoint of the `Get` attribute. As a result, they will be added as query string parameters when doing the request.

With our API interfaces defined, it's finally time to bridge the gap between our repositories and the actual API calls.

Integrating Refit

Let's integrate Refit into our repositories to make the API calls a breeze. It all starts with adding the Refit NuGet package to the `Recipes.Client.Repositories` project. To make integrating Refit even easier and avoid duplicate code later on, let's first add a new `ApiGateway` abstract class to the `Recipes.Client.Repositories` project. The purpose of this class is to help us in executing a call and mapping the `ApiResponse` result to another type. This is what the `InvokeAndMap` method's signature looks like:

```
protected async Task<Result<TResult>>
    InvokeAndMap<TResult, TDtoResult>(
    Task<ApiResponse<TDtoResult>> call,
    Func<TDtoResult, TResult> mapper)
{
}
```

This method returns a `Task<TResult>` object and takes in two parameters:

- The `call` parameter is the API call to make, which returns an `ApiResponse<TDtoResult>` object
- The `mapper` parameter is a method that takes in the `TDtoResult` object from the response and maps it to the `TResult` object that the `InvokeAndMap` method returns

The implementation is fairly straightforward: the method must execute the provided `call` parameter. If the resulting `ApiResponse` instance indicates success, the passed-in `mapper` parameter will be used to map the result from `TDtoResult` to `TResult`, which is wrapped in a `Result` object that indicates success. If the response doesn't indicate success, a failed result is returned, containing the response's status code. The following code block shows how it's done:

```
try
{
    var response = await call;

    if (response.IsSuccessStatusCode)
    {
        return Result<TResult>
```

```
                .Success(mapper(response.Content));
    }
    else
    {
        return Result<TResult>.Fail("FAILED_REQUEST",
            response.Error.StatusCode.ToString());
    }
}
...
```

On top of that, we also need to be wary of potential exceptions being thrown, which we can handle as shown here:

```
try
{
...
}
catch (ApiException aex)
{
    return Result<TResult>
        .Fail("ApiException",
            aex.StatusCode.ToString(), aex);
}
catch (Exception ex)
{
    return Result<TResult>.Fail(ex);
}
```

When an exception occurs, we should return a `Result` object that indicates failure, containing relevant data about the exception.

A note on robustness

When developing mobile applications, it's important to remember that network conditions can be unpredictable. Mobile devices might move between different network zones, causing unstable connections. As a best practice, always consider implementing resilience patterns such as **retry** or **circuit breaker** when making API calls. A library such as **Polly** makes this straightforward, allowing you to define policies for handling transient faults and network hiccups. Leveraging such tools can greatly enhance the reliability of your app, ensuring a smoother user experience even under challenging network conditions. The abstract `ApiGateway` class is the perfect spot to add this kind of retry logic instead of directly returning a `Fail` result. Find out more about Polly here: `https://github.com/App-vNext/Polly`.

In situations where the data type returned by the API interface is identical to the type we wish to encapsulate in a `Result` object, we can provide an overloaded `InvokeAndMap` method that eliminates the need for a type mapper. This is particularly useful when dealing with primitive types. The following snippet shows this overload:

```
protected Task<Result<T>>
    InvokeAndMap<T>(<ApiResponse<T>> call)
    => InvokeAndMap(call, e => e);
```

This base class will drastically simplify the mapping of a DTO returned by the API to a domain entity that gets encapsulated in a `Result` object. Now, let's have a look at how we can utilize this `InvokeAndMap` method in our repositories:

1. First, make sure that all of our repositories (`FavoritesApiGateway`, `RatingsApiGateway`, and `RecipeApiGateway`) inherit this abstract `ApiGateway` class by adding the following code:

    ```
    internal class FavoritesApiGateway : ApiGateway,
      IFavoritesRepository { ... }
    internal class RatingsApiGateway : ApiGateway,
      IRatingsRepository { ... }
    internal class RecipeApiGateway : ApiGateway,
      IRecipeRepository { ... }
    ```

2. Next, each of these repositories should get its corresponding API interface injected through its constructor. Let's see what this looks like for `RatingsApiGateway`:

    ```
    internal class RatingsApiGateway : ApiGateway,
      IRatingsRepository
    {
        readonly IRatingsApi _api;
    ...
        public RatingsApiGateway(IRatingsApi api)
        {
            _api = api;
        }
    }
    ```

3. The injected `IRatingsApi` interface can now be used to do the network calls and retrieve the requested data from the API. The following code block shows the implemented `GetRatings` method:

    ```
    public Task<Result<IReadOnlyCollection<Rating>>>
        GetRatings(string recipeId)
        => InvokeAndMap(
            _api.GetRatings(recipeId), MapRatings);
    ```

The GetRatings method calls the InvokeAndMap method of the base class. The GetRatings API call is passed in as a parameter, as well as the MapRatings method, which maps the RatingDto array returned by the API to an IReadOnlyCollection of Rating objects. The MapRatings method is a static method on the static RatingsMapper class. We can directly access RatingsMapper's static mapping methods inside this class without explicitly needing to prepend its name because the following using statement is added to the class:

```
using static Recipes.Client.Repositories.Mappers
    .RatingsMapper;
```

4. We can now do the exact same thing for the GetRatingsSummary method on this class:

```
public Task<Result<RatingsSummary>>
    GetRatingsSummary(string recipeId)
    => InvokeAndMap(_api.GetRatingsSummary(recipeId),
        MapRatingSummary);
```

5. Analogous to the previous examples, the implementation of the FavoritesApiGateway class can be done following the same pattern: inject the IFavoritesApi interface and use its methods to retrieve data from the API, leveraging the InvokeAndMap method of the ApiGateway base class:

```
internal class FavoritesApiGateway : ApiGateway,
    IFavoritesRepository
{
    readonly IFavoritesApi _api;

    public Task<Result<Nothing>> Add(
        string userId, string id)
        => InvokeAndMap(_api.AddFavorite(userId,
            new FavoriteDto(id)));

    public Task<Result<string[]>> LoadFavorites(
        string userId)
        => InvokeAndMap(_api.GetFavorites(userId));

    public Task<Result<Nothing>> Remove(string userId,
    string recipeId)
        => InvokeAndMap(_api.DeleteFavorite(userId,
            recipeId));

    public FavoritesApiGateway(IFavoritesApi api)
    {
        _api = api;
    }
}
```

All of these methods in the `FavoritesApiGateway` use the overloaded `InvokeAndMap` method, which doesn't do additional mapping: the data type returned by the API interface is the same as the one the repository returns, but it's encapsulated in a `Result` object.

6. The implementation of the `RecipeApiGateway` class shouldn't contain any surprises; it only contains more mapping. But at its core, it follows the exact same pattern as the previous two classes. First, a field of type `IRecipeApi` needs to be added as a member and constructor parameter, as the following snippet shows:

```
internal class RecipeApiGateway : ApiGateway,
    IRecipeRepository
{
    readonly IRecipeApi _api;
...
    public RecipeApiGateway(IRecipeApi api)
    {
        _api = api;
    }
}
```

The `LoadRecipes` method and the mappings it uses look like this:

```
public Task<Result<LoadRecipesResponse>>
    LoadRecipes(int pageSize, int page)
    => InvokeAndMap(_api.GetRecipes(pageSize, page),
        MapRecipesOverview);
```

`LoadRecipes` calls the `InvokeAndMap` method, passing in the `GetRecipes` method of the API interface. The `MapRecipesOverview` method is used to map the resulting object of type `RecipesOverviewItemsDto` to a `LoadRecipesResponse` object.

And finally, we can implement the `LoadRecipe` method. It can use the `GetRecipe` method of the `IRecipeApi` to get the data. The result will be mapped using the static `MapRecipe` method of the static `RecipeMapper` class. Take a look:

```
public Task<Result<RecipeDetail>> LoadRecipe(
    string id)
    => InvokeAndMap(_api.GetRecipe(id), MapRecipe);
```

We also need to update our `ServiceCollectionExtension` class. Because every repository now has a dependency on a particular API interface, we need to make sure these dependencies get registered as well. But first, we might want to add a new `RepositorySettings` class to the `Recipes.Client.Repositories` project. This class should be a way to pass settings from the app to the repositories, such as a specific `HttpClient` instance that needs to be used, for example. As the following code block shows, there's not much to this class for this particular demo project. But in more complex applications, things such as particular serialization or authentication settings can be added here as well:

```
public class RepositorySettings
```

```
{
    public HttpClient HttpClient { get; }

    public RepositorySettings(HttpClient httpClient)
    {
        HttpClient = httpClient;
    }
}
```

Let's fit the final pieces of the puzzle together, update the `ServiceCollectionExtension`, and call it from our app. Here's what we need to do:

1. Add the `RepositorySettings` class, as shown earlier, to the `Recipes.Client. Repositories` project.

2. Add a parameter of type `RepositorySettings` to the `RegisterRepositories` extension method of the `ServiceCollectionExtension` class, as shown here:

    ```
    public static class ServiceCollectionExtension
    {
        public static IServiceCollection
            RegisterRepositories (
            this IServiceCollection services,
            RepositorySettings settings)
        {
            ...
            return services;
        }
    }
    ```

3. As we saw earlier, Refit's `RestService.For` method can be used to generate implementations of the API interfaces. The following snippet shows how we can register the generated implementations in the DI container:

    ```
    services.AddSingleton((s) =>
      RestService.For<IRatingsApi>(settings.HttpClient));
    services.AddSingleton((s) =>
      RestService.For<IRecipeApi>(settings.HttpClient));
    services.AddSingleton((s) =>
    RestService.For<IFavoritesApi>(settings.HttpClient));
    ```

The `RestService.For` method accepts an instance of `HttpClient` that will be used by Refit to do the API communication. An `HttpClient`, should be configured in the app and passed-in via the `RepositorySettings`.

4. Finally, in the `MauiProgram` class, we can call the updated `RegisterRepositories` and pass-in a configured `HttpClient` as shown here:

```
var baseAddress = DeviceInfo.Platform ==
    DevicePlatform.Android
    ? "https://10.0.2.2:7220"
    : "https://localhost:7220";

var httpClient = HttpClientHelper
    .GetPlatformHttpClient(baseAddress);

builder.Services.RegisterRepositories(
    new RepositorySettings(httpClient));
```

As the Android emulator runs in an isolated network environment behind a virtual router, it cannot directly access the development machine using `localhost`. Instead, the emulator provides a special `10.0.2.2` alias that routes to the development machine's loopback interface, enabling you to access local web services.

The `Recipes.Mobile` project contains an `HttpClientHelper` class that configures an `HttpClient` instance to be used for connecting to local web services. This is needed as some additional configuration specific to each platform needs to be done in order to effectively communicate to web services hosted locally.

> **Connecting to local web services**
>
> While developing software, it's typical to run a local web service and access it using an app in either an Android emulator or an iOS simulator. Some additional configuration is needed in order for the app to communicate with your local web service. More information about connecting to a local web service and how to configure each platform can be found here: `https://learn.microsoft.com/dotnet/maui/data-cloud/local-web-services`.

If you want to debug the *Recipes!* app, we need to tell Visual Studio to run both the mobile app and the API. To do this, right-click **Solution 'Recipes App'** in the **Solution Explorer** and select **Properties**. In the pop-up, select **Multiple startup projects** and set the **Action** of both the **Recipes.Mobile** and **Recipes.Web.Api** projects to **Start**.

As we wrap up this chapter, let's briefly turn our attention to how we can call APIs from ViewModels, deal with loading indicators, and handle potential errors, all while providing a seamless user experience.

API communication from ViewModels

When navigating to the `RecipeDetailPage`, you'll see some data on the screen while the recipe is being loaded. The data being shown is the values defined as `FallbackValue` or `TargetNullValue` in the binding statements as a result of the data in `RecipeDetailViewModel` not being loaded yet. Although effective, I don't think it looks pretty. Let's see how we can improve this by showing a loading indicator while the data is being loaded.

Showing a loading indicator

One of the simplest yet effective ways to improve user experience is to provide visual feedback during API calls. Consider the following code snippet:

```
private bool _isLoading = true;

public bool IsLoading
{
    get => _isLoading;
    set => SetProperty(ref _isLoading, value);
}

private async Task LoadRecipe(string recipeId)
{
    IsLoading = true;
...
    await Task.WhenAll(loadRecipeTask,
        loadIsFavoriteTask, loadRatingsTask);

...
    IsLoading = false;
}
```

Here, we set the IsLoading property of the RecipeDetailViewModel to true before we start loading the data and it is reverted back to false afterward. Thanks to the use of async/await, the UI thread is not blocked during this operation, allowing UI elements such as loading indicators to be updated and rendered.

You can bind this property to a loading spinner in your XAML like so:

```
<Grid>
    <ScrollView>
        ...
    </ScrollView>
    <Grid
        BackgroundColor="GhostWhite"
        IsVisible="{Binding IsLoading}">
        <ActivityIndicator
            HorizontalOptions="Center"
            IsRunning="{Binding IsLoading}"
            VerticalOptions="Center" />
    </Grid>
</Grid>
```

As a result of this setup, whenever the API call – or any long-running process, for that matter – is in progress, the user receives a visual cue, indicating that the app is currently busy. In the preceding example, we've used a `Grid` property that overlays the entire page and contains an `ActivityIndicator`. However, you're not limited to this approach; you could also use a message, an animation, or any other UI element that best suits your app's design and user experience.

Using a property to indicate that a task is in progress, and binding this property to the UI, is a common MVVM pattern for managing longer-running operations. The responsiveness is made possible by the async/await construct, which keeps the UI thread unblocked, allowing for a smoother user experience.

Earlier in this chapter, we already saw how the `Result` object can help us elegantly handle successful and unsuccessful results. Now, let's take it a step further by enhancing the user experience by handling a `Result` object that indicates failure.

Handling failures

Earlier in this chapter, we introduced the `Result` object as a way to elegantly handle failures. The object's `IsSuccess` property indicates whether an operation is completed successfully or not. We've already seen that in successful cases, the `Data` property gives us access to the result. However, when `IsSuccess` is `false`, it's crucial not to leave the user guessing. Instead, we should provide clear feedback and offer a way to resolve the issue. Let's see how this is tackled in the `LoadRecipes` method of `RecipesOverviewViewModel`:

```
private async Task LoadRecipes(int pageSize, int page)
{
    LoadFailed = false;

    var loadRecipesTask =
        recipeService.LoadRecipes(pageSize, page);
    ...
    if(recipesResult.IsSuccess)
    {
        //Set TotalNumberOfRecipes property
        //Fill Recipes collection
        ...
    }
    else
    {
        LoadFailed = true;
        ReloadCommand =
            new AsyncRelayCommand(
            () => LoadRecipes(pageSize, page));
    }
}
```

As you can see, when the task isn't successful, the `LoadFailed` property is set to `true`. Also, the `ReloadCommand` property gets initialized. The following code block shows how both properties are data-bound to the UI and will provide the user with some information and the ability to retry loading the list of recipes:

```xml
<Grid>
    <CollectionView>
    ...
    </CollectionView>
    <Grid
        BackgroundColor="{StaticResource Primary}"
        HorizontalOptions="Fill"
        IsVisible="{Binding LoadFailed}"
        VerticalOptions="Fill">
        <VerticalStackLayout
            HorizontalOptions="Center"
            VerticalOptions="Center">
            <Label Text="Unable to load recipes" />
            <Button Command="{Binding ReloadCommand}"
                Text="Retry" />
        </VerticalStackLayout>
    </Grid>
</Grid>
```

Additionally, we could show a custom error message to the user when a specific failure occurs. The `ErrorMessage`, `ErrorCode`, and `Exception` properties of the `Result` object could be used for that. This approach eliminates the need for scattering various exception-handling blocks throughout our ViewModels, thereby creating a more streamlined, readable, and maintainable code base.

Summary

We kicked off this chapter by revisiting the architecture of our *Recipes!* app to include repositories. This addition was aimed at adhering to the principle of SoC and minimizing our app's dependency on the API itself. We also introduced the `Result` object, a transformative component in our error-handling strategy. This single object encapsulates both success and failure states, making our ViewModels more robust and intelligible. By using the `Result` object, we've made it easier to handle anticipated errors in a graceful manner, while still keeping exceptions reserved for critical failures.

After setting this architectural foundation, we moved on to explore the power and simplicity of Refit, a type-safe REST client. Refit has substantially streamlined the way we interact with APIs, making the code more readable and maintainable.

We also looked at how the `Result` object elegantly fits into our ViewModels, making it far easier to handle expected errors and providing a uniform approach to error management. Alongside this, we discussed practical UI considerations, including loading indicators and error overlays, to offer the user an engaging and informative experience.

You should now have a solid understanding of how to make API calls, manage responses, and provide real-time user feedback, all in a resilient and easily maintainable way.

In the next chapter, we will be looking at how to create MVVM-friendly controls.

Further reading

To learn more about the topics that were covered in this chapter, take a look at the following resources:

- Refit documentation: `https://reactiveui.github.io/refit/`
- Consuming a REST-based web service with `HttpClient`: `https://learn.microsoft.com/dotnet/maui/data-cloud/rest`

Part 3: Mastering MVVM Development

This final part is all about refining and hardening your .NET MAUI app. We will delve deep into crafting controls that seamlessly integrate with MVVM. You will learn how to expand your app's reach with techniques for localization and fortify your code base with robust unit testing, ensuring stability and reliability. And when things don't go as planned, you will be able to rely on valuable troubleshooting and debugging tips to steer back on course.

This part has the following chapters:

- *Chapter 11, Creating MVVM-Friendly Controls*
- *Chapter 12, Localization with MVVM*
- *Chapter 13, Unit Testing*
- *Chapter 14, Troubleshooting and Debugging Tips*

11

Creating
MVVM-Friendly Controls

Up to this point, we've navigated through a wide spectrum of topics in MVVM and .NET MAUI – from the fundamental design pattern to data binding, navigation, and even working with remote data. Now, let's dig into another important topic – **custom controls**.

Sometimes, the built-in controls might fall short in catering to specific user interface requirements or unique design elements. As a consequence, you'll need to create your own by combining individual UI elements into a single, more effective unit. Making these elements MVVM-friendly and reusable throughout your app is our goal.

In this chapter, we'll focus on the following:

- Building a custom control with bindable properties
- Enabling interactions on custom controls
- Working with control templates

By the end of this chapter, you'll know how to make custom controls that not only look good but are also easy to manage in an MVVM setup. Ready to dive in?

Technical requirements

We'll continue to enhance the *Recipes!* app by diving into custom controls and control templates, all designed with an MVVM architecture in mind. To follow along with the code, make sure to visit the GitHub repository at https://github.com/PacktPublishing/MVVM-pattern-.NET-MAUI/tree/main/Chapter11. The Start folder has the initial code set up to begin this chapter, while the Finish folder contains the completed code for your reference.

Building a custom control with bindable properties

Building a feature-rich application often requires more than just the standard set of UI controls. When you have a combination of controls appearing together across multiple parts of your application – such as an input field with a list of validation errors or a button that's always used with an activity indicator – it makes sense to package these into custom controls. These custom, reusable elements not only make the code base more maintainable but also align perfectly with MVVM architecture when made bindable.

The focus of this section is not only to create custom controls but also to make them "bindable," seamlessly integrating them into our MVVM architecture. By crafting controls that are bindable, you enable straightforward communication with your ViewModel. This is key to ensuring that the UI is always up to date with an application's data and logic.

So, how do we achieve this?

Over the next few pages, we'll see how to combine existing controls into a custom, bindable control. We'll also discuss how to add custom properties and behavior to controls, ensuring they can effortlessly fit into an MVVM-based application architecture.

> **Note**
>
> While we will be creating a custom control in XAML throughout this chapter, it's important to note that everything we do can also be done entirely in code if preferred.

As we dive into creating custom controls with data binding capabilities, it's important to recall the concept of a binding target, which we covered in *Chapter 3, Data Binding Building Blocks in .NET MAUI*. In .NET MAUI, a binding target is typically a `BindableProperty` on a UI element or another `BindableObject`. To make our custom controls serve as effective binding targets, they need to inherit from `BindableObject`. Additionally, any properties that we intend to bind must be of type `BindableProperty`. This ensures that our custom controls will integrate seamlessly into the MVVM data-binding architecture.

Implementing FavoriteControl

In our *Recipes!* app, displaying whether a recipe is marked as a favorite or not is a recurring theme. The "favorite" icon appears across various parts of our app. Each time this icon appears, it behaves the same way – changing colors when the recipe is marked as a favorite. Instead of repeating the same code everywhere, we can encapsulate this pattern into a reusable `FavoriteControl`. By doing so, we make our code more maintainable and pave the way for future improvements – such as additional gestures or animations – without needing to alter multiple sections of the code base.

Let's go ahead and look at the steps needed to create our `FavoriteControl`:

1. In the **Solution Explorer**, right-click the `Controls` folder in the `Recipes.Mobile` project and select **Add | New Item…**.

2. Select **.NET MAUI ContentView (XAML)** in the dialog window (*Figure 11.1*) and enter `FavoriteControl.xaml` as the name of the new item. Click **Add**.

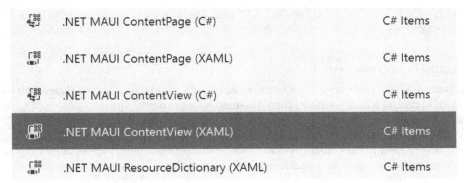

	.NET MAUI ContentPage (C#)	C# Items
	.NET MAUI ContentPage (XAML)	C# Items
	.NET MAUI ContentView (C#)	C# Items
	.NET MAUI ContentView (XAML)	C# Items
	.NET MAUI ResourceDictionary (XAML)	C# Items

Figure 11.1: Select ContentView from the dialog

By following these steps, two new files will be created – `FavoriteControl.xaml` and its code-behind file, `FavoriteControl.xaml.cs`, as shown in *Figure 11.2*:

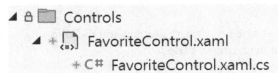

Figure 11.2: Files making up FavoriteControl

The generated `FavoriteControl` inherits the `ContentView` class, which itself is a descendant of `BindableObject`. This allows `FavoriteControl` to define `BindableProperties`, which is essential to make the control bindable. Speaking of which, `FavoriteControl` should contain a `BindableProperty` called `IsFavoriteProperty` and an `IsFavorite` property of type `bool`. The following code snippet shows what this looks like:

```
public static readonly BindableProperty IsFavoriteProperty
 =
    BindableProperty.Create(nameof(IsFavorite),
        typeof(bool), typeof(FavoriteControl));

public bool IsFavorite
{
```

```
    get { return (bool)GetValue(IsFavoriteProperty); }
    set { SetValue(IsFavoriteProperty, value); }
}
```

Defining a `BindableProperty` can be confusing or unclear at first. If this concept is still vague, *Chapter 3, Data Binding Building Blocks in .NET MAUI,* covers it in more depth.

With this in place, we can dive into XAML and start working on the visual layer of this `FavoriteControl`.

> **Data binding in a custom control**
>
> When building a custom control, it's recommended to design it so that it doesn't depend on its `BindingContext`, which it inherits from its parent page or control. Instead of depending on its `BindingContext`, the custom control should be self-contained and interact directly with its own bindable properties. This approach makes your control more modular and reusable, freeing it from dependencies on any specific ViewModel or data source. Element binding or relative binding is instrumental in achieving this independence. However, it's worth noting that using data binding within the control is not mandatory. Handling all the logic and value assignments programmatically in the control's code-behind is also a solid approach. This mostly depends on personal preference.

Let's have a look at how to define the control's appearance and see how we can efficiently bind to its `IsFavorite` property:

1. Open the `FavoriteControl.xaml` file, and add the following `local` and `toolkit` XML namespaces and the `x:Name` attribute:

    ```
    <ContentView
        x:Class="Recipes.Mobile.Controls.FavoriteControl"
        xmlns="http://schemas.microsoft.com/dotnet/
          2021/maui"
        xmlns:x="http://schemas.microsoft.com/winfx/
          2009/xaml"
        xmlns:local="clr-namespace:
          Recipes.Mobile.Controls"
        xmlns:toolkit="http://schemas.microsoft.com/
          dotnet/2022/maui/toolkit"
        x:Name="root">
    ```

2. With the `toolkit` namespace in place, which refers to the .NET MAUI Community Toolkit, we can add an instance of `BoolToObjectConverter` to the control's `Resources`. This converter can be copied over from `RecipesOverviewPage` or `RecipeDetailPage`. The next code block shows what it looks like:

```
<ContentView.Resources>
    <toolkit:BoolToObjectConverter
        x:Key="isFavoriteToColorConverter"
        x:TypeArguments="Color"
        FalseObject="#E9E9E9E9"
        TrueObject="#FF0000" />
</ContentView.Resources>
```

As a reminder, this converter (as it is configured here) will convert a `bool` value into a color – `false` will become a color with the hex value of `"#E9E9E9E9"` while `true` will be converted to `"#FF0000"`.

3. Next, we can add the `Image` control to display the `"favorite.png"` icon. We also want this Image control to match the dimensions specified for `FavoriteControl`. Here's how to set this up:

```
<Image
    x:Name="icon"
    HeightRequest="{Binding HeightRequest,
      Source={RelativeSource AncestorType={x:Type
        local:FavoriteControl}}}"
    Source="favorite.png"
    WidthRequest="{Binding WidthRequest, Source=
      {RelativeSource AncestorType={x:Type
        local:FavoriteControl}}}">
```

In this code snippet, we're using relative binding to connect the `HeightRequest` and `WidthRequest` properties of the Image control to those of `FavoriteControl`. By doing so, we ensure that the image scales according to the dimensions defined for `FavoriteControl`.

4. Finally, to control the tint of the `Image`, depending on the favorite status, we use `IconTintColorBehavior`, as shown here:

```
<Image.Behaviors>
    <toolkit:IconTintColorBehavior
        TintColor="{Binding IsFavorite,
        Source={x:Reference root},
        Converter={StaticResource
        isFavoriteToColorConverter}}" />
</Image.Behaviors>
```

This setup closely mirrors what we used on `RecipesOverviewPage` and `RecipeDetailPage`. The key difference lies in the source of the binding. Here, we bind directly to the `IsFavorite` property we just created. We achieve this using element binding (via `x:Reference root`), which refers back to `FavoriteControl` itself. This is necessary because relative binding isn't suitable here. Behaviors, unlike other UI elements, are not part of the visual tree, so they can't perform relative binding or find ancestors in the same way that other elements can.

With these steps completed, we've successfully created our first custom control, `FavoriteControl`. Now, we can go ahead and replace the existing image and `IconTintColorBehavior` setup, used to indicate favorite recipes on both `RecipesOverviewPage` and `RecipeDetailPage`, with this custom control. Let's do this in the following steps:

1. Go to `RecipesOverviewPage` and add an `xml` namespace, referring to the namespace containing the newly created `FavoriteControl`, as shown here:

    ```
    xmlns:controls="clr-namespace:Recipes.Mobile.Controls"
    ```

2. The XML namespace (`xmlns:toolkit`) pointing to the .NET MAUI Community Toolkit can be removed, as we won't be using any of its functionalities anymore on this page. This is now encapsulated in our custom control.

3. Remove the `Image` UI element along with its associated behavior, which until now served as the favorite indicator for a recipe.

4. In place of the deleted `Image`, insert the `FavoriteControl` we just created. Here's how to do it:

    ```
    <controls:FavoriteControl
        Margin="5"
        HeightRequest="45"
        HorizontalOptions="End"
        IsFavorite="{Binding IsFavorite}"
        IsVisible="{Binding IsFavorite}"
        VerticalOptions="Start"
        WidthRequest="45" />
    ```

The layout properties such as margin, size, visibility, and alignment options are unchanged from the removed `Image`. Also, observe how easily we can bind the `IsFavorite` property of our `FavoriteControl` to the corresponding `IsFavorite` property on the page's `BindingContext`.

For `RecipeDetailPage`, we can follow a similar approach. Include an XML namespace that points to `Recipes.Mobile.Controls` and swap out the `Image`, which previously signaled whether the recipe was a favorite, with the newly created `FavoriteControl`. This is what the result looks like:

```
<ContentPage
    x:Class="Recipes.Mobile.RecipeDetailPage"
    xmlns="http://schemas.microsoft.com/dotnet/2021/maui"
    xmlns:x="http://schemas.microsoft.com/winfx/2009/xaml"
    xmlns:controls="clr-namespace:Recipes.Mobile.Controls"
    ...>
...
    <Grid ColumnDefinitions="*, Auto">
        <Label FontAttributes="Bold" FontSize="22"
            Text="{Binding Path=Title, Mode=OneWay}"
            VerticalOptions="Center" />
        <controls:FavoriteControl Grid.Column="1"
            Margin="5" HeightRequest="35"
            IsFavorite="{Binding IsFavorite}"
            VerticalOptions="Center" WidthRequest="35" />
    </Grid>
...
</ContentPage>
```

By consolidating the favorite indicator into a single, reusable `FavoriteControl`, we've achieved multiple objectives. Firstly, we've centralized the code, making it easier to manage and update. Secondly, this control can now be used consistently across different pages of the app, ensuring a uniform user experience. Finally, by doing so, we've also enhanced the readability and maintainability of our code base. *Figure 11.3* shows `FavoriteControl` on different pages of the app. Although nothing has visibly changed for the user, the code and its maintainability profit immensely from this reusable control.

Figure 11.3: FavoriteControl on different pages

Let's see how we can improve this control a bit more, making the app more attractive to the user.

Animating state changes

As a quick example of reacting to state changes, let's explore how to add a subtle animation to `FavoriteControl` whenever the `IsFavorite` property changes. We'll use the `propertyChanged` delegate method of `IsFavoriteProperty` to trigger this animation. Let's dive in!

1. Modify `IsFavoriteProperty` by adding a `propertyChanged` delegate, like this:

```
public static readonly BindableProperty
  IsFavoriteProperty =
        BindableProperty.Create(nameof(IsFavorite),
        typeof(bool),
        typeof(FavoriteControl),
        propertyChanged: OnIsFavoriteChanged);

private static void OnIsFavoriteChanged(BindableObject
  bindable, object oldValue, object newValue)
{
}
```

With this modification, the static `OnIsFavoriteChanged` method will be invoked each time the value of the `IsFavorite` property changes. The `BindableObject` that gets passed in is the instance on which `BindableProperty` is set. In this case, it will be an instance of `FavoriteControl`. The `oldValue` and `newValue` parameters are self-explanatory, as they provide the previous and new values of the property, respectively.

2. Next, let's add the animation we want to play when the control's state changes. Here's how we can add it:

```
private async Task AnimateChange()
{
    await icon.ScaleTo(1.5, 100);
    await icon.ScaleTo(1, 100);
}
```

The `AnimateChange` method will scale the `Image` holding the icon to 1.5 times its size over a period of 100 milliseconds. Afterward, it will be scaled down again to its original size over the same amount of time.

3. Finally, we need to call this method from the static `OnIsFavoriteChanged` method. The following code block shows how this can be done:

```
private static void OnIsFavoriteChanged(
    BindableObject bindable,
    object oldValue, object newValue)
    => (bindable as FavoriteControl).AnimateChange();
```

The bindable parameter can safely be cast to `FavoriteControl`, allowing us to call the `AnimateChange` method, triggering the animation.

Run the app to see the changes in action! You'll observe a subtle animation on the `RecipeDetailPage` each time a recipe is toggled as a favorite. Introducing this custom control brings the convenience of unified animations across the application. Any modification made to the animation within the custom control gets automatically reflected everywhere it's used. Without such a control, we'd need to manually update the animation at each individual instance throughout the app. Overlooking even a single instance would lead to inconsistent behavior. Thus, custom controls ensure both consistency and streamlined maintainability.

> **Note**
>
> This example underscores an important point – even when you're fully committed to using the MVVM pattern, there will be scenarios where writing code in the code-behind is not just acceptable but necessary. This is especially true when creating custom controls, where using code-behind is not only inevitable but also perfectly appropriate.

Next, let's explore how to add interactions to a custom control by leveraging commanding, thereby further aligning it with MVVM concepts.

Enabling interactions on custom controls

In real-world applications, controls often serve dual roles – they both display data and allow users to interact with it. In this section, we'll further enhance our `FavoriteControl` to not only support user interactions through `IsFavoriteChangedCommand` but also to facilitate two-way data binding. These features will make the control more interactive and further align it with MVVM concepts. We want to allow users to tap the `Image` on the `FavoriteControl`. When `FavoriteControl`'s `IsEnabled` property is set to `true`, the `IsFavorite` property will be updated and `IsFavoriteChangedCommand` will be executed.

Let's take a look at the first part of this functionality – updating the `IsFavorite` property when a user taps on the image and making sure the value bound to this property gets updated as well.

User actions and reflecting state

To start with, let's add the ability for users to toggle their favorite state by tapping on the control. This user action will then update the `IsFavorite` property of the control, which, in turn, will reflect back to update the bound property. The following steps show how to achieve this:

1. Add a `GestureRecognizer` to the `FavoriteControl`'s `ContentView`, as shown here:

```
<ContentView.GestureRecognizers>
    <TapGestureRecognizer
```

```
        Tapped="TapGestureRecognizer_Tapped" />
    </ContentView.GestureRecognizers>
```

A `GestureRecognizer` allows you to handle user interaction events, such as tapping, pinching, and swiping, on a UI element. By adding a `TapGestureRecognizer` to the `ContentView`, we effectively instruct the application to listen for a tap event on this control.

Here's the `TapGestureRecognizer_Tapped` event handler in the code-behind:

```
private void TapGestureRecognizer_Tapped(
    object sender, TappedEventArgs e)
{
}
```

This method will be triggered when a user taps on the `FavoriteControl`.

2. Now, let's implement the logic needed to update the `IsFavorite` property in the `TapGestureRecognizer_Tapped` method:

```
private void TapGestureRecognizer_Tapped(
    object sender, TappedEventArgs e)
{
    if (IsEnabled)
    {
        IsFavorite = !IsFavorite;
    }
}
```

Note how we first check the `IsEnabled` property before updating the `IsFavorite`. It's crucial for custom controls to behave consistently with developers' expectations. In this case, setting the `IsEnabled` property of a `VisualElement` to `false` should disable the control. As a result, we check the `IsEnabled` property before toggling the value of `IsFavorite`.

If we run the app and navigate to `RecipeDetailPage` at this point, tapping `FavoriteControl` should update its state. The animation we defined earlier also plays as a reaction to the `IsFavorite` property being updated. However, the state change is not reflected on the ViewModel. You might wonder why this is the case. It's because `IsFavoriteProperty` has a default binding mode of `OneWay`. That's why the updated value doesn't flow from the control back to the ViewModel. This can easily be adjusted – change the `IsFavoriteProperty`'s default binding mode to `TwoWay`, or update the binding statement on the `RecipeDetailPage` and explicitly set it to `TwoWay`. Here's what the first approach – updating the default binding mode – looks like:

```
public static readonly BindableProperty
IsFavoriteProperty =
    BindableProperty.Create(nameof(IsFavorite),
        typeof(bool),
```

```
    typeof(FavoriteControl),
    defaultBindingMode: BindingMode.TwoWay,
    propertyChanged: OnIsFavoriteChanged);
```

Alternatively, we can leave the default binding mode to `OneWay` and update the binding statement on `RecipeDetailPage`, as shown here:

```
<controls:FavoriteControl
    Grid.Column="1"
    Margin="5"
    HeightRequest="35"
    IsFavorite="{Binding IsFavorite, Mode=TwoWay}"
    VerticalOptions="Center"
    WidthRequest="35" />
```

Either way, the `IsFavorite` property on the `FavoriteControl` will now reflect its state on the ViewModel. How can we verify this? By adding breakpoints in code of course, but also by simply tapping the control – note how the visibility of the **Add as favorite** and **Remove as favorite** buttons also update, as their visibility depends on the `IsFavorite` property on the ViewModel.

> **Note**
>
> When defining a bindable property, it's crucial to select the `defaultBindingMode` that aligns best with the control's primary intended behavior or the binding mode that will be most commonly used. In the rare instances where different behavior is required, the developer can always override the default by specifying a different binding mode in the binding statement.

Two-way data binding is a powerful feature that allows your custom control to interact with the underlying data. While this brings your control to life, adding support for command-based interactions allows developers to tie more meaningful, custom behavior to your control. This is particularly useful in scenarios where simply updating a data property may not be sufficient to capture the complexity of a user interaction. Specifically, in our scenario, simply updating the `IsFavorite` property won't result in the underlying model being updated. Let's delve into how we can incorporate commands into our `FavoriteControl` to make it even more versatile.

Adding command-based interactions

Let's further enhance our `FavoriteControl` by exposing a command property – `ToggledCommand`. This command will be invoked whenever the `IsFavorite` property is toggled via a tap gesture on the control. To make this even more robust, the command will send the updated `IsFavorite` bool value as a parameter.

Adding command-based interactions to custom controls is pretty straightforward, as the following steps show:

1. It all starts by adding a `BindableProperty` and a property of type `ICommand`. This code block shows how to add the `ToggledCommand` property and its corresponding `BindableProperty` to our `FavoriteControl`:

```
public static readonly BindableProperty
  ToggledCommandProperty =
    BindableProperty.Create(
        nameof(ToggledCommand),
        typeof(ICommand), typeof(FavoriteControl));

public ICommand ToggledCommand
{
    get => (ICommand)
        GetValue(ToggledCommandProperty);
    set => SetValue(ToggledCommandProperty, value);
}
```

2. Next, we can call the command's `Execute` method whenever the user has tapped the control and, thus, has updated the `IsFavorite` property. Here's what the updated `TapGestureRecognizer_Tapped` method looks like:

```
private void TapGestureRecognizer_Tapped(
    object sender, TappedEventArgs e)
{
    if (IsEnabled)
    {
        IsFavorite = !IsFavorite;
        ToggledCommand?.Execute(IsFavorite);
    }
}
```

Note that we're using the null-conditional operator (?) to prevent a `NullReferenceException` in case `ToggledCommand` is null.

3. The following code block shows the `FavoriteToggledCommand` that we can add to the `RecipeDetailViewModel`, and which we will bind to the `ToggledCommand` of the `FavoriteControl`:

```
...
public IRelayCommand FavoriteToggledCommand { get; }
...
public RecipeDetailViewModel(...)
{
```

```
    ...
    FavoriteToggledCommand =
        new AsyncRelayCommand<bool>(FavoriteToggled);
    ...
}
...
```

4. Next, let's add the `FavoriteToggled` method, which is called by `FavoriteToggledCommand`. Here's what it looks like:

```
private async Task FavoriteToggled(bool isFavorite)
{
    if(isFavorite)
    {
        await favoritesService.Add(recipeDto.Id);
    }
    else
    {
        await favoritesService.Remove(recipeDto.Id);
    }
}
```

The `ToggledCommand` of the `FavoriteControl` sends the updated `isFavorite` value as a parameter. We can use this parameter to decide what method to call on the `favoritesService`.

5. With this in place, we can also quickly refactor the existing `AddAsFavorite` and `RemoveAsFavorite` methods in order to avoid code duplication, as shown here:

```
private Task AddAsFavorite()
    => UpdateIsFavorite(true);

private Task RemoveAsFavorite()
    => UpdateIsFavorite(false);

private Task UpdateIsFavorite(bool newValue)
{
    IsFavorite = newValue;
    return FavoriteToggled(newValue);
}
```

The `UpdateIsFavorite` method is added. This method takes in the new value that the `IsFavorite` property should get. It assigns this value to the property and calls the `FavoriteToggled` method that we just introduced. From the `AddAsFavorite` and `RemoveAsFavorite` methods, this new `UpdateIsFavorite` method can now be called, passing in just a `bool` value.

6. The only thing that is left to do is to bind `FavoriteToggledCommand` of `RecipeDetailViewModel` to the `ToggledCommand` property of the `FavoriteControl` on the `RecipeDetailPage`. Here's how:

```
<controls:FavoriteControl
    Grid.Column="1"
    Margin="5"
    HeightRequest="35"
    IsFavorite="{Binding IsFavorite, Mode=TwoWay}"
    ToggledCommand="{Binding FavoriteToggledCommand}"
    VerticalOptions="Center"
    WidthRequest="150" />
```

If we run the app now, we'll see that not only does the `IsFavorite` property updates when the `FavoriteControl` is tapped but the bound `FavoriteToggledCommand` is also invoked, allowing for seamless interaction and data updates in our application. This completes the integration of a very basic command-based interaction into our custom control. Let's continue and make the control better and more intuitive for both the users of our app and other developers.

Improving developer and user experience

While the previous example provided a foundational understanding of how to integrate command-based interactions into our custom control, it merely scratched the surface. Developers aiming to integrate this control across diverse use cases and the end-users who will interact with it both anticipate a solution that's more polished and adaptable. For instance, we could enhance the user experience by providing visual cues that indicate the control is clickable. On the developer side, we want our control to be predictable; developers expect things to work in a certain way. Ideally, our control should adhere to the bound command's `CanExecute` method and adjust its behavior accordingly. In my experience, poorly designed or inadequately thought-through controls have often created headaches for both myself and my colleagues. The goal is to make a custom control intuitive enough that it doesn't require extensive explanation for straightforward tasks. Let's see how we can bring our `FavoriteControl` to another level!

Let's first introduce a new property called `IsInteractive` to `FavoriteControl`. This property will be set to `true` when the `IsEnabled` property of the control is set to `true`, the `ToggleCommand` is set, and its `CanExecute` method returns `true`. In all other situations, the value of the `IsInteractive` property needs to be `false`. This property can then be checked inside the control prior to executing an action. Let's go through this step by step:

1. Add the `IsInteractive` property to `FavoriteControl`, as shown here:

```
public bool IsInteractive { get; private set; }
```

2. The following code snippet shows the `UpdateIsInteractive` method. This method is responsible for setting the `IsInteractive` property:

```
private void UpdateIsInteractive()
    => IsInteractive = IsEnabled
    && (ToggledCommand?.CanExecute(IsFavorite)
    ?? false);
```

3. Update the `TapGestureRecognizer_Tapped` method, as shown in the next code block:

```
private void TapGestureRecognizer_Tapped(
    object sender, TappedEventArgs e)
{
    if (IsInteractive)
    {
        IsFavorite = !IsFavorite;
        ToggledCommand?.Execute(IsFavorite);
    }
}
```

By updating the code that is shown here, we only allow the `IsFavorite` property to be toggled when the `IsInteractive` property is set to `true`. This means the control is enabled, its `ToggleCommand` is set, and the `ToggleCommand`'s `CanExecute` method returns `true`.

Next, we need to make sure that the `UpdateIsInteractive` method is called when its value needs updating. That's the case in the following three situations:

- When the value of the `IsEnabled` property changes
- When the `ToggleCommand` property is updated
- When the `CanExecuteChanged` event of the command is triggered

In the following steps, we'll put everything in place so that the `UpdateIsInteractive` method is called in the aforementioned situations:

1. In the `FavoriteControl` class, override the `OnPropertyChanged` method. This method gets called by the control's properties in order to trigger the `PropertyChanged` event, just like we typically have in our ViewModels. Let's see what we can do with it:

```
protected override void OnPropertyChanged(
    [CallerMemberName] string propertyName = null)
{
    base.OnPropertyChanged(propertyName);

    if(propertyName == nameof(IsEnabled))
    {
```

```
                    UpdateIsInteractive();
            }
    }
```

Whenever the passed-in `propertyName` matches the `IsEnabled` property, we want to trigger the `UpdateIsInteractive` method. This ensures that whenever the `IsEnabled` property is updated, the `IsInteractive` property gets re-evaluated.

2. Next, we move on to make sure that the `IsInteractive` property gets updated when `ToggledCommand` is updated. Let's start by adding a `propertyChanged` delegate to `ToggledCommandProperty`, as shown here:

```
public static readonly BindableProperty
    ToggledCommandProperty =
        BindableProperty.Create(nameof(ToggledCommand),
            typeof(ICommand), typeof(FavoriteControl),
            propertyChanged: ToggledCommandChanged);

private static void ToggledCommandChanged(
        BindableObject bindable,
        object oldValue, object newValue)
{
        var control = bindable as FavoriteControl;
        control.UpdateIsInteractive();
}
```

The `ToggledCommandChanged` method is called when the value of the command is updated. This is the ideal place to call the `UpdateIsInteractive` method so that the `IsInteractive` property gets updated, based on the new `ToggledCommand`.

3. Finally, our `IsInteractive` property isn't solely reliant on the `IsEnabled` property and the presence of the `ToggledCommand`. It also takes into account the `CanExecute` method of the defined command. To achieve this, we need to listen for changes in the command's `CanExecute` state by subscribing to its `CanExecuteChanged` event. Here's how we can update the `ToggleCommandChanged` method for that purpose:

```
private static void ToggledCommandChanged(
        BindableObject bindable,
        object oldValue, object newValue)
{
        var control = bindable as FavoriteControl;

        if (oldValue is ICommand oldCommand)
        {
            oldCommand.CanExecuteChanged -=
```

```
                control.CanExecuteChanged;
    }

    if (newValue is ICommand newCommand)
    {
        newCommand.CanExecuteChanged +=
            control.CanExecuteChanged;
    }

    control.UpdateIsInteractive();
}
```

After setting the new command, we're not just subscribing to its `CanExecuteChanged` event; we're also making sure to unsubscribe from the same event on the previous command. This is crucial to ensure that our control only reacts to the current command's `CanExecute` state. The `CanExecuteChanged` event handler merely calls the `UpdateIsInteractive` method, as shown here:

```
private void CanExecuteChanged(
    object sender, EventArgs e)
    => UpdateIsInteractive();
```

In summary, the `IsInteractive` property serves as the gateway for user interactions with the control. Its state is determined by a combination of factors – the `IsEnabled` property of the control, the presence of a command, and that command's `CanExecute` method. Importantly, the `IsInteractive` state is dynamically re-evaluated every time any of these contributing factors change.

Let's see this in action! For demo purposes, let's add a maximum number of times the favorite state of a recipe can be toggled via `FavoriteControl`. The `canExecute` delegate of the `FavoriteToggledCommand` on the `RecipeDetailViewModel` should return `true` as long as this number is not exceeded. Let's see how we can implement this:

1. Let's start by adding the following two fields to `RecipeDetailViewModel`:

   ```
   int updateCount = 0;
   int maxUpdatedAllowed = 5;
   ```

2. Next, update the `FavoriteToggledCommand` so that it includes the `canExecute` predicate, as shown here:

   ```
   FavoriteToggledCommand = new AsyncRelayCommand<bool>(
       FavoriteToggled,
       (e) => updateCount < maxUpdatedAllowed);
   ```

3. Finally, update the `FavoriteToggled` method so that it keeps track of the number of times it was invoked, as shown here:

```
private async Task FavoriteToggled(bool isFavorite)
{
    ...

    updateCount++;
    FavoriteToggledCommand.NotifyCanExecuteChanged();
}
```

Not only does this method now keep track of the number of times it was invoked, but it also triggers the `NotifyCanExecuteChanged` event of the `FavoriteToggledCommand`. As a result, the `CanExecuteChanged` method on `FavoriteControl` will get called, which will eventually call the command's `CanExecute` method to see whether it still can be executed.

With this in place, we can run the app and see how the `FavoriteControl` reacts to the `ToggleCommand`'s `CanExecute` method. Go to the detail page of a recipe and press the `FavoriteControl` a couple of times. You'll notice the favorite state will be updated until you've clicked five times. After that, the `ToggleCommand`'s `CanExecute` method returns `false`, resulting in `IsInteractive` being set to `false` as well. Any following interactions with the control will be ignored because of this. Additionally, on the `RecipesOverviewPage`, you'll find that `FavoriteControl` is not tappable due to the absence of a defined `ToggleCommand`. Both scenarios illustrate that the controls behave as expected!

Now that we've established how the `IsInteractive` property works, let's turn our attention to leveraging it for a more intuitive user experience. Specifically, we'll explore how to use this property to provide a visual cue that indicates whether or not the control is tappable. There's not that much we can do about our `FavoriteControl` to make it really clear that it's tappable. For the purposes of this demo, we'll add a simple indicator – a black border around the heart icon when it's tappable. Here's how we can do this:

1. Open the `FavoriteControl.xaml` file and surround the existing `Image` control with `Grid`, as shown in the following snippet:

```
<Grid>
    <Image x:Name="icon" ...>
        ...
    </Image>
</Grid>
```

2. Inside this grid, add the following `Image`, prior to the existing one:

```
<Grid>
    <Image
        HeightRequest="{Binding HeightRequest,
            Source={x:Reference icon}}"
```

```
        WidthRequest="{Binding WidthRequest,
            Source={x:Reference icon}}"
        IsVisible="{Binding IsInteractive,
            Source={RelativeSource
            AncestorType={x:Type
            local:FavoriteControl}}}"
        Scale="1.2"
        Source="{Binding Source,
            Source={x:Reference icon}}" />
    <Image x:Name="icon" ...>
        ...
    </Image>
</Grid>
```

Grid allows controls to be placed on top of each other. The added Image will be rendered below the existing favorite icon. Its HeightRequest, WidthRequest, and Source properties are bound to those of the existing Image. Do note its Scale property – it's set to 1.2. As a result, this new Image will be a bit bigger than the Image on top. This creates the visual effect of a border surrounding the icon. Also, take a look at the IsVisible property – it's bound to the IsInteractive property we introduced earlier. Because of this, the underlying Image will only be rendered when the control is tappable, giving a user a visual cue.

3.   Lastly, it's crucial not to forget to trigger the PropertyChanged event for the IsInteractive property whenever it is updated. Otherwise, the binding engine wouldn't be notified about the updated value. The following snippet shows how we can update the UpdateIsInteractive method to do that:

```
private void UpdateIsInteractive()
{
    IsInteractive = IsEnabled
    && (ToggledCommand?.CanExecute(IsFavorite)
    ?? false);
    OnPropertyChanged(nameof(IsInteractive));
}
```

When running the app now and navigating to a RecipeDetailPage, you should see a black border around the favorite icon, indicating that the control is interactive. This border isn't visible on the RecipeOverviewPage because of the absence of a ToggledCommand. Moreover, when tapping FavoriteControl on a RecipeDetailPage a few times, after the fifth time, the border will disappear because FavoriteToggledCommand's CanExecute method returns false. This visual cue informs a user that the control is no longer interactive. *Figure 11.4* shows the FavoriteControl on the RecipeDetailPage in all its different states:

Figure 11.4: FavoriteControl in different states

Now that we've fine-tuned the user and developer experience, let's take it a step further by making our control's design as adaptable as its functionality.

Working with control templates

So far, we've been dealing with a hardcoded look and feel, but what if we want to offer more flexibility without forcing developers to rewrite or extend our control? By supporting control templates, we can expose the structure of our control's visual tree, enabling both styling and structural changes while retaining its core functionality. This is an excellent way to ensure that our custom control seamlessly fits into a diverse array of user interfaces, providing an even greater degree of customization.

You might wonder how this is relevant to MVVM. Consider the following – a control template serves to separate the logic and behavior of a control from its visual representation, much like how MVVM achieves loose coupling between the ViewModel and the View. In this sense, the control effectively serves as a ViewModel for the control template. It exposes properties that the template binds to. The control template, in turn, can be considered as the View. So, just like we are used to, we can use data binding in the control template and use a relative binding source set to `TemplatedParent` to bind to the properties of the control that the template is applied to.

> **TemplateBinding and TemplatedParent**
>
> In the upcoming examples, we'll use binding statements with their `RelativeSource` set to `TemplatedParent`. It's worth noting that this approach performs the same function as the now-obsolete `TemplateBinding` markup extension. Essentially, setting `RelativeSource` to `TemplatedParent` manually accomplishes what `TemplateBinding` used to do automatically, creating a binding whose source is the control to which the template is applied. However, since .NET 7, the `TemplateBinding` markup extension has been marked as "obsolete."

I want to quickly discuss control templates, as they reflect the MVVM philosophy. Whether you're extending the visuals of existing controls or creating new ones from scratch, knowing how to properly structure and utilize control templates will make your development process more efficient and your applications more maintainable. I also think that being proficient in the aspects of XAML and data binding directly contributes to effectively applying the MVVM pattern in your projects. Without further ado, let's dive in!

The next steps show how to define a control template and apply it to the `FavoriteControl`:

1. On `RecipeDetailPage`, we can add a `ControlTemplate` to the page's `Resources`, as shown in the following snippet:

```
<ControlTemplate x:Key="FavoriteTemplate">
    <VerticalStackLayout>
        <Label
            FontSize="10" HorizontalOptions="Center"
            Text="Favorite?" />
        <Switch
            HorizontalOptions="Center"
            InputTransparent="True"
            IsEnabled="{Binding IsInteractive,
             Source={RelativeSource TemplatedParent}}"
            IsToggled="{Binding IsFavorite, Source=
                {RelativeSource TemplatedParent},
                    Mode=OneWay}"
        />
    </VerticalStackLayout>
</ControlTemplate>
```

    Note how this template uses `TemplatedParent` as `RelativeSource` in its binding statements. By doing this, we bind to the public properties exposed by the control where this template will be applied, as we will see later on.

2. The following code snippet shows how we can use the key associated with the `ControlTemplate` (`FavoriteTemplate`), together with the `StaticResource` Markup extension, to assign it as the template of our `FavoriteControl`:

```
<controls:FavoriteControl
    ...
    ControlTemplate="{StaticResource
      FavoriteTemplate}"
    ... />
```

While maintaining the functionality of the `FavoriteControl`, this template gives an entirely different look to the control, as you can see in *Figure 11.5*:

Favorite?

Classic Caesar Salad

Last updated: Friday, July 3, 2020 | Sally Burton

Figure 11.5: FavoriteControl with an alternative template

However, there is one thing missing. Remember the animation we had on the original control? The animation was triggered by the following code:

```
private async Task AnimateChange()
{
    await icon.ScaleTo(1.5, 100);
    await icon.ScaleTo(1, 100);
}
```

The original visual tree of the control is replaced by the new visual tree defined in the `ControlTemplate`. Therefore, the original elements are not visible and are not part of the current visual tree. However, those original elements do still exist in memory if you have references to them in your code-behind. Even though they are detached from the visual tree and are not visible, you can still interact with them using code. They just won't have any impact on what a user sees because they are not in the visual tree anymore. As a result, the code responsible for the animation won't crash, but there won't be any visual effect on the screen. Let's see how we can access visual elements defined on a `ControlTemplate`.

Accessing elements from a template

Traditionally, when working with custom controls, UI elements are defined directly within the control. These controls, when given an `x:Name` attribute, can be accessed and manipulated from the control's code-behind, which is a perfectly valid approach to defining and working with custom controls. However, when fully embracing the power of control templates, the need for directly defined UI elements lessens. Instead, the default appearance of the control should ideally be encapsulated within a `ControlTemplate`.

For illustration, let's consider `FavoriteControlTemplated`, which is a variant of `FavoriteControl`. Unlike the original, this version doesn't have UI elements defined directly within it. Instead, its default appearance is declared in a `ControlTemplate`, defined in the control's `Resources`. Here's how it looks in XAML:

```
<ContentView
    ...>
    <ContentView.Resources>
        <toolkit:BoolToObjectConverter
```

```
                    ... />
        <ControlTemplate x:Key="DefaultTemplate">
            <Grid>
                <Image
                    HeightRequest="{Binding HeightRequest,
                     Source={x:Reference TemplatedParent}}"
                    IsVisible="{Binding IsInteractive,
                      Source={RelativeSource
                        TemplatedParent}}"
                    Scale="1.2"
                    Source="{Binding Source, Source=
                      {x:Reference scalableContent}}"
                    WidthRequest="{Binding WidthRequest,
                     Source={x:Reference scalableContent}}"
                        />
                <Image
                    x:Name="scalableContent"
                    HeightRequest="{Binding HeightRequest,
                      Source={RelativeSource
                        TemplatedParent}}"
                    Source="favorite.png"
                    WidthRequest="{Binding WidthRequest,
                      Source={RelativeSource
                        TemplatedParent}}">
                    <Image.Behaviors>
                        ...
                    </Image.Behaviors>
                </Image>
            </Grid>
        </ControlTemplate>
    </ContentView.Resources>
    <ContentView.GestureRecognizers>
        ...
    </ContentView.GestureRecognizers>
</ContentView>
```

As you can see in the next code block, in the constructor of the `FavoriteControlTemplated` class, a default template is assigned when no other template is specified:

```
public FavoriteControlTemplated()
{
    InitializeComponent();
    if(ControlTemplate == null)
    {
```

```
            var template = Resources["DefaultTemplate"];
            ControlTemplate = template as ControlTemplate;
    }
}
```

If the `ControlTemplate` property is null, it means the developer hasn't specified a different template. In that case, the default template from the control's `Resources` is retrieved and assigned.

The `OnApplyTemplate` method is called when the control template is fully loaded. This is where the `GetTemplateChild` method can be used to access specific elements within the template, like `Image` in our template, which we assigned the name `scalableContent`. The following snippet shows how we use the `GetTemplateChild` method to get a `VisualElement` named `scalableContent`:

```
VisualElement scalableContent;

protected override void OnApplyTemplate()
{
    base.OnApplyTemplate();
    scalableContent =
        GetTemplateChild("scalableContent")
        as VisualElement;
}
```

Once a `VisualElement` with the name `scalableContent` is retrieved, it can be manipulated programmatically. For example, in the `AnimateChange` method, scaling animations can be applied to it:

```
private async Task AnimateChange()
{
    if (scalableContent is not null)
    {
        await scalableContent.ScaleTo(1.5, 100);
        await scalableContent.ScaleTo(1, 100);
    }
}
```

By adopting control templates and leveraging methods such as `GetTemplateChild`, we can maintain a clean separation between the logic and visual representation of our control, allowing more flexible and reusable components.

Let's update the `FavoriteTemplate` we created earlier on `RecipeDetailPage` by giving a certain UI element the name `scalableContent`, using `FavoriteControlTemplated` instead of `FavoriteControl`. Here's how:

1. On `RecipeDetailPage`, update the `FavoriteTemplate`, as shown here:

    ```
    <ControlTemplate x:Key="FavoriteTemplate">
        . . .
            <Switch
                x:Name="scalebleContent"
                … />
        </VerticalStackLayout>
    </ControlTemplate>
    ```

    By assigning `scalebleContent` as the name of the `Switch` control, it can be picked up later by the `FavoriteControlTemplated` control and have animations applied to it.

2. As shown in the next code block, let's use the `FavoriteControlTemplated` custom control instead of the `FavoriteControl` from earlier:

    ```
    <controls:FavoriteControlTemplated
        Grid.Column="1"
        Margin="5"
        ControlTemplate="{StaticResource
          FavoriteTemplate}"
        IsFavorite="{Binding IsFavorite, Mode=TwoWay}"
        ToggledCommand="{Binding FavoriteToggledCommand}"
        VerticalOptions="Center" />
    ```

    If you run the app at this stage, you'll notice the updated favorite indicator. When we tap the control, you'll notice the `Switch` is scaled. This is because it was named `scalableContent` in the template. If you update `RecipeDetailPage` and leave out the assignment of the `ControlTemplate` property (`ControlTemplate="{StaticResource FavoriteTemplate}"`) and run the app again, you'll see the visualization using the hearts we had earlier. That's because when no `ControlTemplate` is assigned explicitly, the control will load the default control template.

It's worth noting that any control template that includes an element named `scalableContent` will be compatible with this code. In other words, as long as the template has a UI element with the name `scalableContent`, our `FavoriteControlTemplated` class will be able to retrieve it and apply the scaling animation. However, what if there's no `scalableContent` element in the template? No worries – the control is designed to degrade gracefully. If the element isn't found, all functionalities of the control will remain intact; only the animation will be absent. This flexibility allows developers to create a wide array of visual styles while the behavior of the control remains intact.

The principle of separation of concerns is central to MVVM and vital to creating maintainable software. When you're crafting custom controls, this same principle can be extended through the use of control templates. However, it's worth mentioning that fully implementing control templates may not always be necessary. For simpler controls that are unique to your application and maintain a consistent appearance, directly defining UI elements within the control itself is both a practical and valid approach. This allows you to balance complexity with flexibility, enabling you to choose the approach that best suits your project's specific requirements.

Summary

In this chapter, we explored the powerful possibilities offered by custom controls and control templates in .NET MAUI, all within the context of the MVVM architecture. From understanding the basics of custom controls to creating bindable properties, we've delved into the intricacies of data binding on custom controls. We also explored how to add interactivity to our control and how commands can be exposed and dealt with. Furthermore, we dived deep into the flexibility and scalability offered by control templates. Collectively, these techniques enhance reusability and adhere to the principles of separation of concerns. Mastering the art of creating UIs – whether through XAML or code-behind – and understanding how to craft MVVM-friendly controls with bindable properties and commands contributes tremendously to being proficient in MVVM. Whether it's a simple control with a hardcoded appearance or a complex, template-driven control, the key takeaway is understanding when and how to appropriately apply these approaches to create maintainable, adaptable, and highly customizable UI components.

In the next chapter, we'll explore localization within the context of MVVM, enabling our UI components to be not only flexible and maintainable but also globally adaptable.

Further reading

To learn more about the topics that were covered in this chapter, take a look at the following resources:

- Create a custom control using handlers: `https://learn.microsoft.com/dotnet/maui/user-interface/handlers/create`

- Customize controls with handlers: `https://learn.microsoft.com/dotnet/maui/user-interface/handlers/customize`

- More about control templates: `https://learn.microsoft.com/dotnet/maui/fundamentals/controltemplate`

- Bind to a templated parent: `https://learn.microsoft.com/dotnet/maui/fundamentals/data-binding/relative-bindings#bind-to-a-templated-parent`

12

Localization with MVVM

So, we've built this fantastic *Recipes!* app, and we're quite pleased with its design and features. However, as it stands, the app is entirely in English. What about culinary enthusiasts from different parts of the world? The answer is localization, specifically focusing on translating all aspects of our app to make it accessible and user-friendly to a global audience.

In this chapter, we'll tackle localization through the lens of MVVM. We'll be looking at translating the hardcoded `copy` labels that are baked into the app, but also at effectively fetching language-specific data from the API. To accomplish this, we'll delve into the following topics:

- Working with cultures, resource files, and localization

- Looking at a localization solution for MVVM

- Using a custom `Translate` markup extension

- Fetching localized data from APIs

As we dive into this chapter, remember that our journey through localization also showcases thoughtful app design with MVVM principles. By the end, not only will we have the tools and knowledge to extend the reach of our app to a diverse, global audience through the UI, but we'll also see how the right design choices ensure that every layer of our app, down to the data we present, is coherent and organized.

Technical requirements

As always, for hands-on experience and to keep pace with the content, head over to our GitHub repository at `https://github.com/PacktPublishing/MVVM-pattern-.NET-MAUI/tree/main/Chapter12`. Begin with the code in the `Start` folder, and, for a comprehensive view, you can always refer to the `Finish` folder, which houses the polished, end-of-chapter code.

Working with cultures, resource files, and localization

Before we jump into the actual coding bits and look at how we can integrate localization in MVVM, let's make sure we're all on the same page about what we mean by *culture* in the .NET MAUI context. Culture, in this case, refers to the settings that determine the language to be used and the display format for items such as dates, times, currency, and so on.

Let's start with how to retrieve the user's culture in .NET MAUI.

Getting the user's culture

The `CultureInfo` class is part of the `System.Globalization` namespace in .NET and serves as a central point for obtaining culture-specific information, such as language, country, date formats, number formats, and more. It also contains `CurrentCulture` and `CurrentUICulture` properties that can be used to get or set the user's current culture and "UI culture."

> **CurrentCulture versus CurrentUICulture**
>
> `CurrentCulture` defines how data types such as dates, numbers, and currencies should be formatted in the application. This ensures that the look and feel of the data aligns with the user's cultural context. On the other hand, `CurrentUICulture` dictates the language used for the UI elements and text resources. `CurrentCulture` determines *how things look* (formatting), while `CurrentUICulture` controls *which language is being used* (localization).

The user's current culture settings can be easily obtained with the following lines of code:

```
var currentCulture = CultureInfo.CurrentCulture;
var currentUICulture = CultureInfo.CurrentUICulture;
```

This will get the device's culture settings, which the user has set up in their system settings. Let's see how we can set a different culture.

Setting a different culture

Setting a particular culture is as easy as assigning it to the relevant properties on the `CultureInfo` class:

```
var cultureInfo = new CultureInfo("fr-FR");
CultureInfo.CurrentCulture = cultureInfo;
CultureInfo.CurrentUICulture = cultureInfo;
CultureInfo.DefaultThreadCurrentCulture = cultureInfo;
CultureInfo.DefaultThreadCurrentUICulture = cultureInfo;
```

The DefaultThreadCurrentCulture and DefaultThreadCurrentUICulture properties are used to set the default culture settings for all threads in a .NET application, including background threads that you may spin up for various tasks.

> **Note**
>
> For the sake of simplicity and to keep our focus on the overall process of localization, throughout this chapter we won't be making a distinction between CurrentCulture and CurrentUICulture unless explicitly mentioned. When we talk about updating the culture settings, we'll be updating both CurrentCulture and CurrentUICulture, as well as their DefaultThread counterparts.

If we want, we can allow users to select a culture from a list of supported cultures and save it for future sessions. Here's a simplified example using Microsoft.Maui.Storage.Preferences to store the chosen culture:

```
Preferences.Set("SelectedCulture", "fr-FR");
```

Retrieving and assigning the previously stored selected culture can be done like this:

```
var storedCulture = Preferences.Get("SelectedCulture",
"en-US");
```

The Preferences's Get method accepts a second parameter that serves as a default value to return when no existing value for the given key exists. The string value that we retrieved can now be used to instantiate a new CultureInfo object, which we can then use to set the application's culture. Take a look:

```
var cultureInfo = new CultureInfo(storedCulture);
CultureInfo.CurrentCulture = cultureInfo;
```

As mentioned earlier, the CurrentCulture property defines how particular data types are being displayed. So, let's have a quick look at what we mean by that.

Displaying formatted data

Culture settings have a direct impact on how data types such as dates and numbers are formatted when they are displayed in the UI. When you set CultureInfo.CurrentCulture, it will also influence the formatting in data-binding scenarios. This means that DateTime values, for instance, will be displayed according to the format rules of the set culture.

Let's say we have a DateTime property in our ViewModel:

```
public DateTime LastUpdated { get; set; } = new
DateTime(2020, 7, 3);
```

And we are binding this property to a `Label` in XAML:

```
<Label Text="{Binding LastUpdated}" />
```

Because we are not specifying how the data should be formatted, the `ToString` method will be called on the `DateTime` object, and that result will be shown on the screen. The `ToString` method will take the current culture settings into account. As a result, if the culture is set to US English (`en-US`), the date will be formatted as `7/3/2020 12:00:00 AM`, whereas if the culture is set to French (`fr-FR`), the date will appear as `03/07/2020 00:00:00`.

The `StringFormat` property in XAML binding expressions allows us to define custom formatting for data types such as `DateTime`. What's great is that `StringFormat` will also respect the current culture settings, so it's a fantastic way to combine customization with localization. For instance, we could use `StringFormat` in XAML to specify how you'd like that date to appear:

```
<Label Text="{Binding LastUpdated, StringFormat='{0:MMMM d,
    yyyy}'}" />
```

In this example, `StringFormat` is set to display the full month name, the day, and the full year. In US English, it will be displayed as `July 3, 2020`, whereas when the app's culture is set to French, the date will automatically adjust to `juillet 3, 2020`. The format specified in `StringFormat` remains consistent, but the actual string values for the day and month adapt to the set culture.

The same principles apply to number formatting. Different cultures have various ways of representing numbers, particularly when it comes to separating thousands and decimal points. By being mindful of the culture settings, we ensure that our application displays numbers in a format that is both familiar and understandable to the user.

In contrast to the `CurrentCulture` property, the `CurrentUICulture` property determines the language that is being used in the app. So, let's have a look at how this can be managed through resource files.

What are Resources Files?

Resources Files are a core feature of the .NET ecosystem, used to facilitate localization across a wide array of application types. Typically named with a `.resx` extension, these XML-based files allow you to define key-value pairs where the key represents a specific piece of text or asset in your application, and the value represents its localized equivalent. Visual Studio even provides an editor for `.resx` files, allowing developers to easily define keys and their value (*Figure 12.1*):

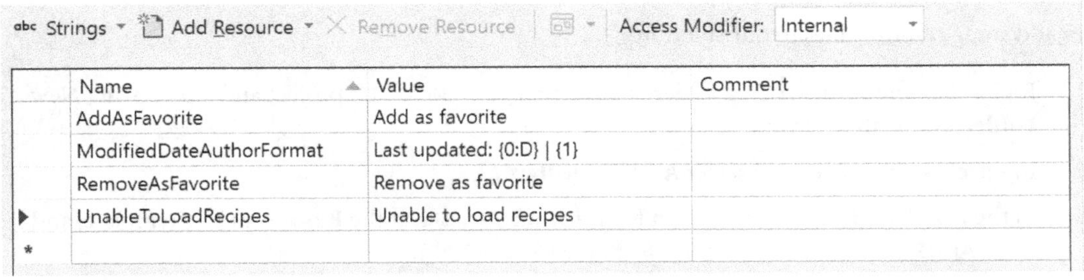

Figure 12.1: Visual Studio .resx designer

What's particularly handy is that a strongly typed class is automatically generated when you create a .resx file. This class allows us to access localized resources programmatically in a type-safe manner, eliminating the need to manually look up resource keys in your code. The name of this autogenerated class is derived from the name of the resx file itself. For example, if the resource file is named AppResources.resx, the generated class will be named AppResources.

By suffixing the name of the file, we can specify which culture a specific resource file belongs to – for example, AppResources.resx for the default culture of the app (let's say English), AppResources.fr-FR.resx for French, AppResources.es-ES.resx for Spanish, and so on.

.NET MAUI will look in the .resx file that corresponds with the set culture for the requested value. Fetching a localized string can be done as shown here:

```
var s1 = AppResources.
    ResourceManager.GetString("AddAsFavorite");
```

If the current UI culture is set to French (fr-FR), .NET MAUI will automatically look for AddAsFavorite in the AppResources.fr-FR.resx file. If there is no resource file matching the current UI culture, the default file (the one without a suffix) will be used.

Alternatively, retrieving a value for the AddAsFavorite key can also be done as follows:

```
var s2 = AppResources.AddAsFavorite;
```

A static property will be generated in the AppResources class for every key in the .resx file. These properties utilize ResourceManager's GetString method to retrieve the corresponding value.

> **Note**
>
> It's important to note that the generated class will only be based on the default resource file. This means that only properties will be generated for the keys in the default file. So, it is very important to have the same keys in each of the different culture-specific files! Resolving a value for a key that is not present in the resource file of the current UI culture will result in an exception!

Let's add some resource files to our solution:

1. Right-click the `Resources` folder in the `Recipes.Mobile` project and select **Add | New Folder**. Name this folder `Strings`.

2. Right-click this folder and select **Add | New Item…**.

3. In the **Add New Item** popup, search for `resources`, select the **Resources File** template, and enter `AppResources.resx` as the name (*Figure 12.2*):

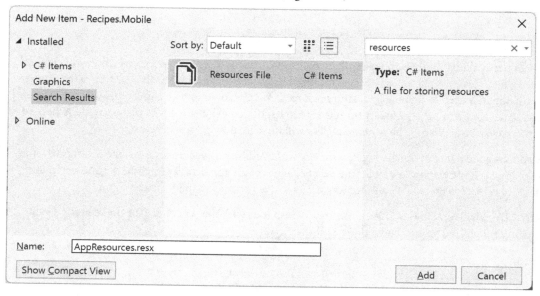

Figure 12.2: Creating a new Resources File

4. Double-check the newly created file's properties in the **Properties** window. The **Build Action** property should be set to **Embedded resource**, and the **Custom Tool** property should be set to **ResXFileCodeGenerator**, as *Figure 12.3* shows:

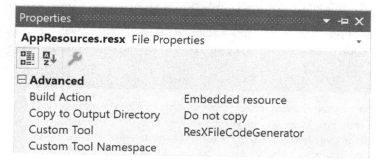

Figure 12.3: Properties of the AppResources.resx file

5. Add a second **Resources File** and name it `AppResources.fr-FR.resx`. Note that only the default resource file has its **Custom Tool** property set to **ResXFileCodeGenerator**. Other resource files will not have this property set, but their **Build Action** property does have to be set to **Embedded resource** as well.

6. In the `Chapter 12/Resources` folder, you will find an `AppResources.resx` file and an `AppResources.fr-FR.resx` file containing the English and French resources respectively. Copy them over to the `Strings` folder in Visual Studio and override the files you just created.

With this in place, let's have a look at how we can get those values on the screen.

Getting localized resources on the screen

In its simplest form, we can use the `x:Static` markup extension. This markup extension is used to reference static fields or properties from a specified class. As mentioned earlier, the generated `AppResources` class has a static property for each of the keys in the **Resources File**. This allows us to leverage the `x:Static` markup extension to reference the localized values. Let's see how we can add this:

1. Add the following code to the `CreateMauiApp` method of the `MauiProgram` class:

```
public static MauiApp CreateMauiApp()
{
    var builder = MauiApp.CreateBuilder();
    ...
    var french = new CultureInfo("fr-FR");
    CultureInfo.CurrentCulture = french;
    CultureInfo.CurrentUICulture = french;
    ...
}
```

This will force the app's culture to French.

2. Go to `AppShell.xaml` and add an XML namespace pointing to the namespace of the `AppResources` class:

```
xmlns:strings="clr-namespace:Recipes.Mobile.Resources.Strings"
```

3. Next, update the `Title` property of the first `Tab` element to the following:

```
Title="{x:Static strings:AppResources.Tab1Title}"
```

By leveraging the `x:Static` markup extension, we are pointing to the static `Tab1Title` property of the `AppResources` class.

4. The `Title` property of the second `Tab` element should point to the `Tab2Title` property as shown here:

```
Title="{x:Static strings:AppResources.Tab2Title}"
```

5. And finally, for this first example, head over to `RecipeDetailPage` and find the `MultiBinding` on the label that shows the `LastUpdated` and `Author` properties. The `x:Static` markup extension can also be used on the `StringFormat` property on a binding statement, as shown here:

```
<MultiBinding StringFormat="{x:Static
    strings:AppResources.ModifiedDateAuthorFormat}">
    <Binding Path="LastUpdated" />
    <Binding Path="Author" />
</MultiBinding>
```

It's worth mentioning that `ModifiedDateAuthorFormat` contains a D format specifier that represents a long date pattern. As a result, the notation of the date will be different depending on the selected culture. For example, when `CurrentCulture` is set to French (`fr-FR`), July 3, 2020, will be shown as `vendredi 3 juillet 2020`.

If we now run the app, we should immediately see that the titles of the two main tabs are now in French, as *Figure 12.4* shows:

Figure 12.4: Localized tab titles

When navigating to `RecipeDetailPage`, the label showing the `LastUpdated` and `Author` properties is now also translated. Now, go ahead and change the culture in the `CreateMauiApp` method to `nl-BE`. Run the app, and you should see the localized labels in English. That's because there is no resource file for this culture, so the default one is used. Do note that the date is being formatted according to the Dutch (Belgium) notation: `vrijdag 3 juli 2020`.

As said, this approach is the simplest form of getting the localized resources on the screen. This is a perfectly valid approach, but it's not very MVVM-friendly, and it has its limitations:

*   The biggest limitation is that `x:Static` doesn't react to changes. If you change the value of the static property at runtime, the UI will not update to reflect the new value. This makes it unsuitable for scenarios where the localized text might change dynamically, such as when a user switches languages in-app. Only when navigating to a new page will the `x:Static` markup extension load the required values for the newly selected culture. When navigating (back) to pages that are in memory, the values of the previous culture will still be there.

- There is no way to access these resources from within our ViewModels. This can be an issue if we want to show dialogs or alerts from a ViewModel.

So far, we've laid down the essential groundwork for understanding localization in .NET MAUI, including the role of resource files, the `CultureInfo` class, and the `x:Static` markup extension. While the methods and concepts we've discussed so far form the essential backbone of localization in .NET MAUI, our next section will explore how to seamlessly integrate them into MVVM. Ultimately, our goal is to make use of data binding to connect our UI to localized values. This enables dynamic updates: if the user switches languages or cultures during runtime, the displayed text will automatically reflect these changes.

> **Note**
>
> The properties on a binding statement such as `StringFormat`, `FallbackValue`, and `TargetNullValue` aren't bindable properties. This means that the only way to assign values from a resource file to these properties is by leveraging the `x:Static` markup extension, with its limitations.

Looking at a localization solution for MVVM

In this section, we'll look at a solution that's not just functional but also fits well with the MVVM architectural pattern. Whether you need to localize text within your ViewModels or dynamically update language in your UI, this approach has you covered. It's a solution that I've personally implemented in numerous projects over the years. While I've made some refinements along the way, the core concept has stood the test of time and proven its effectiveness in real-world applications.

> **Warning – culture settings are thread-specific**
>
> When allowing the user to switch cultures inside the app, we should be wary of the fact that when updating `CultureInfo` inside `async` operations, those changes will not automatically propagate to the parent thread. A localization strategy needs to be designed with this in mind to avoid inconsistencies.

In the code accompanying this chapter, two new projects have been added: `Localization` and `Localization.Maui`. The primary objective of the `Localization` project is to provide a framework-agnostic approach to manage and access localization settings and resources. By encapsulating this localization logic within its own project, we facilitate easy code sharing across different projects, paving the way for potential packaging and reuse in other projects.

On the other hand, the `Localization.Maui` project is tailored specifically for .NET MAUI. It houses the code responsible for storing and retrieving localization information. Putting this logic separately from the rest of our *Recipes!* app code allows us to ensure that it remains modular and reusable for other .NET MAUI applications. Let's discuss the `Localization` project first.

The Localization project

Let's take a look at the `ILocalizationManager` interface in the `Localization` project:

```
public interface ILocalizationManager
{
    void RestorePreviousCulture(
        CultureInfo defaultCulture = null);

    void UpdateUserCulture(CultureInfo cultureInfo);

    CultureInfo GetUserCulture(
        CultureInfo defaultCulture = null);
}
```

The `ILocalizationManager` interface defines three methods for managing localization settings:

- `RestorePreviousCulture` is a method that can be used to restore the previous culture used by the user. The `defaultCulture` parameter can be used to specify a fallback culture in case there is no previous culture set.
- `UpdateUserCulture` updates and stores the culture settings for the current user. The `cultureInfo` parameter specifies the new culture to use.
- The `GetUserCulture` method retrieves the stored culture settings. The `defaultCulture` parameter can be used to specify a fallback culture in case there is no culture set.

The primary intent behind this interface is to abstract tasks related to the persistence and retrieval of user-specified cultures. In the context of a .NET MAUI-specific implementation, we might, for instance, opt to save the most recently chosen `CultureInfo` within `Preferences`, ensuring it's available the next time the app launches so that it can be restored. We'll delve deeper into this specific approach shortly.

The second interface in the `Localization` project is the `ILocalizedResourcesProvider` interface. Let's see what this looks like:

```
public interface ILocalizedResourcesProvider
{
    string this[string key]
    {
        get;
    }

    void UpdateCulture(CultureInfo cultureInfo);
}
```

At its core, this interface facilitates the retrieval of localized string values that align with the user's chosen CultureInfo. It provides a read-only indexer to fetch the localized string corresponding to a specified key. Additionally, the UpdateCulture method lets you modify the current CultureInfo, ensuring that subsequent localized string retrievals reflect the updated cultural context.

Next, we'll explore the Localization project's concrete implementation of the ILocalizedResourceProvider interface – namely, LocalizedResourcesProvider. Let's start by looking at its constructor:

```
ResourceManager resourceManager;
CultureInfo currentCulture;

public static LocalizedResourcesProvider Instance
{
    get;
    private set;
}

public LocalizedResourcesProvider(
    ResourceManager resourceManager)
{
    this.resourceManager = resourceManager;
    currentCulture = CultureInfo.CurrentUICulture;
    Instance = this;
}
```

The constructor takes a single parameter, resourceManager. This is the ResourceManager that needs to be used to retrieve the localized values. The currentCulture field is initialized with a default value, being the current UI culture. Within the constructor, the current instance is assigned to the static Instance property. This allows us to access this LocalizedResourcesProvider implementation through a static property, which will be handy in data-binding scenarios, as we'll see later on.

> **Note**
>
> Assigning the current instance of LocalizedResourcesProvider to the static Instance property means there can only be one LocalizedResourcesProvider implementation throughout the app. While this is a limitation to be wary of, it should not pose a significant problem.

The indexer of this class allows us to get the localized string value for a given key. Here's how this is implemented:

```
public string this[string key]
    => resourceManager.GetString(key, currentCulture)
    ?? key;
```

When the key exists within our resources, the method fetches the corresponding localized string using the currentCulture. However, if the provided key doesn't match any resource key, the key itself is returned as a fallback. It's crucial to observe that we're passing the currentCulture explicitly when calling GetString. This ensures that the resourceManager fetches values specific to the provided currentCulture, rather than defaulting to the CultureInfo of the currently executing thread. This design choice addresses potential challenges arising from culture settings being thread-specific.

Now, let's look at the UpdateCulture method within the LocalizedResourcesProvider:

```
public void UpdateCulture(CultureInfo cultureInfo)
{
    currentCulture = cultureInfo;
    OnPropertyChanged("Item");
}
```

This method updates the currentCulture field. As a result, any subsequent calls to the class's indexer will retrieve the localized string value for the given key, based on the updated currentCulture. Additionally, the method calls the OnPropertyChanged method, sending Item as its argument. In scenarios involving data binding, this prompts a re-evaluation of all bindings linked to the indexer. Consequently, any values that are data-bound to this indexer will refresh, returning the localized strings of the updated CultureInfo. Let's transition our focus to the Localization.Maui project.

The Localization.Maui project

The LocalizationManager class in the Localization.Maui project is an implementation of the ILocaliazationManager. It has a dependency on ILocalizedResourcesProvider, as you can see here:

```
readonly ILocalizedResourcesProvider _resourceProvider;

public LocalizationManager(
    ILocalizedResourcesProvider resoureProvider)
{
    _resourceProvider = resoureProvider;
}
```

By having this reference, we can, later on, call its UpdateCulture method, keeping the updated culture in sync with the ILocalizedResourcesProvider.

The `LocalizationManager` class should also store the selected `CultureInfo` so that it can be retrieved on subsequent app launches and restore the previous `CultureInfo`. The following code block shows how the `UpdateUserCulture` uses the `Preferences` API to store the given `CultureInfo`, assigns the updated value to the `currentCulture` field, updates the static properties on the `CultureInfo` object, and calls the `ILocalizedResourcesProvider`'s `UpdateCulture` method:

```
public void UpdateUserCulture(CultureInfo cultureInfo)
{
    Preferences.Default.Set("UserCulture",
        cultureInfo.Name);
    SetCulture(cultureInfo);
}

private void SetCulture(CultureInfo cultureInfo)
{
    currentCulture = cultureInfo;
    Application.Current.Dispatcher.Dispatch(() =>
    {
        CultureInfo.CurrentCulture = cultureInfo;
        CultureInfo.CurrentUICulture = cultureInfo;
        CultureInfo.DefaultThreadCurrentCulture =
            cultureInfo;
        CultureInfo.DefaultThreadCurrentUICulture =
            cultureInfo;
    });
    _resourceProvider.UpdateCulture(cultureInfo);
}
```

Notice how the updates on the `CultureInfo` object are dispatched to the main thread. Remember the note about `CultureInfo` being bound to the current thread? We want to ensure that the main thread's `CultureInfo` is updated to maintain consistency. Failing to apply these changes to the main thread could result in data binding using the outdated or previous `CultureInfo`. This misalignment can lead to inaccuracies when formatting data, such as displaying `DateTime` objects.

The `GetUserCulture` method first checks if its `currentCulture` field is set. If it is, that value is returned directly. If not, the method tries to retrieve the culture based on the `UserCulture` key from `Preferences`. If no value is found there, it either resorts to the provided `defaultCulture` parameter or, in its absence, the current system culture. Once determined, this culture is assigned to the `currentCulture` field, which is then returned. Take a look:

```
public CultureInfo GetUserCulture(
    CultureInfo defaultCulture = null)
{
```

```
    if (currentCulture is null)
    {
        var culture = Preferences.Default.Get(
            "UserCulture", string.Empty);
        if (string.IsNullOrEmpty(culture))
        {
            currentCulture = defaultCulture
                ?? CultureInfo.CurrentCulture;
        }
        else
        {
            currentCulture = new CultureInfo(culture);
        }
    }
    return currentCulture;
}
```

Finally, the `RestorePreviousCulture` method uses the `GetUserCutlure` method to retrieve the previously used culture and passes this on to the `SetCulture` method, as you can see here:

```
public void RestorePreviousCulture(
    CultureInfo defaultCulture = null)
    => SetCulture(GetUserCulture(defaultCulture));
```

This method can be used when the app starts to set the current culture to the culture that the user selected previously.

Now that we're familiar with the roles and workings of these classes, let's integrate them into the *Recipes!* app. This will enable us to handle localization in a manner that complements the MVVM architectural pattern. Here's a step-by-step guide:

1. Go to `MauiProgram.cs` and add the following line of code to the `CreateMauiApp` method:

    ```
    builder.Services.AddSingleton<ILocalizationManager,
        LocalizationManager>();
    ```

    This registers an instance of `LocalizationManager` to the DI container.

2. Create an instance of `LocalizedResourcesProvider`. Pass the `ResourceManager` of `AppResources` to its constructor, allowing `LocalizedResourceProvider` to access the resources defined in the `AppResources` files:

    ```
    var resources = new LocalizedResourcesProvider(
        AppResources.ResourceManager);
    ```

3. Let's register this `LocalizedResourcesProvider` as `Singleton` to the DI container, as shown here:

```
builder.Services
    .AddSingleton<ILocalizedResourcesProvider>(
    resources);
```

By doing this, we're ensuring a single instance of the `LocalizedResourcesProvider` class is used throughout the app. Any time this instance is resolved through DI, it's guaranteed to be the same as that referred to by the `LocalizedResourcesProvider`'s static `Instance` property. This is essential for accessing localized resources consistently across the application.

This sets the foundation for a solid localization solution that is ready to be used in our app. Let's see how we can integrate the `LocalizedResourcesProvider` and `LocalizationManager` in our app.

Using the LocalizedResourcesProvider and LocalizationManager

Let's take a look at how we can use the `LocalizedResourcesProvider` and `LocalizationManager` to access localized resources from within a ViewModel. On the `SettingsPage`, the user can select a new language through the `PickLanguagePage`. When selecting a language, a prompt should ask, in the current language, whether the user wants to switch. After switching, an alert in the updated language should confirm the update. Here's how we can do this:

1. First, let's add the following two fields to `SettingsViewModel`:

```
readonly ILocalizedResourcesProvider _resources;
readonly ILocalizationManager _localizationManager;
readonly IDialogService _dialogService
...
public PickLanguageViewModel(
    INavigationService navigationService
    IDialogService dialogService,
    ILocalizedResourcesProvider resourcesProvider,
    ILocalizationManager localizationManager)
{
    _dialogService = dialogService;
    _resources = resourcesProvider;
    _localizationManager = localizationManager;
    ...
}
...
```

The DI container will automatically inject these additional dependencies into the constructor.

2. Next, we can update the `ConfirmSwitchLanguage` method to this:

```
private Task<bool> ConfirmSwitchLanguage()
    => _dialogService.AskYesNo(
        _resources["SwitchLanguageDialogTitle"],
        _resources["SwitchLanguageDialogText"],
        _resources["YesDialogButton"],
        _resources["NoDialogButton"]);
```

See how we use the `_resources` field to fetch localized strings, which are then passed to the `IDialogService`'s `AskYesNo` method. The keys exactly match the keys present in the `AppResources` files.

3. Likewise, we can also update the `NotifySwitch` method, as shown here:

```
private Task NotifySwitch()
    => _dialogService.Notify(
        _resources["LanguageSwitchedTitle"],
        _resources["LanguageSwitchedText"],
        _resources["OKDialogButton"]);
```

4. Lastly, we need to add the following line of code to the `SwitchLanguage` method:

```
private void SwitchLanguage()
{
    CurrentLanguage = newLanguage;
    _localizationManager
        .UpdateUserCulture(
        new CultureInfo(SelectedLanguage));
}
```

This method is called when the user has confirmed switching to the new language. By calling the `_localizationManager`'s `UpdateUserCulture`, we'll be persisting the selected culture, updating the `CultureInfo` properties, and notifying the `ILocalizedResourcesProvider` about the updated culture. As a result, subsequential calls to the `_resources` field will retrieve the localized values for the updated `CultureInfo`.

We can now run the app, go to the `SettingsPage`, and click through to the `PickLanguagePage`, where we can change the language of the app. Once a new language is chosen, we automatically navigate back to the `SettingsPage`, where we'll get a prompt in the current language of the app (*Figure 12.5*):

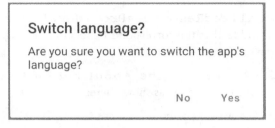

Figure 12.5: Prompt in English

After confirmation, the language will be updated, and we'll see an alert in the new language (*Figure 12.6*):

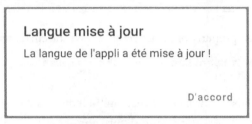

Figure 12.6: Alert in French

The fact that we can switch cultures from within our ViewModels and retrieve localized string values for the currently set culture is already very exciting! But how do we handle the localization in our Views if we want them to update to the newly selected culture as well? Let's have a look!

1. Go to `SettingsPage.xml` and add the following XML namespace:

    ```
    xmlns:localization="clr-namespace:
        Localization;assembly=Localization"
    ```

    This namespace points to the `Localization` namespace of the `Localization` project.

2. Update the `Text` property of the **Select Language** button to the following:

    ```
    Text="{Binding Path=[ChooseLanguage], Source={x:Static
    localization:LocalizedResourcesProvider.Instance}}"
    ```

    This binding statement might seem complex at first glance. Let's break it down. The `Source` property is set to the `LocalizedResourcesProvider.Instance` static property, leveraging the `x:Static` markup extension. The `Path` property is set to `[ChooseLanguage]`. What this basically means is that we want to access the indexer on the source object and pass `ChooseLanguage` as the key. Effectively, this binding statement binds to the following:

    ```
    LocalizedResourcesProvider.Instance["ChooseLanguage"]
    ```

As we saw in the `LocalizedResourcesProvider`'s implementation, the indexer takes a provided key and fetches the corresponding localized string using the configured `ResourceManager`.

3. Let's also update the text of the **About** button to make use of the `LocalizedResourcesProvider`, as shown here:

```
{Binding Path=[About], Source={x:Static
localization:LocalizedResourcesProvider.Instance}}"
```

And while we're at it, let's also update the page's title as well:

```
Title="{Binding Path=[SettingsTitle], Source={x:Static
localization:LocalizedResourcesProvider.Instance}}"
```

4. Take a look at the `Text` property of the label that shows the current selected language:

```
Text="{Binding CurrentLanguage, StringFormat=
  'Language: {0}'}"
```

In order to localize this label, we will need to use multi-binding, as shown in the following snippet:

```
<Label FontSize="14" HorizontalOptions="Center">
    <Label.Text>
        <MultiBinding StringFormat="{}{0}: {1}">
            <Binding Path="[Language]"
                     Source="{x:Static localization:
                        LocalizedResourcesProvider
                        .Instance}" />
            <Binding Path="CurrentLanguage" />
        </MultiBinding>
    </Label.Text>
</Label>
```

We've extracted the hardcoded `Language` part from the `StringFormat` property and defined two placeholders. By leveraging multi-binding, we can indicate the first placeholder should get the value associated with `Language` in the `AppResources`. The second placeholder is bound to the `CurrentLanguage` property on the ViewModel.

Note that the `StringFormat` property starts with `{}`. Putting just `{0}: {1}` in there is not allowed, because the `{` curly brace is a special character in XAML, often signaling the start of a markup extension. `{}` is an escape sequence to handle this.

With these changes in place, run the app again. Go to the `SettingsPage` and select a different language. After confirming to switch the language of the app, you should not only see the alert in the updated language appearing but also see that the labels on the `SettingsPage` instantly update (*Figure 12.7*)!

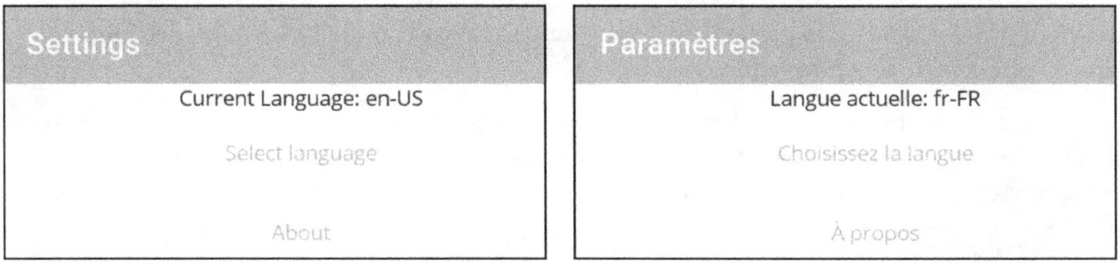

Settings	
Current Language: en-US	
Select language	
About	

Paramètres	
Langue actuelle: fr-FR	
Choisissez la langue	
À propos	

Figure 12.7: The Settings page before (left) and after (right) switching to French

The magic happens because our bindings target the indexer of the `LocalizedResourcesProvider` class. Thus, any trigger of the `PropertyChanged` event (with `Item` as the property name) will prompt a re-evaluation of these bindings. Triggering the `PropertyChanged` event is done because the `LocalizationManager` calls the `UpdateCulture` method on its `_resourceProvider` field.

Currently, the selected culture isn't persisted across app launches. To be exact: the selected culture does get stored, but it is not being restored when the application starts. We can easily add that functionality by updating the constructor of the `App` class:

```
public App(INavigationInterceptor navigationInterceptor,
    ILocalizationManager manager)
{
    manager.RestorePreviousCulture();
...
}
```

By calling the `RestorePreviousCulture` on the injected `ILocalizationManager` interface, the previously set culture is being restored. It's done in the constructor of the `App` class so that it is applied early on in the application's life cycle.

Personally, I think this is a beautiful and very MVVM-friendly solution to localization; well, except for the rather complex data-binding statements we have to put in place. In the next section, we'll see how we can improve on that.

Using a custom Translate markup extension

We previously set up a localization solution for our app. While it works effectively, the data-binding statements were a bit verbose and would have to be repeated for each string. Building on that foundation, in this section, we'll introduce a streamlined approach: a custom markup extension designed specifically for translations.

But before we proceed, let's briefly revisit what markup extensions are. **Markup extensions** provide a way to compute or retrieve property values at runtime rather than just setting them to static values.

This functionality makes them particularly handy for tasks such as resource lookups, data binding, or, in our case, simplifying translation retrieval.

It's important to note that we're not changing how we leverage data binding to bind to our resources. Instead, we're just making the XAML code easier to write and read. The actual data-binding process stays the same. This is essentially what the `Translate` markup extension will look like in XAML:

```
Title="{mauiloc:Translate SettingsTitle}"
```

This is synonymous with the following:

```
Title="{Binding Path=[SettingsTitle], Source={x:Static
   localization:LocalizedResourcesProvider.Instance},
     Mode=OneWay}"
```

The `Translate` markup extension is a wrapper around a conventional data-binding statement. Let's take a look at the `TranslateExtension` class in the `Localization.Maui` project. This class implements the generic `IMarkupExtension` interface, and as a result, it needs to implement the following methods:

```
object IMarkupExtension.ProvideValue(IServiceProvider
   serviceProvider);
T ProvideValue(IServiceProvider serviceProvider);
```

The non-generic `ProvideValue` method will be called at runtime and must return the value we want to be using in our XAML. In this case, we want to return a `Binding`. Here's how it's implemented:

```
[ContentProperty(nameof(Key))]
public class TranslateExtension :
    IMarkupExtension<Binding>
{

    public string Key { get; set; }

    object IMarkupExtension.ProvideValue(
        IServiceProvider serviceProvider)
        => ProvideValue(serviceProvider);

    public Binding ProvideValue(
        IServiceProvider serviceProvider)
        => ...

}
```

The non-generic `ProvideValue` method calls its generic version, which returns a `Binding`. The class has a property named Key, which represents the key used to fetch the localized value. This Key property can be assigned in the markup extension, as shown here:

```
Title="{mauiloc:Translate Key=SettingsTitle}"
```

Thanks to the `ContentProperty` attribute applied to this class, we can omit the Key= segment, simplifying our markup extension's use even more. `ContentProperty` specifies the default property that is to be used when no identifier is specified in XAML. Remember how we don't need to explicitly state `Path=` in a data-binding statement and can simply write the path? This `ContentProperty` attribute is exactly what drives that! Let's finally see what the generic `ProvideValue` method returns:

```
public Binding ProvideValue(
    IServiceProvider serviceProvider)
    => new Binding
    {
        Mode = BindingMode.OneWay,
        Path = $"[{Key}]",
        Source = LocalizedResourcesProvider.Instance
    };
```

The `ProvideValue` method returns a `Binding` object. Its `Source` value is set to the static `Instance` property of `LocalizedResourcesProvider`, equivalent to this:

```
{x:Static localization:LocalizedResourcesProvider.Instance}
```

For the `Path` property, when the `Key` value is `SettingsTitle`, it translates to `Path=[SettingsTitle]`. The Binding's Mode is set to OneWay to ensure it listens for the PropertyChanged event and updates the bound value when needed.

The `Translate` markup extension provides a convenient way to define the exact same binding statements we had earlier. Let's go ahead and update some of our Views so that they leverage this `Translate` markup extension:

1. Go to `SettingsPage` and add the following XML namespace, which points to the `Localization.Maui` namespace of the `Localization.Maui` project:

    ```
    xmlns:mauiloc="clr-namespace:Localization.Maui;
        assembly=Localization.Maui"
    ```

2. Update the binding statements on the `SettingsPage`, as shown here:

    ```
    ...
    Title="{mauiloc:Translate SettingsTitle}"
    ...
    Text="{mauiloc:Translate ChooseLanguage}"
    ```

```
. . .
Text="{mauiloc:Translate About}"
. . .
```

3. In `AppShell.xaml`, add the same XML namespace that we previously added to `SettingsPage` in *step 1*.

4. Now, update the binding statements on `AppShell.xaml`, as shown in the following snippet:

```
<Tab Title="{mauiloc:Translate Tab1Title}">
    . . .
</Tab>
<Tab Title="{mauiloc:Translate Tab2Title}">
    . . .
</Tab>
```

The `Translate` markup extension offers an elegant approach to what is typically considered a complex task. Everywhere hardcoded text is used, we can very simply replace it with this `TranslateExtension`. Note that the `TranslateExtension` can still be improved: all the typical data-binding properties such as `Converter`, `ConverterParameter`, and so on can be added to this class as well and be used in the `Binding` object that is being returned.

Now that we know how to localize hardcoded `copy` labels, let's have a look at how we can fetch localized data from APIs.

Fetching localized data from APIs

Before we wrap up this chapter, let's have a quick look at how we could pass the user's language to the API so that it can return localized data. One approach is to include a language parameter in every service and repository method, allowing the ViewModel to pass the user's current language. However, I believe adding such parameters can clutter the code. A cleaner alternative is to handle this within the repositories. Let's see how:

1. First, let's update the `IRecipeAPI` interface by adding a `language` parameter of type `string` to the `GetRecipes` method. The following snippet shows how we can configure Refit to pass this additional parameter as an `Accept-Language` request header when executing the API call:

```
Task<ApiResponse<RecipeOverviewItemsDto>>
    GetRecipes([Header("Accept-Language")] string
        language, int pageSize = 7, int pageIndex = 0);
```

We could pass this language parameter as a query string parameter as well by leaving out the `Header` attribute, but I think this approach is a lot cleaner.

2. It's the `RecipeApiGateway` class that invokes the updated `GetRecipes` method. In order for it to access the current culture, let's inject an instance of the `ILocalizationManager`, as shown here:

```
readonly ILocalizationManager _localizationManager;
...
public RecipeApiGateway(IRecipeApi api,
    ILocalizationManager localizationManager)
{
    _api = api;
    _localizationManager = localizationManager;
}
```

3. The next code block shows how we can now use the `_localizationManager` field to access the current user culture and pass its `Name` property to the `GetRecipes` method:

```
public Task<Result<LoadRecipesResponse>>
    LoadRecipes(int pageSize, int page)
    => InvokeAndMap(_api.GetRecipes(
        _localizationManager.GetUserCulture().Name,
        pageSize, page), MapRecipesOverview);
```

While directly using `CultureInfo.CurrentCulture.Name` might seem straightforward, accessing the culture via our `ILocalizationManager` ensures greater consistency, as mentioned earlier.

4. Accessing the `Accept-Language` that's now being sent with this API call can be achieved by updating the `GetRecipes` endpoint in the `Program.cs` file inside the `Recipes.Web.Api` project. Here's what the updated code looks like:

```
app.MapGet("/recipes", (int pageSize, int pageIndex,
    [FromHeader(Name = "Accept-Language")] string
        language) =>
    {
        //use language to retrieve recipes
        return new RecipeService()
            .LoadRecipes(pageSize, pageIndex);
    })
    .WithName("GetRecipes")
    .WithOpenApi();
```

In contrast to the data-bound values on the screen, changing the app's language won't automatically fetch any localized data coming from the API anew. So, how can we tackle this? In *Chapter 7*, *Dependency Injection, Services, and Messaging*, we already discussed thoroughly how ViewModels can communicate with each other in a loosely coupled manner through `Messaging`. `Messaging` offers a solution to this challenge: `SettingsViewModel` can send a message notifying other ViewModels about the updated language. ViewModels can react to this and re-fetch their data. Let's implement this:

1. Add a new class called `CultureChangedMessage` to the `Messages` folder of the `Recipes.Client.Core` project. Here's what it looks like:

   ```
   public class CultureChangedMessage :
       ValueChangedMessage<CultureInfo>
   {
       public CultureChangedMessage(CultureInfo value) :
           base(value)
       { }
   }
   ```

2. Update the `SwitchLanguage` method on `SettingsViewModel`, as shown here:

   ```
   private void SwitchLanguage(string newLanguage)
   {
       CurrentLanguage = newLanguage;

       var newCulture = new CultureInfo(newLanguage);

       _localizationManager
           .UpdateUserCulture(newCulture);

       WeakReferenceMessenger.Default.Send(
           new CultureChangedMessage(newCulture));
   }
   ```

3. Finally, in the constructor of the `RecipesOverviewViewModel`, we can add the following code that listens for the `CultureChangedMessage` to arrive so that we can reload the list of recipes:

   ```
   WeakReferenceMessenger.Default
       .Register<CultureChangedMessage>(this, (r, m) =>
   {
       Recipes.Clear();
       (r as RecipesOverviewViewModel).LoadRecipes(7, 0);
   });
   ```

   We don't need to bother with passing the updated culture or language around. Once the message is received, the `LocalizationManager` is already updated to the selected culture and will return the newly selected culture. This ensures that any new recipe fetch will use the updated culture.

When running the app and changing the language on the `SettingsPage`, the `RecipesOverviewViewModel` will reload its recipes. If you debug and set a breakpoint in the API, you'll observe that the language parameter consistently matches the newly selected language.

Summary

We kicked off this chapter with an introduction to localization, understanding its importance in ensuring our app resonates with users globally. Before diving deep, we explored the basics of how localizable values can be statically bound, offering a foundational approach.

Building on this, we introduced a more dynamic localization framework. This allowed for more flexible updates and interactions. Following this, we delved into simplifying our XAML through the `Translate` markup extension. While it made our data-binding statements sleeker, the underlying mechanism remained unchanged.

Next, we discussed getting localized data from our APIs. We found a neat way to tell the API about the user's language choice without making our code messy. By using the `ILocalizationManager`, we kept our approach consistent. And, with `Messaging`, our app knows when to fetch new data if a user changes their language.

The big takeaway? All our steps respected the key MVVM idea of "separation of concerns." Each part of our app has its job, making things organized and easier to manage.

> **Note**
>
> Be aware that what we've seen throughout this chapter doesn't completely cover everything there is to localizing your apps, such as localizing the app's name or localizing images. Take a look at `https://learn.microsoft.com/dotnet/maui/fundamentals/localization` to find out more!

As we wrap up this chapter, we've truly come a long way in building the *Recipes!* app, while adhering to the MVVM principles. But, of course, no app development journey is complete without ensuring its robustness. And that's where the next chapter comes in. We'll dive into how MVVM isn't just about structuring our app effectively, but also about setting the stage for thorough and effective unit testing.

Further reading

To learn more about the topics that were covered in this chapter, take a look at the following resources:

- The ResourceManager class: `https://learn.microsoft.com/dotnet/api/system.resources.resourcemanager?view=net-8.0`
- *XAML markup extensions*: `https://learn.microsoft.com/dotnet/maui/xaml/fundamentals/markup-extensions`
- *Create XAML markup extensions*: `https://learn.microsoft.com/dotnet/maui/xaml/markup-extensions/create`

13

Unit Testing

Let's dive into something critical: **unit testing**. Think of it as your safety net. It's not just about knowing your app runs smoothly now, but ensuring that after every tweak, update, or overhaul, your app keeps on ticking without hiccups or unexpected surprises. Regression bugs? We're looking at you! With MVVM and the right testing practices, we can effectively guard against these potential issues.

In this chapter, we're going to tackle the following:

- The importance of unit testing
- Setting up a unit test project
- Generating data with Bogus
- Mocking dependencies with Moq
- Testing MAUI-specific code

While we won't be diving deep into the weeds (after all, the intricacies can vary widely depending on the tools you use), I'll guide you using a set of tools I'm familiar with: **xUnit**, **Bogus**, **AutoBogus**, and **Moq**. These are my go-to building blocks, but let's remember: the .NET ecosystem is vast and versatile. There are several other fantastic frameworks and libraries out there, such as **NUnit**, **AutoFixture**, **NSubstitute**, and more. The principles we cover will largely remain the same; it's just a matter of which tools resonate with your workflow. At the end of the day, it's all about personal preference.

By the end of this chapter, you should be firmly convinced of the immense value unit tests offer. Additionally, you'll have a clear view of how to effectively use tools and techniques for writing unit tests.

Technical requirements

To ensure you're in sync with the upcoming content, make your way to our GitHub repository: `https://github.com/PacktPublishing/MVVM-pattern-.NET-MAUI/tree/main/Chapter13`. Kick off with the materials in the `Start` folder. And remember – if you're ever in need of a consolidated reference, the `Finish` folder holds the final, refined code at the chapter's close.

The importance of unit testing

A lesson I learned the hard way forever transformed my stance on software development: *never underestimate unit testing.*

Years ago, I was part of a dedicated team crafting an ambitious app. Our expertise in C# and the platform was undeniable. Yet, we overlooked unit tests, placing our faith in manual testing and our **Quality Assurance (QA)** team. The end product was highly recognized and praised, but the journey was a tumultuous one. Feedback from QA often revealed bugs, making each code adjustment feel risky.

Nearing deadlines was synonymous with sleepless nights, hasty bug fixes, and a looming fear of regressions. Post-project, I collaborated with diverse developers and encountered a colleague profoundly devoted to **test-driven development (TDD)**. It was a true eye-opener, not just for the essence of unit testing but also for the flaws in our previous design choices.

My evolving journey underscored the real benefits of unit tests:

- **Efficiency**: No more long-lasting deployments before manual verifications. Unit tests swiftly validate my code, streamlining development.

- **Quality and confidence**: With each test, the software's quality rises, as does my confidence. It becomes a safety net, allowing explorative coding without the fear of unintended consequences.

- **Guarding against regressions**: Unit tests ensure alterations don't unintentionally break existing features.

With time, I've also observed that unit tests serve as an evolving documentation. New team members can determine the expected behavior and logic from these tests, facilitating quicker integration and more confident code modifications.

My old teammates and I still meet up from time to time. We chat about the old days and our shared experiences. In our conversations, a shared realization stands out: after our time together, each of us matured in our individual projects. This often leads us to a mutual reflection: if we had embraced unit testing in that project we did years ago, our work lived might have been a lot smoother. Don't get me wrong; our clients were happy with what we delivered. But for all of us, on a personal level, having tests from the get-go could have saved many stressful nights, health issues, and uncertainties.

While unit testing enjoys acclaim in many developer circles, I still witness hesitancy, especially in parts of the .NET world. My advocacy isn't about achieving a coverage metric or TDD fanaticism. It's about recognizing unit tests for their benefits, from ensuring code reliability to uplifting team morale.

Unit testing is not about achieving an abstract notion of perfection. It's about having a safety net, allowing for code acrobatics without fearing a misstep. Do I write tests for every single line of code I have? In all honesty: no. Is all my code easy to test? Not always. But the tests I write really do help. They let me know quickly if things work, if I broke something, or if I fixed a bug the right way. And that gives me confidence in my work. When a bug is being reported, the first thing I do is write a failing test, exposing this bug. I can then go ahead and work on this bug, and as soon as the test passes, I know I've fixed it. And not only is the bug now fixed, but with the additional test (or tests), the code has become even more robust and protected against future regressions.

As software continuously evolves in our fast-paced world, unit testing is not just best practice; it's a lifeline. The peace of mind it offers is unparalleled, ensuring that the software not only functions but is robust against inevitable change.

To those beginning their developer journey or reevaluating unit tests: don't mimic my initial oversight. See tests not as a chore but as a trusty companion.

Having said that, it's time to pivot from the *why* to the *how*. For those still with me, let's delve into the details: setting up unit tests for ViewModels. Believe me, it's simpler than it seems!

Setting up a unit test project

In this section, we will be walking through the steps of setting up a unit test project and creating a first test. We'll be using xUnit in this section. We're not going to get all tangled up in the tiny details of this specific library because there are tons of other awesome ones. No matter what you choose, the big takeaways should stick with you. So, without further ado, let's dive in and start setting the stage for effective ViewModel testing!

Creating a unit test project

Let's start by creating an xUnit Test project. In xUnit, one of the things I appreciate is its simplicity. Test classes and methods are just normal classes and methods, without the need for special base classes or complex setups. Here's how:

1. In the **Solution Explorer** in **Visual Studio**, right-click **Solution 'Recipes App'** and select **Add | New Project…**.

2. In the **Add a new project** dialog, type `xunit` in the search box and select **xUnit Test Project** from the list (*Figure 13.1*):

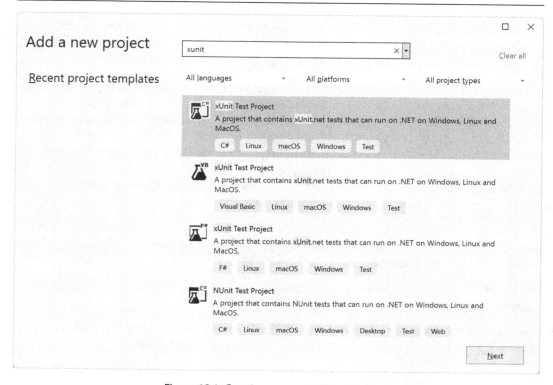

Figure 13.1: Creating a new xUnit test project

3. Click the **Next** button and enter `Recipes.Client.Core.UnitTests` as the project name. Click **Next**.

4. When prompted, select **.NET 8.0 (Long Term Support)** from the **Framework** list and hit the **Create** button.

5. Once the project is generated, right-click on it, select **Add | Project Reference...**, and select the `Recipes.Client.Core` project from the list.

With the project and its reference to the `Recipes.Client.Core` project in place, we can start writing our unit tests. Let's go ahead and write our first one!

Creating unit tests

Let's start by testing something pretty straightforward: testing the initialization of the `RecipeListItemViewModel`. Here's how:

1. Delete the generated `UnitTest1.cs` file.

2. Add a new C# class called `RecipeListItemViewModelTests` to the project.

3. Make the class public and add a public method called `ViewModel_Initialized_PropertiesSetCorrectly`, as shown in the following snippet:

```
[Fact]
public void
  ViewModel_Initialized_PropertiesSetCorrectly()
{

}
```

Note how the `Fact` attribute is added to this method. This attribute signals that this is a test method. Without it, the method won't be identified as a test and therefore won't be executed as one during test runs.

4. Add the following code to this method:

```
//Arrange
string id = "id1";
string title = "title1";
bool isFavorite = false;
string image = "image1";

//Act
var sut = new RecipeListItemViewModel(id, title,
    isFavorite, image);

//Assert
Assert.Equal(id, sut.Id);
Assert.Equal(title, sut.Title);
Assert.Equal(isFavorite, sut.IsFavorite);
Assert.Equal(image, sut.Image);
```

This creates and validates a `RecipeListItemViewModel` instance. This code block first creates an instance of the `RecipeListItemViewModel` class using sample data. It then calls a series of assertions to confirm that the object's properties were initialized as expected.

In unit testing jargon, our instantiated object is named `sut`, which stands for **system under test**. This is a name commonly used in unit tests.

Lastly, the role of the `Assert` statements, inherent to the xUnit framework, deserves special mention. `Assert` methods play a pivotal role in validating object states to ensure they meet our expectations. `Assert.True`, `Assert.Empty`, `Assert.Contains`, and many more are at our disposal. The `Assert.Equal` method, as shown in this example, evaluates if the expected value matches the object's actual value. In this context, it ensures that properties of our `sut` object, such as `Id`, `Title`, `IsFavorite`, and `Image`, were initialized as expected.

In the previous code snippet, you may notice the clear structure, which is guided by comments: `//Arrange`, `//Act`, and `//Assert`. This corresponds to a fundamental pattern in unit testing known as **Arrange-Act-Assert (AAA)**. Let's delve briefly into what each stage signifies:

- `Arrange`: This stage involves setting up any prerequisites for a test. We establish the conditions our test operates under. This might include initializing variables, creating mock objects, or setting up resources. In our example, this is where we define our sample data: `id`, `title`, `isFavorite`, and `image`.

- `Act`: Here, we perform the action that we intend to test. This is where the `sut` object is invoked, and it's typically a single action. In our context, it's the instantiation of `RecipeListItemViewModel` with the sample data we arranged.

- `Assert`: This final stage is where we verify if the test has passed or failed by checking the outcome against the expected results. In our example, this is done using the `Assert.Equal` method to ensure that our `RecipeListItemViewModel` object's properties match the values we initialized them with.

Following the AAA pattern ensures that tests are organized and readable, making it easier for you, or anyone reviewing your code, to understand the purpose and behavior of each test.

Go ahead and run the test! This can be done by right-clicking inside the test method you want to test and selecting **Run Tests**. Alternatively, you can choose **Debug Tests**, which runs your test and breaks on any breakpoints you have added, allowing you to step through the unit test. Test methods are also visible in the **Test Explorer** in **Visual Studio**. From there, you can easily run multiple tests. This pane also shows the current status of your tests: which ran successfully and which failed, alongside other relevant info, as shown in *Figure 13.2*:

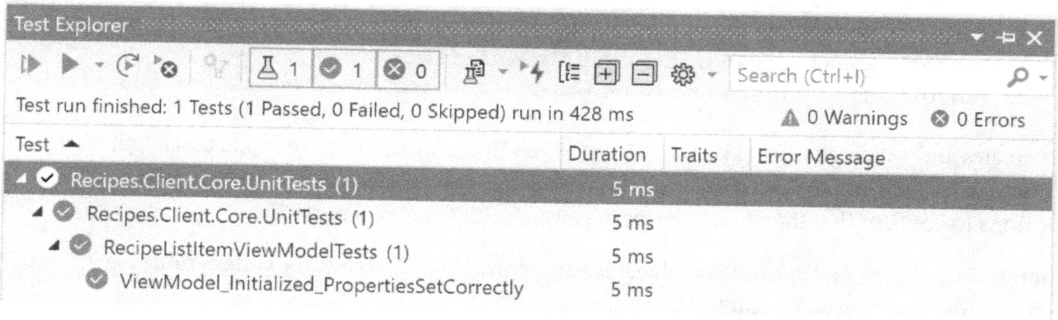

Figure 13.2: Visual Studio's Test Explorer

Let's add a couple more tests! Each instance of a `RecipeListItemViewModel` should listen for a `FavoriteUpdateMessage` and when such a message arrives, its `IsFavorite` property should be updated accordingly. So, let's first write a test that validates that a newly instantiated

`RecipeListItemViewModel` is registered as a recipient for a `FavoriteUpdateMessage` message. Secondly, in separate tests, we can check if the class reacts as expected to such a message:

1. Let's start off by adding the following test to the `RecipeListItemViewModelTests` class:

```
[Fact]
public void
  VM_Initialized_SubscribedToFavoriteUpdateMessage()
{
    //Arrange, Act
    var sut = new RecipeListItemViewModel(
        "id", "title", true, "image");

    //Assert
    Assert.True(WeakReferenceMessenger.Default
        .IsRegistered<FavoriteUpdateMessage>(sut));
}
```

The `WeakReferenceMessenger.Default.IsRegistered` method allows us to check whether a particular object is registered for a particular message. We expect our `sut` to be registered for the `FavoriteUpdateMessage`, so we can call this method and validate the outcome to be true with `Assert.True`.

2. We should also validate that when a `FavoriteUpdateMessage` is received by the `sut`, the `IsFavorite` property is updated accordingly – only, of course, when the id sent by the message matches the id of the `sut`. Take a look:

```
[Fact]
public void
  FavoriteUpdateMsgReceived_SameId_FavoriteUpdated()
{
    //Arrange
    var id = "id";
    var originalValue = false;
    var updateToValue= !originalValue;
    var sut = new RecipeListItemViewModel(
        "someid", "title", originalValue, "image");

    //Act
    WeakReferenceMessenger.Default.Send(
        new FavoriteUpdateMessage(
            id, updatedFavorite));

    //Assert
```

```
        Assert.Equal(updatedFavorite, sut.IsFavorite);
    }
```

The `FavoriteUpdateMessage` sends the inverse of the `originalValue` value that is used to instantiate the sut. After sending the message, which contains the same `RecipeId` as the sut, we can check whether the value of the `IsFavorite` property equals the value we've sent.

3. As a last test, we might want to validate that a `RecipeListItemViewModel` doesn't react to a `FavoriteMessage` with a different `RecipeId`. This is very similar to our previous test, as you can see here:

```
[Fact]
public void FavoriteUpdateMsgReceived_DifferentId
    _FavoriteNotUpdated()
{
    //Arrange
    var originalValue = false;
    var updateToValue= !originalValue;
    var sut = new RecipeListItemViewModel(
        "someid", "title", originalValue, "image");

    //Act
    WeakReferenceMessenger.Default.Send(
        new FavoriteUpdateMessage(
            "otherid", updatedFavorite));

    //Assert
    Assert.Equal(originalValue, sut.IsFavorite);
}
```

Because the message sends a different `RecipeId` than the ID on the `RecipeListItemViewModel`, we want to validate that the `IsFavorite` property on the sut is still the same as the originally set value.

The "unit" in unit tests

When we talk about *unit tests*, that *unit* part is crucial. It's all about keeping things small and focused. Take a peek at the tests we just created. The first one ensures the ViewModel is registered for incoming `FavoriteUpdateMessages`, while the other one checks how the ViewModel responds to an incoming message. Sure – the latter indirectly verifies the message listener too, but that doesn't mean we can skip the first test. Each *unit* test should stick to checking one tiny piece of the puzzle to make sure every bit is working as it should.

With our first test passing, let's see how we can make them more data-driven.

Looking at data-driven tests

Data-driven tests are a concept in software testing that refers to the strategy of creating test methods that can be executed with multiple sets of input data. Instead of writing individual tests for every possible input value or scenario, data-driven testing allows you to define a single test method and then feed it multiple different inputs. Notice in the first test that we wrote earlier how we are explicitly passing `false` as the third parameter. Now, if we were to remove `IsFavorite = isFavorite;` from the `RecipeListItemViewModel` class's constructor, our test would deceptively still pass – a classic example of a false positive in testing. This is because, by coincidence, the default value of `IsFavorite` is `false`, but in fact, it is never assigned the value we passed in as a parameter. We could create another test method with different values in the **Arrange** step to address this. But we don't like code duplication, do we? A more elegant solution is to utilize xUnit's `Theory` and `InlineData` attributes to leverage data-driven tests.

In xUnit, while the `Fact` attribute denotes a straightforward unit test that runs once, there's another powerful feature: the `Theory` attribute. Paired with the `InlineData` attribute, `Theory` allows us to create parameterized tests. This means we can run the same test logic with different input values, ensuring our code is robust against a variety of scenarios without duplicating our test methods. Let's dive in and refactor our earlier test to take advantage of this capability:

1. Modify the `ViewModel_Initialized_PropertiesSetCorrectly` method to include the following parameters:

    ```
    public void
      ViewModel_Initialized_PropertiesSetCorrectly(
        string id, string title, bool isFavorite,
        string image)
    ```

2. Within the method, we can skip the entire `Arrange` phase and use the provided parameters directly to instantiate our ViewModel:

    ```
    //Arrange, Act
    var sut = new RecipeListItemViewModel(id, title,
        isFavorite, image);

    //Assert
    Assert.Equal(id, sut.Id);
    Assert.Equal(title, sut.Title);
    Assert.Equal(isFavorite, sut.IsFavorite);
    Assert.Equal(image, sut.Image);
    ```

3. Let's now remove the Fact attribute and add a Theory attribute and some InlineData attributes to this method:

```
[Theory]
[InlineData("id1", "title1", false, "image1")]
[InlineData("id2", "title2", true, "image2")]
[InlineData("foo", "bar", true, null)]
[InlineData(null, null, false, null)]
```

The Theory attribute is used to mark a test method as being a data-driven test. This means that the test method will be executed once for each set of data values specified using the InlineData attribute. Each of those runs of the test will have access to the data values provided by InlineData. When the Theory method is executed, xUnit will create a new instance of the test class for each set of data values specified in the InlineData attribute, and then execute the test method using those data values. The values provided in the InlineData attribute should exactly match the number and types of parameters on the method that is being tested.

Here's how we can update the FavoriteUpdateMsgReceived_SameId_FavoriteUpdated method to turn it into a data-driven test method:

```
[Theory]
[InlineData(true, false)]
[InlineData(false, true)]
[InlineData(true, true)]
[InlineData(false, false)]
public void
    FavoriteUpdateMsgReceived_SameId_FavoriteUpdated(
    bool originalValue, bool updateToValue)
{
    //Arrange
    var id = "id";
    var sut = new RecipeListItemViewModel(
        id, "title", originalValue, "image");

    //Act
    WeakReferenceMessenger.Default.Send(
        new FavoriteUpdateMessage(id, updateToValue));

    //Assert
    Assert.Equal(updateToValue, sut.IsFavorite);
}
```

The `FavoriteUpdateMsgReceived_DifferentId_FavoriteNotUpdated` can be updated similarly, as shown here:

```
[Theory]
[InlineData(true, false)]
[InlineData(false, true)]
[InlineData(true, true)]
[InlineData(false, false)]
public void FavoriteUpdateMsgReceived_
  DifferentId_FavoriteNotUpdated(
bool originalValue, bool updateToValue)
{
    //Arrange
    var sut = new RecipeListItemViewModel(
        "someid", "title", originalValue, "image");

    //Act
    WeakReferenceMessenger.Default.Send(
        new FavoriteUpdateMessage(
        "otherid", updateToValue));

    //Assert
    Assert.Equal(originalValue, sut.IsFavorite);
}
```

By adopting the `Theory` and `InlineData` attributes, we've enhanced our testing capability significantly. These updated test methods can now validate across a diverse set of values, ensuring that our ViewModel behaves consistently in varied scenarios. It's an elegant way to increase test coverage without adding redundant code.

Sometimes, it's beneficial to have test data generated for us, especially when we're more concerned about the logic than the specific values. That's where tools such as Bogus and AutoBogus come into play, helping us effortlessly generate diverse test values without manual intervention. Let's have a look!

Generating data with Bogus

While handpicked data has its place in unit tests, it often comes with inherent bias: because we've written the functionality that we want to test, we have a certain expectation about the format of the values being used. To combat this, many tests benefit from randomized or generated data, especially when the specific input matters less than the resulting outcome. Bogus is a powerful tool tailored for those moments when you need reliable, unbiased test data without the manual labor.

In this section, we'll introduce Bogus and AutoBogus and explore some of its basic capabilities. However, it's worth noting that we're merely scratching the surface here. These tools offer many features, but for the sake of brevity and focus, we'll keep our discussion high-level, touching only upon a few fundamental use cases.

Let's start off by adding AutoBogus (and thus also Bogus) to our project:

1. In **Visual Studio**, right-click the `Recipes.Client.Core.UnitTests` project and select **Manage NuGet Packages…**.

2. In the **NuGet Package Manager**, search for `autobogus` and install the **AutoBogus** package:

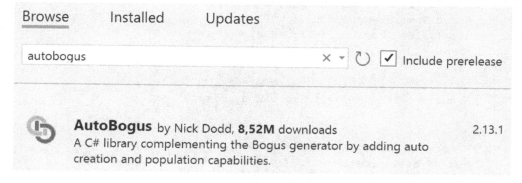

Figure 13.3: AutoBogus NuGet Package

Now that we have installed these packages, let's put this library into practice by testing the `EmptyOrWithinRangeAttribute` class:

1. Create a new class called `EmptyOrWithinRangeAttributeTests`.

2. Place the following member variables into the new class:

```
const int MinValueStart = 5;
const int MinValueEnd = 10;
const int MaxValueStart = 11;
const int MaxValueEnd = 15;

readonly EmptyOrWithinRangeAttribute sut;
```

In this class, we'll be putting our `sut` object as a class member. This allows us to write the instantiation code of the `sut` object once in the constructor (or inline), preventing repeatable code in each test for setting everything up. As each test method runs in a separate instance of the `EmptyOrWithinRangeAttributeTests` class, this also has no side effects on other tests.

3. Add a constructor to the class and add the following code:

```
sut = new Faker<EmptyOrWithinRangeAttribute>()
    .RuleFor(r => r.MinLength, f =>
        f.Random.Int(MinValueStart, MinValueEnd))
```

```
        .RuleFor(r => r.MaxLength, f =>
            f.Random.Int(MaxValueStart, MaxValueEnd))
        .Generate();
```

Instead of manually creating an instance of the `EmptyOrWithinRangeAttribute` class, we are delegating this to the Bogus framework. We do this by instantiating a new `Faker` class, passing in the type we want it to generate. With the `RuleFor` methods of the `Faker` class, we can configure the values for the individual properties.

In a `RuleFor` method, we first need to point to the property we want to configure. The next parameter of this method is a function with a `Faker` class as a parameter that allows us to define the value of the property. In this case, we use the `Faker`'s `Random.Int` method to indicate we want it to be a generated int value between two values.

By calling the `Generate` method, the Bogus framework will generate an instance of the type we want, adhering to the rules we've defined. This gives back the instance of the `EmptyOrWithinRangeAttribute` we want to work with.

Let's go ahead and implement a test that checks if `EmptyOrWithinRangeAttribute` validates input correctly:

1. Add the `Value_WithinRange_IsValid` to this class, as shown here:

    ```
    [Fact]
    public void Value_WithinRange_IsValid()
    {
        //Arrange
        var input = new Faker().Random.String2(
            sut.MinLength, sut.MaxLength);

        //Act
        var isValid = sut.IsValid(input);

        //Assert
        Assert.True(isValid);
    }
    ```

    In the `Arrange` step, we're using Bogus' `Faker` class to generate a random string with a length that falls between the `MinLength` and `MaxLength` properties of the `sut`. Remember – these `MinLength` and `MaxLength` properties are values generated by Bogus. This generated string value can now be used to check whether the `IsValid` method of the `EmptyOrWithingRangeAttribute` does what we expect it to do. The returned value should be `true`, which we can easily check with the `Assert.True` method.

2. Similarly, we can add a `Value_TooShort_IsNotValid` method that checks that the `IsValid` method returns `false` when the provided value isn't correct:

```
[Fact]
public void Value_TooShort_IsNotValid()
{
    //Arrange
    var input = new Faker().Random.String2(
        1, MinValueStart - 1);

    //Act
    var isValid = sut.IsValid(input);

    //Assert
    Assert.False(isValid);
}
```

3. While we're at it, let's also add a check to see if an empty string is returned as being valid. This is shown in the following code block:

```
[Fact]
public void Value_Empty_IsValid()
{
    //Arrange
    var input = string.Empty;

    //Act
    var isValid = sut.IsValid(input);

    //Assert
    Assert.True(isValid);
}
```

Notice how short and straightforward these test methods are! Adding extra checks for input values being too long or null really isn't hard labor. And because we are not working with hardcoded data, we can be pretty confident the `IsValid` method of the `EmptyOrWithingRangeAttributes` class works as expected in many different scenarios. On top of that, think about the speed and efficiency with which we're validating this `ValidationAttribute` class. We haven't deployed our app or clicked through its interface. Still, we're already certain about the correctness of our code. That's a significant boost in development efficiency!

Remember the `VM_Initialized_SubscribedToFavoriteUpdateMessage` method in the `RecipeListItemViewModelTests` class we wrote earlier? This method checks whether an instance of the `RecipeListItemViewModel` is registered as a receiver for the `FavoriteUpdateMessage`. In this test method, we had to initialize our sut. However, the values that were used to create it aren't of any value inside the test: whichever values are used, the instance should listen for the FavoriteUpdateMessage. This is an ideal scenario to introduce AutoBogus. Just take a look at the updated code of the VM_Initialized_SubscribedToFavoriteUpdateMessage method:

```
//Arrange, Act
var sut = AutoFaker.Generate<RecipeListItemViewModel>();

//Assert
Assert.True(WeakReferenceMessenger.Default
    .IsRegistered<FavoriteUpdateMessage>(sut));
```

With the static Generate method of the AutoFaker class, we can generate an instance of RecipeListItemViewModel. The Faker class typically requires a default constructor for the object type we want to instantiate. The RecipeListItemViewModel doesn't have a default constructor and that's where AutoFaker comes into play: it will automatically provide fake values for the parameters. We basically don't care which values are used to create this class. All that we are interested in in this test, is the fact the instantiated class is registered for the FavoriteUpdateMessage.

In other test methods, such as those in RecipeListItemViewModelTests, we've relied on hardcoded dummy data. We can use AutoBogus to get rid of these hardcoded values as well. Take a look at the updated FavoriteUpdateMsgReceived_SameId_FavoriteUpdated method:

```
public void
    FavoriteUpdateMsgReceived_SameId_FavoriteUpdated(
    bool originalValue, bool updateToValue)
{
    //Arrange
    var id = AutoFaker.Generate<string>();
    var sut = new RecipeListItemViewModel(id,
        AutoFaker.Generate<string>(),
        originalValue,
        AutoFaker.Generate<string>());

    //Act
    WeakReferenceMessenger.Default.Send(new
        FavoriteUpdateMessage(id, updateToValue));

    //Assert
    Assert.Equal(updateToValue, sut.IsFavorite);
}
```

In this previous code block, we're leveraging AutoBogus' Generate method to generate random data for us.

Bogus and AutoBogus automate .NET testing by generating unbiased, randomized test data, eliminating manual and potentially biased inputs.

Instead of merely providing fake data, we often need to mock entire components or behavior. This is where a dedicated mocking framework, such as Moq, becomes invaluable. Let's delve into how Moq empowers us to effectively mock dependencies and streamline our testing process.

Mocking dependencies with Moq

Testing frequently involves scenarios where our system under test interacts with external dependencies, whether they are databases, APIs, or other services. Running tests against these real dependencies can lead to slow, unpredictable outcomes and potentially unwanted side effects. Mocking provides a solution by simulating these dependencies, ensuring our tests focus purely on the component at hand. Through mocking, we gain control over external interactions, ensuring our tests are swift, reliable, and free from external influences.

> **Integration tests**
>
> When writing unit tests, we typically want to mock external dependencies as much as possible. However, it is often valuable to also test the integration of different components to ensure they work together seamlessly. This is where integration tests come in. Unlike unit tests, which focus heavily on mocking to test units in isolation, integration tests often involve fewer mocks. This ensures that components interact with each other in the exact manner we expect, verifying that they behave correctly as a unified whole.

The principles of DI and separation of concerns accentuate this approach. When we design our components to be decoupled and inject their dependencies, it becomes seamless to replace real dependencies with mock versions during testing. Think of DI, SoC, and mocking as interlocking puzzle pieces, each complementing the other, leading to a comprehensive and maintainable testing strategy. Now, let's dive into how Moq assists us in achieving this goal.

When we inspect the `RecipeDetailViewModel`'s constructor, it's evident that it depends on several services:

```
public RecipeDetailViewModel(
    IRecipeService recipeService,
    IFavoritesService favoritesService,
    IRatingsService ratingsService,
    INavigationService navigationService,
    IDialogService dialogService)
{
    ...
}
```

To effectively test this ViewModel, we need to abstract away its external dependencies. Mocking the recipeService parameter can be achieved like this:

```
var recipeServiceMock = new Mock<IRecipeService>();
```

The mocked value can then be passed-in the RecipeDetailViewModel as follows:

```
var sut = new RecipeDetailViewModel
   (recipeServiceMock.Object, ...);
```

This is where it gets interesting: we can provide recipeServiceMock with fake method implementations. We can configure our mock object with specific method behaviors. Consider the LoadRecipe method of IRecipeService:

```
Task<Result<RecipeDetail>> LoadRecipe(string id);
```

Here's how to instruct Moq to mimic this method:

```
recipeServiceMock
    .Setup(m => m.LoadRecipe(It.IsAny<string>()))
    .ReturnsAsync(
    Result<RecipeDetail>.Success(new RecipeDetail(...));
```

With the Setup method, we can tell Moq which method we want to simulate. In our example, we're targeting the LoadRecipe method. It.IsAny<string> is a matcher, which signifies that we're indifferent to the exact value passed into the method. In simpler terms, any string value will trigger the behavior we're defining here. Speaking of which, ReturnsAsync specifies the result our mock method should produce. For example, we're returning a successful result containing dummy RecipeDetail data. In essence, this code configures recipeServiceMock to always produce a specific result for any call to LoadRecipe, ensuring our tests are predictable and not reliant on real implementations. Let's see how we can add a set of new tests.

Applying mocking in our ViewModel tests

To start testing RecipeDetailViewModel, let's add a new class named RecipeDetailViewModelTests to the test project and follow these steps:

1. Add the following fields to the RecipeDetailViewModelTests class:

    ```
    readonly Mock<IRecipeService> _recipeServiceMock;
    readonly Mock<IFavoritesService>
        _favoritesServiceMock;
    readonly Mock<IRatingsService> _ratingsServiceMock;
    readonly Mock<INavigationService>
        _navigationServiceMock;
    ```

```
readonly Mock<IDialogService> _dialogServiceMock;

readonly RecipeDetailViewModel sut;
```

2. Instantiate these fields in the class's constructor, as shown here:

```
public RecipeDetailViewModelTests()
{
    _recipeServiceMock = new();
    _favoritesServiceMock = new();
    _ratingsServiceMock = new();
    _navigationServiceMock = new();
    _dialogServiceMock = new();

    _ratingsServiceMock
        .Setup(m =>
            m.LoadRatingsSummary(It.IsAny<string>()))
        .ReturnsAsync(Result<RatingsSummary>.Success(
            AutoFaker.Generate<RatingsSummary>()));

    sut = new RecipeDetailViewModel(
        _recipeServiceMock.Object,
        _favoritesServiceMock.Object,
        _ratingsServiceMock.Object,
        _navigationServiceMock.Object,
        _dialogServiceMock.Object);
}
```

In this previous code block, we're instantiating all of our mock classes and using them to instantiate the sut object. By putting this in the constructor, we don't have to repeat this code in every unit test. We can even already provide some default mock implementations, as shown with _ratingServiceMock. If, for a specific test, we need a different behavior for _ratingServiceMock, we can easily override the default behavior set in the constructor in the test itself. When we specify a new behavior in the test method, Moq will use the most recent setup, ensuring flexibility in our tests.

3. In the first test, we want to validate that the parameter that is being used to navigate to the detail page, is effectively being passed to the injected IRecipeService's LoadRecipe method to retrieve the detail information. Start by adding the following method to this class:

```
[Fact]
public async Task OnNavigatedTo_Should_Load_Recipe()
{
    ...
}
```

4. Let's have a look at this test's `Arrange` step:

```
//Arrange
var recipeId = AutoFaker.Generate<string>();

var parameters = new Dictionary<string, object> {
    { "id", recipeId }
};

_recipeServiceMock
    .Setup(m => m.LoadRecipe(It.IsAny<string>()))
    .ReturnsAsync(Result<RecipeDetail>
    .Success(AutoFaker.Generate<RecipeDetail>()));
```

In the `Arrange` step, we're generating a `recipeId` using `AutoFaker`. This value is put in a Dictionary named parameters which we'll use in the next step. We're also configuring the behavior of the `_recipeServiceMock`'s `LoadRecipe` method. As we're not interested in what exactly is being returned in this test, we'll leave it to `AutoFaker` to generate a `RecipeDetail` instance.

5. Add the following code below the `Arrange` steps:

```
//Act
await sut.OnNavigatedTo(parameters);
```

By calling the ViewModel's `OnNavigatedTo` method and passing a dictionary, we can mimic navigating to the ViewModel. This should trigger the load of the recipe's detail information, using the passed-in `"id"` item from the dictionary.

6. Validating whether the `LoadRecipe` method of the injected `IRecipeService` is correctly called can be achieved like this:

```
//Assert
_recipeServiceMock.Verify(
    m => m.LoadRecipe(recipeId), Times.Once);
```

The `Verify` method on a `Mock` object allows us to check whether a specific method was invoked or not. Note that we're explicitly specifying that the `LoadRecipe` should have been called with the `recipeId` parameter. Also, with `Times.Once` we define that the method, with the given parameter, should have been called exactly once. If that isn't the case, an exception will be thrown that will fail the test.

This powerful feature of Moq ensures that certain interactions (method calls) take place as expected. But by using Moq, we can also make our tests predictable, allowing us to check for particular output values. The following test shows how we can validate whether the data returned by the IRecipeService's LoadRecipe method is correctly mapped on to the ViewModel:

```
[Fact]
public async Task OnNavigatedTo_Should_Map_RecipeDetail()
{
    //Arrange
    var recipeDetail = AutoFaker.Generate<RecipeDetail>();

    var parameters = new Dictionary<string, object> {
        { "id", AutoFaker.Generate<string>() }
    };

    _recipeServiceMock
        .Setup(m => m.LoadRecipe(It.IsAny<string>()))
        .ReturnsAsync(Result<RecipeDetail>
        .Success(recipeDetail));

    //Act
    await sut.OnNavigatedTo(parameters);

    //Assert
    Assert.Equal(recipeDetail.Name, sut.Title);
    Assert.Equal(recipeDetail.Author, sut.Author);
}
```

A generated recipeDetail is what the _recipeServiceMock's LoadRecipe method returns. After navigating to the ViewModel, we can check whether the properties match the value of the returned recipeDetail variable, assuring us the values are correctly mapped.

Thin UI, deep tests

One of the pinnacle benefits of the MVVM pattern, especially when coupled with DI, is the depth of our unit testing capability. Let's look at an example that demonstrates this. Traditionally, interactions such as dialog prompts or navigation might be considered to be UI testing. But here, we'll see how we can validate these interactions through simple unit tests. The IDialogService and INavigationService, while seeming intrinsically linked to UI, are injected as platform-independent dependencies. This abstraction ensures that our tests remain agnostic to the final UI layer, whether it's a mobile app, a web interface, or desktop software. As a result, the UI layer remains incredibly thin, and our confidence in the bulk of our application logic – verified through these tests — remains high. Let's dive into an example: when the RecipeDetailViewModel is unable to load the recipe detail, a prompt should be shown asking the user to retry. If the user selects **No**, the app should automatically navigate back to the previous page. Here's what this test looks like:

```
[Fact]
public async Task FailedLoad_Should_ShowDialog()
{
    //Arrange
    var parameters = new Dictionary<string, object> {
        { "id", AutoFaker.Generate<string>() }
    };

    _recipeServiceMock
        .Setup(m => m.LoadRecipe(It.IsAny<string>()))
        .ReturnsAsync(Result<RecipeDetail>
        .Fail(AutoFaker.Generate<string>()));

    _dialogServiceMock
        .Setup(m => m.AskYesNo(It.IsAny<string>(), ...))
        .ReturnsAsync(false);

    //Act
    await sut.OnNavigatedTo(parameters);

    //Assert
    _dialogServiceMock.Verify(m =>
        m.AskYesNo(It.IsAny<string>(), ...), Times.Once);
    _navigationServiceMock.Verify(m => m.GoBack(),
        Times.Once);
}
```

In the previous code block, we're configuring `_recipeServiceMock` so that it returns a `Fail` result every time the `LoadRecipe` method is called. `_dialogServiceMock` is configured so that when the `AskYesNo` method is invoked, a `false` value is returned. This mimics the user selecting No in the presented dialog. With all this in place, we can check that the dialog is being shown and that back navigation is triggered as a result of the user selecting No in the retry dialog.

This demonstrates how, with the right architecture and tools, even intricate interactions that touch upon UI elements can be captured, controlled, and tested – all without direct dependency on platform-specific components. This platform-independent unit testing not only ensures that our application remains both maintainable and reliable but also hardens its adaptability across various platforms. It underscores the power of the MVVM pattern!

However, there is still some code to be tested that is platform-specific. Let's have a look at that before we end this chapter.

Testing MAUI-specific code

As shown in the previous examples, the majority of our code can be tested independently of the platform. But let's not forget that there is code in our MAUI project as well that could benefit from some unit tests.

Let's start by adding a new project to hold our tests for the `Recipes.Mobile` project:

1. Add a new **xUnit Test Project** type, just as we did at the beginning of this chapter. Name this project `Recipes.Mobile.UnitTests`.

2. Once the project has been created, add a reference to the `Recipes.Mobile` project.

3. Add the **AutoBogus** NuGet package to this project.

The `Recipes.Mobile.UnitTests` project doesn't target any specific frameworks other than `net8.0`. Because of that, we need to make sure `net8.0` is on the list of target frameworks of the MAUI project as well. Also, we need to make sure that when the `Recipes.Mobile` project targets this additional `net8.0` framework, it doesn't output an EXE file. Let's see how to properly configure this:

1. Open the `Recipes.Mobile.csproj` file by clicking on the project name in the **Solution Explorer** in **Visual Studio** or by right-clicking the project and selecting **Edit Project File**.

2. Add `net8.0` to the `TargetFrameworks` tag, as shown here:

   ```
   <TargetFrameworks>net8.0;net8.0-android;net8.0-
   ios;net8.0-maccatalyst</TargetFrameworks>
   ```

3. Find the `OutputType` tag in the `.csproj` file and update the following:

   ```
   <OutputType Condition="'$(TargetFramework)' !=
   'net8.0'">Exe</OutputType>
   ```

4. In the **Solution Explorer**, right-click the `Recipes.Mobile` project and select **Unload Project**. Once unloaded, right-click it again and select **Reload Project**.

Once the `Recipes.Mobile` project is configured, we also need to add one thing to the `Recipes.Mobile.UnitTests` project. In its `.csproj` file, find the first `PropertyGroup` tag and add the following: `<UseMaui>true</UseMaui>`.

With all of this in place, writing tests for functionality in the `Recipes.Mobile` project isn't any different from the tests we've written so far. Let's have a look at how to test the `RatingToStarsConverter` class:

1. Start by creating a new class called `RatingToStarsConverterTests`.

2. This converter makes for a good data-driven test. We can specify the input and expected output through method parameters, as shown in the following code block:

```
public void Convert_Should_Return_ExpectedOutput(
    object input, string expectedOutput)
{
    //Arrange
    var sut = new Converters.RatingToStarsConverter();

    //Act
    var result = sut.Convert(input,
        null, null, null);

    //Assert
    Assert.Equal(expectedOutput, result);
}
```

The passed-in input value is the value we want our converter to convert. The result is compared to the converted value by using Assert.Equal.

3. Add the Theory attribute and the following InlineData attributes for different – edge-case – scenarios to this method:

```
[InlineData("foo", "")]
[InlineData(-1d, "")]
[InlineData(6d, "")]
[InlineData(1d, "\ue838")]
[InlineData(2d, "\ue838\ue838")]
[InlineData(2.2d, "\ue838\ue838")]
[InlineData(2.5d, "\ue838\ue838\ue839")]
[InlineData(2.9d, "\ue838\ue838\ue839")]
```

This test method successfully validates if the RatingToStarsConverter converts a given value to a string representing star-icons. Not only are happy paths tested, but also the expected behavior when passing in invalid data.

One other thing we can test is the InstructionsDataTemplateSelector class. The following steps show you how this can be done:

1. Add a new class InstructionsDataTemplateSelectorTests to the Recipes. Mobile.UnitTests project.

2. Here's what a test for this TemplateSelector could look like:

```
[Fact]
public void SelectTemplate_NoteVM_Should_Return
    _NoteTemplate()
```

```
    {
        //Arrange
        var template = new DataTemplate();
        var sut = new InstructionsDataTemplateSelector();
        sut.NoteTemplate = template;
        sut.InstructionTemplate = new DataTemplate();

        //Act
        var result = sut.SelectTemplate(
            AutoFaker.Generate<NoteViewModel>(), null);

        //Assert
        Assert.Equal(template, result);
    }
```

In this test, we're creating a template that gets assigned to the `NoteTemplate` property of the sut. The `SelectTemplate` method of the sut gets invoked, passing in a generated `NoteViewModel`. We expect the returned `DataTemplate` to be the one we created and assigned to the `NoteTemplate` property.

With simple tests like these, we can easily validate the behavior of a `TemplateSelector` without deploying and running our app once! Testing if the `InstructionsDataTemplateSelector` works as expected for an `InstructionViewModel` or an unsupported ViewModel, should be pretty straightforward.

Summary

In this chapter, we delved into unit testing within the MAUI framework, specifically focusing on testing ViewModels and some MAUI components. It's worth noting that while we focused on these areas, the tools and techniques discussed are equally effective for testing services, repositories, and other integral parts of your application. Beyond just validating the code's functionality, unit testing acts as a safety net, ensuring maintainability and robustness by reducing the chances of regression bugs. This powerful approach empowers us to iterate faster, removing the constant need for cumbersome deployments or manual checks. Leveraging mock implementations, we can seamlessly mimic and validate countless scenarios, and this validation remains ingrained in our code base. As we add or modify features, this ensures every intricate use case remains covered. A key takeaway is the significant portion of our app that can be tested independently of platform-specific details. This not only enhances adaptability but solidifies the effectiveness of the MVVM pattern. In conclusion, unit testing in MAUI isn't just a checkbox; it's a foundational element that drives us to build robust applications with agility and confidence. In the next and final chapter of this book, we'll be looking at some troubleshooting and debugging tips that might come in handy when building an MVVM app with .NET MAUI.

Further reading

To learn more about the topics that were covered in this chapter, take a look at the following resources:

- xUnit: `https://xunit.net/`
- Bogus for .NET: `https://github.com/bchavez/Bogus`
- AutoBogus: `https://github.com/nickdodd79/AutoBogus`
- Moq: `https://github.com/devlooped/moq`
- *Unit testing C# in .NET Core using dotnet test and xUnit*: `https://learn.microsoft.com/dotnet/core/testing/unit-testing-with-dotnet-test`

Troubleshooting and Debugging Tips

Congratulations on making it this far in your journey to mastering the MVVM pattern in .NET MAUI! By now, you've learned about the intricacies of data binding, dependency injection, converters, and various other components that make up your *Recipes!* app. However, as any seasoned developer will tell you, even the most experienced experts encounter roadblocks from time to time.

MVVM, with all its benefits, can sometimes feel like navigating a complex maze. When you encounter issues, it's not always obvious where to find the root cause or how to fix it. That's where this chapter comes in. In this short but invaluable chapter, we'll shine a light on common pitfalls and challenges you may face during your MVVM journey.

We'll explore three areas where issues often tend to occur:

- Common data binding issues
- Services and Dependency Injection pitfalls
- Frequent custom control and converter problems

Let's get started on our journey through these common stumbling blocks. By the end of this chapter, you'll be better equipped to troubleshoot and conquer the challenges that MVVM in .NET MAUI may throw your way.

Technical requirements

To ensure you're in sync with the upcoming content, make your way to our GitHub repository at `https://github.com/PacktPublishing/MVVM-pattern-.NET-MAUI/tree/main/Chapter14`. Kick off with the materials in the `Start` folder. And remember, if you're ever in need of a consolidated reference, the `Finish` folder holds the final, refined code at the chapter's close.

Common data binding issues

One of the cornerstones of the MVVM pattern is data binding. It forms the link between your View and ViewModel, ensuring seamless communication between them. While data binding offers powerful capabilities, it's also an area where developers often face challenges. This section aims to shed light on common data binding and ViewModel issues and how to troubleshoot them:

- **Typos and mismatched names**: One of the simplest yet surprisingly common issues developers encounter is typos or mismatched property names. A small typo in your XAML markup or ViewModel code can disrupt the entire data binding process.

- **Incorrect binding modes**: Data binding supports various modes such as `OneWay`, `TwoWay`, and `OneTime`, each with its own purpose, as we've seen in *Chapter 4, Data Binding in .NET MAUI*. Using the wrong mode can lead to unexpected behavior in your app.

- **Binding incompatible data types**: Obviously, binding a property of type `int` to a property of type `Color` on a UI control won't work, despite XAML supporting implicit type conversion in certain cases.

- **PropertyChanged event not fired**: ViewModel properties must notify the view of changes by raising `PropertyChanged` events. What happens when these events don't trigger as expected? The View will not be updated to reflect the changes in the ViewModel's data.

- **Updating collections**: More or less related to the previous point, handling collections in MVVM is often misunderstood, especially when working with `ObservableCollection`. Make sure your collections update correctly and avoid the pitfall of inadvertently assigning a new `ObservableCollection`.

- **Data binding scope confusion**: When you bind data within a `ListView` or `CollectionView`, keep in mind that each item in the collection creates its own data binding scope. This means that when attempting to bind a property or command that resides in the ViewModel rather than the individual item, you'll need to use techniques such as relative or element binding to correctly reference the desired context.

- **Data binding in behaviors**: Behaviors exist outside the visual tree, which means they do not have the same capability for locating ancestors as other UI elements do.

> **Note**
>
> Some of these pitfalls, such as typos in property names and binding incompatible data types, can be avoided by leveraging compiled bindings, as stipulated in *Chapter 4, Data Binding in .NET MAUI*.

As you can see, a lot of issues related to data binding can arise. Luckily, some of them aren't that hard to spot and fix, as long as you know where to look. Let's start off by looking at some tools in Visual Studio.

Checking the Output and XAML Binding Failures window

With both the **Output** window and **XAML Binding Failures** window in Visual Studio, typos or mismatched property names can easily be spotted. Here's how:

1. Let's first introduce two faulty data binding statements in our code. On `RecipesOverviewPage`, update the `Image` and `Label` elements in the `CollectionView`'s `ItemTemplate`, as shown here:

```
<CollectionView.ItemTemplate>
    <DataTemplate>
        . . .
            <Image
                Aspect="AspectFill"
                HorizontalOptions="Fill"
                Source="{Binding IsFavorite}"
                VerticalOptions="Fill" />
            . . .
            <Label
                Grid.Row="1"
                Margin="20,5,20,40"
                FontSize="16"
                HorizontalOptions="Fill"
                HorizontalTextAlignment="Start"
                MaxLines="2"
                Text="{Binding Titel}"
                TextColor="Black"
                VerticalOptions="Center" />
        . . .
    </DataTemplate>
</CollectionView.ItemTemplate>
```

2. Run the app. While the app is running, head over to Visual Studio and open up the **Output** window. If it's not already open, you can open it through **Debug | Windows | Output**. Notice the following:

```
[0:] Microsoft.Maui.Controls.Xaml.Diagnostics.Binding
Diagnostics: Warning: 'False' cannot be converted to
type 'Microsoft.Maui.Controls.ImageSource'
[0:] Microsoft.Maui.Controls.Xaml.Diagnostics.Binding
Diagnostics: Warning: 'Titel' property not found on
'Recipes.Client.Core.ViewModels.RecipeListItemView
Model', target property: 'Microsoft.Maui
.Controls.Label.Text'
```

See how the **Output** window warns us about two things. The first warning notifies us about an incompatible data type: a `bool` value cannot be converted to an `ImageSource` type. The second warning signals that a property named `Titel` cannot be found on the `RecipeListItemViewModel`. That, of course, is a typo!

3. Alternatively, let's have a look at the **XAML Binding Failures** window in Visual Studio. This can be opened through **Debug | Windows | XAML Binding Failures**. *Figure 14.1* shows what this window looks like:

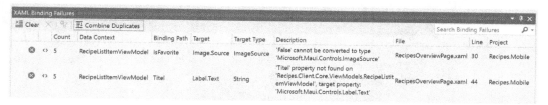

Figure 14.1: XAML Binding Failures window

This window gives us the same information as the **Output** window. Additionally, it shows extra information such as where the failing binding statement is located and how many times this issue has occurred. The best thing about this window? When clicking on an item in this list, Visual Studio will open the XAML file where the faulty binding statement is located and will put the pointer on the exact data binding statement that contains the error.

Whenever you have a binding failure in your application, the **XAML Binding Failures** window and the **Output** window in Visual Studio will provide information about what went wrong. The **XAML Binding Failures** window, especially, provides immediate insight into typos, missing properties, or data type issues. Always keep an eye on this window when developing your views.

Another way to troubleshoot or debug data binding issues is by creating and leveraging a specialized converter. Let's have a look!

Debugging with a DoNothingConverter

A `DoNothingConverter` is an invaluable tool for debugging. By placing it in your binding pipeline, you can inspect the values being passed during the binding process. If you see unexpected values or none at all, it can help pinpoint where the breakdown occurs. Here's the implementation of the `DoNothingConverter`:

```
public class DoNothingConverter : IValueConverter
{
    public object Convert(object value,
        Type targetType, object parameter,
        CultureInfo culture)
    {
```

```
        // Break here to inspect value during debugging
        return value;
    }
    public object ConvertBack(object value,
        Type targetType, object parameter,
        CultureInfo culture)
    {
        // Break here to inspect value during debugging
        return value;
    }
}
```

To add and use this converter in your binding statements, follow these steps:

1. Add a DoNothingConverter to the Resources of the page where you want to debug a binding statement. Here's how we can add it to RecipesOverviewPage:

```xml
<ContentPage
    x:Class="Recipes.Mobile.RecipesOverviewPage"
    ...
    xmlns:conv="clr-namespace:
      Recipes.Mobile.Converters"
    ... >
    <ContentPage.Resources>
        ...
        <conv:DoNothingConverter
            x:Key="doNothingConverter" />
    </ContentPage.Resources>
    ...
</ContentPage>
```

2. Add the converter to the binding statement you want to debug, as shown here:

```xml
<Image
    ...
    Source="{Binding IsFavorite,
    Converter={StaticResource doNothingConverter}}"
    VerticalOptions="Fill" />
...
<Label
    ...
    Text="{Binding Titel,
    Converter={StaticResource doNothingConverter}}"
    TextColor="Black"
    VerticalOptions="Center" />
```

3. Insert a breakpoint in the Convert or ConvertBack method of the DoNothingConverter.

4. If the breakpoint is hit during runtime, it indicates a successful binding to an existing property on the ViewModel. You'll notice that the breakpoint in the Convert method will not be hit for the Titel binding as this property doesn't exist.

5. If the breakpoint isn't hit on subsequent updates of the property value, check the binding mode of the statement and ensure that the PropertyChanged method is triggered when the property gets updated.

6. When the breakpoint is hit, you can easily inspect the bound value and compare it to your expectations.

7. You can also examine the targetType parameter, which represents the type of the target property. Keep in mind that while XAML supports implicit type conversion in certain cases, it's essential to be aware of the specific conversions supported.

8. The ConvertBack method should be called when the property on the UI controls is updated and the binding mode is set to TwoWay or OneWayToSource. If you expect this to work but the ConvertBack method is not called, check the binding statement's binding mode.

By following these steps and utilizing the DoNothingConverter tool, you can effectively troubleshoot data binding issues in your MVVM application.

Let's discuss another cause of potential data binding issues: collections.

Troubleshooting collections

When working with collections, especially ObservableCollection, developers frequently encounter challenges related to updates and bindings.

If you're using an ObservableCollection or any collection implementing the INotifyCollectionChanged interface, it's usually assigned once during the initialization of your ViewModel. Here's an important nuance to keep in mind: the setter for this property doesn't trigger the PropertyChanged event. Instead, when you add or remove items from the collection, it triggers the CollectionChanged event on the collection instance. This event, in turn, updates the bound control, assuming it supports binding to ObservableCollection. To verify whether a specific control works well with the INotifyCollectionChanged interface, consult the control's documentation.

However, there's a critical point to be aware of: if the ObservableCollection is assigned anew, the binding will effectively be *lost*, unless, of course, the PropertyChanged event is properly raised. This means that if you reassign the entire collection with a new instance of ObservableCollection, you need to ensure that the PropertyChanged event is correctly triggered. To check whether this event is effectively raised, you can utilize the DoNothingConverter.

In contrast, when you're working with a collection that doesn't implement INotifyCollectionChanged (as in the case of a standard List or similar collections), adding or removing items won't be automatically detected by the UI layer. In this scenario, the PropertyChanged event must be explicitly triggered when items are added to or removed from the collection. Consequently, the entire list will be re-rendered in the UI when you make changes.

When troubleshooting issues related to collections, pay close attention to whether you're using ObservableCollection or non-observable collections, and ensure that you trigger the appropriate events to keep your ViewModel and UI in sync. Understanding these dynamics will help you navigate the complexities of collections in your MVVM application more effectively and prevent potential issues.

When working with collections, remember that you don't need to trigger a PropertyChanged event on the collection itself when a property of an item within the collection changes. Instead, the key lies in raising the PropertyChanged event on the instance of the specific item that underwent modification. This ensures that the UI is notified of changes at the item level and reflects the updated state accurately. In essence, you're focusing the update event precisely where it matters, minimizing unnecessary updates to the entire collection.

The data binding pitfall on Behaviors

It's very easy to oversee this while writing XAML, but relative source binding won't work on Behaviors. That is because Behaviors exist outside the visual tree. In fact, a Behavior can even be reused by multiple UI elements, hence a relative source binding won't be able to retrieve a parent object. When applying relative source binding to a Behavior, your app will crash, preceded by an exception of type System. InvalidOperationException. The exception states the following: **Operation is not valid due to the current state of the object**. This exception alongside this message should be an indication that there is a faulty data binding statement defined on a Behavior. There will be no further indication in the exception or in the **Output** window whatsoever. The only thing you can do is systematically go through the Behaviors in your code and look at their binding statements.

In many cases, the relative source binding can be replaced by element binding, as demonstrated here:

```
<!-- RelativeSource binding fails on Behaviors! -->
<toolkit:IconTintColorBehavior
    TintColor="{Binding IsFavorite,
    Source={RelativeSource AncestorType={x:Type local:
    FavoriteControl}}, Converter=..." />
```

This code snippet will fail because of the usage of RelativeSource binding in the IcontTintColorBehavior. This can be bypassed by leveraging element binding, as shown in the next code block:

```
<ContentView
    ...
```

```
        x:Name="root">
    ...
            <toolkit:IconTintColorBehavior
                TintColor="{Binding IsFavorite,
                Source={x:Reference root},
                Converter=...}" />
    ...
</ContentView>
```

Next, let's discuss the things to look out for when working with Dependency Injection.

Services and Dependency Injection pitfalls

In your MVVM journey, DI plays a crucial role in providing essential functionality to your application. However, even in the world of DI, there can be pitfalls waiting to catch you off guard. This section is dedicated to unveiling the most common pitfalls and equipping you with the knowledge to navigate them effectively.

Unable to resolve service for type

A `System.InvalidOperationException` stating **Unable to resolve service for type** ... is one of the most frequent exceptions when working with DI. The cause is pretty simple: we ask the DI container to resolve an instance of an object that has some dependencies that can't be resolved. In other words, we haven't registered all dependencies for this class. *Figure 14.2* shows what this exception would look like if we didn't register the `RecipesOverviewViewModel` in the DI container:

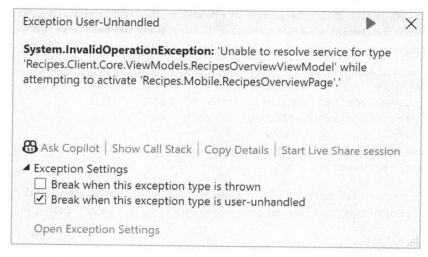

Figure 14.2: InvalidOperationException thrown

The exception gives you all the information you need as it clearly states what type is missing while trying to create a particular type.

Registering the missing dependency in the `MauiProgram` class (or anywhere you do your registrations) should fix the issue.

Let's have a look at another common exception in the context of DI.

No parameterless constructor defined for type

A `System.MissingMethodException` can be thrown in the following scenario:

- Shell is used to perform navigation
- The BindingContext (a ViewModel) of a page is injected through the page's constructor
- The page isn't registered in the DI container

As long as a page doesn't have any dependencies that need to be injected through the constructor, it doesn't need to be registered in the DI container, as its default constructor is being used by Shell to instantiate the page. However, when the page has one or more dependencies, we need to register it in the DI container. That way, Shell can ask the container to resolve an instance of the needed page.

Registering the page in the DI container solves this issue.

A much more subtle pitfall when it comes to DI is not registering the services appropriately. Let's have a look.

Incorrect service registration

In the context of DI, one common pitfall stems from improperly registering services, leading to issues that can affect your application's functionality:

- **Resource intensiveness**: If you register a service as transient when it should be a singleton, you may encounter resource-intensive behavior. This occurs because a new instance of the service is created every time it's requested. For services that involve resource-intensive operations, such as establishing database connections or managing file handles, this frequent creation can lead to performance bottlenecks and resource exhaustion. Such issues can significantly impact your application's performance and stability.
- **Unintended shared state**: Conversely, if you mistakenly register a service as a singleton when it should be transient, you may inadvertently introduce an unintended shared state. In this scenario, changes made to the service's state or properties affect all parts of your application that depend on that service. This shared state can lead to unpredictable behavior and make debugging challenging, as the source of the problem may not be immediately apparent. It's crucial to align the service's registration with its intended usage to avoid such pitfalls.

To mitigate these issues, carefully consider the intended scope and usage of each service during registration. Ensure that services requiring a single shared instance across your application are registered as singletons, while services that should have unique instances for each request are registered as transient. By making informed decisions about service registration, you can prevent these common pitfalls and ensure your application functions as intended.

In the final section, let's have a look at common problems around custom controls and value converters.

Frequent custom control and converter problems

Most of the issues that arise when working with custom controls regularly have to do with bindable properties. Often, a small typo or a little oversight might cause your custom control to not react as expected or to display the wrong data.

Troubleshooting bindable properties

On a custom control, there is a lot of ceremony needed to define bindable properties. It's very easy to make a mistake that is very hard to spot when troubleshooting. Here are a couple of things to look out for:

- The `propertyName` parameter in the `Create` method: Make sure the `propertyName` parameter matches the exact naming of the property:

```
public static readonly BindableProperty
  IsFavoriteProperty =
    BindableProperty.Create(nameof(IsFavorite), …);


public bool IsFavorite
{
    ...
}
```

As this code sample shows, it is advised to use the `nameof` expression to prevent typos!

- The `returnType` parameter in the `Create` method: The second parameter of the `BindableProperty`'s `Create` method is the `returnType`, which must match the type of the property:

```
public static readonly BindableProperty
  IsFavoriteProperty =
    BindableProperty.Create(nameof(IsFavorite),
    typeof(bool), …);


public bool IsFavorite
{
```

```
    ...
}
```

- The declaringType parameter in the Create method: This parameter should be the type of the class where the property is defined:

```
public partial class FavoriteControl : ContentView
{
    public static readonly BindableProperty
      IsFavoriteProperty =
            BindableProperty.Create(...
                typeof(FavoriteControl),...);

    public bool IsFavorite
    {
        ...
    }
}
```

- It's also important to make sure the getter and setter of the property call the GetValue and SetValue, passing in the correct BindableProperty:

```
public static readonly BindableProperty IsFavoriteProperty = ...

public bool IsFavorite
{
    get => (bool)GetValue(IsFavoriteProperty);
    set => SetValue(IsFavoriteProperty, value);
}
```

Whenever there is a discrepancy between the provided values in the BindableProperty's Create method and the values on the control itself, or when the property doesn't get or set the value correctly on the BindableProperty, the bindable property will not work as expected. So, it's crucial to double-check these values!

Binding to the BindingContext

As already stipulated in *Chapter 11, Creating MVVM-Friendly Controls,* it is crucial that custom controls don't depend on their BindingContext! The reason is that you can't control that, as it is inherited from the parent the custom control is used on. Instead, you should only bind to the (bindable) properties that you've defined on the control itself. This can easily be achieved by leveraging relative or element binding, just like we did with the FavoriteControl:

```
<Image
      HeightRequest="{Binding HeightRequest,
        Source={x:Reference icon}}"
```

```
IsVisible="{Binding IsInteractive,
    Source={RelativeSource AncestorType={x:Type
        local:FavoriteControl}}}"
... />
```

Any binding statements on a custom control that don't have an explicit source set will bind to the `BindingContext` of the parent, which we don't control. When a custom control works in one place but not in the other, chances are high that there is some binding going on that is not relative to the control itself. So, always double-check the binding statements in your custom control!

Finally, let's have a quick look at the issues that might arise when working with value converters.

Value converter issues

Converters play a crucial role in data transformation within your app. However, their logic might not always behave as expected. It's a seemingly trivial issue, but one that is frequently underestimated. The solution? Simple yet powerful: write unit tests! In *Chapter 13, Unit Testing*, we've highlighted how easy it is to unit test value converters. Paying attention to the logic within converters, testing them rigorously, and handling special cases will ensure that your converters perform reliably.

Summary

Now that we've reached the end of this short chapter, I hope you've gained valuable insights and tips for effectively troubleshooting issues that can arise in an MVVM context. Remember, the road to mastering MVVM is an ongoing journey, and troubleshooting and debugging are indispensable companions on this path. These challenges, though sometimes frustrating, are valuable teachers that will deepen your understanding and proficiency in MVVM. Embrace them as opportunities to grow, and in doing so, you'll become a more proficient and confident MVVM developer. Your journey doesn't end here; it evolves with each issue you resolve.

As we wrap up this final chapter, I want to extend my heartfelt congratulations to you for completing this book's journey into the world of MVVM in .NET MAUI. Throughout this book, you've delved into the intricacies of the MVVM pattern, explored the capabilities of .NET MAUI, and built your very own *Recipes!* app.

Once again, congratulations on your accomplishment, and may your MVVM and .NET MAUI journey continue to be rewarding and filled with exciting projects!

Further reading

To learn more about the topics that were covered in this chapter, take a look at the following resource:

XAML data binding diagnostics: `https://learn.microsoft.com/en-us/visualstudio/xaml-tools/xaml-data-binding-diagnostics?view=vs-2022`

Index

Symbols

Packt.com

Subscribe to our online digital library for full access to over 7,000 books and videos, as well as industry leading tools to help you plan your personal development and advance your career. For more information, please visit our website.

Why subscribe?

- Spend less time learning and more time coding with practical eBooks and Videos from over 4,000 industry professionals

- Improve your learning with Skill Plans built especially for you

- Get a free eBook or video every month

- Fully searchable for easy access to vital information

- Copy and paste, print, and bookmark content

Did you know that Packt offers eBook versions of every book published, with PDF and ePub files available? You can upgrade to the eBook version at packt.com and as a print book customer, you are entitled to a discount on the eBook copy. Get in touch with us at customercare@packtpub.com for more details.

At www.packt.com, you can also read a collection of free technical articles, sign up for a range of free newsletters, and receive exclusive discounts and offers on Packt books and eBooks.

Other Books You May Enjoy

If you enjoyed this book, you may be interested in these other books by Packt:

.NET MAUI for C# Developers

Jesse Liberty, Rodrigo Juarez

ISBN: 978-1-83763-169-8

- Explore the fundamentals of creating .NET MAUI apps with Visual Studio
- Understand XAML as the key tool for building your user interface
- Obtain and display data using layout and controls
- Discover the MVVM pattern to create robust apps
- Acquire the skills for storing and retrieving persistent data
- Use unit testing to ensure your app is solid and reliable

.NET MAUI Cross-Platform Application Development

Roger Ye

ISBN: 978-1-80056-922-5

- Discover the latest features of .NET 6 that can be used in mobile and desktop app development
- Find out how to build cross-platform apps with .NET MAUI and Blazor
- Implement device-specific features using .NET MAUI Essentials
- Integrate third-party libraries and add your own device-specific features
- Discover .NET class unit test using xUnit.net and Razor components unit test using bUnit
- Deploy apps in different app stores on mobile as well as desktop

Packt is searching for authors like you

If you're interested in becoming an author for Packt, please visit `authors.packtpub.com` and apply today. We have worked with thousands of developers and tech professionals, just like you, to help them share their insight with the global tech community. You can make a general application, apply for a specific hot topic that we are recruiting an author for, or submit your own idea.

Share Your Thoughts

Now you've finished *The MVVM pattern in .NET MAUI*, we'd love to hear your thoughts! Scan the QR code below to go straight to the Amazon review page for this book and share your feedback or leave a review on the site that you purchased it from.

`https://packt.link/r/1805125001`

Your review is important to us and the tech community and will help us make sure we're delivering excellent quality content.

Download a free PDF copy of this book

Thanks for purchasing this book!

Do you like to read on the go but are unable to carry your print books everywhere?

Is your eBook purchase not compatible with the device of your choice?

Don't worry, now with every Packt book you get a DRM-free PDF version of that book at no cost.

Read anywhere, any place, on any device. Search, copy, and paste code from your favorite technical books directly into your application.

The perks don't stop there, you can get exclusive access to discounts, newsletters, and great free content in your inbox daily

Follow these simple steps to get the benefits:

1. Scan the QR code or visit the link below

https://packt.link/free-ebook/9781805125006

2. Submit your proof of purchase
3. That's it! We'll send your free PDF and other benefits to your email directly

Printed in the USA
CPSIA information can be obtained
at www.ICGtesting.com
JSHW070542151223
53774JS00011B/189